# NEW WORLDS FROM BELOW

## INFORMAL LIFE POLITICS AND GRASSROOTS ACTION IN TWENTY-FIRST-CENTURY NORTHEAST ASIA

# NEW WORLDS FROM BELOW

## INFORMAL LIFE POLITICS AND GRASSROOTS ACTION IN TWENTY-FIRST-CENTURY NORTHEAST ASIA

EDITED BY TESSA MORRIS-SUZUKI
AND EUN JEONG SOH

Australian
National
University

PRESS

ASIAN STUDIES SERIES MONOGRAPH 9

Published by ANU Press
The Australian National University
Acton ACT 2601, Australia
Email: anupress@anu.edu.au
This title is also available online at press.anu.edu.au

National Library of Australia Cataloguing-in-Publication entry

Title:              New worlds from below : informal life politics and
                    grassroots action in twenty-first
                    century Northeast Asia / Tessa
                    Morris-Suzuki, Eun Jeong Soh, editors.

ISBN:               9781760460907 (paperback) 9781760460914 (ebook)

Series:             Asian studies series ; 9.

Subjects:           Communities--Asia, Northeast--Citizen participation.
                    Community development--Asia, Northeast.
                    Asia, Northeast--Politics and government--Citizen
                    participation.
                    Asia, Northeast--Social conditions.

Other Creators/Contributors:
                    Morris-Suzuki, Tessa, editor.
                    Soh, Eun Jeong, editor.

Cover design and layout by ANU Press. Cover photograph: Tessa Morris-Suzuki.

This edition © 2017 ANU Press

# Contents

# List of Figures and Tables

# Acknowledgements

This book emerged from research and conferences supported by the Australian Research Council's Laureate Fellowship project 'Informal Life Politics in the Remaking of Northeast Asia: From Cold War to Post-Cold War' (Project ID FL120100155) and the Academy of Korean Studies (KSPS) Grant funded by the Korean Government (Ministry of Education) (AKS-2011-BAA-2106). The editors and authors gratefully acknowledge the support of these funding agencies. Our thanks also go to Ms Maxine McArthur for her assistance with the copyediting and final preparation of the manuscript.

# Introduction: Informal Life Politics in Northeast Asia

Tessa Morris-Suzuki

## Liberating Politics

A group of prewar Hokkaido farmers creating their own experiment in communal living; a Chinese village where artists and locals come together to reinvent tradition; fishermen in mercury-polluted Minamata creating a new philosophy of nature; two grieving fathers walking across South Korea in remembrance of children killed in an avoidable disaster; North Koreans setting up a market in the streets of their town, in defiance of official regulations. These are some of the people you will encounter in the pages that follow. None of these people is behaving in an overtly 'political' way, but the argument of this book is that their actions are part of an invisible politics that is quietly transforming aspects of life in Northeast Asia today. Understanding the emergence and nature of this invisible politics is important in order to make sense of contemporary Northeast Asia. Beyond that, it is important because these small experiments in 'politics from below' shed light on some fundamental global dilemmas of 21st-century political life.

'Politics' is constantly defined and redefined. A broadly recognisable definition, though, might be this, which draws on (but slightly rewords) the writings of British political scientist David Runciman: politics is about the collective choices that shape the way people live, and about the nature of the human interrelationships through which those choices are made.[1] In everyday speech we equate politics with the formal mechanisms of government: national constitutions, parliaments, cabinets,

---

1    David Runciman, *Politics: Ideas in Profile* (London: Profile Books, 2014).

prime ministers or presidents, elections, party platforms. We include local institutions like city councils, and international bodies like the United Nations. We also sometimes consider the actions of lobby groups and of organised protest movements. But the activities of such formal and semi-formal political institutions are only a small corner of politics in the full meaning of the word.

For many people, none of the formal institutions of politics—whether local, national or international—seems able or willing to address the life crises that they face, or to assist them in making meaningful choices. In response, these people try to act out aspects of the change they seek in their everyday lives, through autonomous collective responses. The responses may be enacted by the local community of a village or urban area, but may also be enacted by networks dispersed across the boundaries of region or nation. This is 'informal life politics': an act of collected self-protection in the face of the profound deficits of institutional politics. Often, though not always, informal life politics is truly 'survival politics'—an act of desperation in response to direct threats to the physical survival of individuals or the social survival of communities.

This book sets out to explore examples of informal life politics in Northeast Asia, building on the work of scholars like James C. Scott and Benedict Tria Kerkvliet, who have charted and made visible forms of political action embedded in everyday life.[2] Such forms of politics have a long history, but there are impasses in the world of formal governmental politics today that make it particularly important to reconsider the past, present and possibilities of this less visible political realm. How can we reconceive politics to include that realm, and how might our understanding of politics in all its dimensions change if we broaden our vision in this way?

---

2    See, for example, James C. Scott, 'Everyday Forms of Peasant Resistance', in James C. Scott and Benedict J. Tria Kerkvliet eds, *Everyday Forms of Peasant Resistance in South-East Asia* (London: Frank Cass, 1986), 5–35; Benedict J. Tria Kerkvliet, *The Power of Everyday Politics: How Vietnamese Peasants Transformed National Policy* (Ithaca and London: Cornell University Press, 2005).

# Northeast Asia and the Crisis of Democracy

Northeast Asia is a region in the throes of enormous and unsettling change. The opening of the Chinese economy and its subsequent phenomenal growth have brought prosperity, but also massive environmental and social disruption. Japan, following a quarter of a century of economic stagnation, faces profound problems of ageing and population decline, aggravated by the trauma of the 2011 triple disaster and its aftermath. North Korea, in the midst of one of the world's most prosperous regions, remains one of the world's poorest countries; and in South Korea, visions of democratisation and national reunification that captured the popular imagination in the 1990s and early 21st century seem to have given way to a deep sense of social malaise (vividly depicted by Cho (Han) Haejoang in Chapter Seven of this book).

If we take a global perspective, Northeast Asia may indeed be seen as encapsulating profound challenges at the heart of the political order worldwide. The region contains countries that share long-term historical and cultural traditions, but whose modern history has led them in radically divergent directions. Japan became an imperial power, but was then stripped of its colonies and democratised following wartime defeat in 1945. China pursued a path of revolution, becoming a crucible of communist experimentation and social engineering, but has since— without ever formally repudiating its communist past—been transformed into a powerhouse of global capitalism. Taiwan and South Korea both moved from an era of authoritarian dictatorship to democracy, while Hong Kong evolved from colony to 'special administrative region': a precarious hybrid of authoritarian and quasi-democratic political forms. North Korea, meanwhile, is the one communist country that has resisted the global transition towards 'post-socialism', remaining trapped in its own distinctive *Chuch'e* variant of communism. This is therefore a region that spans an unusually wide spectrum of political forms, and, for this very reason, is a region where the nature of the global 'post-democracy' becomes particularly visible.[3]

---

3    See Obsolete Capitalism Collective ed., *The Birth of Digital Populism: Crowd, Power and Postdemocracy in the Twenty-First Century* (Rome and London: Obsolete Capitalism Free Press, 2014); Colin Crouch, *Post-Democracy*, (London: Wiley, 2004).

The end of the Cold War in Europe, coinciding roughly with democratisation of a number of formerly authoritarian states (including the Philippines and South Korea) and the collapse of South African apartheid, promoted a widespread belief that liberal democracy had triumphed worldwide. As Francis Fukuyama proclaimed in the late 1980s, 'a remarkable consensus concerning liberal democracy as a form of government had emerged throughout the world'. Democracy (according to this view) had 'conquered rival ideologies like hereditary monarchy, fascism, and most recently communism'. Fukuyama famously went on to predict that, since liberal democracy was free from the 'grave defects and irrationalities' that marred other regimes of power, its triumph would mark 'the endpoint of man's ideological evolution' and therefore also 'the end of history'.[4] The Arab Spring of 2011 prompted a revival and reassessment of these ideas by those who argued that Fukuyama had been right to foresee the irreversible victory of democracy, even if he was wrong in failing to foresee how prolonged and complex the road to this victory would be.[5]

But by the middle of the second decade of the 21st century, the state of the world was starting to look very different. It is now clear that neither the collapse of communism nor the Arab Spring has ushered in universal liberal democracy. In many former Soviet republics and satellites, the end of communism merely paved the way to new forms of authoritarianism that proved very capable of coexisting with the rapid marketisation of the economy. In China, a fundamentally unreformed once-communist political system has proved be a comfortable bedfellow of globalised capitalism. Meanwhile, in many countries (both longstanding and newer democratic polities), democracy itself, as Indian novelist and activist Arudhati Roy argues, is being 'hollowed out and emptied of meaning'.[6]

Italian economist Lapo Berti, who also speaks of the 'emptying' of democracy, sees a core problem as lying in the deepening power of the globalised corporate system and the intermeshing of economic power and politics elites, which renders politics divorced from the everyday concerns

4    Francis Fukuyama, 'By Way of Introduction', in Francis Fukuyama, *The End of History and the Last Man* (New York: Free Press, 2006), xi; see also Francis Fukuyama, 'The End of History', *The National Interest* 16 (Summer 1989), 3–18.
5    For example, Ewen Harrison and Sara McLaughlin Mitchell, *The Triumph of Democracy and the Eclipse of the West* (London: Palgrave Macmillan, 2014).
6    Arundhati Roy, 'Democracy's Failing Light', *Outlook India*, 13 July 2009, www.outlookindia.com/magazine/story/democracys-failing-light/250418.

of citizens and 'entirely self-referential'. One result is the estrangement of ordinary people from a voting system 'that is more and more perceived as useless, if not ridiculous':

> When people start voting at random because there is no longer any hope of making your voice heard, something is irrevocably broken in the mechanism of representation. And when … abstention reaches nearly half of those entitled to vote, the fracture is serious and it is very unlikely to be reversible in the short term.[7]

Berti is writing of Italian politics, but his words resonate powerfully in Northeast Asia, where all the main democracies have experienced sharply falling voting rates and growing voter cynicism in the past two decades. In South Korea, the voter turnout in the first democratic presidential election of 1992 was over 70 per cent, but it fell below 50 per cent in 2008, recovering only slightly to 54 per cent in 2012.[8] In Taiwan, more than 80 per cent of the electorate voted in the presidential elections of 2000 and 2004, but only 62 per cent in the 2016 election.[9] In Japan, where turnout in the three general elections of the 1980s averaged 69 per cent, and in 1990 reached 73 per cent, less than 53 per cent of voters participated in the 2014 election—the lowest level since the Pacific War.[10]

Voter estrangement from the political process goes hand-in-hand with populism, which (as Lapo Berti argues) emerges when:

> citizens lose their hopes of being the protagonists in democratic life, and therefore search for a surrogate who can represent their aspirations. This person is usually seen as a saviour, a character who imposes himself/herself through his/her communicative skills, which are very often enhanced or made up by the media.[11]

Populist elements have long existed in democratic politics everywhere, but populism in Berti's sense of the word has become an increasingly conspicuous part of political life in Northeast Asia (and elsewhere) since

---

7    Lapo Berti, 'On Micro-Fascism', in Obsolete Capitalism Collective ed., *The Birth of Digital Populism*, 45.

8    International Institute for Democracy and Electoral Assistance, 'Voter Turnout Data for Korea, Republic of', www.idea.int/data-tools/country-view/163/40.

9    International Institute for Democracy and Electoral Assistance, 'Voter Turnout Data for Taiwan', www.idea.int/data-tools/country-view/290/40.

10    International Institute for Democracy and Electoral Assistance, 'Voter Turnout Data for Japan', www.idea.int/data-tools/country-view/155/40.

11    Lapo Berti, 'On Micro-Fascism', in Obsolete Capitalism Collective ed., *The Birth of Digital Populism*, 45.

the end of the 20th century.[12] This populism combines an emphasis on personalities and slogans with nationalism, anti-intellectualism, and 'anti-political politics': its practitioners 'claim to represent the democratic sovereign … the united people … as against the parties or factions that divide it'.[13] Populist leaders, as self-defined saviours and representatives of the democratic sovereign, are typically impatient with the constitutional restraints of traditional liberal democracy. This personalised emphasis on the leader—who is presented as being in direct communication with a homogeneous mass nation—creates elements of convergence between the political styles of democracies like Japan and South Korea (on the one hand) and post-communist (or quasi-post-communist) states like Russia and China (on the other).

Because it privileges media presence and headline-grabbing phrases over policy expertise and the disciplines of democratic process, populism often fails to deliver when confronted with practical crises that affect the everyday lives of citizens. This inherent flaw can create a spiral of disaffection, where one section of the population becomes ever more alienated from the political process, while another redoubles its attempt to find salvation from crisis though identification with the images of strength projected by the populist leader. So populism, despite its rhetoric of a united and homogenous national community, is commonly accompanied by bitter and deepening social antagonisms and competitive narratives of victimhood. These crises of politics in Northeast Asia are particularly clearly illustrated by the cases explored in Chapters Six and Seven of this book.

But if one response to estrangement from politics is a search for the leader as surrogate and saviour, another very different response lies in the search for autonomous and locally generated practical responses to crises. It is this response that we focus on in the pages that follow. The examples discussed in these pages are only tiny fragments of the immensely complex landscape of informal life politics in Northeast Asia today. It is important to emphasise, too, that these examples are not being put forward here as all-encompassing solutions to the profound crises of politics outlined in the previous paragraphs. The crises, of course, need to be addressed at multiple levels—through formal political processes at local, national and international level as well as through the informal politics of everyday life.

---

12   See Pasuk Phongpaichit and Kosuke Mizuno eds, *Populism in Asia* (Singapore: NUS Press, 2009).
13   Margaret Canavan, quoted in Pasuk Phongpaichit and Kosuke Mizuno eds, *Populism in Asia*, 4.

But a focus on the world of informal life politics can, we suggest, enrich our vision of the possibilities of political action, and challenges us to rethink some preconceptions about the very nature of 'the political' itself.

## Mixed Economies, Mixed Polities

One challenge posed by informal life politics is that it impels us to reconsider the boundaries that we conventionally draw between 'the political' and 'the economic'. In all the stories explored in this book, the economic and the political are inextricably intertwined; all actions are inescapably *both* political and economic. But over the past 50 years, while corporate capitalism and state power have become ever more deeply entangled with one another, the intellectual worlds of politics and economics have bifurcated. Integrated notions of political economy have dissolved, and are replaced by two distinct, specialised realms called 'political science' and 'economics', each working according to its own sets of rules. This intellectual bifurcation has given us an economics that rarely addresses underlying questions about the nature and purpose of our economic systems, and a politics incapable of confronting the political problems posed by global corporate capitalism.

In public discourse, 'the economy' is now commonly taken to mean 'the corporate market', and 'politics' is commonly taken to mean the actions of formal governmental institutions and the politicians and bureaucrats who run them. But in fact (as Thomas Picketty observes), 'we live in a mixed economy, different to be sure from the mixed economies that people envisioned after World War II but nonetheless quite real'.[14] Substantial sections of the economy in most countries are operated by non-profit organisations, charitable foundations, household enterprises, and other institutions that work on principles very different from those of the capitalist corporation. A multitude of cooperatives, community and household enterprises, local non-commercial exchange networks and so

14   Thomas Picketty, *Capital in the Twenty-First Century*, trans. Arthur Goldhammer (Cambridge, Mass.: Harvard University Press, 2014).

on play vital economic roles, particularly in the 'majority world' (that is, in the world inhabited by the 85 per cent of the global population who live in low-income countries).[15]

And we all inhabit not just mixed economies, but also mixed polities. Our world is not neatly divisible into good constitutional democracies and bad dictatorships. Though configured in very many differing ways, every country in the world today contains at least some corners where ordinary people make their own collective choices through reasoned debate, and every country contains at least some corners where power is arbitrary and unaccountable. The differences lie in relative weights of both ends of the spectrum, and in the diverse ways in which democratic and the authoritarian elements are configured. We need analytical approaches that do not simply treat the political systems of nations as single totalities: well-oiled machines whose parts all work in unison. Instead, we need to become more aware of the great diversity that exists within each mixed polity. It is important to understand the very varied ways in which collective choices that shape life are made, and the very varied human interrelationships through which those choices are made. This book seeks to contribute to an understanding of that diversity.

As we explore the examples discussed in this volume, we become more aware of the intimate interweaving of the political and the economic. Attempts to restructure village life in Hokkaido, the mountains of Honshu or rural China (see Chapters One, Two and Three) are inescapably both economic and political. Responses to environmental crisis in Minamata, Fukushima and beyond ineluctably weave together the political and the economic, as do responses to disasters like the *Sewol* ferry tragedy in South Korea (Chapters Four, Six and Seven).

In many of these cases a key underlying issue is the expansionary nature of the power of the corporate economy (which is itself inseparably intertwined with the power of the state). As Hannah Arendt observed in the 1950s, modernity is based on endless economic expansion: 'what the modern age so heatedly defended was never property as such but the unhampered pursuit of more property or of accumulation'.[16] Or (to borrow Ellen

---

15   J. K. Gibson-Graham, Jenny Cameron and Stephen Healy, *Take Back the Economy: An Ethical Guide for Transforming our Communities* (Minneapolis and London: University of Minnesota Press, 2013); see also Shahidul Alam, 'Majority World' 2015 (website), www.shahidulalam.com/#pi=38&p=-1&a=0&at=0.

16   Hannah Arendt, *The Human Condition* (Chicago: University of Chicago Press, 1958), 110.

Meiskins Wood's words) modern capitalism is characterised by 'its unique capacity as well as its unique need for constant self-expansion'.[17] But the attempt to treat all things as potentially profit-generating commodities is doomed to disaster. If everything were a commodity:

> human beings would perish from the effect of social exposure; they would die as the victims of acute social dislocation through vice, perversion, crime and starvation. Nature would be reduced to its elements, neighbourhoods and landscapes defiled, rivers polluted, military safety jeopardised, the power to produce food and raw materials destroyed.[18]

A conscious or unconscious urge to 'push-back' against this encroaching commodification of life lies at the heart of many of the stories we shall explore here (and this is a point to which we will return in the epilogue). These stories help us to see commonalities and differences between informal life politics in various parts of East Asia, and to glimpse the possibilities and limitations, the creativity and the challenges, which drive diverse practices of informal politics in everyday life.

## Old and New Informal Life Politics

From the 1970s onwards, grassroots political activism generated much interest and debate around the world. The rise of environmentalism, feminism, alternative lifestyle movements, indigenous and minority rights movements, lesbian, gay and transgender activism and many other forms of 'lifestyle politics' (as they are often termed) has given rise to theories that have expanded the boundaries of traditional political research. Influential scholars like Anthony Giddens and Ulrich Beck identified the rise of this new activism as a symptom of a new, reflexive, 'post materialist' world, transcending the old class-based politics that had been centred on questions of the distribution of material wealth.[19]

This book begins by digging deeper into the past; emphasising the historical roots of the forms of living politics that we are studying. Informal life politics is often (though not always) a politics of the poor.

---

17   Ellen Meiskins Wood, *The Origin of Capitalism: A Longer View* (London: Verso, 2002), 193.
18   Karl Polanyi, *The Great Transformation* (Boston: Beacon Press, 2001, original published in 1944), 76.
19   Anthony Giddens, *Beyond Left and Right: The Future of Radical Politics* (Cambridge: Polity Press, 1994); Anthony Giddens, *The Third Way: The Renewal of Social Democracy* (Cambridge: Polity Press, 1998); Ulrich Beck, *World at Risk* (Cambridge: Polity Press, 2007).

Rather than simply emerging when societies reach a stage of development that transcends materialism, it has a history that stretches back at least to the start of East Asian industrialisation in the early 20th century. The cross-border links between cooperatist thought and action in Japan and Russia—carefully traced by Sho Konishi in Chapter One—are a reminder of this long history of grassroots efforts to create new social forms in response to the challenges of rapid, state-imposed industrialisation and modernisation. Small-scale local attempts to create 'another modernity' were inspired by the spread of ideas across the borders of nations and continents. Russian cooperatist anarchism, British and French utopian socialism, and non-Darwinian accounts of natural evolution were among the forces that shaped such social experiments in early 20th-century Japan, and indeed in many other parts of the world.

Chapters Two and Three show how these ideas and social experiments have crossed spatial and temporal boundaries. Ou Ning, himself actively involved in a village revival movement in China, traces the flow of ideas through which prewar Japanese images of the 'New Village' (themselves inspired by concepts imported from Russia and elsewhere) were in turn taken up and reworked in Republican China, where they played a part in shaping the rural reconstruction movement. This tradition has been rediscovered in China since the 1990s, providing inspiration for new efforts to reconstruct rural life from below. In Japan meanwhile, the same stream of ideas continues to feed informal life politics actions in rural areas affected by depopulation and ageing (see Chapter Three).

Informal life politics in Northeast Asia today draws on this long lineage of ideas and experiences, but reinterprets them in the light of a rapidly and radically changing world. By the 1970s, new currents of environmental thought were added to the mix of ideas. In Chapter Four, Simon Avenell explores the neglected way in which exchanges of environmental ideas in the 1970s and 1980s helped to extend 'translocal' links between the grassroots actions of communities in various parts of Asia threatened by industrial pollution. The creative intermingling of old and new ideas of nature and humanity is illustrated in Chapter Five by Shoko Yoneyama's study of living politics in two areas devastated by environmental disaster: the Minamata region and the areas affected by the 2011 tsunami and nuclear meltdown. Other variants of that intermingling and reworking emerge in the critical rethinking of 'development' that followed the *Sewol* disaster in South Korea (Chapter Seven), and in the community arts experiments of Hong Kong's Wooferten and Seoul's Mullae-Tong (Chapter Eight).

While most of the chapters in this book look at specific local responses to crisis in particular countries of the region, Chapter Ten offers a broader comparative perspective on grassroots action in Asia from the perspective of the concept of social innovation. This final chapter draws on a large-scale study by Seoul-based The Hope Institute, which aims to encourage bottom-up sustainable approaches to addressing social problems. The Hope Institute's work highlights some common threads in emerging forms of Asian grassroots social innovation, and extends the story to encompass cases from South and Southeast as well as Northeast Asia.

## Common Themes in the Politics of Improvisation

When we place the diverse stories in this book together, connecting themes emerge. Fundamental to all of these grassroots experiments is an unease at the way that the modern corporate growth economy defines and shapes human beings and the natural world. The first chapters of the book trace a long history of critiques of the mechanised separation of humans from nature, the erosion of community cooperation by the pressures of economic competition, and the devaluing of spiritual and creative capabilities that cannot readily be turned into financial profit. Miyamoto Kenichi, whose work inspires the Miyamoto School (discussed in Chapter Three), reinterprets Marx's notion of 'immiseration'. In Marx's day, immiseration meant sheer material poverty. Today (Miyamoto suggests) it means phenomena like pollution, urban congestion and rural depopulation, the displacement of people and the destruction of social support systems etc., produced both by the rampant profit seeking of corporations and by state policies imposed from above to support this profit seeking.[20] Though the terms they use may vary, most of the grassroots groups discussed in this book share a critical perspective on the human and environmental burdens imposed by the ever-expanding global corporate economy.

The response to this immiseration involves efforts to revive local livelihoods and to find support and recompense for people whose lives have been disrupted by environmental damage or failed state policies;

---

20   Miyamoto Kenichi, *Gendai shihonshugi to kokka* [Contemporary Capitalism and the State] (Tokyo: Iwanami Shoten, 1981), 135–42.

but it also goes further than this. Many of the groups discussed in this book are engaged in a search for ways to reconceptualise the relationship between humans and nature, and to redefine notions of 'development', 'prosperity', 'citizenship' and 'community'. One theme that repeatedly emerges is a re-evaluation of the significance of the human spirit. In conventional models of democratic state politics, formal religions often play an important role (since many political parties have explicit or implicit religious links), but the notion of individual spirituality tends to be treated with caution and even suspicion, as something likely to lead into the murky quicksands of superstition and irrationality. By contrast, several of the experiments in living politics discussed in this book challenge that approach by bringing notions of spirituality and ritual into the light of day. We find this in the ritual practices developed by cooperative farmers in prewar Hokkaido (Chapter One), in Japanese re-evaluations of animism following the Minamata and Fukushima disasters (Chapter Five) and in the use of shamanic and other religious rituals by the families of *Sewol* ferry victims (Chapter Seven).

At the same time, though, the actions discussed in this book cannot be slotted into any single clearly defined ideological framework. Rather, they challenge us to reconsider the very notion of 'ideology' itself. The classic 18th- and 19th-century political philosophies that still influence our understandings of politics were commonly based on visions of the social world as a closed system whose rules were derived from a foundational first principle, often seen as lying in the original state of nature. Such images of society provide fertile ground for ideological certainties about the solutions to our present-day human predicaments. But as philosopher William Connolly suggests, in our complex contemporary age it may make more sense to see the world as a multitude of coexisting partially open systems in a state of becoming; and if we do so, the ideological certainties dissolve. We are in the midst of an immensely complicated and changing nexus of existence, in which relatively small events may trigger large and unpredictable changes. There are no iron laws of historical evolution, and there is no pure unsullied nature into which utopians can withdraw to build ideal communities. We have to start from where we are, and this means that 'when a new crisis of possibility emerges, you must often experiment to ascertain where and how to engage it'.[21]

---

21　William Connolly, *A World of Becoming* (Durham, NC, and London: Duke University Press, 2011), 37.

Some of the forms of living politics that we explore in this book arise from relatively well-articulated politico-social philosophies. But many begin as experiments in response to crisis—environmental crisis, the drastic restructuring of the social landscape or the failures of state policy. The participants in these projects, rather than starting out with clearly defined philosophies, grope their way gradually towards a deeper understanding of the forces behind the particular crisis that they are trying to address. Their lack of firm ideological framework may be seen as a liability and a source of vulnerability. But it can also be a source of flexibility and dynamism. The world of living politics—small in scale, grounded in everyday life, protean and often ephemeral—provides scope for a wide diversity of experiments. It allows for the multiplicity of ideas and practices that is lacking in the mental monocultures of institutional politics. And, even more importantly perhaps, it allows room for failure without triggering catastrophe. Informal life politics is a space for the action that Brian Massumi sees as central to biological and social becoming: improvisation—the 'margin of manoeuvre', the 'power of variation'.[22] It allows groups of people, in responding to profound politico-economic challenges to try, and see what happens.

Informal life politics also impels us to think again about the notion of 'community'. The term 'community' recurs in many of the chapters that follow. People in Bishan and Mochizuki, Minamata and Ansan, Yau Ma Tei and Wonju try to restore and re-create community connections eroded by rapid social and economic change. But it is important to emphasise that none of these communities is a self-contained or closed entity. In fact, a clear common theme of the stories in this book is the crucial importance of interaction between insiders and outsiders— between those who have spent all their lives in a particular location, and those who have arrived recently, bringing new ideas and experiences with them. These communities are therefore very different from the Weberian notion of *Gemeinschaft*. They are networks, linking people in diverse social situations and spatial locations, and sometimes linking people across the boundaries of the nation. The dynamics of interaction within these networks is a particularly important topic for future study as we explore the evolving world of living politics in East Asia.

---

22   Brian Massumi, *What Animals Teach us about Politics* (Durham, NC, and London: Duke University Press, 2014), 12–13.

North Korea seems the outlier: the 'outsider' to all political and economic analyses of East Asia. It is certainly important to recognise the peculiarities that make North Korean political circumstances different from those of neighbouring countries. But although North Korea has absolutely no visible 'civil society' or independent 'social movements', Eun Jeong Soh's analysis in Chapter Nine suggests that even in North Korea, types of informal life politics are quietly changing the way people make collective decisions that shape their futures, and interpret the decisions that they have made. Soh shows that networks linking traders to one another and to local officials become a vital part of informal livelihood creation, and state notions both of autonomy and collective effort are reinterpreted to justify the rise of survival strategies from below.

## A New Beginning

The chapters in this book do not, of course, speak in unison. They are written by historians, anthropologists and sociologists, by scholars and by those directly engaged in living politics actions in the region. The diversity of approaches adopted by the grassroots movements explored in the book is matched by the diversity of approaches taken by those who write about them. But, by placing these accounts side by side, we hope that we can create space for a conversation about previously neglected dimensions of the political life of Northeast Asia, and contribute to a wider discussion about the role of informal life politics in the 21st-century world.

If, as we have suggested earlier, all polities are mixed polities, then informal life politics is only one dimension of the mix. But it is an important, complex, and insufficiently understood dimension. The stories told in the following pages offer no conclusions, but we believe that they do offer starting points on a journey to a deeper understanding of the many ways in which people around Northeast Asia are (to borrow Davina Cooper's words) 'creating the change they wish to encounter, building and forging new ways of experiencing social and political life'.[23]

---

23   Davina Cooper, *Everyday Utopias: The Conceptual Life of Promising Spaces* (Durham, NC, and London: Duke University Press, 2014), 2.

# 1

# Provincialising the State: Symbiotic Nature and Survival Politics in Post-World War Zero Japan

Sho Konishi

This chapter explores the idea and practice of what I have called elsewhere 'cooperatist anarchist modernity'. It looks at one particular moment in the long historical development of this vision and practice of progress, the period following the Russo-Japanese War of 1904–05, when an anarchist scientific turn occurred. Some historians have called this war 'World War Zero', in reference to its status as the first of the modern, all-encompassing global wars of the 20th century.[1] The scientific turn in the wake of the war was integral to the dynamic development of anarchism in Japan and would in turn generate a wave of innovative thought and cultural practices. By introducing the popularised notion of symbiotic nature as the driver of evolution and civilisational progress[2] and its temporality in post Russo-Japanese War Japan, this chapter demonstrates the cooperatist anarchist cultural overturning of the idea and practice of progress fashioned after

---

1    John Steinberg, Bruce W. Menning, David Schimmelpenninck van der Oye, David Wolff, and Shinji Yokote eds, *The Russo-Japanese War in Global Perspective: World War Zero* (Leiden: Brill, 2005), 349–64.
2    The notion of 'symbiotic nature' contrasted with the Darwinist notion of competition as the source of progress and natural evolution.

the West that provincialised the state.[3] This historic overcoming of Western modernity served as the epistemological and cultural foundation of survival politics of the everyday, an understanding from which contemporary informal life politics may be meaningfully discussed and discerned. The chapter reveals not what ordinary people did on the main floor of shops and institutions during the day, but what they did upstairs at night. We will visit public intellectuals not at their imperial universities, but when they gathered in the evenings on the second floor of a sweet shop or a people's hospital after closing time. Then I would like to introduce a place 50 miles from nowhere on the northernmost island of Hokkaido in order to talk about ordinary farmers who, I argue, consciously adopted and put into practice the concept of cooperatist anarchist progress and thereby conceived of themselves as standing at the forefront of modern progress and civilisation. In doing so, these former tenant farmers, overcoming tremendous fear, managed to survive liberation from tenancy in the most severe living conditions.

In 1906, less than a year after the Portsmouth Treaty that ended the Russo-Japanese War, two of the most popular writers in late Meiji-Taisho Japan, Tokutomi Roka and Arishima Takeo (who was then in America), made separate pilgrimages to the homes of figures that they saw as symbols of international peace, civilisation and progress. Both traced the major sites of inspiration for human civilisational development, and culminated their respective travels at the homes of Russian anarchist thinkers, Peter Kropotkin and Lev Tolstoy. It was in the immediate post-war period that the faces of Tolstoy and Kropotkin, symbols of the Japanese Nonwar Movement in the Russo-Japanese War, appeared arm-in-arm on the Japanese cultural scene, to the point that we might call it a phenomenon of Tolstoy-Kropotkinism. It would be difficult to read the public prominence of these particular figures without an understanding of anarchism and its provincialising of the nation-state in early 20th-century Japan.

After winning the Russo-Japanese War, people in Japan had an unprecedented opportunity to engage with the wider world afresh. And the 'world' was watching with great anticipation to see what the people of Japan would bring to the world. It is hardly a coincidence that some

---

3     This anarchist notion of 'provincialising the state' may be contrasted with that of Dipesh Chakrabarty's 'provincialising Europe', which focuses on indigenous sources of modern state- and nation-building. Dipesh Chakrabarty, *Provincializing Europe: Postcolonial Thought and Historical Difference* (Princeton, NJ: Princeton University Press, 2000).

historians begin the history of decolonisation movements from 1905 because of the perceived significance of the war for the colonised world. Our historiography has given only one historical meaning to this war for Japanese history in the wider world: Japan's entry into the group of elite civilised sovereign nation-states and its embarkation onto the path of Western modernity. At the time, however, a number of people in fact came to share a very different view of the war, that it represented a *retrogression* of human progress. Their view of world order was also ideologically opposed to the most basic assumptions of the rising decolonisation movements. Decolonisation movements were political movements that sought to liberate the nation from imperialism, by transferring power to indigenous hands in order to found a sovereign nation-state modelled after the West.[4] Yet in the Japanese Nonwar Movement's imagination of free transnational, non-state relations among 'people' around the world was an ideology of emancipation from that very territorial utopia of Western modernity founded on the modern nation-state.

I suggest that the war served as a pivotal experience that made salient a deep conflict between competing visions of human progress and civilisation. The view of the Nonwar Movement, probably the most successful peace movement in a time of war in modern history as scholar Hyman Kublin has suggested,[5] sharply contrasted with the ideology of Western modernity that sanctioned, if not celebrated, Japan's entry into the community of nation-states as a result of its victory in war and empire building. The experience of the war only helped to solidify a cooperatist anarchist historical consciousness that would take the form of social action. Historians have long overlooked this vision and corresponding practices, which did not fit the narrative of Western modernity ('History'). 'History' has been that familiar narrative of the rise and development of the nation-state toward a Western modern form of political and economic liberty, or Hegelian Reason. Japan has been narrated according to this History as 'late'.[6]

---

4    Prasenjit Duara, 'Introduction: The Decolonisation of Asia and Africa in the Twentieth Century', in Prasenjit Duara ed., *Decolonisation: Perspectives From Now and Then* (London: Routledge, 2004), 1–20.

5    Hyman Kublin, 'The Japanese Socialists and the Russo-Japanese War', *Journal of Modern History* 21 (March–December 1950): 322–39.

6    On the conceptualisation of the war as a retrogression of civilisation and development by the Nonwar Movement, see Konishi, 'The Absence of Portsmouth in an Early Twentieth-Century Imagination of Peace', in Steven J. Ericson, Allen Hockley, *The Treaty of Portsmouth and Its Legacies* (Hanover and London: University Press of New England, 2008), 98–105.

I argue that in the immediate aftermath of the war, what I call a 'history slide', (*rekishi no jisuberi* 歴史の地滑り) occurred, a slide of historical consciousness that produced a reconceived subjectivity of the present as a point of moral action in the here and now to attain that new future. Nonwar participants perceived their location in the given space and time as backward. The present as a product of Western progress was now perceived as behind and no longer morally justifiable. History thus slid from narratives of the past to justify the present to a narrated future vision. In what would develop into an anarchist theory of social change, the 'present' had become the urgent moment to rectify history for the future. As Arishima wrote in 1905, history was to be '*kiyome tadasu*' (morally cleansed and rectified 清め正す). Inferiority was now assigned not to a given space but to a belonging to a certain sense of time or temporality.

Certainly, among the supporters of the Nonwar Movement, neither the Portsmouth Peace Treaty nor the Nobel Peace Prize consequently awarded to Theodore Roosevelt for brokering that treaty was a part of their discussions of peace. One could even say that members of the movement were completely disinterested in the peacemaking achievements of the international community in ending the war between Russia and Japan. Despite the participants' seeming reticence in relation to the international community and its territorial utopia of Western modernity, the Nonwar Movement's ideological redrawing of the concept of peace attracted many people in Japan.

I chose to translate the term Japanese participants used for their movement, *hisen undō* 非戦運動, as 'Nonwar Movement'. References to the movement have translated *hisen undō* as 'Antiwar Movement', without distinguishing it from the more contemporary Japanese term *hansen undō* 反戦運動. This translation not only fails to reflect the intellectual universe of the movement, but may be misleading, for the term *hansen* as it has been used in the post–Asia-Pacific War period refers to an oppositional position against a particular war, as in the Antiwar Movement in America during the Vietnam War. At the same time, the *hisen undō* of the Russo-Japanese War did not express a philosophical position of pacifism, the total negation of violence.

In fact, *hisen* was a term historically specific to the Russo-Japanese War, with the war being the only time that the term would ever be used. Inherent in the language of *hisen* was a construct of civilisation and progress that was distinguished from Western modernity. According to their construct, imperialist wars were not a part of that modernity, and therefore *hi*, 'absent'. We may thereby conceive this movement as an intellectual phenomenon *for* a given understanding of progress and civilisation, rather than *against* a particular war or *against* violence on absolute terms.

## Anarchist Science

In this context of wide-ranging questioning of the progressiveness of Western modernity following the war, science became the vessel through which the 'true nature' of human behaviour and society could be discerned. In my view, the end of the war simultaneously marked what may be called a scientific turn. The anarchist Ōsugi Sakae was emblematic of this turn. He developed a deep interest in scientific knowledge of astronomy, evolutionary biology and animal behaviour that in turn inspired him to realise that he was an 'anarchist' at this time.

Ōsugi made a direct link between human society and the centreless nature of the universe and claimed that the interdependent relationship between humans and nature was such that it logically followed that humans had no choice but to harmonise society with the most advanced scientific knowledge of space matter and the natural world. This devotion to scientific knowledge that was selectively interpreted by anarchists to represent the future of human society is what I call 'anarchist science'.[7] Ōsugi believed that human subjectivity and social relations ought to reflexively mirror scientific findings about the nature and 'logic' of the physical and natural universe around and within human beings. This perspective on the human world rooted in a scientific view of the logic and functioning of nature and biological evolution helped inspire a new wave of Japanese interest in anarchism after the war. The definitive postwar moment of the history slide when anarchist ideas of progress were adopted was accompanied by this scientific turn.

---

7     Sho Konishi, 'The Science of Symbiosis and Linguistic Democracy in Early Twentieth-Century Japan', *Interdisciplinary Description of Complex Systems* (INDEKS) 13, no. 2 (2015): 299–317. See also Sho Konishi, *Anarchist Modernity: Cooperatism and Japanese-Russian Intellectual Relations in Modern Japan* (Cambridge, Mass.: Harvard University Press, 2013), 296–327.

Ōsugi was certainly not the only one to develop a deep interest in natural science immediately following the war. During his transnational pilgrimage to Kropotkin's home, Arishima held on to one book, written by the Russian embryologist and microbiologist Ilia Mechnikov, who would win the Nobel Prize for his work on micro-organisms and immunity in 1908.[8] It is curious that at this critical moment immediately after the war, Arishima chose to read, not revolutionary texts of revolt or texts on international relations, but a text by a Russian microbiologist. How can one possibly grasp the place of micro-organisms in the embrace of anarchism in this period? In the broader context of war and imperialist expansion, terrorism and assassination by anarchists worldwide, and government persecution of anarchists and socialists, anarchists in Japan like Arishima turned to Mechnikov's universe of bacteria and phagocytes and, later, the spiders, dung beetles and wasps of the French entomologist Jean Henri Fabre, in their search for answers to the world problems at hand. If Theodore Roosevelt and the Nobel Peace Prize of 1906 did not represent their idea of peace, then certainly the Nobel Prize in science awarded to Mechnikov two years later represented perfectly their idea of peace and civilisational progress.

Kōtoku Shūsui, a theoretical leader of anarchism and the Nonwar Movement, echoed the notion of the centreless universe. In his introduction to Darwin's theory that helped popularise ideas of evolution in Japan, Kōtoku wrote that after Charles Darwin, 'there will be no more debate about the beginningless and endless composition of nature'.[9] Japanese anarchists embraced what astronomer Mark Davis characterises today as 'negative discovery', the understanding:

> That Earth is *not* the center of the Universe.
>
> That the Sun is *not* the center of the Universe.
>
> Our galaxy is *not* the center of the Universe.
>
> Our type of matter is *not* the dominant constituent of the Universe (dark matter predominates instead).
>
> Our Universe (seen and unseen) is *not* the only Universe.[10]

---

8   On Mechnikov's work on immunology, see Alfred I. Tauber and Leon Chernyak, *Metchnikoff and the Origins of Immunology: From Metaphor to Theory* (New York, Oxford: Oxford University Press, 1991).

9   'Dāwin to Marukusu' [Darwin and Marx], *Heimin shimbun* 47 (2 October 1904): 5.

10   Davis is quoted in Daniel Boorstin, *Cleopatra's Nose: Essays on the Unexpected* (New York: Vintage Press, 1995), 7.

The centre of the universe was scattered everywhere and nowhere at the same time. Kropotkin expressed this idea in his work *Anarchism:*

> It is to this dust, to these infinitely tiny bodies that dash through space in all directions with giddy swiftness, that clash with one another, agglomerate, disintegrate, everywhere and always, it is to them that today astronomers look for an explanation of the origin of our solar system, the movements that animate its parts, and the harmony of their whole … Thus the center, the origin of force, formerly transferred from the earth to the sun, now turns out to be scattered and disseminated: it is everywhere and nowhere. With the astronomer, we perceive that solar systems are the work of infinitely small bodies; that the power which was supposed to govern the system is itself but the result of the collisions among those infinitely tiny clusters of matter, that the harmony of stellar systems is harmony only … a resultant of all these numberless movements uniting, completing, equilibrating one another.[11]

Supported by the findings of natural science, Japanese anarchists removed the distinction between high and low, subverted the centrality of the state for human progress, advocated the multiplicity of ever-changing cultures, and promoted voluntary associations for an interdependent world. Mechnikov, who suddenly became a topic of discussion among some prominent Japanese cultural figures following the Russo-Japanese War, is emblematic of the kind of interest in natural science in Japan during this time. Mechnikov discovered the symbiotic functions of the natural world within the human body itself by examining the symbiotic interdependencies of bacteria and other micro-organisms that thrived within the body. For Japanese anarchists, the human body discovered by Mechnikov was a body functioning in mutual interaction and interdependence with its environment from both within and without and was a reflection of the cosmological universe. Mechnikov's understanding of multiple levels of 'social' relations among organisms within and outside the human body led him to reflect in his writings on how an understanding of humans' symbiotic relations with the very microbiotic world within themselves can prolong individual lives.[12] From the perspective of Japanese anarchists,

11    Peter Kropotkin, *Anarchism: Its Philosophy and Ideal*, 3rd ed. (San Francisco: Free Society, 1898), 3–4.
12    See Elie Metchnikoff, *The Prolongation of Life: Optimistic Studies* (London: Heinemann, 1910). Ilia Mechnikov's older brother Lev was a Russian revolutionary and an anarchist who became a well-recognised scholar of Japanese studies after he travelled to Japan to witness the revolution there in the 1870s. See Sho Konishi, 'Reopening the "Opening of Japan": A Russian-Japanese Revolutionary Encounter and the Vision of Anarchist Progress', *The American Historical Review* 112, no. 1 (2007): 101–30.

then, interdependent and symbiotic relations from the very internal workings of human beings themselves at the smallest microbiotic level of life negated Malthusian assumptions about the struggle for survival promoted by social Darwinism.

Unlike Freud's urging of a civilisational departure from nature, Mechnikov argued in *Nature of Man* that the happiness and well-being of man lay in his attainment of harmony with the order of nature that lay both within his own body and without, in his environment. For man's adaptation to nature and harmony with the environment was far from complete, a disjuncture rooted in the profound changes achieved in his evolutionary development, Mechnikov observed. He believed that the exact sciences should serve to remedy the organic disharmonies within humans, thereby offering solutions to the problems of human happiness.[13]

This would be the intellectual foundation of anarchist science that would much later be picked up by the cell biologist Lynn Margulis, one of the most influential biologists in contemporary times. Margulis saw the evolution of cells through the lens of symbiotic dependencies in a similar way to Mechnikov. Prompted by her findings of the symbiotic origins of evolution, Margulis codeveloped the theory of global symbiosis called 'Gaia'.[14] According to this theory, the earth consists of a self-regulating biosphere dependent on micro-organisms' and plants' unconscious maintenance of the environment in a homeostasis favourable for life. Similar in style of thought, the anti-capitalist conclusions drawn by Margulis herself remind one of the manner in which Japanese anarchists of the early 20th century reflected on Mechnikov's findings about micro-organisms to develop their claims of the relevance of anarchism for human culture and civilisational progress. The controversy prompted by studies of bacteria and other micro-organisms as a dynamic starting point for thinking about the nature of evolution—and 'progress' itself—was as compelling in early 20th-century Japan as it is today.

Through their translations of scientists' writings, anarchists subsequently played a leading role in the popularisation of the natural sciences in Japan in the early 20th century at large. State officials felt threatened by the massive popularity of anarchist introductions of the biological sciences,

---

13   See, for example, Elie Metchnikoff, *Nature of Man: Studies in Optimistic Philosophy*, translated by Sir Peter Chalmers Mitchell (New York: G.P. Putnam's Sons, 1905), 209–15; Metchnikoff, 'The Haunting Terror Of All Human Life', *New York Times*, 27 February 1910.

14   Lynn Margulis, *Symbiotic Planet: A New Look at Evolution* (New York: Basic Books, 1998).

and the government banned their translations of Fabre's entomological study of the dung beetle in *Konchū Shakai* (Insect Society 昆虫社会).[15] Fabre's observations of the insect world verified a view of nonhierarchical nature in which each species or form of creature had its own naturally endowed virtue, its own talent, specialised knowledge and ability. Through Fabre's insects, anarchists have helped shape early childhood imagination and perceptions of the natural world. Despite (and sometimes because of) the government's initial ban on translations of Fabre, anarchist translations of his studies of insects in the early 1920s came to capture the national imagination. Even today, Fabre's writings continue to be a sort of 'Mother Goose' of Japan, read by Japanese children as a staple of children's literature and childhood imaginations. The once-banned dung beetle has far outlasted any state regimes and ideologies that banned it, yet our historiography that has focused on the state has silenced the dung beetle from historical memory. If the social knowledge of childhood has the power to order imaginations of the future, then the popularity of anarchists' representations and definition of childhood meant that anarchists had a powerful hand on future visions in Japan, however hidden from history.

The turn to anarchist science on popular grounds interacted discursively with the Western modern construct of civilisational progress. When stripped down to its most basic intellectual foundations, that construct of Western modernity may be most simply understood as a movement away from 'nature' and toward 'culture'. Ishikawa Sanshirō, an anarchist leader and the founder of the influential women's journal *Sekai Fujin* 世界婦人 with Fukuda Hideko, saw this as the frightening product of the conception of nature as the enemy of civilisation and the antithesis of human culture. He proposed instead to embrace boundless nature, leading to a deep connection of the limited human life to the limitless world of nature. If there were to be any progress in his own life, Ishikawa wrote, that progress was to aim at that idea of a human civilisation deeply interconnected with nature.[16]

---

15    In English, see Jean Henri Fabre, *The Insect World of J. Henri Fabre*, trans. Alexander Teixeira De Mattos (New York: Dodd, Mead & Company, 1949).

16    Ishikawa Sanshirō, *Hi shinkaron to jinsei* [Non-Evolutionary Theory and Human Life] (Tokyo: Hakuyōsha Shuppan, 1925).

# Cultural Revolution

Once the concept of nature was redefined, so was the idea of culture. In the roughly 20 years following the Russo-Japanese War, Japanese cooperatist anarchists overturned the meaning of culture and the cultured. By so doing, they provincialised the state to meet the expectations of anarchist progress. I call this reconstruction of the concept of culture an anarchist cultural revolution. This 'revolution' in culture was the product of shifts from high culture to popular, state to non-state, institution to non-institution, sociolinguistic Darwinism to multiplicity and diversity of cultural development, and formal to informal realms of everyday life as the sites, times and sources of cultural expression.

The dualism between the concepts of 'culture' and 'nature' that fed the foundational idea of civilisational progress also disappeared. 'Culture' became the varied, creative expressions of each individual's virtue gifted from nature. Producers of anarchist forms of culture believed that civilisational progress was reliant on these individual expressions for the symbiotic process of social improvement. The anarchist concept of culture thereby inverted both the modern Western notion of civilisation and the ideological foundations of the Japanese imperial state.

A number of distinctive cultural movements and intellectual developments followed one after another to constitute the multifaceted conceptual turns in culture. Such varied expressions and fields of study in early 20th-century Japan as religion, primatology, microbiology, literature, theatre, popular music, agriculture, language, and children's art and *mingei* (民芸) folk art responded to the cultural revolution. These cultural expressions were in tune with the formulations of multiplicity, democracy, mutual aid, and symbiosis in scientific nature. The widely recognised and pioneering primatologist Imanishi Kinji, who was fundamentally influenced by 'anarchist science' at this time, developed his influential and radical studies of culture in the primate world—culture in nature—that continue to orient the work of primatologists around the world today. In religion, Tolstoyan anarchist religion was embraced nationwide, leading Tolstoy to become the most translated writer in the modern history of Japan.[17] In folk art, Yanagi Sōetsu, who introduced Mechnikov's microbiology in Japan after the war, would develop the folk art movement called People's Art, *Mingei,* from this discourse. In 1911, Yanagi had published a well-known article on Mechnikov, 'Mechnikov's Scientific View on Human Life'.[18] Yanagi was a member of the White Birch Group that was heavily inspired by its most senior member, Arishima Takeo. Without a conductor to harmonise them, the various cultural expressions nonetheless appeared as if they had been orchestrated to overturn the concept of culture.

Culture was reproduced as knowledge that did not flow from the classrooms of state schools and imperial universities to shape the popular Japanese mind. The production and circulation of knowledge took place instead in unofficial sites of knowledge dissemination and production such as local shrines, rural homes that housed poetry reading groups, churches, village schools, the second floor of the Nakamuraya sweet shop in Tokyo, inns and pubs, the second floor of the *Heimin Byōin* 平民病院 hospital, pharmacies, the shops and homes of neighbourhood book lenders, dormitories within the imperial universities, and urban 'People's Cafeterias' (*Heimin Shokudō* 平民食堂). These cafeterias came to be widely known as *Taishū Shokudō* (mass cafeterias 大衆食堂), referring here not to the labouring class of Marxist language, but to the anarchist notion of 'everyone' regardless of class. It would be this *Taishū*, inclusive of everyone, that the so-called 'Marxist' Yamakawa Hitoshi would later call for, as '*Taishū e*' ('*v Narod*' in Russian or 'Going to the People'), using the anarchist concept of the 'people' developed in the course of the Nonwar Movement. People educated themselves and discussed the latest findings in social studies and the natural sciences. Their meetings occurred primarily in the evenings. From day to night, from imperial university campuses to unofficial sites, the places and times where and when the reverse flow of knowledge was developed and disseminated were themselves part of the cultural revolution.[19]

---

17   For example, Russian scholar Kim Rekho writes, 'in terms of the breadth and depth of the study of Tolstoy's works, Japan without question occupies a special place among other countries … Nowhere, except Russia, have the works of Tolstoy been published as many times as in Japan. Nowhere outside Russia have they written about Tolstoy so much as Japan'. Kim Rekho, 'Lev Tolstoi i Vostok' [Lev Tolstoi and the East], in Kim Rekho ed., *Lev Tolstoi i literatury Vostoka* [Lev Tolstoi and the Literature of the East] (Moscow: IMLI RAN, Nasledie, 2000), 6. Tolstoy's collected works, ranging from 10 to 47 volumes, have been published at least 13 times in Japan.

18   Yanagi Sōetsu, 'Mechinikofu no kagakuteki jinsei kan' [Mechnikov's Scientific View on Life], in his *Kagaku to jinsei* [Science and Life] (Tokyo: Momiyama Shoten, 1911), 133–326.

19   Konishi, 'Epilogue', *Anarchist Modernity*, 331.

Despite the powerful Western origins of the term 'democracy', a notion of anarchist democracy developed in this period without reference to the nation-state.[20] The Japanese imagination of 'the people' as *heimin*, without class or national belonging, was the subject for a just democratic sociopolitical order that I have described elsewhere as an 'invention of the "people" without the state'. The invention of 'the people' as *heimin* may be compared to the invention of 'the people' in America, which Edmund Morgan demonstrates was integral to American democracy as representative government.[21] Yet anarchist culture came to define 'the people's' practice of everyday democratic life, given expression in such phrases as '*kurashi no chikara* 暮らしの力' (the power of everyday life) by the anarchist physician Katō Tokijirō. 'Democracy' for cooperatist anarchists meant the pursuit of the progressive principle of mutual aid in everyday life, a notion outlined by the anarchist Peter Kropotkin in his work *Mutual Aid: A Factor of Evolution*.[22] The promise of anarchist democracy, aligned with the notion of progress as ever changing and developing human civilisation, drew numerous people to participate in the expansion of cooperatist anarchism. Their idea of 'democracy' became inseparable from active popular practices of mutual aid to overcome economic hardship. Anarchist democracy became the practical means to solve people's everyday problems and concretely improve their lives in an equitable and mutually beneficial manner through spontaneous associations of people to cooperatively solve shared problems through mutual aid. In this way, cooperatist anarchism gave ideological shape to the development of cooperatist society and sociality, or 'anarchist civil society' if you like.

Anarchists in Japan gave progressive meaning to the everyday cooperative practices of ordinary people, and their corresponding antihierarchical relationality and subjectivity. 'Cooperative living', ranging from the micro-level of everyday life to transnational-scale interdependence between peoples of different ethnicities, races and cultural backgrounds, was identified as the key to achieving democratic society on a global scale.

---

20   Sho Konishi, 'Translingual World Order: Language Without Culture in Post-Russo-Japanese War Japan', *Journal of Asian Studies* 72, no. 1 (February 2013).

21   Edmund Morgan, *Inventing the People: The Rise of Popular Sovereignty in England and America* (New York: W.W. Norton & Co., 1988).

22   Peter Kropotkin, *Mutual Aid: A Factor of Evolution* (London: W.W. Heinemann, 1902).

Functioning within this intellectual universe, *Heimin Igaku* 平民医学 (The People's Society for Medical Knowledge), *Heimin Shokudō* (The People's Cafeteria) and *Heimin Byōin* (The People's Hospital) were founded and supported as cooperative institutions by anarchists to directly address its members' practical needs for hospital treatment, medical knowledge, and meals. In the People's Cafeteria, for example, cafeteria 'regulations' stated that the cafeteria was a 'part of the larger project for Mutual Aid'. This particular people's cafeteria drew on average 700–800 ordinary people every day, with 13,387 people using the cafeteria just in the month of March 1918, for example.[23] Their spontaneous activities from below to solve real everyday problems on the spot were reminiscent of the popular phrase '*Kayui tokoro ni te ga todoku*' (the dexterous hand is able to itch just the right spot かゆいところに手が届く).

Ishikawa Sanshirō coined a new term for this democracy as everyday practice. He created the term '*domin seikatsu* 土民生活', or 'the life of people on the soil'. While *domin seikatsu* stirs up images of farmers tending to the soil, Ishikawa was in fact referring to the organic rootedness of all people in their God-given nature, or virtue. Ishikawa believed that each individual has a will (*ishi* 意思) or subjectivity/virtue (*jitsusei* 実性), which was uniquely different in each person. This will, or talent, may be realised only through hard work and the repeated practice of it. Ishikawa called this activity of work and practice '*nenriki* 念力', which is the energy or power everyone has to work on and realise their virtue. He called the resulting force that is created in realising one's virtue '*katsudō* 活動', or active motion in society. 'Freedom' (*jiyū* 自由) was the possibility given to each individual to discover and realise his or her own personal God-given will and virtue. This freedom was the very source of human development, which he called '*sensa banshu* 千差万種' (one thousand differences, one million kinds). This realisation of the plurality of individual development, the so-called 'million ways' of participation in the human community, was what Ishikawa meant when he reinvented democracy as '*domin*

---

23  On Katō Tokijiro and the beginnings of these institutions, see Narita Ryūichi, *Katō Tokijiro* (Tokyo: Fuji Shuppan, 1983).

*seikatsu*'.[24] Ishikawa saw democracy as an expression of what he called the 'new cosmology' defined by the centreless universe. He described the 'unity in multiplicity' that would lead to independence and equality in human society. For Ishikawa, the infinity that characterised our centreless universe dictated the absence of an absolute subject of power and the limitlessness of possibilities for human interaction and cultural invention.

It was in this context that the Esperanto language was named the biggest fad just after the Russo-Japanese War by *Asahi* newspaper. Once again, the near perfect contrast between the popularity of Esperanto on the ground and the absence of any discussion of Esperantism in the historiography of modern Japan is striking.[25] The language was studied and discussed by elites and non-elites alike in non-insitutional spaces such as in rural homes, coffee shops, and even on the farm (as occurred in the case of the renowned novelist and social thinker Miyazawa Kenji), often at night when institutions privileged by state and financial power had closed.[26] By looking at these space-times outside the realms of state guidance, we become privy to an imagination of peace and world order that operated outside the international relations of the nation-state. The history of this cultural-linguistic movement offers us a rare window into a popular concept of world order in Asia. By the mid-1920s, Japan had the highest number of Esperanto speakers by far of any non-European country including the US. Many Esperantists, including leading figures in the anarchist cultural revolution like Ōsugi Sakae, believed that the language, often called '*Minsaigo* 民際語', the people's language on the non-state level, in contrast to '*Kokusaigo* 国際語' (international language or, literally, 'language between states') as the language of the nation-state

---

24  Ishikawa Sanshirō, *Kinsei domin tetsugaku* [Philosophy of Democracy], in Tsurumi Shunsuke ed., *Kindai Nihon shisō taikei* [Collection of Modern Japanese Thought] 16 (Tokyo: Chikuma Shobō, 1976), 39–111. See also Ishikawa, 'Nōhonshugi to domin shisō' [Agrarianism and Democratic Life], in *Ishikawa Sanshirō chosakushū* 3 (Tokyo: Seidōsha, 1978), 96–100; 'Shakai bigaku toshite no museifushugi' [Anarchism as Social Aesthetics], in *Ishikawa Sanshirō chosakushū* 3 (Tokyo: Seidōsha, 1978), 190–206; and 'Dōtai shakai bigaku toshite no museifushugi' [Anarchism as Aesthetic Dynamic], in *Ishikawa Sanshirō chosakushū* 3 (Tokyo: Seidōsha, 1978), 207–17. See also Kitazawa Fumitake, *Ishikawa Sanshirō no shōgai to shisō* [The Thought and Life of Ishikawa Sanshirō], 3 vols (Tokyo: Hatonomori Shobō, 1974).

25  On the Esperanto movement in the early 20th century as an expression of an understanding of what I call 'translingual world order', see my article, 'Translingual World Order'. On the history of Esperanto in Japan, see also Ian Rapley, 'When Global and Local Culture Meet: Esperanto in 1920s Rural Japan', *Language Problems & Language Planning* 37, no. 2 (2013): 179–96. For Rapley's insightful overall treatment of the topic, see his 'Green Star Japan: Language and Internationalism in the Japanese Esperanto Movement, 1905–1944', (DPhil diss., University of Oxford, 2013).

26  Konishi, 'The Science of Symbiosis and Linguistic Democracy'.

and international relations, was designed to promote the multiplicity of cultures that interdependently coexist and evolve. This distinguished it from the international languages of English or French, for example, that essentially belonged to particular culture(s) and, given power in the context of civilisation discourse of the time, expanded through political, economic and cultural imperialism—'linguistic Darwinism'.

At the heart of anarchist democracy and the modern progress formulated by anarchists were the domestically rooted cooperatist activities found in agrarian communities, the most unlikely place for civilisational progress. Anarchists like Itō Noe identified the cooperatist practices that she observed in her own rural home region to be 'the reality of anarchism in Japan'. Itō saw in those everyday practices a global significance for human progress. She concluded that anarchism has been and continues to exist in everyday practice, and it was therefore this 'reality' that 'we should consciously work on'.[27]

## Cooperative Living in Hokkaido

Let me now turn to the concrete manifestation of these ideas on the most unlikely site, Hokkaido, the experimental site for the realisation of Western modernity in the late 19th and early 20th century. From the first years of the Meiji period, modern agricultural practices were promoted in the vast expanses of Hokkaido as a means to achieve Japan's colonisation of its northern territory and, later, its imperialist expansion into other territories. The farm that had belonged to the father of *Shirakaba* (White Birch 白樺) Group activist Arishima Takeo was an embodiment of this colonial effort, and Arishima's inheritance of the farm contradicted his anarchist beliefs and practices. He was serving at this time as an unusually popular professor at Hokkaido University where he taught anarchist values in the heart of Japan's colonisation efforts. In distinct polemic with the Japanese Government's modern vision of agriculture modelled after America, Arishima liberated his tenant farmers in 1921, granting them cooperative ownership of the land. He departed from the farm and its affairs entirely upon liberation, believing in the farmers' own abilities to democratically run the farm. Arishima's liberation of

---

27 Itō Noe, 'Museifushugi no jijitsu' [The Reality of Anarchism], in *Itō Noe zenshū* [The Complete Works of Itō Noe] 2 (Tokyo: Gakugei Shorin, 1970), 222–35.

his tenant farmers and founding of a farm cooperatively owned by the farmers on his former estate in Hokkaido in 1921 became a model and symbol of the progressiveness of cooperative practices among rural non-elites. Named Cooperative Living Farm, and widely known as Arishima Farm, the success of the farm was talked about across Hokkaido and well beyond, drawing numerous farmers from across northern Japan to apply for membership. The farm's modern, cooperatist anarchist perception of the world and its integration into the broader agricultural community of Hokkaido suggests that the farm was quite different from the nomadic, self-peripheralised fugitive communites that fled the state, featured in James Scott's anarchist history of Southeast Asia.[28]

The existing view of this famous site of tenant farmer liberation is that of a 'futile utopian project' that failed with Arishima's suicide in 1923. A frequently used Japanese history textbook epitomised this view by describing Arishima's suicide as having 'effectively sealed the fate of this noble but poorly executed experiment'.[29] Arishima himself, in his liberation speech to the farmers, warned them of the struggles they would face to survive, while 'surrounded by malevolent capitalism'.[30]

In contrast, my interviews with former members of the farm reveal that the farmers themselves felt not only that they were surviving, but that they were at the very forefront of modern progress.[31] As one member used to say, he felt as if he had 'climbed atop a mountain of jewels' when he and his family became members of the farm.[32] This sense of achievement and progress came not from concrete material improvement in their lives, of which there was little in the first decades of the farm's existence, but from the shared sense of mutual ownership of the farm and cooperative living in the midst of 'malevolent capitalism'.

---

28   James C. Scott, *The Art of Not Being Governed: An Anarchist History of Upland Southeast Asia* (New Haven, CT: Yale University Press, 2009).

29   David Lu, *Japan: A Documentary History* (Armonk, NY and London, England: M.E. Sharpe, 1997), 400.

30   Arishima Takeo, 'Kosakunin e no kokubetsu' [Farewell to Tenants], *Izumi* 1 (1 October 1 1922): 43.

31   Sho Konishi, 'Ordinary Farmers, Competing Time: Arishima Cooperative Farm in Hokkaido, 1922–1935', *Modern Asian Studies* 47, no. 6 (November 2013): 1845–87.

32   A former member of the farm, Kiriyama Katsuo, recalled his father Tokiji saying this to his family and neighbours on numerous occasions. Kiriyama Katsuo, interview by author, Niseko, Japan, 2000.

As evidenced by the farm's handbook, members interpreted their cooperative farm as the progressive materialisation of anarchist thought on nature, even as their practices relied on common-sense rural traditions of mutual aid interrupted by the expansion of tenant farming. Every member of Cooperative Living Farm carried a copy of the *Cooperative Living Handbook*. It is the only written document we have from that period. Arishima's liberation speech served as the anchoring centrepiece of the coop book. 'Anyone knows that the source of all production, land, water, air … should not be owned privately but should be shared and used for the mutual benefit of all human beings.'[33] Along with Arishima, the anarchists Kropotkin and Tolstoy were specifically mentioned as cohorts who shared their ideas of progress based on the principle of *Sōgo Fujo* 相互扶助, Mutual Aid.

The new spaces created by the members of Cooperative Living Farm on the one hand, and their new modern subjectivity of cooperative progress on the other, emerged in reciprocal relation to each other. New spaces created on the farm continuously gave new shape to the community, guiding those who conducted everyday life in those spaces. In tandem with the growing experience of cooperative community-making, these spaces silently gained in sacredness.

The Shintō shrines that dotted the colonial landscape visible atop its farms' highest points have been commonly described as authoritative, patriarchal and forbidding. They were a spatial symbol of colonial control over the lands, which were laid under the shrine's gaze. Behind the gaze were the landlords who built the shrines with the encouragement of the Colonisation Bureau. The shrines represented a masculine patriarchical order that was a foundation for the emperor-centred ideology of the nation-state. The shrines culturally and religiously authenticated settlers' participation in the national colonisation project in Hokkaido. In contrast, Iyateru Shrine of Cooperative Living Farm stood out for its modesty. After Arishima inherited the shrine, he physically removed it from its place atop the farm's highest point on Miya Mountain overseeing the colonial property, to its current position halfway up a small hill, modestly nestled among the other hills of the estate. Following liberation, the shrine became a focal point for community activities, where the farm's annual deliberative meetings, festivals and other community gatherings were

---

33  *Kyōsan nōdan techō* [Arishima Cooperative Living Farm Handbook], Arishima Takeo Museum and Archive, Niseko, Japan, 8-7-90.

held. The farmers themselves further added a new sacred meaning of their own to the shrine. They installed a hidden back window in the shrine, behind which they erected a sacred six-sided stone structure dedicated to the goddesses. When the window was opened for annual ceremonies of cultivation and harvest, it served as a window to the goddesses.

At first glance, the stone appears to be quite similar to numerous pentagonal worship stones erected in the region surrounding the farm to honour the Taishō emperor as a part of State-sponsored Shintōist practices. Many of the stones were erected in the years immediately following the new emperor's enthronement, in 1914–16.[34] However, close comparison with the many five-sided *jijin* at other farms in the region reveals that Cooperative Living Farmers erected their stone independently, for the added purpose of paying tribute to their liberation and the founding of the farm.

Members had added an entirely unique sixth side to the traditional five-sided stone of the five goddesses of production. Their hexagonal stone was engraved with the date August 1924, to commemorate the second anniversary of the liberation of the farm and the establishment of their community. The stone thus made it appear as if the emergence of Cooperative Living Farm was being embraced by the five goddesses, inscribed on the remaining five sides. It seemed the goddesses themselves had given birth to Cooperative Living Farm. This was consistent with the farm's shared ideology of the divine nature of the land, which was the deities' 'gift' foundational to the emergence of the community in 1922. The divine givenness of the soil took away the landlord's right to the land. This sixth side was an invention of the Cooperative Living Farmers, who had inserted their realm of cooperative virtue into the sacred realm of the goddesses.

The goddesses of production represented a cosmological foundation of human relations of interdependency with nature, and with other human beings. This most fundamental existence of human beings as they understood it, their dependency on nature and on one another for survival, provided a foundation for their non-hierarchically constituted practices

---

34 See the works by the local history study group of Kutchan, the neighbouring village of Niseko, Ishida Suteo, Takei Shizuo, and Ono Taizō, *Nono shinbutsu* [Gods of the Field] (Kutchan: Kutchan Local History Study Group, 1987), and Kutchan chō kyodōbunkazai hozonkai ed., *Kutchan no jijinsan batōsan* [The Jijinsan and Batōsan of Kutchan] (Kutchan: Kutchan Chō Kyodō Bunkazai Hozonkai, n.d.).

of mutual aid. The sacred stone stood at the centre of the farm's annual spring planting and fall harvest festivals, which began with ceremonial offerings to the goddesses. The stone thereby further altered the patriarchal authority of the shrine, by reconditioning it with a localised folk religion of the soil. It was as if 'State Shintōism' had never reached here.

Members also erected a water god stone, another unique structure. The stone overlooked and made sacred the farm's dam, which served as the centre point for its irrigation system. Together, the worship stones of water, soil and air completed and concretised the cooperative imperative and delivered the anarchist notion of non-ownership and cooperative utilisation of natural resources for mutual benefit. They represented the foundational ethic of the farm itself, the imperative of shared cultivation and utilisation of the natural resources for the purpose of co-survival with nature.

Technology was neither opposed to nor superior to nature in farm members' understanding. It was seen rather to complement and enhance the gifts of nature. The farm thus vigorously pursued technological advancement. It experimented with some of the latest technological advancements necessary to pipe in water for the paddies. They applied new techniques for temperature moderation of the icy water tapped from the adjacent mountain.[35] The conversion to rice promised both material and symbolic progress. Back in early Meiji, the Hokkaido Colonisation Office had emphasised the importation of large-scale farming with agricultural technologies from the West that centred on foods like potatoes, corn, beef and dairy. No other farm in the region surrounding Cooperative Living Farm had yet experimented with rice cultivation. The shiny white rice was thus the taste of cooperative living progress. The rice became a part of their identity, as it set the farm apart from the rest of the farms. Within a decade or so, bags of their rice decorated with large red labels 'Arishima mai' [Arishima Rice] were found in stores across the region. Members were convinced of the progressiveness of their existence as a new modern community of mutual aid. Adopting new technologies took considerable place in this progressive self-image. The linkage between

---

35  Blueprint of the irrigation plan and 'Request to Begin Construction of Irrigation', Arishima Takeo Museum and Archive, 1-6-101. See also *Arishima no sato: Arishima nōjō jidai no seikatsu* [Arishima's Homeland: Life in Arishima's Farming Period] (Hokkaido). Self-publication in the Arishima Takeo Museum and Archive, 24–7.

technology and the advancement of cooperative living may be contrasted with surrounding tenant farms, where the benefits of technology were hardly returned to the tenant farmer.

According to former farm member Kiriyama Katsuo, another aspect of their new life on the farm that members had to work on was gift-giving. Kiriyama recalls that members meticulously practised the giving of gifts in carefully measured equal number to each member of the farm. The practice of gift-giving was constructed to horizontalise relations among members of the community. Members consciously contrasted this new practice with the old times of tenancy, when the gift was often used in a vertical bi-directional manner between managers and the labourers who worked for them, functioning to enhance the power relations between them. A gift to the landlord or the manager used to grease the machinery of the tenant–landlord relationship of dependency. Usually given in a single direction to those with power, the gift might anticipate or follow a request for a loan, or some other sort of necessity. It might simply put the tenant in the landlord's favour. In turn, gifts or demonstrations of favour from the landlord served to concretise the benevolent status of the landlord in relation to his tenants.[36] On Cooperative Living Farm, what might be called the practice of multidirectional gift-giving appears to have functioned as the demonstration of mutual interdependency and the preservation of the non-hierarchy of members' recognition and value to one other. Overall, it helped to dislodge privilege from community relations.

Kiriyama's distinct recollection of his farm's gift-giving practices in interviews revealed members' conscious efforts to habitualise the practice into a new farm tradition. Each family drew on their own particular resources and abilities for simultaneous gift-giving in equal measure. Members looked forward to the deliveries of gifts from multiple directions, and they knew that no more would be given to any particular member

---

36  Nagatsuka Takashi, *The Soil: A Portrait of Rural Life in Meiji Japan*, trans. Ann Waswo (London and New York: Routledge, 1989), gives a realistic account of tenant–landlord relations in the early 1900s. On landlord benevolence, see e.g. 39–40. For an anthropological discussion of gift-giving practices in light of psychology and time, see Pierre Bourdieu, *Outline of a Theory of Practice* (Cambridge: Cambridge University Press, 1977), 3–8.

than the other.[37] The power once given to the former 'master' dissipated in the multidirectional material exchange of things. The practice of multidirectional gift-giving was now a practice of 'new' time.

Interestingly, at a time of mass tenant farmer unrest across the country, the All-Hokkaido Agricultural Industrial Cooperative Association also began to speak in the language of cooperatist anarchist, rather than Marxist, progress in the early 1920s. The association was the representative organ for agricultural industrial cooperatives found across Hokkaido, in every town and village. In 1926, the cooperative association published the first issue of its farming journal *Kyōei* (共栄 Co-prosperity), which outlined the ideals and goals of this large organisation. The journal sought to put the 'world in perspective', to promote thinking among agricultural labourers about world affairs. Situating themselves in a historical time of cooperatist progress, the journal stated that while the 'Great Project' of the Meiji Ishin had fulfilled the political tasks assigned it, the *cultural* resurrection in modern Japan had not yet been achieved. The declaration of the Hokkaido-wide cooperative called in essence for a second, cultural Ishin, through the 'cooperatist movement'. Farmers themselves were writing history. In accord with the larger History Slide, the cooperative's declaration stated:

> In the social life of today's civilisation, we are trying to conduct a life of less anxiety, more pleasure and hope, a life of more creativity, mutual love and mutual aid. Relying on Social Darwinism will never lead to making a society of peace. It is Kropotkinism or Cooperatism that we believe in. To realise this ideal of both the material and spiritual world, *sangyō kumiaism* (industrial cooperativism) is nothing but Kropotkinism.[38]

Their association represented agricultural practices with anarchist ideas of progress in the very space of Hokkaido, the nation's most intense and complete experimental project of Western modernity, most vividly symbolised by its vast glittering mechanised farms and farming industries. The inversion of Western modernity was now complete.

---

37 Kiriyama Katsuo, interview by author, Niseko, Japan, 2000. For example, Kiriyama recalled that every year, a family receiving persimmons from relatives on Honshu counted the number of people in each household on the farm and delivered a single fruit for each person in each household. Neighbours came to expect that in the autumn, that household would bring them each a persimmon. The fruits were delivered personally, not losing thereby the cooperative meaning of the gift.

38 'Sangyō kumiai sengen' [Industrial Cooperative Declaration], part I, *Kyōei: Hokkaido Sangyō Kumiai zasshi* [Coprosperity: Hokkaido Industrial Association Journal] (June 1929): 6–10.

Tellingly, many years later during the US Occupation of Japan, when American representatives of the Supreme Commander for the Allied Powers (SCAP) came to judge whether Arishima Farm's practices were democratic or not, they couldn't make sense of the farm. This was not 'democracy' as Americans understood it, yet it looked very democratic. Nor was it 'Communist', yet it looked very communal. Giving up on finding a label for it, the Americans left it up to the farmers to decide whether their farm community belonged to the new postwar era.

This particular modernity imagined, lived and experienced by cooperatist anarchists in Japan *uprooted* and *overturned* the very state-centred modernity of the West. In this sense, the notions of 'resistance' and 'being overcome by Western modernity' were inadequate to describe this history. By provincialising the state, cooperatist anarchists also naturally provincialised Europe. This was the opposite, I might add, to what postcolonial scholars have attempted to achieve through theories of so-called hybrid cultures and alternative modernities modelled on Western political structures of the state. Even the postcolonial project to 'Provincialise Europe'[39] has in a way re-emphasised the centrality of Western modernity. In contrast, 'survival' in this discourse of cooperatist anarchism, and indeed the survival *of* this discourse, depended on the successful liberation in both thought and practice from the temporality and the territorial utopia of the modern nation-state of Western modernity.

---

39   Chakrabarty, *Provincializing Europe: Postcolonial Thought and Historical Difference.*

# 2

# Social Change and Rediscovering Rural Reconstruction in China[1]

Ou Ning

## The Origins of the Rural Reconstruction Movement

Rural reconstruction, one of the most important insurmountable problems in China's relentless pursuit of modernity, has had its ups and downs over the last 100 years. It again has emerged as a lens through which to examine the role of different political and intellectual forces in China's process of social reform. This chapter explores this historical legacy and the recent re-emergence of rural reconstruction as a source of inspiration for Chinese social change.

Chinese elites began exploring the concept of rural reform in the late Qing dynasty, when Mi Jiansan and his Japan-educated son Mi Digang, members of a distinguished local family in the village of Zhaicheng in Ding county of Hebei province, experimented with the idea of 'village government' (*cunzhi* 村治) in 1902, through literacy campaigns, civic education and local self-government. County magistrate Sun Faxu developed their idea further as he took the post of governor in neighbouring Shanxi province, and it was later also embraced by the

---

1    This chapter is a revised version of an essay first published in Ou Ning ed., *The South of Southern: Space, Geography, History and the Biennale* (Beijing: China Youth Press, 2014).

warlord Yan Xishan, who effectively controlled Shanxi in the Republican era and turned the province into a model of rural reconstruction. The 'Village Government Group' (*cunzhipai* 村治派) was established as a school of thought in 1924, when some north China landed gentry, including Wang Hongyi, Mi Digang, Mi Jieping, Peng Yuting, Liang Zhonghua, Yi Zhongcai and Wang Yike, launched the *Zhonghua Daily* (*Zhonghua ribao* 中华日报) and the *Village Government Monthly* (*Cunzhiyuekan* 村治月刊). In 1925, the then four-year-old Chinese Communist Party, having realised the importance of farmers to its revolution, decided to mobilise support in the countryside with their 'Letter to Farmers' (*gao nongmin shu* 告农民书), encouraging the establishment of farmers' unions. The ensuing class struggles and land revolution provoked urban intellectuals into seeking different approaches to rural reform.

The 30 May 1925 shooting of protesters in the Shanghai International Settlement sparked a nationwide labour and anti-imperialist movement, and many parts of China saw a surge of rural reconstruction experiments. By 1934, official statistics show that there were more than 600 rural reconstruction groups and over 1,000 experiments across China.[2] Newspapers and magazines were filled with reports, commentaries and debates on rural reconstruction. The two most influential experiments were those conducted by Liang Shuming's Rural Reconstruction Institute in Zouping county, Shandong province, and Y. C. James Yen's Mass Education Association in Ding county, Hebei province. Liang, inspired by the 'Village Government Group', developed a Confucianism-based philosophy for rural reconstruction and thus was considered a member of the 'Old Group' (*jiupai* 旧派) while Yen, who was Christian and received funding from the United States, belonged to the 'New Group' (*xinpai* 新派).

## The Politics of Rural Reconstruction

In the 13th volume of *The Cambridge History of China*, historian John K. Fairbank devoted a whole section, 'The Rural Reconstruction Movement', to the massive rural reconstruction campaigns of the time. Fairbank

---

2    Zhang Yuanshan and Xu Shilian eds, *Xiangcun jianshe shiyan* [Experiment of Rural Reconstruction] Volume 2, (Shanghai: Zhonghua Book Company, 1935), 19.

identified six types of campaigns: 1) Western-influenced (James Yen); 2) nativist (the 'Village Government Group', Liang Shuming and Tao Xingzhi, the founder of the Xiaozhuang Normal College in Nanjing); 3) educational (James Yen and Tao Xingzhi); 4) military (Peng Yuting, who established a local defence regime in Zhenping county, Henan province); 5) populist (James Yen and Tao Xingzhi); and 6) bureaucratic (the two 'experimental counties' administered by the Nanjing authorities in Lanxi, Zhejiang province and Jiangning, Jiangsu province). But Fairbank's volume overlooked several other important experiments—those carried out by Lu Zuofu's Chongqing Beibei Defence Bureau in the Gorges region along the Yangtze tributary Jialing River; Gao Jiansi's Jiangsu Provincial Institute of Education in Huangxiang, Wuxi, Jiangsu province; and Huang Yanpei's National Association of Vocational Education of China in Xugongqiao, Kunshan, Jiangsu province.

*The Cambridge History of China* stated that all rural reconstruction experiments were linked inextricably to politics:

> To revitalise the countryside through educational and economic reforms meant working out relationships of patronage and protection with political authorities. This was surely because any attempt to work with the peasantry in an organised project inevitably raised questions of political orientation and legitimacy, whether or not the project had any explicitly political aims or activities.[3]

Owing to political uncertainty, these educational, social and economic reforms—though not without a local effect—were unable to provide a comprehensive solution to China's rural problems. Politics was not only a barrier to China's rural reconstruction but a key factor contributing to its ultimate failure. Yen first claimed that his experiment had nothing to do with politics, but had to admit later that 'given the circumstances, we couldn't keep ourselves away from politics'.[4] Liang said that the 'two major difficulties' he encountered were 'the inevitable need to rely on the

3    Philip A. Kuhn, 'The Rural Reconstruction Movement', in John K. Fairbank and Albert Feuerwerker eds, *The Cambridge History of China*, vol. 13, *Republican China 1912–1949, Part 2* (Cambridge: Cambridge University Press, 1986), 359.
4    Y. C. James Yen, 'Pingmin jiaoyu yundong de huigu yu qianzhan' [The Past and Future of the Mass Education Movement], in Enrong Song ed., *Gaoyu renmin* [To the People] (Guilin: Guangxi Normal University Press, 2003), 197.

authorities to push for social reform and farmers' indifference to the rural reconstruction movement'.[5] Rural reconstruction was doomed to failure if it did not seek 'a political solution'.[6]

In fact, the multitude of experiments that focused on local self-government, mass education and agricultural development were preceded by the brief existence in China of a utopian philosophy called 'New Village-ism' (*xincunzhuyi* 新村主义)—a mixture of Japanese writer Mushanokōji Saneatsu's idea of *Atarashiki-mura* (New Village, 新しき村), Peter Kropotkin's theory of mutual aid, and Lev Tolstoy's view of labour and the North American practice of combining studies with part-time work. Mushanokōji's philosophy was part of the 'White Birch Group' (*Shirakaba-ha* 白樺派), for the name of the literary magazine he founded in 1910, 'White Birch' (on this movement see also Chapters One and Three). In 1918, in the mountains of Miyazaki Prefecture in Kyushu, members of the White Birch Group carried out their plan to build an intentional community without government, exploitation or social class and to live an idyllically pastoral life. Chinese writer Zhou Zuoren was a long-time subscriber to the commune's literary magazine *Atarashiki-mura,* expressing his support for the movement in his articles 'Humanist Literature' (*Rende wenxue* 人的文学) and 'Japan's New Village' (*Ribende xincun* 日本的新村), published in 1918 and 1919 in the influential magazine *La Jeunesse,* during China's New Culture Movement of the 1910s and 1920s. Zhou even visited Miyazaki himself and in 1920 founded a branch of the *Atarashiki-mura* commune in his Beijing home, attracting early communist leaders such as Li Dazhao, Mao Zedong, Cai Hesen and Yun Daiying.

The same year, a similar and influential experiment was started in the village of Xiaowuying of Xihua county, Henan province, by Wang Gongbi, a member of the former *Tongmenghui,* a revolutionary alliance absorbed by the Kuomintang in 1912. Xiaowuying was soon renamed Youth Village (*qingniancun* 青年村). Mao Zedong was also an admirer of 'New Village-ism', but chose the path of revolution in the end. It was only after the founding of the People's Republic of China in 1949 that

---

5    Liang Shuming, *Xiangcun jianshe lilun* [Rural Reconstruction Theories] (Shanghai: Shanghai Century Publishing Group, 2006), 368.

6    Cao Lixin made an in-depth analysis of the political dilemma faced by the rural reconstruction movement in the Republican era in comparison with the rural revolution of the Communist Party of China. See Cao Lixin, 'Zouxiang zhengzhi jiejue de xiangcun jianshe' [Rural Reconstruction: Toward a Political Solution], *Twenty-First Century* 91 (October 2005).

Mao would transform this utopian philosophy into people's communes. The idealistic values of 'New Village-ism', unlike the pragmatic approach of the rural reconstruction movement, soon fell into decline in China. In fact, 'New Village-ism' was not only a Japanese import but a continuation of ancient Chinese Agrarianism (*nongjia* 农家), the most marginalised and overlooked of all the schools of thought, and one that dates back to the golden age of Chinese philosophy from 770 to 221 BC. Agriculturalism was discussed in a volume ('Treatise on Literature', *yiwenzhi* 艺文志) of the *Book of Han* (*hanshu* 汉书), a history written in the Han dynasty:

> The first Agrarianists may have been agriculture officials, who grew different kinds of grain and encouraged people to till land and plant mulberry trees to produce enough food and clothing. Food is so important that it ranks first among the eight major areas of a state's policy, followed by property. The merit of early Agriculturalists is their emphasis on food production, which Confucius said should be a priority for any ruler. However, their vulgar successors, who believe that a saint-king in the Confucian sense would be useless, attempt to disrupt the social hierarchy by calling on rulers to plough alongside their people.

In his book *Debt: The First 5000 Years*, American anthropologist and anarchist David Graeber referred to Agrarianism as an anarchist movement in the pre-Qin period.[7]

## Crisis and Revival

The rural reconstruction movement turned out to be short-lived as well. Reformers saw their hopes crushed in 1937, when the national crisis following Japan's invasion took precedence over rural impoverishment and decline as the most urgent problem faced by the country. Still, had the war not broken out, the rural reconstruction movement would have eventually failed because of its own limitations. In 1930, Peng Yuting was assassinated by a rival faction and Chiang Kai-shek ordered Tao Xingzhi to close his Xiaozhuang Normal College. Wang Dazhi, one of Tao's students,

---

7   'In China, while many of the founders of the "hundred schools" of philosophy that blossomed under the Warring States were wandering sages who spent their days moving from city to city trying to catch the ears of princes, others were leaders of social movements from the very start. Some of these movements didn't even have leaders, like the School of the Tillers, an anarchist movement of peasant intellectuals who set out to create egalitarian communities in the cracks and fissures between states.' David Graeber, *Debt: The First 5000 Years* (New York: Melville House, 2012), 237.

carried on the work of his alma mater after being appointed principal of the Xin'an Primary School. He organised the Xin'an Traveling Group (*xinan luxingtuan* 新安旅行团), whose students spent more than 10 years visiting different parts of China and calling for resistance to the Japanese invasion. As different political forces joined the resistance movement, Liang Shuming's Shandong Rural Reconstruction Institute was disbanded and James Yen's Mass Education Association moved to Chongqing with the Kuomintang Government. But Yen did not give up his rural reform efforts. In Chongqing, he established the Chinese Institute of Rural Reconstruction, which was declared a 'reactionary organisation' and taken over by the local Military Control Commission in 1950. Nevertheless, his International Institute of Rural Reconstruction, founded in 1960 in the Philippines, still operates today. Yen dedicated his whole life to rural reconstruction.

These reformers were often criticised for their superficial understanding of the complexity of Chinese society, especially China's stubborn social problems. In 1936, the New Knowledge Bookstore (*Xinzhi Shudian* 新知书店) published *Critiques of China's Rural Reconstruction* (*Zhongguo xiangcun jianshe pipan* 中国乡村建设批判), a collection of commentaries on Liang's and Yen's experiments written by pro-Communist intellectuals such as Qian Jiaju and Li Zixiang. Qian pointed out that Yen and his associates did not fully understand Chinese society:

> They attribute China's social ills to the ignorance, poverty, weakness and selfishness of farmers, who account for over 85 percent of China's population, and believe they need to address those four problems to save Chinese society. But they overlook the fact that farmers' ignorance, poverty, weakness and selfishness are only the symptoms of China's social ills. The root cause cannot be removed simply by treating the symptoms.[8]

Qian argued that Liang, as a 'rural philosopher', had a more in-depth understanding of Chinese society than Yen, but offered only an old solution repackaged as a new one:

> Mr. Liang's new approach appears to be a perfect solution that could immediately lead people into 'a kingdom of liberty, equality and fraternity'. But that is actually just an old trick invented by Confucius, who once said, 'The people only need to be told what to do but not why

---

8    Qian Jiaju, 'Zhongguo nongcun jianshe zhi lu hezai' [Where Is the Path to China's Rural Reconstruction?], in *Zhongguo xiangcun jianshe pipan* [Critiques of China's Rural Reconstruction] (Shanghai: New Knowledge Bookstore, 1936), 101.

they should do it'. His theories of rural reconstruction, under the new disguise of farmer organisations and farmer education, are nothing more than a clever redesign of the current social order.[9]

These two kinds of experiments, Qian suggested, would lead China astray. Although he did not put forward any feasible solution in his articles, it can be inferred from his arguments that he advocated anti-imperialist, anti-feudal class struggles aimed at subverting the established system. The theory of class struggle also served as the ideological basis for the Chinese Communist Party's revolution.

If the only viable option for the Communist Party at that time was to seize power through revolution, what would it do about the unresolved issue of rural reconstruction after its revolution succeeded? Shortly after the People's Republic of China was founded in 1949, private ownership was abolished in the countryside through the agricultural cooperative movement. People's communes were introduced in 1958 as a quintessential example of Mao's vision of rural reconstruction. The concept of people's communes is a blend of the utopian 'New Village-ism', Liang Shuming's theory of combining politics with education, and Peng Yuting's military-style management. Land and labour were pooled to boost agricultural production so that China could build a communist society, in which people would work to their best ability and have all their needs satisfied. However, before being gradually dismantled by the new market economy created in 1984, the communes did not bring about any fundamental improvement in the rural economy or farmers' lives. Instead, they severely damaged Chinese rural society. The concentration of land and other means of production disrupted traditional small-scale farming; intense class struggles and frequent political movements destroyed the family structure and ethics in rural areas; forced labour and egalitarianism demoralised farmers.

Thanks to the household responsibility system adopted in 1982, rural China was revitalised temporarily. But the fast-growing urbanisation that followed has left the countryside increasingly deprived and marginalised and has given rise to myriad problems, including agricultural decline, the loss of agrarian land, rural emigration, reliance on imported food, poor land-use planning (new homes are mostly built on the periphery of a village, leaving the centre with abandoned, dilapidated houses),

---

9    Qian Jiaju, 'Zhongguo de qilu' [China's Wrong Road], in *Zhongguo xiangcun jianshe pipan* (Critiques of China's Rural Reconstruction) (Shanghai: New Knowledge Bookstore, 1936), 142.

insufficient public resources, local gangs, rural–urban imbalance and social conflicts, especially the numerous mass protests staged against arbitrary land acquisitions by the government. Rural reconstruction has re-emerged as a critical issue for China.

In 2003, researcher Wen Tiejun, who coined the phrase 'three rural problems' (rural people, rural society and the rural economy, *sannong wenti* 三农问题), founded the James Yen Rural Reconstruction Institute at the village of Zhaicheng of Hebei province, where Mi Jiansan, Mi Digang and James Yen had done their pioneering work.[10] Farmers from all parts of China arrived at Zhaicheng to participate in his project, which generated significant media coverage. In 2004, Wen was appointed Dean of the School of Agricultural Economics and Rural Development at Remin University in Beijing. He also founded the Liang Shuming Rural Reconstruction Center, a branch of which he moved to Renmin in 2005. The founding of this research institute with multiple affiliate organisations suggested a considerable revival of the rural reconstruction movement of the Republican era. The same year, the Fifth Plenum of the 16th Central Committee of the Communist Party of China resolved to create a 'new socialist countryside' (*shehuizhuyixin nongcun* 社会主义新农村) to address the 'three rural problems'. As Wen and other intellectuals became more involved in rural reconstruction in different parts of the country, governments of all levels were ready to implement the Party's new policy. For example, Sichuan province and Chongqing municipality launched experimental projects to coordinate rural and urban development. The issue of rural reconstruction returned to public view, attracting the attention of both the government and civil society.

Wen was sent to live and work in rural Shanxi province during the Cultural Revolution. He went to Renmin University to study journalism in 1979 and joined the Rural Policy Research Office of the Party's Central Committee in 1985, where he assisted Du Runsheng, an important promoter of the household responsibility system, in research and fieldwork. Thus he gained first-hand experience of the hardships of rural life. Wen studied at the University of Michigan in 1987 and at Columbia University in 1991. He visited Cornell University and the University of

---

10  All quotations from Wen Tiejun in this chapter are taken from 'Sannong wenti: shiji mo de fansi' [The Three Rural Problems: Some Reflections at the End of the Twentieth Century], *Dushu*, December 1999. For the longer version of this article, see Tiejun Wen, *Sannong wenti yu shiji fansi* [The Three Rural Problems and Some Reflections at the End of the Twentieth Century] (Beijing: Joint Publishing, 2005).

Southern California as a visiting scholar in 1991. However, compared with James Yen, who also received Western academic training and embraced an international perspective, Wen has been able to make more insightful observations about the 'three rural problems' and put forward theories in a broader context by using the research methodology he learned from the distinguished economist Wu Jinglian.

Familiar with the philosophy behind the rural reconstruction movement of the Republican era and the rural revolution of the Communist Party, Wen argues that owing to China's enormous population and limited available land, 'neither the revolution nor the reform led to anything other than "equal" distribution of arable land'. He believes that the main cause of the social conflicts in rural areas, unknown to his predecessors, is the excessive extraction of agricultural surplus, which undermines 'the property and income distribution system inherent in the small-scale peasant economy'. That system, in his opinion, is the norm and a stabilising factor for Chinese society, and is 'naturally resistant to the Western Industrial Revolution and the ensuing "social progress" in the capitalist sense'. Wen asserts that China, like the West, has been passing on the huge institutional costs of industrialisation and urbanisation to its countryside.

He also believes that China's development strategy, oriented toward industrial capital, international trade and economic globalisation, not only has imposed an onerous burden on farmers, rural society and agriculture but involves significant risk itself because excessive dependence on imported food and resources means potential vulnerability to global shocks, especially financial crises. Wen often says in self-mockery that his attitude toward urbanisation is too 'conservative' but, in a country obsessed with urban life and high economic growth, his commitment to rural reconstruction is more likely to be considered radical. Compared with the pioneers in the Republican era, he has accomplished more with fewer resources. But he has encountered the same problem as his predecessors— local authorities shut down the James Yen Rural Reconstruction Institute in 2006 on the grounds that it had built an environmentally friendly building without official approval, missed the annual inspection by the local government and advised farmers on petition matters.

Nevertheless, Wen and his followers are as resilient as James Yen. After the institute was closed, Qiu Jiansheng, who had joined the cause of rural reconstruction because of Wen, launched new projects in Hainan and Fujian provinces. One of Wen's PhD students, He Huili, continued to work as assistant to the mayor of Kaifeng city, Henan province, and help local farmers form cooperatives. The Liang Shuming Rural Reconstruction Center is still in operation, encouraging university students to do their part for rural reconstruction, though its former director Liu Xiangbo died in a car accident in 2011. The Little Donkey Farm in the western suburbs of Beijing is working on ecological agriculture and devising new methods to provide organic produce for city dwellers. They all have benefitted from Wen's theories and support, sharing resources among themselves.[11] In addition to Wen's movement, there are other important projects such as the ones run by He Xuefeng in Hubei province, Li Changping in Henan province and Liao Xiaoyi in Sichuan province. By combining the traditional approach to rural reconstruction focused on mass education and agriculture with their insights into contemporary problems, these people have developed various new programs and concepts such as community colleges, community-supported agriculture, ecological villages and 'Workers' Homes', programs targeting migrant workers living in cities (*gongyouzhijia* 工友之家).

Many urban writers and artists have settled in the countryside and become involved in the rural reconstruction movement either because they have noticed the inextricable link between rural and urban areas or because they aspire to rediscover and revive the traditional culture eroded by urbanisation. A well-known example is Johnson Chang Tsong-zung and Hu Xiangcheng's project in the small town of Jinze near Shanghai. They transformed an abandoned industrial site there into a village featuring architecture typical of traditional buildings in the region. Their project covers a number of areas, including reviving traditional folk arts, developing organic farming (they are running a farm as part of the project) and restoring traditional values.[12] Other examples include writer Ye Fu's experiment in representative democracy and rural drama in Luojiang county, Sichuan province, and Li Yinqiang's China Rural Library, a non-government organisation (NGO) that often invites urban writers and intellectuals to give talks to rural children. The strength of these projects lies in their ability to leverage the unique cultural resources at their disposal.[13]

---

11    For more information about the rural reconstruction movement led by Wen Tiejun, see Hong Liang, 'Xingdong zai dadi' [Action on Land], *Chutzpah!*, January 2011.

12    Australian writer Tony Perrottet visited and wrote about Jinze. See Tony Perrottet, 'The Shock of the Old', *The Wall Street Journal Magazine*, 28 June 2012, online.wsj.com/article/SB1000142405270 2304765304577482580429791656.html.

13    For more information about these projects, see 'Tamen de xiangjian' [Their Rural Reconstruction], in *ChinaFortune*, November 2011.

China's urban–rural relations first came to my attention when I was doing research and making documentary film in Guangzhou's urban village San Yuan Li from 2002 to 2003. I realised that urban villages and slums were actually rooted in the failure of the rural economy. From then on, I became interested in studying rural issues, learned about Wen Tiejun's theories and work, and read the biography of James Yen as well as works on the rural reconstruction movement of the Republican era. Before starting my own project, the Bishan Commune (*Bishan Gongtongti* 碧山共同体), in the village of Bishan of Yi county, Anhui province, in 2011, I spent years studying rural society and social movements. I visited the closed James Yen Rural Reconstruction Institute, Qiu Jiansheng's project in Fujian and He Huili's workplace in Henan. I attended the 'Ecology and the Revival of Rural Culture' seminar hosted by Wen Tiejun, talked with intellectuals engaged in rural movements in Taiwan, and examined the diverse body of literature on Chinese rural society.

I also watched Ogawa Shinsuke's documentaries about rural Japan, visited Thai artists Rirkrit Tiravanija and Kamin Lertchaiprasert's Land Foundation in Chiang Mai, and read about Indian writer Arundhati Roy's criticism of the controversial Narmada Dam project and of the Indian Government's armed actions against the Maoist insurgents supported by rural populations. My Bishan Commune thus turned out to be a melting pot of fascinating ideas—a mixture of the benevolent society described in Peter Kropotkin's *Mutual Aid: A Factor of Evolution*, the concept of 'direct action' advocated by neo-anarchism, the utopian artist collective *Neue Slowenische Kunst* established by Slovenian artists, the rural reconstruction movement of the Republican era, and the vision of contemporary reformers like Wen Tiejun.

## The Bishan Project

In 2011, Zuo Jing and I purchased two antique Hui-style houses in the villages of Bishan and Guanlu of Yi County to start our project. We raised funds to hold the first Bishan Harvestival (*bishan fengnianij* 碧山丰年祭), a cultural feast in the form of a harvest celebration. Based on a project called 'Craftsmanship in Yi County' (*yixian baigong* 黟县百工), the event invited artists, architects and designers from other parts of the country to work with local craftsmen and folk artists to create modern versions of traditional objects, which were put on display in

Bishan's ancestral halls and old granaries. There were also exhibitions of historical documents about Bishan village and the region, performances by musicians from other places and local Chinese opera groups, poetry classes for local children, the screening of documentary and dramatic films about rural China, seminars on rural reconstruction attended by participants from both mainland China and Taiwan, and farmers' fairs.[14]

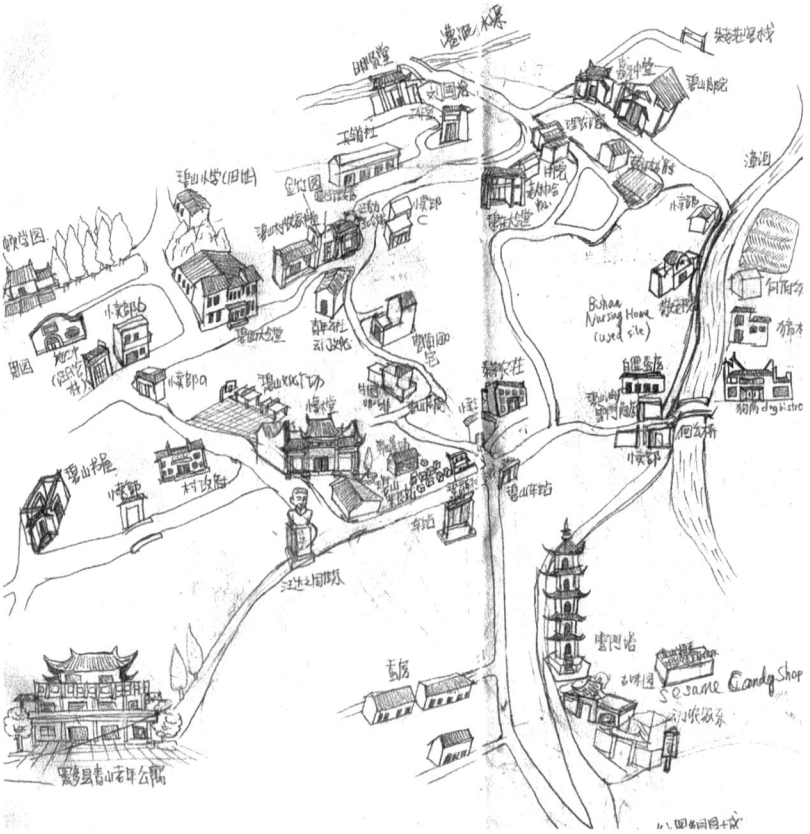

Figure 1: Schematic image of Bishan community.
Source: Ou Ning.

---

14    For details about the Bishan Harvestival, see Zhao Qian's report in the October 2011 issue of *Leap*.

As the first step of our plan, the Bishan Harvestival (a portmanteau of the words 'harvest' and 'festival') aimed at reinvigorating public life in rural areas. We believed that reviving traditional folk arts was, at that stage, the only way to transform our cultural resources into job opportunities and tangible economic benefits for farmers because, although Bishan attracts many tourists every year thanks to its proximity to the beautiful Mount Huangshan, its heavy reliance on admission charges to generate tourism revenue may be unsustainable. However, we hoped that the Bishan Commune would go beyond arts and culture and take on economic and social dimensions by encouraging farmers to engage in 'exchange of labour' (*jiaogong* 交工), for example, and through other forms of mutual aid so that they can depend less on public services.

My own project in Bishan gave me a deeper understanding of the difficulties of rural reconstruction. First of all, since the Republican era, rural reconstruction, as a spontaneous movement independent of the government, always has faced a major constraint—its legitimacy and social space depend on its delicate relationship with politics. Any misstep can lead to failure, as in the examples of Tao Xingzhi's Xiaozhuang Normal College, Peng Yuting's experiment in Zhenping and Wen Tiejun's James Yen Rural Reconstruction Institute. So we need to be cautious about engaging local authorities ourselves and avoid compromising the independence and sustainability of the Bishan Commune when seeking the government's support. The second thing that I learnt from this project is that, although rural reconstruction needs financing, corporate and government funds would undermine the movement's independence while funding from the general public is inadequate at this time and will not be a viable source of financing without persistent effort. James Yen received funding from the Rockefeller Foundation but was criticised for relying on 'imperialism'. His case, though successful in a sense, was an exception that cannot serve as an example to everyone. A fundamental element of Wen Tiejun's rural reconstruction philosophy is his disapproval of 'big capital'. Wen refuses funding from large corporations and even NGOs, which means that his colleagues may be doing their work for its own sake without any material reward. At the Bishan Commune, we secured the necessary funding by including our programs in the budgets of the large arts exhibitions and events we are commissioned to organise, paying from our own pockets or asking our friends for donations. None of these methods, nevertheless, is sustainable.

Third, local communities' understanding of rural reconstruction is sometimes at odds with the lofty ideals of intellectuals. Local people seldom recognise the value of outsiders' work if they don't perceive any practical benefits. Some of them even become your enemies if other groups are helped at their expense. For example, cotton farmers in Ding county were grateful to James Yen because the cooperatives he helped to form made it unnecessary for them to borrow from banks or through intermediaries and thus reduced their costs. But, as a result, many local banks went bankrupt. Failed banks laid siege to Yen's Mass Education Association and demanded it leave the county. Similarly, we found it both amusing and frustrating when some villagers called the Bishan Harvestival, which was free to all local farmers, a profitable investment in tourism.[15]

So why bother engaging in rural reconstruction if it is so difficult? Wen once said, 'Personally, it's because I can't stand doing nothing about it. Humans, particularly intellectuals, inevitably possess a feminine kindness. If intellectuals, as part of the social mainstream, didn't have that quality or didn't reflect on this issue, the social mainstream would be a masculine one or, in other words, would have a tendency toward extreme beliefs'.[16] As a man who was born in rural China, struggled to find his footing in the city and then aspired to return to the countryside, I do not sense in Wen's words any condescension but a genuine compassion for his fellow Chinese.

---

15  Editors' note: In the first half of 2016, the Chinese authorities cut off the electricity and water supply and closed the main cultural centre that Ou Ning had established in Bishan, forcing Ou to leave the village, though the ideals of the project appear to live on in many aspects of village life; see Calum Macleod, 'Crushed Dreams of Utopia in Rural China', *The Times*, 2 May 2016.

16  Hong Liang, 'Xingdong zai dadi,' [Action on Land] *Chutzpah!*, January 2011.

# A Century of Social Alternatives in a Japanese Mountain Community

Tessa Morris-Suzuki

## The Storyteller and the Stories

The village of Motai in Nagano Prefecture, Japan, is about 2,000 kilometres away from Bishan in China, where Ou Ning and his fellow residents have developed the grassroots social visions described in Chapter Two. As far as I know, these two places have no direct connection with one another. Both suffer from the problems that assail so many small rural communities throughout East Asia and beyond—ageing populations, limited employment opportunities—but other than that, they are not particularly alike. Bishan, which once lay at the heart of the prosperous mercantile Huizhou region, is a place of old stone and brick buildings, some of which are now lovingly being restored. Motai and its slightly larger neighbouring town of Mochizuki—both now merged into the artificial Saku City—were once post-towns on the Nakasendō, one of the great roads that ran like arteries across the landscape of premodern Japan. Their old buildings are wooden-fronted; their warehouses have crumbling earthen walls.

But these small places in Japan and China are like springs of water that, although far apart, are fed by the same network of underground watercourses—deep, invisible, complicated watercourses running quietly under the familiar landscape of East Asian history. On the surface sit

China, the emerging superpower whose rampant capitalism has signally failed to give birth to liberalism and democracy, and Japan, whose increasingly assertive nationalist government struggles to extract the nation from the economic quagmire of two-and-a-half 'lost decades'. But in Bishan and the Mochizuki area, dreams are being pursued that (in anthropologist Tom Cliff's words) 'run perpendicular' to the state dreams for both countries.[1] These little local dreams have similarities that are not coincidental: they spring from the same fluid and meandering current of political and social ideas that has been flowing under the surface of East Asia for at least a century.

You can hear the similarities echoing in the words that fly about in the community halls of the two places—words like 'autonomy', 'mutual aid', 'endogenous development', 'cooperatives', 'counter-urbanisation'. You can also see and feel similarities in the symbolic sites and events that make the dreams tangible. The mixture of tradition and critical modernity enacted in the spectacle of Bishan's Harvestival (see Chapter Two), for example, is mirrored on a smaller scale by an event in Motai that I attended on a warm spring day in 2014.

This event was the launch of the year's new *saké* (rice wine 酒), celebrated with speeches and *taiko* (太鼓) drumming in the courtyard of an ancient brewery under a cloudless sky. The brewery, founded in the 17th century, stands at the heart of the village. A member of the local assembly arrived to offer his congratulations. Young and old tried their hand at pounding rice into *mochi* in a wooden vat whose surface wore the patina of generations of use. The tables were laden with home-grown and home-made delicacies. It seemed like a perfect evocation of 'traditional Japan'.

---

1    Tom Cliff, 'Pastoral Dreams: Bishan Village, Anhui, China'. On the website 'Survival Politics: ARC Laureate Project "Informal Life Politics"'. survivalpolitics.org/case-study/china-2/pastoral-dreams-bishan-village-anhui-china/.

Figure 2: The Motai *saké* festival.
Source: Tessa Morris-Suzuki.

But after the familiar phrases of greeting, the speeches took a less predictable turn. The eminent environmental economist Miyamoto Kenichi was loudly applauded as he condemned the government's heavy-handed top-down development projects, and drew connections between local social problems and the sufferings of the Okinawan people in their struggle against US military bases. Friends and neighbours in the crowd swapped information on the unending aftermath of the Fukushima disaster and a forthcoming demonstration against nuclear power; and on our way home, we dropped off at the nearby house of an elderly resident, to be presented with the libretto of an opera that he and his friends had composed, and regularly perform, in Esperanto. This is not eccentricity or defiance of tradition. It is an alternative quiet, semi-visible tradition that is too often obscured by stereotypes of rural conservatism and Japanese group consciousness. The brand of *saké* being celebrated at this annual festival in Motai is called *Kataribe* かたりべ, which means 'storyteller', and although the brand itself is only quarter of a century old, the stories it tells have origins that go back 100 years or more.

The long-neglected context from which these stories emerge has recently begun to be rediscovered by historians. In Chapter One of this book, Sho Konishi explores the strong current of anti-war cooperatist thought that emerged in early 20th-century Japan, with powerful connections to simultaneous currents in Russia. He also draws attention to the remarkable prewar Japanese enthusiasm for the study of Esperanto, and the broader internationalism in which this enthusiasm was embedded.[2] Robert Stolz's book *Bad Water* reinterprets the early environmentalism of the Meiji era anti-pollution activist Tanaka Shōzō (1841–1913), and shows how Tanaka's vision of 'natural democracy' continued to inspire social thinkers such as Ishikawa Sanshirō (1876–1956, an anarchist and Esperantist, also discussed by Konishi in Chapter One).[3] From a somewhat different perspective, Tetsuo Najita's study *Ordinary Economies in Japan* emphasises the significant role that credit and producer cooperatives played in modern Japanese development, and explores the distinctive visions of economic life that sustained cooperativism, particularly in rural Japan.[4]

Such ideas span a wide political spectrum and defy simple categorisation. They stretch from the radical political thought of anarchists like Ōsugi Sakae (1885–1923) to the more romantic idealism of the White Birch Group (*Shirakaba-ha* 白樺派), who espoused humanism, social utopianism and the folk arts movement. Central figures in this group included novelists Arishima Takeo (1878–1923) and Shiga Naoya (1883–71, also a disciple of Tanaka Shōzō), *Mingei* (folk arts 民芸) movement founder Yanagi Sōetsu (1889–1961), and Mushanakōji Saneatsu (1885–1976). From 1918 onward, Mushanakōji put his social visions into action in the communal life of the utopian 'New Villages' (*Atarashiki Mura* 新しき村), which he established in Kyushu and Saitama Prefecture, and which also influenced the Chinese tradition of rural reconstruction that finds contemporary expression in Bishan.

These social visionaries perceived human life as deeply enmeshed in the wider flows of nature. They did not reject the market per se, but expressed profound concern at the relentless pursuit of economic might and commercial profit in industrialising Japan. They valued the farmer's

---

2    See also Sho Konishi, *Anarchist Modernity: Cooperatism and Japanese-Russian Intellectual Relations in Modern Japan* (Cambridge, Mass.: Harvard University Asia Center, 2013), particularly Chapter 5.
3    Robert Stolz, *Bad Water: Nature, Pollution and Politics in Japan, 1870–1950* (Durham, NC: Duke University Press, 2014).
4    Tetsuo Najita, *Ordinary Economies in Japan: A Historical Perspective, 1750–1950* (Berkeley and London: University of California Press, 2009).

connections to the soil, and dreamed of the re-creation of egalitarian small-scale communities, but they also embraced a form of modern cosmopolitanism symbolised by their enthusiasm for Esperanto. Their heroes (as we have seen) included Lev Tolstoy, William Morris, Peter Kropotkin and the French entomologist Jean-Henri Fabre.[5]

The cooperativist thought discussed by Najita, on the other hand, was more often paternalistic and socially conservative, but in certain moments and places it too embodied ideas of self-help that overlapped with the anarchist radicalism explored by Konishi and Stolz. As Konishi shows in Chapter One, during the 1910s and 1920s experiments in cooperative farming as well as cooperative 'People's Hospitals' and 'People's Cafeterias' flourished in various parts of Japan. Political alliances, indeed, were fluid and ambiguous. Some of those linked to Tanaka Shōzō and the White Birch Group became active in postwar socialist politics, but others, such as Yanagi Sōetsu, were later to be condemned for advocating ideas that all too easily resonated with the imperialist ideologies of wartime Japan.[6] During the Cold War era, the fading visions of these loosely connected groups tended to be dismissed by orthodox Marxists as failed bourgeois idealism, and by advocates of capitalist high growth as muddle-headed if not actively subversive.

This chapter revisits those views by exploring how some of these early 20th-century critical ideas survived and interacted with postwar social and environmental thought, and how they continue to form a vibrant part of local life in corners of rural Japan to the present day. To trace the history of these alternative traditions, I focus on a region of a few hundred square kilometres in the very heart of the island of Honshū—the area largely occupied (in administrative terms) by the present-day city of Saku, Nagano Prefecture.

---

5    See Chapter One of this volume; also Konishi, *Anarchist Modernity*, 297–300.

6    See for example Yuko Kikuchi, *Japanese Modernisation and Mingei Theory: Cultural Nationalism and Oriental Orientalism* (London: Routledge Curzon, 2004); Noriko Aso, 'Mediating the Masses: Yanagi Sōetsu and Fascism', in Alan Tansman ed., *The Culture of Japanese Fascism* (Durham, NC: Duke University Press, 2010), 138–54.

# A Place in the Mountains

The images conjured up by the word 'city' are likely to mislead. Saku, extending across a wide plateau from Mount Tateshina in the southwest towards the foothills of Mount Asama in the northeast, is a city only the most artificial sense of the word. Its population of around 100,000 lives scattered over an area of more than 400 square kilometres.[7] Although the expansion of the highway network in the 1980s and 1990s and the coming of the Shinkansen super-express in 1997 generated a sprawl of shops, houses and factories in the centre of the plateau, many of Saku's inhabitants still live in the towns and villages—Asama, Nozawa, Usuda, Mochizuki, Motai and others—which were strung together to form the city (sometimes in the face of strenuous resistance) during Japan's local government amalgamations of 1961 and 2005. Each of these communities retains its distinct history and sense of identity, and each in turn is a mosaic of smaller hamlets with their own stories to tell. Some, like Motai, found themselves unceremoniously bisected by the new city boundaries: one end of Motai's main street lies in Saku City while the other is in the neighbouring town of Tateshina.

The valleys of Saku, with their volcanic soil and multitude of mountain streams, are good rice-growing and *saké*-brewing country, but the winters are bitterly cold, and the higher mountain slopes produce hard-won crops of vegetables and buckwheat. The area could be seen as a microcosm of rural Japan. Its population is ageing,[8] and enthusiastic schemes to attract investment and tourism fight a constant battle against a lingering pall of economic stagnation. The forces of globalisation stir unease in these valleys, and the road sides are dotted here and there with placards protesting the free-trade Trans-Pacific Partnership (TPP).

The history of popular social thought that I trace here is not (of course) confined to Saku City and its surroundings. It has appeared, disappeared and reappeared in many parts of Japan. Both Konishi and Stolz, for example, show how the ideas of egalitarian cooperatism developed by prewar intellectuals were put into practice in rural communities in

---

7    The total population as of 1 October 2014 was 100,085, and had declined slightly over the past decade: at the beginning of April 2005 it was 101,393; see Saku-shi no jinkō dēta: 5sai kaikyū betsu, www.city.saku.nagano.jp/shisei/profile/tokei/jinkodata02.html. Accessed 6 April 2015.

8    In 2013, 26.6 per cent of Saku City's population was aged over 65, up from 23.7 per cent in 2005; see Saku-shi no jinkō dēta.

Hokkaido.[9] But there are several features that seem to have made Saku and the surrounding areas of Nagano Prefecture particularly fertile ground for nurturing such ideas.

Though a large proportion of the region's pre-Meiji population were poor peasant farmers, the Shinshū area (to use the archaic but still popular name for Nagano) had a relatively high level of education. Divided into a multitude of small domains, it also contained an exceptionally large number of the 'temple schools' (*teragoya* 寺小屋) that provided education for commoners in the Tokugawa Era.[10] As Japan opened new trading links to the rest of the world from the mid-19th century onward, the local silk industry flourished, bringing social change and new ideas to the region. Shinshū activists played an important part in the popular rights movement (*jiyū minken undō* 自由民権運動) of the 1880s, many of them placing particular hope in the role of school education as the path to a freer and more equitable society.[11]

Rather than tracing the history of one particular intellectual group, this chapter takes Saku and its surrounding region as a site for exploring how various streams of thought came together and intermingled in a specific place, and how the legacies of this confluence are still at work in the 21st century. The focus on place directs attention towards the ordinary people who took up and developed ideas propagated by their better known literary and intellectual contemporaries, and helps us to see how ideas and social action are interwoven. Ideas, of course, are not objects handed on intact from generation to generation like material heirlooms. They are communicated from person to person and from group to group in fluid, partial and mercurial ways. Concepts and theories are reinterpreted— sometimes creatively misunderstood—and shaped by changing spatial and temporal circumstances. Diverse intellectual currents come together, colliding and sparking in unexpected ways. Ideas not only influence action but are also themselves the product of action and lived experience. The confluence of ideas and action that has shaped and been shaped by local communities in the Saku region is, I think, particularly worth

---

9    See Chapter One; also Stolz, *Bad Water*, Chapter 5.

10    Sakaguchi Mitsukuni, '"Ni-yon jiken" to Nagano ken kyōiku: "Kyōiku ken Nagano" ni shūshifu o utta "Ni-yon danatsu jiken"' [The '2.4 Incident' and Education in Nagano Prefecture: The '2.4 Repression Incident' which Put a Full-Stop to Nagano's Role as 'Education Prefecture'], *Heiwa to teshigoto* [Peace and Handicrafts], 18 (July 2013): 144–61 (citation from pp. 145–6).

11    See Shinshū no Minken Hyakunen Jikkō Iinkai ed., *Shinshū minken undōshi* [A History of the People's Rights Movement in Shinshū] (Nagano City: Ginga Shobō, 1981).

recovering in the contemporary Japanese political environment, where formal national politics seems devoid of lively debate between alternative visions of the future, and where rising nationalism fuels conflict between Japan and its neighbours.

## Kobayashi Tatsue and the Legacy of the New Village and White Birch Teachers

The origins of the social visions at work in Mochizuki, Motai and other parts of Saku City today can be traced to the activities of a group of residents—most of them local school teachers—who were inspired by the writings of the White Birch Group, but who put those ideas to work in distinctive ways. One central figure was Kobayashi Tatsue, the son of a farmer from Kyōwa Village (now part of Saku City), who was born in 1896 and had entered of Nagano Prefectural Teacher Training College in 1914. Many years later, Kobayashi would recall the moment in 1916 when he first encountered the ideas of the White Birch Group as he browsed the shelves of the college library. There he came upon a 700-page magnum opus by Yanagi Sōetsu—a study by Yanagi of the life and works of the English poet, artist and visionary William Blake—and his life was transformed.[12]

Fascinated by the humanism and respect for life that he found in Yanagi's interpretation of Blake, Kobayashi began reading the work of Yanagi's White Birch associates—Arishima Takeo, Shiga Naoya and Mushanokōji Saneatsu—and soon joined a local reading group who shared his enthusiasm for the White Birch philosophies.[13] For young teachers like Kobayashi, the ideas of the White Birch Group were not just philosophical and aesthetic visions; they pointed to practical education methods radically at odds with the school curriculum imposed by the government.

The modernising Japanese state had created an effective system of universal schooling based on standardised texts, rote learning and substantial doses of nationalism. But the spread of education and the introduction

---

12   Kobayashi Tatsue, '"Shirakaba" no koro' [The Time of 'White Birch'], in Kobayashi Tatsue no Hon Henshū Iinkai ed., *Heiwa to teshigoto: Kobayashi Tatsue 104-sai no tabi* [Peace and Handicrafts: The 104-year Journey of Kobayashi Tatsue] (Tokyo: Fukinotō Shobō, 2001), 16–26.
13   ibid., 16–18.

of foreign ideas brought with them trends that alarmed Japan's rulers. The writings of European anarchists, socialists, pacifists and individualists found their way across Japan's borders alongside the scientific, technical, economic and legal texts needed to advance the nation's place in the global order. The response of the state education system to these undesirable influences was to reinforce the emphasis on discipline, patriotism and self-sacrifice. When Kobayashi entered teachers training college, the ethics (*shūshin* 修身) texts used in primary schools had recently been revised to place greater emphasis on loyalty to the nation.[14]

All this was anathema to the 'White Birch teachers' (*Shirakaba-ha Kyōin* 白樺派教員), as Kobayashi and his fellow students and young educators in Nagano Prefecture called themselves. Their readings of Ruskin, Walt Whitman, Romain Rolland, Mushanokōji Saneatsu and others had left them with a profound belief in 'personalist education' (*jinkakushugi kyōiku* 人格主義教育), whose core principles were to 'nurture the self, respect individuality, love beauty and seek peace'.[15] The White Birch teachers organised reading groups and from 1919 to 1921 published their own journal *Chijō* (地上). They attended lectures by Yanagi Sōetsu (with whom Kobayashi Tatsue established a lifelong friendship), Mushanokōji Saneatsu and others. Kobayashi Tatsue was also one of the first White Birch teachers to embark on the long journey southwards to the wilds of northern Kyushu—for some, the longest journey they had ever undertaken—to live and work in Mushanokōji Saneatsu's New Village.

Against the background of rapid Japanese industrialisation and urbanisation, Mushanokōji Saneatsu had conceived of the New Village as a quasi-Tolstoyan farm community where work and wealth would be fairly distributed, and where all would participate equally in manual and intellectual labour, and take part in communal decision-making. The original New Village was created by 16 pioneers, including Mushanokōji and his wife, in the Hyūga district of Kyushu in 1918, though Mushanokōji himself retreated to the more familiar world of urban society in the mid-1920s, and in 1939 almost the entire community

---

14    Byron K. Marshall, *Learning to be Modern: Japanese Political Discourse on Education* (Boulder, CO: Westview Press, 1994), 107.

15    Yoshikawa Tōru, 'Heiwa to teshigoto o kataritsuzuketa kyōikusha Kobayashi Tatsue' [Kobayashi Tatsue, the Educator Who Kept on Speaking of Peace and Handicrafts], in Saku no Senjin Kentō Iinkai / Saku-Shi Kyōiku Iinkai ed., *Saku no senjin - kentō jigyō* [Saku Pioneers: An Investigative Project] (Saku-Shi: Saku-Shi Bunka Jigyōka, 2012), 26–7; see also Sakaguchi, '"Ni-yon jiken"', 148.

moved to Moroyama in Saitama Prefecture, where it still exists today.[16] The New Village was not a rejection of modernity or internationalism; on the contrary, Mushanokōji advocated scientific and technological development as a means to lighten the burden of human labour, and believed that people should become fluent 'not only in their own language but also in the world language' (by which he meant Esperanto).[17] But the village aimed to be the seed bed of a radically different version of modernity where 'all the world's human beings would fulfil the will of Heaven, and the self which dwells within each individual would be enabled to grow to the full'.[18] As well as its permanent residents, the village attracted many short-term residents and visitors, and Kobayashi Tatsue proved to be one of these. He joined the village soon after its establishment in 1918, which was also the year of his graduation from college, but soon after arriving there he became seriously ill and had to return home to Nagano Prefecture.[19] As a result, he probably did not meet the prominent Chinese intellectual Zhou Zuoren (brother of the even more famous Lu Xun), who arrived in the New Village for a visit there in the summer of 1919. But Zhou's arrival symbolises yet another way in which the ripples of the White Birch movement spread out from its small group of founders to resonate in complex ways across Japan and East Asia, initiating the process of diffusion traced by Ou Ning in Chapter Two.

Meanwhile, Kobayashi had come home to a region in turmoil; for his fellow White Birch teachers had begun to put their ideas into action in their Nagano Prefecture classroom. Their aims—'to nurture the self, respect individuality, love beauty and seek peace'—inevitably soon fell foul of a state education system that emphasised obedience, discipline and loyalty to nation and empire.[20] In 1919, at a school in the mountain village of Togura (now part of Chikuma City), a group of White Birch teachers transformed the curriculum, replacing the official ethics textbooks with readings from works like Tolstoy's *Ivan the Fool* and Romain Rolland's *Jean-Christophe*. In place of the officially prescribed glorification of the

16   Mushanokōji Saneatsu, *Atarashiki mura no sōzō* [Imagining the New Village] (Tokyo: Fuzanbō, 1977).
17   Mushakoji, Saneatsu, *Atarashiki mura no seikatsu* [Life in the New Village] (Tokyo: Shinchōsha, 1969), 24.
18   Kobayashi Tatsue, 'Ko Mushinokōji Saneatsu shi to Shinshū' [Mushanokōji Saneatsu and Shinshū], in Kobayashi Tatsue no Hon Henshū Iinkai ed., *Heiwa to teshigoto*, 34–7; quotation from p. 36.
19   Kobayashi Tatsue no Hon Henshū Iinkai, 'Kobayashi Tatsue 104-sai no ayumi' [The 104-year Trajectory of Kobayashi Tatsue], in Kobayashi Tatsue no Hon Henshū Iinkai ed., *Heiwa to teshigoto*, 266–9; Yoshikawa, 'Heiwa to teshigoto'.
20   Yohsikawa, 'Heiwa to teshigoto'; Sakaguchi, '"Ni-yon jiken"'.

imperial line and the Japanese military, the White Birch teachers promoted pacifism and criticised Japan's colonial expansion into Korea. Questions were soon raised in the Prefectural Assembly, and the activities of the Togura reformers were crushed. Two teachers were dismissed, while others were temporarily suspended, demoted or transferred.[21]

But some persisted. Kobayashi Tatsue's close friend Nakatani Isao was one of those who took part in the reform attempt and was transferred to another school in the village of Yamato (now part of Matsumoto City) following the Togura Incident. Nakatani, a passionate and popular teacher, continued to put his ideas into practice in quiet ways, taking his pupils for long nature walks and contributing the White Birch teachers' journal *Chijō*. But another purge soon followed. This time, the teachers' main offence was to celebrate Christmas with a school performance of Mushanokōji's dramatised and mildly subversive reworking of the Japanese folktale 'The Old Man who Made Trees Blossom' (*Hanasaku Jijii* 花咲爺). Nakatani was dismissed from his teaching position, sank into deep depression and died soon after at the age of 25.[22]

Kobayashi Tatsue himself was not directly caught up in these events, but he was profoundly affected by them. From then on, as a White Birch teacher, he would find his life subjected to intense scrutiny by the education authorities. In an atmosphere of growing repression, he tried to keep his ideals alive in inconspicuous ways, through organising public lectures and other events centred on the ideas of the White Birch Group, and by collecting and promoting local folk art. But he and other like-minded teachers faced continual battles with the education authorities, and were repeatedly transferred from one school to the next in an effort to limit their influence in the classroom.[23] In early 1933, a further wave of repression resulted in the arrest of over 600 people, mostly in Nagano Prefecture, under the 'Peace Preservation Law' (Chian Iji Hō 治安維持法) of 1925. About one-third of those rounded up were teachers who were regarded as having expressed radical views. Many of those who avoided arrest were cowed into silence by the threat of dismissal and

---

21 Sakaguchi, '"Ni-yon jiken"', 149; also Kobayashi, '"Shirakaba" no koro', 22–3.
22 Kobayashi, '"Shirakaba" no koro', 23–24.
23 Yoshikawa, 'Heiwa to teshigoto', 26.

imprisonment. Among them was Kobayashi, whose sense of remorse at his failure to speak out against the political repression of the 1930s became a major impetus behind his postwar social activism.[24]

From one point of view, there can be no doubt that the White Birch education movement in Nagano failed. Its liberal and anti-war sentiments were unable to withstand the rising tide of militarism, and by the late 1930s the group's members had been scattered and silenced. As a practical step towards a new society, Mushanokōji's New Village, too, can easily be dismissed as a failure. Its founder dreamed of new villages sprouting spontaneously all over Japan, and so transforming society from below; but this did not happen, and in retrospect it seems clear that there was never any prospect of its happening. Yet the New Village had another, less tangible, significance: it was a symbol that provoked people in many places to debate and rethink the possibilities of rural life. And the fact that there was at least one real New Village in existence made the symbol much more powerful than it would have been had it merely been a utopia described on paper. That surely is one reason why the echoes of this century-old 'failed' experiment still reverberates in Bishan, Mochizuki and many other places today.

Judgments of historical success and failure are partly a matter of time. The rise of militarism, the slide into war and the suppression of the White Birch teachers were not the end of the story. Kobayashi Tatsue's life spanned the entire 20th century, and (in evolving forms) carried the ideas of early 20th-century humanism into the 21st century. Shortly before his 100th birthday in 1996, his friends and supporters created a small meeting place and museum, the Kobayashi Tatsue Peace and Handicraft Folk Arts Hall, perched on a hilltop overlooking Mochizuki, to house the teacher's large collection of craft objects. This has become a focus for ongoing local movements to promote social education, sustainable development and local peace initiatives.

---

24    Interview with Yoshikawa Tōru, Mochizuki, 25 May 2015.

# Social Education and Visions of a Local Future

Looking back at his youthful ideals from the vantage point of postwar Japan, Kobayashi Tatsue wrote:

> the consistent element in the White Birch group was the notion of 'cultivating the self' Japan's defeat has created a painful awareness of the importance of building individuality on firm foundations. To lack your own beliefs and perceptions, and to follow the herd wherever others lead you, is the source of all evil and misery.[25]

The failure of the White Birch intellectuals and other Japanese humanists actively to resist militarism and imperial expansionism has often been emphasised,[26] but what is rarely noted is the deep sense of guilt about that failure that impelled some of them to embark on postwar social activism. Kobayashi Tatsue was one of those people. Haunted by memories of his own inability to speak out against the arrests of his colleagues, he devoted his postwar life to promoting their ideals—the ideals of peace and of people's art—with consequences that are still being felt in his home region today.[27]

As a schoolteacher, writer and social activist in the 1950s, Kobayashi won support from the local education committee to create a folk craft collection that was exhibited and used as a focus for events such as lectures by Yanagi Sōetsu and the British *Mingei* movement potter Bernard Leach. He studied and practised traditional textile dyeing techniques, and wrote and published widely on the importance of nurturing human creativity and on peace and nuclear disarmament. He participated in a local protest movement against plans to establish a US military training base on the slopes of nearby Mt Asama, and in 1981, at the age of 85, launched a successful local journal, *Kyōwa Tsūshin* (*Kyōwa News* 協和通信), which he continued to edit and publish for the next 10 years. The title was a telling play on words: *Kyōwa* means 'harmony' or 'oneness', but also happens to be name of the village where Kobayashi was born and spent the last years of his life.[28]

---

25   Kobayashi, '"Shirakaba" no koro', 17.
26   See, for example, Aso, 'Mediating the Masses'.
27   Yoshikawa Tōru, 'Kankō ni atatte' [On the Occasion of Publication], in Kobayashi Tatsue no Hon Henshū Iinkai ed., *Heiwa to teshigoto*, 1–8, citation from p. 4.
28   Kobayashi Tatsue no Hon Henshū Iinkai, 'Kobayashi Tatsue 104-sai no ayumi', 268–9.

Like the philosophies of his White Birch predecessors, Kobayashi's idealist enthusiasm for folk arts and peace can be (and sometimes has been) criticised as naive and impractical. But its tangible impact is vividly described by Yoshikawa Tōru, a teacher and activist who first arrived in Mochizuki as a young graduate from Tokyo in the early 1960s and has lived there ever since. Amongst the postwar generation who came in contact with Kobayashi and his fellow former White Birch teachers, Yoshikawa writes:

> There were those who said 'I understand the theory all right, but I just can't live the way our teacher does'. And those who studied with him often said, 'I can't follow what he's saying'. I have to say that I sometimes felt the same way myself. But the people who had been taught by the White Birch Teachers as children, even for a short time, were influenced in a way that affected the rest of their lives. In old age they were still talking about their recollections of that time with such enjoyment that, seeing their expressions, I would wonder what the secret of those teachers was.[29]

In the postwar era, a web of local human interaction brought ideas inherited from the White Birch and craft movements into contact with new forces of agrarian and peace protest. The allied occupation of Japan resulted in the liberalisation of education, and in land reform that greatly improved the lives of farmers. As the Japanese economy began to revive from the devastation of war, a wave of enthusiasm for grassroots education, self-improvement and democratisation was expressed in the appearance all over the country of 'study circles' (*sākuru* サークル), where farmers, factory workers, housewives and others studied topics such as local history, political ideas, arts and literature. 'Social education' (*shakai kyōiku* 社会教育) became the buzzword of the era.

In rural Nagano Prefecture, a focus for this postwar passion for self-improvement was provided by the *Seinendan* (Youth Groups 青年団) to which most young villagers, male and female, belonged.[30] Before and during the Pacific War, the rural youth groups were generally seen as hotbeds of nationalism, and became a central element of the militarising state's pyramid of social control.[31] But in parts of postwar Japan, the *Seinendan* came to play a very different role. In its early postwar years, the

---

29  Yoshikawa, 'Kankō ni atatte', 2.
30  Interview with Shimizu Noriko, Shimizu Kiyoshi and Itō Kimiko, Kyōwa, 28 May 2015.
31  Mikiso Hane, *Peasants, Rebels, Women and Outcasts: The Underside of Modern Japan* (Lanham, NJ: Rowman and Littlefield, 2003), 61–2; Sally Ann Hastings, *Neighbourhood and Nation in Japan, 1905–1937* (Pittsburgh, PA: University of Pittsburgh Press, 1995), 109–22.

rural grassroots enthusiasm for study and self-improvement was driven by a passion for agricultural modernisation. New farm machinery began to appear in local fields, and villagers immersed themselves in the latest American-inspired manuals on farm management. But by the late 1950s, a more critical element was also entering the debates that took place in night-time gatherings in the village halls of Saku and surrounding areas— an element that reflected the changing face of Japanese farming. The rural young were not immune from the critical social ideas that, by the 1960s, were radicalising Japan's students and urban youth. In some areas of Japan *Seinendan* members, inspired partly by left-of-centre intellectuals who moved to the countryside to disseminate their social ideas, launched music and drama groups, discussed visions of a new Japan, and participated in strikes for higher produce prices and protests against environmentally damaging development projects.

Following the signing of the San Francisco Peace Treaty and of the Security Treaty (commonly known as *Ampō*) with the US in 1951, the Japanese Government entered into negotiations with the US on military security assistance (MSA) from America to Japan. The agreement, finally signed in 1954, included a somewhat convoluted arrangement under which Japan would buy surplus agricultural produce from the US, and in return, the US would pay back part of the proceeds to the Japanese Government as aid for heavy industrial development (including support for Japan's reviving armaments industry).[32] The inflow of cheap US agricultural produce into Japan dealt a serious blow to Japanese farmers, who suddenly found the prices for their wheat or milk undercut by dumped US goods. In 1960, frustration at the MSA flared up into a strike and protest demonstrations by Japanese dairy farmers at the dumping of US milk powder on the Japanese market. Farmers from Mochizuki and other parts of Saku City were key figures in the protest—the first strike by farmers in Japanese history.[33]

Criticism of the MSA agreement also flowed into rising opposition to the introduction of a revised Security Treaty, and by 1960 some young farmers were explicitly linking their own struggles to stay on the land with problems of the Japan–US military alliance and with a broader critique of

---

32  See John L. Weste, 'Salvation from Without: Mutual Security Assistance and the Military-Industrial Lobby in Post-War Japan' in Stephen S. Large ed., *Showa Japan: Political, Economic and Social History, 1926-1989*, vol. 3 (London and New York: Routledge, 1998), 24–43, particularly p. 35.
33  Interview with Kobayashi Tetsuo, Saku City, 16 May 2015; interview with Itō Morihisa, Mochizuki, 29 May 2015.

the trajectory of Japanese industrialisation.[34] One farmer who joined the Mochizuki Youth Group in 1955 recalls how in 1960 he and his fellow members would get up before dawn and ride their bicycles over the rough rural roads to the nearest railway station, over 20 kilometres away, to catch the train to Tokyo and take part in the mass anti-Ampō demonstrations that precipitated the resignation of Prime Minister Kishi Nobusuke.[35]

These activities made local people more aware of a need to understand the world they lived in. A group of young farmers who had been involved in the milk strike therefore lobbied for the creation of a social education centre in Mochizuki. The man appointed to run the centre, Yoshikawa Tōru, was a newcomer to the region—a recent graduate from Tokyo who threw himself wholeheartedly into the task, working closely with local elder Kobayashi Tatsue. During the early 1960s, study circles in and around Mochizuki were meeting almost every evening, discussing social issues like the Cold War, industrialisation and the growing outflow of young people to the expanding metropolitan areas. Here, themes from the prewar White Birch philosophies reemerged in new form: the value of peace; the search for human creativity; respect for craft traditions; concern at the corrosive effects of corporate capitalism on society and community. The study groups met in the village halls (kōminkan 公民館) that existed in almost every hamlet, and participants ate, drank and talked deep into the night around the charcoal braziers that filled the halls with their thick haze of smoke.[36] Arts and self-expression, in the form of choirs and drama groups, went hand-in-hand with heated debates on political and social ideas. Kobayashi Tatsue, as director of the village hall and a frequent speaker at their classes, influenced the artistic as well as the intellectual lives of the young farmer-students, helping them to raise money to buy books and even to acquire a record player and records—still luxuries in the village at that time.[37]

---

34  Kobayashi Setsuo, 'Nagano Ken chiiki jūmin daigaku ni itaru zenshiteki haikei to shiteki kansō: Sengo no nōbunkyō no undō kara chiiki jūmin daigaku ni itaru made' [Early Historical Background and Personal Impressions of the Nagano Prefectural Residents' University: From the Postwar Nōbunkyō Movement to the Regional Residents' University], in Nagano Ken Chiiki Jūmin Daigaku Gakushū Undōshi Henshū Iinkai ed., *Tagayashi, manabi, kangaeru: Sengo Nagano ken gakushū undōshi* [Tilling, Learning, Thinking: The Postwar Nagano Prefecture Educational Movement] vol. 1 (Nagano City: Nagano Ken Chiiki Jūmin Daigaku, 2013), 43–159.
35  Interview with Shimizu Noriko, Shimizu Kiyoshi and Itō Kimiko, Kyōwa, 28 May 2015.
36  Interview with Yoshikawa Tōru, Mochizuki, 1 July 2013.
37  Interview with Shimizu Noriko, Shimizu Kiyoshi and Itō Kimiko, Kyōwa, 28 May 2015.

The overtly critical political tone of Mochizuki social education alarmed more conservative members of the local government. In 1970, following a workshop that questioned local government agricultural policy, the local authorities moved to cut the financial support they had been giving to the social education programs, and only energetic protests by students managed to save Yoshikawa Tōru's teaching position. But the Japan of the 1960s was a very different place from the Japan of the 1910s and 1920s, when the activities of the White Birch teachers had so easily been crushed by the heavy hand of the state. Protests by students and their supporters succeeded in not only preserving but even expanding the Mochizuki social education program,[38] and the experience of protest itself became part of the educational experience. Itō Morihisa, the son of a local dairy farmer and an eager participant in the social education classes of the 1960s, recalls:

> Mr Yoshikawa had an accordion, and we would have musical gatherings, but at the same time we could also learn about social issues and so forth together. I think that was the real basis of our ongoing movement. I was head of the local *Seinendan* at the time, and it was through involvement in the struggle to save Mr Yoshikawa's position as the social education director that I developed my own view of the world and a sense of my place in society.[39]

The central message of the social education movement was 'think for yourself'. Participants were encouraged not to accept the dictates of government, but to create their own visions for the future of their region.[40] And as high-tech industrialisation transformed the face of Japan, this was to lead to new struggles both with and within the formal structures of local government.

## The Body Politic—Rural Medicine and Social Visions in Saku Central Hospital

Meanwhile, the local world of grassroots ideas and activism was being influenced by other currents of thought that came from cooperatism and social medicine. The focal point from which these ideas radiated was Saku

---

38   Interview with Itō Morihisa, Mochizuki, 29 May 2015.
39   Interview with Itō Morihisa, Mochizuki, 1 July 2013.
40   Interview with Yoshikawa Tōru, Mochizuki, 1 July 2013.

Central Hospital (*Saku Sōgō Byōin* 佐久総合病院), founded at the height of the Asia-Pacific War. The hospital first opened its doors in January 1944, at a time when the overriding aim of state medical policy was 'to secure "human resources"—in other words soldiers for the battlefront and workers for wartime industry—in order to pursue of the war effort'.[41] But it was also part of Japan's extensive cooperative movement, which, as Tetsuo Najita persuasively argued, has played a central though long-neglected role in economic and social development. As Sho Konishi observes in Chapter One, cooperatively run 'people's hospitals' (*heimin byōin* 平民病院) had formed a crucial element of the cooperatist/anarchist movements of the 1910s and 1920s.

Like a number of other medical centres throughout the country, Saku Central Hospital was an offshoot of a local agricultural cooperative. Its second director, appointed six months before Japan's defeat in war, was physician Wataksuki Toshikazu (1910–2006), who had been a member of a prewar Marxist study group at the University of Tokyo. Wakatsuki had been arrested twice for his political views, and had spent a year in prison shortly before his appointment to Saku Central Hospital. He was encouraged by a mentor to take a post in this rural mountain community in the hope that this would help him to evade the unwelcome attentions of the thought police. To obtain release from prison, Wakatsuki had been induced to sign a statement of 'conversion' (*tenkō*) renouncing his subversive views (an act about which he expressed lifelong regret), but the influence of his early encounters with Marxist, socialist and humanist ideas continued to influence his thought and medical practice in profound ways.[42] Following Japan's defeat, these ideas interacted with the longing for a better life felt by many local residents in Saku and surrounding regions as they recovered from the disasters of war and faced the massive tasks of rebuilding their community. From this interaction, Saku Central Hospital emerged as a pioneer of rural social medicine within Japan and beyond.

In the second half of the 1940s, the hospital confronted a massive health crisis. Malnutrition and diseases like tuberculosis were rife. Thousands of displaced people were returning to the local area from Japan's lost empire.

41    'Saku Byōinshi' Sakusei Iinkai ed., *Saku Byōinshi* [A History of Saku Hospital] (Tokyo: Keiso Shobō, 1999), 33.

42    Kawakami Takeshi, 'Wakatsuki Toshikazu sensei no shigoto to seishin' [The Work and Spirit of Dr Wakatsuki Toshikazu], *Bunkaren jōhō* [Bunkaren Report], 344 (2006): 33–6; Wakatsuki Toshikazu, *Nōson iryo ni kaketa 30-nen* [Thirty Years Spent in Rural Medicine] (Tokyo: Ie no Hikari Kyōkai, 1976), 34–5.

Medicines and medical equipment were in desperately short supply. In these conditions, the Saku medical staff strongly resisted proposals to transfer their hospital to the control of government, and insisted that it should remain part of the cooperative system, even though they fought running political battles with some of the more conservative figures in the local agricultural coop[43].

The hospital, whose slogan was (and still is) 'Together with the Farmers' (*Nōmin to tomo ni* 農民とともに), was literally sustained by the support of the local farm community, particularly after a fire destroyed much of the hospital compound in 1949. The funds for reconstruction were raised by local residents, and local farmers and the hospital together worked out ways to cooperate in linking hospital treatment to community health. For example, it soon became clear that the recovery of patients discharged from hospital was hampered by poor nutrition, so a system was devised where farmers provided vegetables and other produce, and hospital staff cooked these into nutritious meals to be delivered to recuperating patients. Very unusually for a Japanese hospital at that time, Saku Central encouraged patients' relatives to be present during operations.[44] The hospital also evolved into the focus of a series of patient self-help associations. The members of the first club, made up of patients suffering from the crippling and (in the 1940s) incurable Pott's Disease (tuberculosis of the spine), were soon producing their own journal— *Sebone* 背骨 (Backbone)—which published both medical information on advances in treatment and articles by patients and their families.[45]

So hospital staff, patients and local residents developed a view of social medicine that integrated hospital and community, transforming the conventional image of the role of a hospital as an island of technical expertise in a sea of potential patients. 'Health' from this point of view, is not just a matter of the treatment of disease, but a matter of life as a whole. Saku Central Hospital became the site of a monthly informal discussion group including medical staff, young farmers and others, and ranging over a wide spectrum of social and political issues. The hospital drama group toured villages presenting plays on problems of health, welfare and society (often in a lighthearted, seriocomic style). Wakatsuki Toshikazu described

43   'Saku Byōinshi' Sakusei Iinkai, *Saku Byōinshi,* 50.
44   ibid., 36–8 and 41–2.
45   ibid., 62–3; see also Honda Toru, 'Health Equity: Japan's Post-War Strides towards Universal Health Coverage from a Grassroots Perspective', *Global Health Check* (11 November 2014), www. globalhealthcheck.org. Accessed 17 January 2015.

the interaction as a form of mutual education: hospital staff passed on knowledge about health issues and at the same time learnt about the lives of their patients in ways that 'humanised' their medical practice.[46] When Saku Central, known to local conservatives as 'the Red Hospital', was threatened by the allied occupation's purge of suspected 'communists', local residents rallied to its support, and some 45,000 of them signed a petition to defend their hospital.

At a personal level, Wakatsuki and his medical staff formed close relationships with Kobayashi Tatsue, Yoshikawa Tōru and others involved in the social education movement, and after Wakatsuki's death in 2006, younger doctors whom he trained and influenced have continued his tradition of social activism. The hospital's study circles interacted with the study circles of the social education movement, and participants in both took part in a series of protests that profoundly influenced the nature of local economic and social development from the 1970s onward.

## The Miyamoto School and Endogenous Development

It is a scorching August afternoon, and a group of several dozen people are holding their regular gathering in the Kobayashi Tatsue Peace and Handicraft Folk Arts Hall. The speakers include Yoshikawa Tōru and his former student Itō Morihisa—a farmer and social reformer who has also served as a member of the local government assembly. They are joined by Irohira Tetsurō, a doctor from Saku Central Hospital; and Miyamoto Kenichi, from whom the group takes its name. This is a gathering of the Shinshū Miyamoto School (*Shinshū Miyamoto Juku* 信州宮本塾), a discussion circle that has been meeting on a regular basis for over two decades to explore visions of sustainable and endogenous development for their region. On tables and shelves all around the room stand rows of the thickly glazed vases and blue patterned plates collected by Kobayashi Tatsue to celebrate the simple beauty of folk crafts. An old weaving loom fills one corner of the hall, and photos of Kobayashi and his heroes, among them Yanagi Sōetsu, Gandhi and Roman Rolland, look down, benign but unsmiling, on the participants.

---

46    Wakatsuki Toshikazu, *Nōson iryo ni kaketa 30-nen*; Wakatsuki Toshikazu, Acceptance speech for the 1976 Ramon Magsaysay Award, 1976, www.rmaf.org.ph/newrmaf/main/awardees/awardee/profile/221. Accessed 18 January 2015.

Figure 3: A meeting of the Shinshū Miyamoto School.
Source: Tessa Morris-Suzuki.

The Miyamoto School emerged from the social education experiments of the 1960s, 1970s and 1980s, and from the protest movements that these precipitated. By the 1980s, urban drift and the decline and ageing of rural populations were becoming major challenges for regions like Saku. In an effort to stave off economic decline, the local government put forward a series of development proposals centred on attracting large metropolitan firms to invest in the area. These included plans for golf courses, for industrial waste disposal plants, and (in the early 1990s) for a giant off-course betting centre that, it was hoped, would attract punters from all over eastern Japan. The farmers who had taken part in the social education movement, many of whom were now entering middle age, saw the grand designs of the local authorities as threatening the natural and social environment of their region and offering few if any real benefits to local people. Their response was to question the plans both from outside and inside formal politics.

A series of small protest movements sprang up in towns and villages across the region. In 1994, for example, a former 1960s member of the Mochizuki *Seinendan*, who had just retired from a career in local administration, joined with an elderly woman resident to lead protests against plans to build a potentially highly polluting industrial waste dump and incinerator in the mountains close to Mochizuki. This was the start of a 10-year struggle, which ultimately ended in victory for the protestors in the spring of 2003.[47] Yoshikawa Tōru, Itō Morihisa and others, meanwhile, were helping to organise public demonstrations against the off-course betting centre scheme, which also led to the scheme being abandoned.[48] But the very success of their opposition left the protestors with a challenge: to devise alternative strategies that could at least do something to resolve the real social and economic problems confronting their region. They were not conservatives, simply seeking to hold back the encroaching tide of change. But finding coherent and persuasive *alternative* forms of change that fitted the values they espoused was no easy matter. It was here that the advice of Miyamoto Kenichi proved crucial.

Miyamoto's origins lie outside the Saku region. Born in colonial Taipei in 1930, he spent much of his career teaching economics at Osaka City University. During the 1970s and 1980s, Miyamoto became internationally known both as an anti-pollution activist taking part in the movements discussed by Simon Avenell in Chapter Four, and as a theorist of the relationship between economic structure and environmental crisis. Miyamoto's work draws on but adapts Marxist economic theory to emphasise the role of the state and of state infrastructure policy as a cause of ecological destruction, and highlights the vital role of grassroots action in preserving the environment.[49] By the late 1980s, he was turning his attention particularly to development from below, or endogenous development (*naihatsuteki hatten* 内発的発展)—a concept whose key elements are that local people devise and manage plans for their community's future, drawing on local resources, and that the value added

---

47    Asahi Kensetsu no shōkyakuro ni hantai suru taisaku iinkai, *Asahi Kensetsu no noyaki, sanpai shōkyakuro ni hantai suru jūmin no kiroku* [A Record of the Residents' Movement against Asahi Construction's Open-Air Burning and Industrial Waste Incinerator] (Mochizuki: Asahi Kensetsu no Shōkyakuro ni Hantai suru Taisaku Iinkai, 2009); interview with Iijima Katsuhiko, Mochizuki, 26 May 2015.
48    Interview with Yoshikawa Tōru, Mochizuki, 1 July 2013.
49    See Simon Avenell, *Making Japanese Citizens: Civil Society and the Mythology of the Shimin in Postwar Japan* (Berkeley and London: University of California Press, 2010), 153–5; Tessa Morris-Suzuki, *A History of Japanese Economic Thought* (London: Routledge, 1989), 151–3.

from development should be returned to the local area.[50] Miyamoto had become a friend of Saku Central Hospital's rural medicine pioneer Wakatsuki Toshikazu, and was eager to develop closer links to the Saku region so that he and his students could refine their ideas in direct dialogue with small-scale farming communities. His ideas in turn resonated with the emphasis on human creativity and respect for crafts traditions that the former White Birch teachers had passed on to the postwar generation in the Saku region. Miyamoto bought a house in mountains of Saku where he spent extended periods of time, particularly after his retirement from Osaka City University, and from this base became increasingly closely involved in Saku community life.

The Miyamoto School was formed in 1992, as a venue where local people from Mochizuki and the surrounding area could come together to study the principles of endogenous development and to share their ideas for the future of their region with one another and with Miyamoto and other academic experts. The group meets once a month, except in the depth of winter, and has gradually extended its bounds to include participants from a widening area of Nagano Prefecture. Its meetings are not lectures, where outside experts instruct local people on the proper paths of development, but are forums for a sharing of ideas amongst equals. The school has organised field trips to other areas of Japan facing similar economic challenges, and has published two 'Residents' White Papers' (*Nōsonhatsu Jūmin Hakusho* 農村発住民白書), setting out local projects for endogenous development.

One of the first of these projects for 'development from below' was the launch in 1993 of the *Kataribe saké* brand. Itō Morihisa joined hands with Motai's 300-year-old brewery, supplying them with special low-chemical farmed rice for this brand, which has become a successful 'export' product, sold to other parts of Japan as well as to locals and visitors to the region. Over the years, the range of local endogenous development schemes has gradually grown. A project was established to help city people start new lives as farmers in the Saku region, with a particular emphasis on organic farming, and this has succeeded in bringing a number of new

50    Miyamoto Kenichi, *Kankyō keizaigaku* [Environmental Economics] (Tokyo: Iwanami Shoten, 1989); Tanaka Natsuko, 'Chūsankanchi no naihatsuteki hatten to chiikizukuri no nettowāku: Kita-Saku gun Mochozuki machi ni okeru chiikizukuri jūmin soshiki no ayumi to kadai' [Endogenous Development in a Mountain District and the Regional Development Network: History and Issues of a Regional Development Citizens' Orgainzation in Mochizuki Town, North Saku District]. *Nagano Daigaku kiyō* [Annals of Nagano University] 19, no. 1 (1997): 49–61.

farm families to the district. Itō Morihisa has created an educational program that allows school groups of urban children to stay on his farm and experience agriculture at first-hand. In 2001, a local currency system was launched in the nearby city of Ueda, and its 200-odd members are now engaged in a range of local development and education schemes. An award-winning restaurant serving locally grown soba has been developed by a chef who also continues Kobayashi Tatsue's tradition of researching and preserving local folk crafts.[51] The network around the Miyamoto School has also maintained its particularly close link to Saku Central Hospital, campaigning for the support and development of its rural medicine model, and creating its own health initiatives, such as support schemes for elderly residents.[52]

Over the years, the Miyamoto School has debated local problems like the Saku City amalgamation, as well as larger national issues such as Japan's postwar pacifist constitution. Today, much interest focuses on nuclear power and the international free-trade negotiations surrounding the Trans-Pacific Partnership. The participants in the school are not adherents of a particular political party or a specific ideology, and there is no party line on these matters, though the principles of endogenous development inform all their discussions. A characteristic of the school, though, is to try to take discussion of problems beyond the purely local framework; to consider, for example, not just how the Trans-Pacific Partnership will affect local farm sales, but also how it affects other parts of Asia, and (as in the case of the MSA and the 1960 Security Treaty renewal) how trade and military issues are interwoven.

## The Next Hundred Years

How do we judge the success or failure of a grassroots movement? If longevity is a mark of success, the residents of Saku surely deserve credit for keeping a lineage of alternative social thought alive for almost a century. Interestingly, they have done this without any enduring institutional structure, but simply through the transmission of ideas and experiences from individual to individual within a fluid and changing

---

51    Shinshū Miyamoto Juku ed., *Nōsonhatsu jūmin hakusho dai-2 shū: Tomo ni ikiru* [A Citizens' White Paper Initiated from the Villages, vol. 2: Living Together] (Mochizuki: Shinshū Miyamoto Juku, 2013); interview with Itō Morihisa, Mochizuki, 29 May 2015.
52    Interview with Shimizu Noriko, Shimizu Kiyoshi and Itō Kimiko, Kyōwa, 28 May 2015.

network of grassroots groups. The ideas they embrace have left tangible traces on the life of the region. Without their existence, it is likely that Saku City would have had more large-scale corporate development projects of the sort promoted by many Japanese local governments in the 1970s and 1980s, and less organic farming and craft-style production, exemplified by local products like *Kataribe saké*. The rural medicine developed by Wakatsuki and the doctors he trained has also left its mark—the Saku region is widely recognised for the high quality of its health care.[53]

But while a formal political party might judge success by election victories or the fulfilment of its party platform, the aims of the Saku region's endogenous development networks are broad, open-ended and evolving, so assessing their overall achievements is much more difficult. As some problems have been overcome, others have come into focus—issues, for example, of gender and generation. The social education movement of the 1960s and 1970s was overwhelmingly male-dominated. Though women performed large amounts of labour on local farms, agricultural management was largely in the hands of men, as was leadership in social life. In the 1950s and 1960s *Seinendan*, for example, the convention was that the leader would always be a young man and the deputy a young woman.[54] Over the past 20 years or so, the social hierarchy has been changing. Many women now play increasingly important parts in the Miyamoto School and endogenous development schemes, among them Tsuru Bunka University professor Tanaka Natsuko, a leading Japanese expert on the cooperative movement; Mochizuki-born editor and publisher Hata Yumiko; and Yoshikawa Tōru's daughter Yūko, who is a member of Saku City Council. But change has been gradual, and there is still surely scope for women's voices to play a greater role in the shaping of the network's ideas. A glance around the room at meetings of the Miyamoto School, as at the gatherings of many grassroots groups in Japan today, reveals an ageing population of participants. There are many grey heads and many backs bent by lives of hard work. This partly reflects the ageing of the Saku population as a whole; but, as Yoshikawa, Itō and other readily acknowledge, engaging the younger generation is a challenge.

Meanwhile, Saku's social alternatives face a mass of larger challenges from the outside world. For the farmers of the district, climate change is not an abstract concept but a reality faced every day, in plants that ripen out

---

53    See for example Honda, 'Health Equity'.
54    Interview with Shimizu Noriko, Shimizu Kiyoshi and Itō Kimiko, Kyōwa, 28 May 2015.

of season and monsoon rains that fail to arrive on time. Yet, rather than focusing on the huge challenges of global warming and of Japan's pressing need for new and safe sources of energy, the national government's policy is directed above all to a pursuit of national might through ever-deepening economic and military commitment to the US alliance—a policy that raises the defence budget, opens the agricultural market to cheap imports and destabilises East Asian relations in ways that many local people find deeply alarming. Indeed, the political landscape of Japan appears to have undergone a subtle change in recent decades. The metropolitan areas, once the main centres of progressive politics, are now dominated by right-wing local administrations, while in some rural areas growing currents of unease are disrupting the traditional image of the countryside as the backbone of conservative politics.

When the White Birch teachers started their educational experiments in unpromising circumstances a century ago, would they have imagined that their ideas would still be reverberating in the valleys of Saku 100 years later? Did they see themselves as pioneers of a social revolution that would soon sweep the world, or as voices in the wilderness? The story of the legacy that grew from their actions provides an illustration of the quiet ways in which ideas can survive and grow even in sometimes hostile environments. The concepts of humanist schooling and social education, of rural community medicine and endogenous development nurtured over decades in Saku and surrounding regions have relevance, not just for other parts of Japan, but also for many communities worldwide that face similar challenges today. The survival of these ideas against the odds provides at least some hope that they can be sustained, reshaped and reinvigorated over the century to come.

# 4

# Transnational Activism and Japan's Second Modernity

Simon Avenell

## Introduction

The early 1970s were an important moment of transnational engagement in the Japanese environmental movement. What had until then been a largely domestic phenomenon comprising thousands of local mobilisations against industrial pollution and rampant development expanded to include a new array of transnational initiatives, many with a specific focus on pollution in the countries of East Asia. The initial stimulus for these new movements was scattered media reports and anecdotal accounts that some Japanese companies were relocating their pollutive industrial processes to East Asia in response to stricter regulation in Japan. Such reports came as a rude awakening to many Japanese activists, who realised that so-called 'pollution export' undermined their 'victories' against industrial pollution within Japan. In response, a small number of Japanese activists promptly mobilised movements to address pollution export into countries such as Thailand, South Korea, the Philippines, Malaysia, and Indonesia. Prominent civic activists like the engineer Ui Jun and the novelist Oda Makoto organised international conferences with Asian activists, while others began publishing monthly newsletters on the issue in English and Japanese. A number of Japanese activists also travelled to the affected countries to inform local activists about the Japanese pollution experience and the successful strategies they had employed in their domestic struggles. Impressively, these meetings sometimes resulted in coordinated transnational actions between protestors on the ground in East Asia and supporters back in Japan. This kind of transnational activity was an entirely new phenomenon in the Japanese environmental movement and it marked a significant enhancement in the geographical reach of postwar Japanese environmental activism.

In this chapter, I provide a brief overview of the new sphere of transnational activism in the Japanese environmental movement of the 1970s. As I explain, I believe the transnational movements were glued together by a powerful translocal sentiment in which local struggles and activists combined their strong communal identities with an emergent East Asian grassroots regionalism. Leading activists served as the important 'connective tissue' nurturing this translocal sentiment.[1] Though grassroots movements in the region (as we have seen) have a long history, I believe that transnational involvement nurtured a new reflexivity among the Japanese activists involved, emblematic of the mentalities and consciousness of reflexive or second modernity referred to by Anthony Giddens, Ulrich Beck, and others.[2] If Japanese modernity was marked by a brash and unyielding state-led developmentalism focused on the questions 'how do we grow?' and 'how do we appropriate the resources we need to grow?' as an economy, as a national state, and as individuals, then reflexive modernity has unfolded as a deeply critical project in which some individuals have begun to ask 'what are the consequences of growth (or lack thereof)?' and 'how do we survive?' in a world where the sureties of the national state framework of modernity are threatened and undermined by political, economic, and technological pressures. Transnational involvement had a particularly striking impact on the way the activists involved conceptualised their activist identity. Within the framework of the Japanese nation, civic activists could quite seamlessly position themselves as victims of the state and industry. But transnational involvement upset this schematic by exposing their complicity—albeit indirectly—in the transgressions of Japanese industry abroad. The result, I argue, was a more reflexive activist identity characteristic of the mentalities of reflexive modernity. I begin the chapter by briefly tracing

---

1    Sidney Tarrow, *The New Transnational Activism* (Cambridge, UK: Cambridge University Press, 2005), 206.
2    Ulrich Beck, 'The Reinvention of Politics: Towards a Theory of Reflexive Modernization', in Ulrich Beck, Anthony Giddens, and Scott Lash eds, *Reflexive Modernization: Politics, Tradition, and Aesthetics in the Modern Social Order* (Cambridge, UK: Polity Press, 1994), 1–55.

some of the earliest and most influential of the transnational movements, paying special attention to the role of core activists in bringing people together across borders. The latter part of the chapter examines the new mentalities and ideas born of this transnational interaction.

## Pollution Export and Response

Civic groups were certainly well aware of Japan's troubled legacy in Asia before the mid- to late 1960s but until then their focus had been mainly on resisting conservative rule and the entrenchment of American influence domestically. The pursuit of 'Peace and Democracy' at home, in other words, was seen as the best way to address the misdeeds of the past, particularly in Asia and the Pacific. Coupled with this approach, restrictions on overseas travel until the 1960s also hindered the formation of transnational movement networks. But the outbreak of the Vietnam War and the advent of pollution export almost forced Asia onto the activist agenda by exposing the direct connections of the region to conservative rule, economic growth, and American hegemony at home. What resulted was a period of intensive grassroots regionalisation among some Japanese civic groups that would continue to develop over the coming decades. By 'grassroots regionalisation' I certainly refer to the numerical growth of Japanese NGOs and groups active in East Asia, which was truly significant. But I also allude to what is best described as the regionalisation of an activist mindset that had been largely national or local in focus up to that point. We might say that the late 1960s and early 1970s marked a doubling of the civic mindset as domestic and regional initiatives came to be seen as necessary components of the same struggle. Needless to say, this progressive reengagement with Asia was by no means painless and, in many ways, proved more difficult for activists than for political or corporate elites who could 'buy' their way back into Asian countries. Activists, of course, approached their Asian counterparts with a deep sense of remorse for Japan's problematic history in Asia as well as a sense of responsibility for the pressing issues of the present. Nowhere is this clearer than in movements opposing Japanese industrial pollution export to the region.

Japanese pollution export of the early 1970s had its roots in the Japanese domestic pollution crisis that stretched from the late 1950s to around the early 1970s. I have discussed this domestic history in detail elsewhere but, for the purposes of contextualisation, note the following here.[3] Japan's rise as an economic superpower, coming in waves from around the late 1950s and again in the 1960s, was accompanied by some of the worst cases of industrial pollution in modern global history. As industry spread around the Japanese archipelago local communities were devastated by extreme forms of atmospheric, water, and ground pollution. Industries wilfully pumped dangerous gases into the atmosphere and dumped chemical toxins into bays and rivers. Residents living in surrounding communities bore the brunt of this rampant industrial expansion. In Yokkaichi City, for example, many locals were afflicted with pulmonary diseases and chronic asthma caused by poisonous sulphur dioxide emitted from a nearby petrochemical facility. At Minamata Bay and later in Niigata Prefecture, people were struck down with debilitating motor neuron disease, impaired sensation, and loss of bodily coordination due to their inadvertent consumption of seafood contaminated with methyl mercury dumped by industry (See also Chapter Five). To make matters worse, people in affected communities not only endured harrowing medical complications, they also faced cruel discrimination from an uninformed public.

Nevertheless, as the pollution problem intensified and spread (eventually into big cities like Tokyo and Osaka where air pollution reached dangerous proportions in the 1960s), local communities began to organise protest movements and to take offending industries to court. These protests and court battles sometimes took well over a decade to settle but, by the late 1960s, the Japanese Government and judiciary began to respond. Local governments took the lead by passing stringent regulations and forcing industry into pollution prevention agreements. A reluctant national government followed, first by passing the *Basic Law on Pollution Prevention* in 1967 and then, at the historic Pollution Diet in 1970, amending the *Basic Law* to give it punitive force and passing over a dozen other pieces of pollution prevention legislation. By the early 1970s, Japan had in place some of the strictest industrial pollution regulations in the world and a body of case law strongly on the side of pollution victims. Some even described this outcome as a pollution miracle.

Not entirely by coincidence, there was a marked increase in Japanese foreign direct investment (FDI) into East Asia (and elsewhere) just as the new environmental regulations began to bite in the early 1970s.

---

3    Simon Avenell, 'Japan's Long Environmental Sixties and the Birth of a Green Leviathan', *Japanese Studies* 32, no. 3 (2012): 423–44.

From 1967 to 1973 overall Japanese FDI increased tenfold, and between 1973 and 1976 it essentially doubled that of the preceding 20 years.[4] Along with the quantitative change, Japanese FDI also began to change qualitatively in the early 1970s as polluting industries involved in chemicals and steel became more prominent.[5] To be sure, it would be a mistake to attribute this FDI spike entirely to domestic environmental regulations. Even activists recognised that other factors such as cheap labour and resources played an important role in corporate decisions to go offshore. But there is little doubt that domestic regulation also shaped corporate investment strategies. Important research by Derek Hall has shown that the strict Japanese regulatory regime was very much on the minds of corporate executives and government officials in the early 1970s, to the extent that pollution export even became a 'state strategy' at one point.[6] Utilising a wealth of government and industry publications, newsletters, and public comments, Hall shows beyond doubt that the powerful Ministry of International Trade and Industry (MITI) and mammoth corporations like Mitsubishi openly admitted that environmental regulation was a factor shaping their FDI strategies. In 1970, for example, MITI established a special fund to help relocate the pollutive petrochemical industry abroad while in the same year the Mitsubishi Corporation noted siting difficulties in Japan due to local opposition as one reason for building an oil refinery in Southeast Asia rather than at home.[7] Overt strategy or not, the 1970s witnessed a proliferation of polluting Japanese industries throughout East Asia: hexavalent chromium plants in South Korea, chemical processing plants in Indonesia, mining operations and steel sintering plants in the Philippines, caustic soda plants in Thailand, rare earth mining operations in Malaysia, and asbestos processing in Taiwan.[8]

Japanese environmental activists became aware of the pollution export practice relatively early on thanks to a number of fortuitous transnational encounters. The first was at the historic United Nations Conference on the Human Environment (UNCHE) held in Stockholm in early June 1972.

4    T. J. Pempel, 'Gulliver in Lilliput: Japan and Asian Economic Regionalism', *World Policy Journal* 13, no. 4 (Winter 1996–7): 18; Derek Hall, 'Pollution Export as State and Corporate Strategy: Japan in the 1970s', *Review of International Political Economy* 16, no. 2 (2009): 262.

5    Hall 'Pollution Export', 262.

6    Hall, 'Pollution Export'.

7    Derek Hall, 'Environmental Change, Protest, and Havens of Environmental Degradation: Evidence from Asia', *Global Environmental Politics* 2, no. 2 (2002): 22, 23.

8    Ui Jun, 'Pollution Export', in Shigeto Tsuru and Helmut Weidner eds, *Environmental Policy in Japan* (Berlin: Sigma, 1989), 396, 401.

While participating in the non-governmental forums running parallel to the main conference, Ui Jun and a group of industrial pollution sufferers from Japan met with activists from other East Asian countries. Ui and his group's main objective was to communicate the story of Japanese industrial pollution to the world, so they were deeply shocked to learn from their Asian counterparts that Japanese industrial activity was already causing concern in the region.

On his return, Ui communicated this news to anti-pollution activists through his national environmental network, the Independent Lectures on Pollution (ILP). He scolded himself and fellow activists for their naiveté in assuming that Japanese corporations would simply clean up in response to domestic protest and regulation. Indeed, so insular was their perspective that not until Asian activists alerted them to pollution export had they even considered the concrete implications of Japan's economic penetration into the region. For Ui such realities demanded far deeper and more substantive engagement with East Asian activists.[9] As a first step, Ui and his group began publishing an English-language pamphlet entitled *KOGAI: Newsletter from Polluted Japan*, which ran articles on industrial pollution in Japan and throughout East Asia. ILP sent the newsletter free of charge to subscribers who, in return, provided information about industrial pollution in their countries. In this way, the newsletter served as both a medium for information transmission and a vehicle for connecting anti-pollution protesters across East Asia into a rudimentary transnational grassroots alliance.

The contacts Ui and others formed with Asian activists at UNCHE resulted in substantive, face-to-face interactions and movements in the coming months and years. In late 1972 and early 1973, for example, Matsuoka Nobuo, an activist involved in ILP, travelled to Malaysia and Thailand where he met with environmental groups. In Kuala Lumpur, activists told Matsuoka that they were desperate for technical information about pollution and were actively collecting newspaper clippings on Japanese industrial pollution. The Malaysian activists frankly stated that they were extremely sceptical—if not cynical—about so-called Japanese technical and economic 'assistance' since these were often simply code

---

9   Ui Jun, 'Kokuren kankyō kaigi hōkoku I' [Report from the UN Environmental Conference I], *Kōgai Genron* [Fundamental Studies in Pollution] 13 (July 1972): 17–8. Reproduced in Saitama Daigaku Kyōsei Shakai Kenkyū Sentā ed., *Ui Jun shūshū kōgai mondai shiryō 2 fukkoku 'Kōgai Genron' dai 1-kai haihon dai 3-kan* [Materials on Pollution Problems Collected by Ui Jun, 2, Reprint: 'Fundamental Studies in Pollution', First Distribution, Vol. 3] (Tokyo: Suirensha, 2007), 221–2.

words for Japanese corporate exploitation of cheap labour and resources. As Matsuoka explained, 'if we fail to carefully reconsider what assistance really is, the Japanese run the risk of losing the good faith of our Asian friends to a point where it is irrecoverable'.[10] Later Matsuoka travelled to Chulalongkorn University in Bangkok where he gave a presentation on Japanese pollution to students involved in environmental activism. On learning that the Thai students had previously known nothing about Japan's terrible pollution history, Matsuoka felt an overwhelming sense of guilt and responsibility. From now on, he observed, Japanese activists 'must be prepared to shoulder another heavy load' (i.e. taking responsibility for Japanese corporate activity in neighbouring countries).[11]

Ui, Matsuoka, and others' calls for a new commitment to East Asian environmental problems found a cause almost immediately. Only months after Matsuoka's visit to Thailand, another colleague from the ILP's Asia group, Hirayama Takasada, visited Kasetsart University in Bangkok to meet with members of the university's nature preservation club. During these meetings the club's leader showed Hirayama a newspaper clipping entitled 'No Repeat of the Minamata Tragedy' from the Bangkok daily, *Siam Rath*, reporting that the Thai Asahi Caustic Soda Company—a subsidiary of the Japanese Asahi Glass Company of the Mitsubishi Group—was responsible for dumping effluent containing caustic soda, synthetic hydrochloric acid, liquid chlorine, and mercury into the Chao Phraya River, resulting in a massive fish kill and skin afflictions and diarrhoea among residents who consumed the fish.[12] The discovery of a concrete example of Japanese pollution in Thailand was nothing short of earthshattering for Matsuoka and his visceral response is representative of the way most other Japanese activists reacted:

---

10  Matsuoka Nobuo, 'Tōnan Ajia no tabi kara (Marēshia nite)' [From a Journey to Southeast Asia: Malaysia], *Jishu Kōza* [Independent Lectures] 18 (Sept 1972): 2. Reproduced in Saitama Daigaku Kyōsei Shakai Kenkyū Sentā ed., *Ui Jun shūshū kōgai mondai shiryō 1 fukkoku 'Jishu Kōza' dai 3-kan* [Materials on Pollution Problems Collected by Ui Jun, 1, Reprint: 'Independent Lectures', Vol. 3] (Tokyo: Suirensha, 2005), 346.
11  Matsuoka Nobuo, 'Mō hitotsu no omoni o seou kakugo o: Higashi Ajia no tabi kara (3)' [The Willingness to Take up Another Burden: From a Journey to East Asia], *Jishu Kōza* [Independent Lectures] 20 (Nov 1972): 38. Reproduced in Saitama Daigaku Kyōsei Shakai Kenkyū Sentā ed., *Ui Jun shūshū kōgai mondai shiryō 1 fukkoku 'Jishu Kōza' dai 4-kan* [Materials on Pollution Problems Collected by Ui Jun, 1, Reprint: 'Independent Lectures', Vol. 4] (Tokyo: Suirensha, 2005), 106.
12  Inoue Sumio, 'Bokura wa kōgai yushtsu to tatakai hajimeta' [We Have Begun the Fight against Pollution Export], *Tenbō* [Prospect] 191 (Nov 1974): 50.

What's this!? The evil hand of mercury contamination has reached Thailand! My naïve assumption that full-scale pollution export was yet to come had been betrayed with consummate ease by these cold-hard facts. Utterly surprised, for a time I could say nothing. I was thrown into utter despair by a piercing reality: 'pollution export had begun! Thai Asahi Caustic Soda was just the tip of the iceberg.' I was quickly filled with rage. I could not allow this. I simply could not allow it. Once again I engraved in my mind the purpose of this trip: to communicate the situation of Japanese pollution and to find a way to mobilise an antipollution movement based on cooperation between Japanese and Southeast Asian people.[13]

Throughout 1973 and 1974, Japanese and Thai environmental activists mobilised one of the earliest transnational movements against industrial pollution in postwar East Asian history. In late August 1973, students from Thammasat, Kasetsart, Chulalongkorn, Mahidol universities organised a nature conservation exhibition on the campus of Thammasat University. Around 20 per cent of the exhibition was devoted to displays on Japanese industrial pollution with the remainder focusing on environmental issues in Thailand. Organisers distributed Thai translations of the ILP pamphlet *Polluted Japan* (prepared by Ui and others for UNCHE), which contained detailed information on Japan's pollution experience. They also ran screenings of Tsuchimoto Noriaki's disturbing documentary film *Minamata: The Victims and Their World*.[14] On the Japan side, in September 1973 around 150 activists from anti-war, environmental, and other civic groups marched on the headquarters of the Asahi Glass Company in Tokyo with placards reading 'Asahi Glass, Stop Exporting Pollution!'[15] The Tokyo protest was reported in the *Siam Rath* newspaper days later under the headline 'Japanese people demonstrate in opposition to factory polluting Thailand'. The full-page report contained photographs of the demonstration and interviews with Japanese activists, which generated

---

13    Hirayama Takasada, 'Tōnan Ajia kōgai saihakken no tabi (1) Tai nite' [A Journey of Rediscovery to Southeast Asia: Thailand], *Jishu Kōza* [Independent Lectures] 31 (Oct 1973): 52. Reproduced in Saitama Daigaku Kyōsei Shakai Kenkyū Sentā ed., *Ui Jun shūshū kōgai mondai shiryō 1 fukkoku 'Jishu Kōza' dai 2-kai haihon dai 1-kan* [Materials on Pollution Problems Collected by Ui Jun, 1, Reprint: 'Independent Lectures', Second Distribution, Vol. 1] (Tokyo: Suirensha, 2006), 382.

14    Hirayama Takasada, 'Exporting Pollution (The Export of 'KOGAI')', *KOGAI: The Newsletter From Polluted Japan* 2 (Winter 1974): 7; Inoue, 'Bokura wa', 52.

15    Jishu Kōza Ajia Gurūpu, 'Tai Asahi Kasei Sōda no kasen osen' [The Pollution of Rivers by Asahi Kasei Soda Thailand], *Jishu Kōza* [Independent Lectures] 31 (Oct 1973), 48. Reproduced in Saitama Daigaku Kyōsei Shakai Kenkyū Sentā ed., *Ui Jun shūshū kōgai mondai shiryō 1 fukkoku 'Jishu Kōza' dai 2-kai haihon dai 1-kan* [Materials on Pollution Problems Collected by Ui Jun, 1, Reprint: 'Independent Lectures', Second Distribution, Vol. 1] (Tokyo: Suirensha, 2006), 378.

a great response among Thai citizens.[16] After these protests, activists established the Japan–Thai Youth Friendship Movement (*Nichi-Tai Seinen Yūkō Undō*) to act as the organisational hub for the budding transnational mobilisation.

In the coming months interactions between activists intensified, culminating in a historic simultaneous transnational demonstration in September 1974. As in the previous year, activists in Tokyo marched with banners and placards in Japanese and Thai reading 'Asahi Glass, Get out of Thailand!' Messages of support from Thai activists were read out during the Tokyo protest.[17] In Bangkok, student activists held a three-day exhibition entitled 'Opposing Japanese Export of Pollution', which attracted some 15,000 people. The organisers' aims were twofold: to use the Japanese experience to raise awareness about industrial pollution among the Thai people and to exert pressure on the Thai Government to implement more stringent environmental regulations to control industrial pollution.[18] Visitors to the exhibition were greeted at the entrance by a large banner reading 'POLLUTED JAPAN' and a mock coffin with a photo of a fetal Minamata disease victim. Inside were displays of industrial pollution at Yokkaichi and Minamata, shocking cases of food contamination from arsenic and polychlorinated biphenyl (PCBs), photos of Japanese nuclear power plants, and a series of panels on the Japanese economic penetration of Asia. Over the course of the exhibition, various public discussions were held on pollution in Japan, local residents and pollution, and anti-pollution strategies for youth. Visitors were overjoyed when a statement from the demonstrators in Tokyo was read out and they eagerly signed a petition opposing the proposed construction of a petrochemical plant by Japanese industry in Si Racha in the Gulf of Thailand.[19] Thanks to this pressure, the Mitsui and Mitsubishi Corporations announced that they would be shelving their construction plans. The companies cited increased pollution monitoring by Thai students and intellectuals as one contributing factor.[20] Japanese activists walked away from the demonstration with a deepened

---

16   Inoue, 'Bokura wa', 51.

17   ibid., 52–3.

18   ibid., 53.

19   Okuda Takaharu, 'Nichitai o musubu kōgai hantai undō' [An Anti-Pollution Movement Linking Japan and Thailand], *Jishu Kōza* [Independent Lectures] 44 (Nov 1974): 41–54. Reproduced in Saitama Daigaku Kyōsei Shakai Kenkyū Sentā ed., *Ui Jun shūshū kōgai mondai shiryō 1 fukkoku 'Jishu Kōza' dai 2-kai haihon dai 4-kan* [Materials on Pollution Problems Collected by Ui Jun, 1, Reprint: 'Independent Lectures', Second Distribution, Vol. 4] (Tokyo: Suirensha, 2006), 53.

20   Inoue, 'Bokura wa', 53.

awareness of the entanglement of Japanese industry and pollution with East Asia. As the *KOGAI* newsletter noted in 1975, 'We remember what a Thai friend said to us, "what brings disasters upon [the] Thai people will surely bring them upon [the] Japanese. And conversely, what damages [the] Japanese will also damage [the] Thai people"'.[21]

Deeply concerned about the extent of pollution export, Japanese activists involved in the Thai Asahi movement began to carefully scrutinise Japanese corporate activity elsewhere in East Asia. Their concerns were not unfounded. In mid-February 1974, Hirayama Takasada was alerted to an article in the *Tōyō Keizai Nippō*, a financial newspaper run by resident Koreans in Japan. The article, entitled 'Polluting Plant Exported to South Korea?!', reported how a resident Korean entrepreneur, one Mr Koe, had purchased a mercurochrome plant from the Toyama Chemical Company and reconstructed it in Inch'ŏn City, South Korea, where he was applying for permission to commence operations. Pointing to a possible instance of pollution export, the article noted that Toyama Chemical had decided to sell the Toyama plant in 1973 after running into problems with Japanese regulators over contamination issues.[22] Toyama Chemical had in fact been forced to halt production of mercurochrome—a highly toxic substance—in September 1973 when waters in Toyama Bay were found to have mercury levels equivalent to those in Minamata Bay. In December 1973, tests by the Toyama Prefectural Government revealed toxic levels of mercury contamination in industrial sludge near the plant's drainpipes.[23] It was at this point that managers hatched the 'ingenious' solution of selling the factory to Koe and simply importing mercurochrome from his company once the factory was operational in Inch'ŏn.

In February 1974, Hirayama Takasada and Inoue Sumio—both involved in the Thai movement—met with local civic groups in Toyama, which confirmed the newspaper report. Hirayama and Inoue subsequently produced their own detailed report on the incident and began to mobilise in opposition. In late April, groups gathered in protest in Toyama and

---

21 Okuda, 'Documents', 11.

22 Hirayama Takasada, 'Sōkan no ji' [Some Words on the Launch of the Journal], *Geppō kōgai o nogasuna* 1 [Monthly Journal 'Don't Let the Pollution Escape!'] (1974): 1; 1974/2/15; Inoue, 'Bokura wa', 54.

23 Hirayama Takasada, 'Toyama Kagaku, kōgai yushutsu chūshi!?' [Toyama Chemical: Stop Exporting Pollution!], *Jishu Kōza* [Independent Lectures] 39 (June 1974): 28. Reproduced in Saitama Daigaku Kyōsei Shakai Kenkyū Sentā ed., *Ui Jun shūshū kōgai mondai shiryō 1 fukkoku 'Jishu Kōza' dai 2-kai haihon dai 3-kan* [Materials on Pollution Problems Collected by Ui Jun, 1, Reprint: 'Independent Lectures', Second Distribution, Vol. 3] (Tokyo: Suirensha, 2006), 94.

outside the company's Tokyo headquarters. In Tokyo, ILP members were joined by representatives from the Zainichi Korean Youth League (ZKYL) and the Japanese YWCA. The 200-strong protest group waved placards in Japanese and Korean reading 'Toyama Chemical, Stop Exporting Pollution!' In Toyama, local residents' groups protested outside railway stations and at the Toyama Chemical facilities where they distributed pamphlets to employees.[24] At the Tokyo protest, Hirayama and Inoue were surprised to learn from YWCA participants that women in the Inch'ŏn chapter of the YWCA had been conducting a similar protest against the mercurochrome factory since February 1974. The Inch'ŏn women had apparently learned of the factory relocation from the Korean-language *Christian Newspaper*, which had reproduced the article published earlier in the Japanese *Tōyō Keizai Nippō*. Thereafter the Inch'ŏn YWCA women took the bold step of petitioning the Inch'ŏn Mayor to deny Koe's application to commence mercurochrome production. They did this at substantial personal risk given the nature of authoritarian rule under President Park Chung-hee. The Park regime actively encouraged the establishment of Japanese polluting industries in South Korea by intentionally avoiding pollution regulation and cracking down on local protest.[25] In mid-1973, Park brazenly declared that 'for the purposes of the industrial development of our country, it will be best not to worry too much about pollution problems'.[26]

Faced with mounting pressure in both countries, on April 30, some three days after the protests, NHK television news reported that the Toyama Chemical Company board of directors had decided to abandon their plan to import mercurochrome from the plant in South Korea, effectively ending operations at that end too. Although the nature of political dictatorship in South Korea had made direct coordination impossible, Japanese activists rightly concluded that their protest had been a 'de facto' transnational struggle with the women of the Inch'ŏn YWCA.[27] Indeed, it was thanks to this joint transnational action that they had succeeded.

24   Inoue, 'Bokura wa', 55.
25   Ogawa Hiroshi, 'Ajia no mado: Nihon Kagaku no kōgai yushutsu o kokuhatsu suru' [A Window on Asia: Indicting Nippon Chemical's Pollution Export], *Jishu Kōza* [Independent Lectures] 42 (Sept 1974): 57. Reproduced in Saitama Daigaku Kyōsei Shakai Kenkyū Sentā ed., *Ui Jun shūshū kōgai mondai shiryō 1 fukkoku 'Jishu Kōza' dai 2-kai haihon dai 3-kan* [Materials on Pollution Problems Collected by Ui Jun, 1, Reprint: 'Independent Lectures', Second Distribution, Vol. 3] (Tokyo: Suirensha, 2006), 307.
26   Hall, 'Pollution Export', 269.
27   Inoue Sumio, 'Babanuki no riron o koete: Nihon Kagaku no kuromu tarenagashi to kankoku e no kōgai yushutsu', *Tenbō* 204 (Dec 1977): 89.

As with the Asahi Glass incident in Bangkok, the Inch'ŏn case provided yet another opportunity for Japanese activists to rethink their domestic struggle in a wider regional context and, by consequence, to reevaluate their situation as pollution victims. As one of the placards at the April protest noted, 'We cannot ignore this *mechanism* in which our "affluence" is built on the sacrifice of the South Korean people … . Come on, let's destroy from within Japan the economic invasion and export of pollution into Asia … exemplified by Toyama Chemical's corporate activity'.[28] The statement of the ZKYL expressed a similar sentiment, noting that 'We are committed to transforming this struggle against Toyama Chemical's pollution export into a joint struggle of the Japanese and South Korean people to oppose all forms of pollution export and economic invasion and to intensify our condemnation of responsible corporations'.[29] To this end, in June 1974 Hirayama and Inoue established the monthly publication, *Don't Let the Pollution Escape,* to monitor Toyama Chemical and other companies looking to relocate their polluting activities offshore. What just a few years before had been a domestic struggle between local communities and Japanese corporations was now escalating into region-wide battle against pollution export and political dictatorship throughout East Asia.

The range of movements in ensuing years is too broad to cover here, but one further movement against the Nippon Chemical Company (NCC) deserves attention in the context of my discussion of the emergence of a new reflexivity in 1970s Japanese environmental activism stimulated by transnational involvement. Activists became aware of NCC via a report in the *Nihon Keizai Shinbun* newspaper in June 1974. The article reported that NCC and its South Korean partner were planning to produce sodium bichromate and thenardite at a factory located in the Ulsan industrial region. According to the article, NCC's decision to go abroad was prompted by numerous worker compensation claims, increased regulation, and civic protest relating to the toxic compound hexavalent chromium, a byproduct of sodium bichromate production. NCC's

---

28   Emphasis in original. Hirayama, 'Toyama Kagaku, kōgai yushutsu chūshi!?' 95.
29   Hirayama, 'Toyama Kagaku, kōgai yushutsu chūshi!?' 93.

move was provocatively described as 'a new direction in the development of production bases for pollutive industries by way of international dispersion'.[30]

Hirayama and Inoue of the *Don't Let the Pollution Escape* movement began to investigate NCC immediately. They discovered a record of blatant disregard for environmental regulation and a longer history of transgressions against Asian people. NCC began producing sodium bichromate in 1915 at factories in Tokyo and the surrounding Chiba and Kanagawa prefectures. During World War II, the company actively provided material for munitions manufacture and, more troublingly, operated a chromium mine that made extensive use of forced Korean labour. In the course of their investigations, activists discovered horrific instances of torture and inhumane treatment at this mining operation— all of which they documented (with graphical reproductions) in *Don't Let the Pollution Escape* and other activist newsletters. Adding to its troubled wartime record, in the postwar period NCC began to sell its chromium slag to the construction industry for use in the foundations of domestic dwellings and for filling unused wet rice paddies. Although it would only come to light much later, this slag contained highly toxic chromium that the company was well aware of.[31] Under increasing pressure from residents complaining about foul smells and chemicals leaching from their gardens and cases of pulmonary afflictions in workers and communities around the factories, in 1972 NCC shifted production of sodium bichromate to its Tokuyama factory. Before commencing operations there, the company signed a pollution prevention agreement with Tokuyama City pledging that it would convert all waste material into soluble trivalent chromium.[32] Yet, despite these undertakings, in September 1972 when a ship sank in waters off the coast of Shimonoseki, it was revealed that NCC had been dumping unprocessed chromium slag at sea in direct contravention of the agreement. Subsequent investigations revealed that the company had ocean-dumped an astonishing 5,000 tons of toxic waste material

---

30　Ogawa Yoshio, 'Dai 2 no Toyama Kagaku = Nihon Kagaku no Kankoku e no kōgai yusutsu o yamesaseyo' [Toyama Chemical No. Two: Let's Stop Nippon Chemical from Exporting Pollution to South Korea], *Geppō kōgai o nogasuna! Kankoku e no kōgai yushutsu o kokuhatsu suru* [Monthly Journal 'Don't Let the Pollution Escape!' Indicting Pollution Export to South Korea], 3.

31　Ogawa Yoshio, 'Dai 2 no Toyama Kagaku', 2; Masayoshi Hideo, 'Nikkan no genjō to kōgai yusutsu soshi undō' [The Present Situation of Japan-South Korea Relations and the Movement to Stop Pollution Export], *Geppō kōgai o nogasuna! Kankoku e no kōgai yushutsu o kokuhatsu suru* [Monthly Journal 'Don't Let the Pollution Escape!' Indicting Pollution Export to South Korea] 7 (Dec 1974): 1.

32　Inoue, 'Bokura wa', 59.

since July 1972. As a result, the Tokuyama Municipal Assembly ordered a temporary suspension of production at the factory.[33] It was shortly after this incident the NCC executives hatched the plan to relocate operations to Ulsan in South Korea.

The opposition movement that began to gather steam around mid-1974 is an excellent example of the way growing awareness of the pollution export problem—thanks to the transnational activities of individuals like Ui, Hirayama, and Inoue—encouraged activists in very localised movements within Japan to reconsider the industrial pollution problem on a wider regional canvas and, in turn, reconsider their own sense of victimisation. By acting as the connective tissue between pollution and protest abroad and mobilisations back in Japan, core activists like Hirayama helped to grow this awareness both within themselves and other Japanese activists. As I noted earlier, it was an awareness that resulted in substantive action because some activists began to develop a sense of empathy, comradery and responsibility toward the victims of Japanese pollution export, even though in many cases they would remain physically separated by geographical, cultural and political distance.

The Residents Association to Rid Kōtō, Sumida, and Edogawa Wards of Pollution (RAR) is a case in point. This group initially formed to examine contamination of their neighbourhoods by toxic materials illegally dumped from NCC's factories. With the cooperation of an ethical municipal employee, the RAR was able to identify numerous locations of NCC's illegal chromate slag dumping, some containing levels of chromium 1,300 times in excess of regulatory limits.[34] Importantly, activists in the RAR did not limit their public protests to the local contamination issue. On the contrary, as leaders of the movement explained to Inoue Sumio, a central pillar of their action was to prevent NCC exporting its pollution to South Korea. For these people, NCC's South Korean manoeuvre was part of a single 'structure of discrimination'. People in this downtown area of Tokyo knew all too well that the rich of uptown Tokyo sent all of their unwanted things—trash processing, toxic chemical factories etc.— in their direction. When Tokyo downtowners complained, the company simply relocated out to the Japanese countryside. But the structure now extended even further, with Japan treating Asia in just the same way

---

33    Kawana Hideyuki, *Dokyumento Nihon no kōgai 13: Ajia no kankyō hakai to Nihon* [Document - Pollution in Japan 13: Japan and Asian Environmental Destruction] (Tokyo: Ryokufu, 1996).
34    Kawana, *Dokyumento Nihon no kōgai*, 101.

uptown Tokyoites had treated people downtown. The challenge was to oppose this structure of discrimination through the straightforward logic of 'don't force bad things on others, keep them in your own backyard'.[35] To this end, the RAR organised a series of public protests under the banner 'NCC, Stop Exporting Pollution to South Korea!' The central refrain of participants was that 'there is no valid reason to inflict the pain we are enduring right now onto the South Korean people'.[36] Moreover, as the following extract from an RAR demonstration reveals, local residents had begun to understand the pollution problem not only on a wider regional canvas but also in the context of a fractured history between Japan and its neighbours:

> There could be nothing more disrespectful to South Korea and its people than to impose this [factory] on them simply because it is not possible in Japan. Nippon Chemical must not be allowed to replicate the same 'imperialist mentality' of the war when it forcibly brought Koreans to Japan and imposed abusive labor on them. We will fight until pollution export is stopped so that normal ties of friendship and goodwill lasting for 100 years, 200 years, or forever can be constructed between South Korea and Japan.[37]

For Inoue Sumio, the shift from insular localism to regional awareness was all about activists abandoning the logic of 'Old Maid' for that of a 'dual-frontal attack'. Just as the aim of the Old Maid card game was to deflect the joker card on to other players, for too long local movements in Japan had focused on eradicating pollution from their own backyards without concern for its subsequent destination(s). But things were different now. Activists—even those in very localised movements—were trying to deal with the pollution 'joker' at home. Moreover, even when the pollution joker managed to escape to Thailand, South Korea, or elsewhere in East Asia, activists were now forming transnational ties across borders, effectively mounting 'dual-frontal attacks' on polluting industries.[38]

Of course, we need to keep in mind that these transnational movements were very small in scale and—as in the case of NCC which successfully began sodium chromate production at Ulsan in 1976—that they often

---

35   Inoue, 'Babanuki', 91.
36   'Damatte irarenai: Jimoto higaisha ga dantai o kessei' [We Cannot Remain Silent: Local Victims Band Together], *Tōyō Keizai Nippō* (6 May 1975). Reproduced in *Geppō kōgai o nogasuna! Kankoku e no kōgai yushutsu o kokuhatsu suru* 14 (July 1975): 31.
37   'Damatte irarenai', 31.
38   Inoue, 'Babanuki', 92.

failed. But by connecting activists across borders, by opening their eyes to the regional implications of Japanese corporate activity, and by connecting industrial pollution of the present to transgressions of the past, these movements facilitated a rethinking of extant activist identity built around entrenched notions of victimhood.

## Understanding Aggression

While not all were successful, the rise of transnational movements against pollution export in the 1970s undoubtedly forced Japanese corporate and government elites to tread more carefully in their strategy for economic expansion in East Asia. As Hall explains, 'MITI began criticising the practice [of pollution export] as early as January 1974, when it called for increased surveillance of FDI projects which might constitute pollution export'.[39] Moreover, as we have seen, decisions to abandon industrial projects by Mitsubishi, Mitsui, and other corporations also reveal a greater corporate sensitivity to the problem. But the reverberations of the new transnational movements were also felt in the realm of Japanese civic activism. In this section I look at a few typical examples of how Japanese activists began to rearticulate their activism in light of their experiences in Asia. I see important ideational developments, especially with respect to the degree of reflexivity in activist identity and consciousness. Whereas to date the problems had always been positioned external to the self (i.e. industrial pollution, state power) now some activists began to reconsider their complicity in these problems.

The more activists learned about pollution export, the more they began to suspect that one of the troubling paradoxes of their successful protest at home was how it had—unintentionally, to be sure—encouraged Japanese corporations to take their polluting processes abroad. This realisation came as a rude awakening because it hit at the heart of a victimisation consciousness running very deeply in the Japanese environmental movement and, indeed, in postwar Japanese civil society more broadly. Oda Makoto, the charismatic anti-Vietnam War protestor, of course, had articulated this tension between Japanese activists' sense of victimisation by the state and their complicity as aggressors in the context

---

39   Hall, 'Pollution Export', 274.

of the Indochina conflict.[40] As Oda explained, ordinary Japanese had, to an extent, been victimised by the wartime state and the US fire and atomic bombings at the end of the Pacific War and they were now victims of quasi-American colonisation in the form of military bases and facilities. But this victimisation also made them aggressors toward the Vietnamese people because the US assault on that country was using Japan as a staging ground. The same could be said of the pollution problem: ordinary Japanese people were certainly victims of industrial pollution, but when this pollution was directed abroad these same Japanese victims became unwitting accomplices in Japanese corporate transgressions overseas. After all, to an extent, the affluent daily life and cleaner-living environments of all Japanese were built on the suffering of people throughout Asia.

Such logic pervades the discourse of Japanese environmentalists in the early to mid-1970s, for example, as in the following ideas of a young ILP activist, Aoyama Tadashi, in 1976. From Aoyama's perspective, the Japanese people's battle against the 'contradictions born of high-speed economic growth' had produced impressive results. Thanks to these struggles, the public was now resolutely opposed to industrial pollution and the Japanese natural environment was much cleaner. Yet, despite such successes, the Japanese had been woefully unaware of people overseas 'suffering in the shadows of Japanese affluence', nowhere more so than in Asia.[41] 'Haven't we essentially ignored the voices and existence of our neighbours up until now?' Aoyama asked.[42] If the Japanese were to 'properly comprehend' their future pathway they needed to 'listen to the appeals' of these neighbours and to act accordingly.[43] In this connection, Aoyama felt emboldened by the flowering of the new anti pollution export movements. 'Ours is a small struggle which began as a battle against pollution export and in pursuit of genuine friendship between the people of [Asia] and Japan … But from this starting point it escalated into a new pollution issue causing uproar throughout Japan.' More significantly,

---

40   Oda Makoto, 'Heiwa o tsukuru: Sono genri to kōdō – hitotsu no sengen' [Making Peace: Principles and Action – A Declaration], in Oda Makoto, *Oda Makoto zenshigoto* [The Complete Works of Oda Makoto] 9 (Tokyo: Kawade Shobō Shinsha, 1970), 113–31.

41   Aoyama Tadashi, 'Nikkan jōyaku 10-nen to kōgai yushutsu hantai undō' [Ten Years of the Japan-South Korea Treaty and the Movement to Oppose Pollution Export], *Jishu Kōza* [Independent Lectures] 58 (Jan 1976): 64. Reproduced in Saitama Daigaku Kyōsei Shakai Kenkyū Sentā ed., *Ui Jun shūshū kōgai mondai shiryō 1 fukkoku 'Jishu Kōza' dai 3-kai haihon dai 2-kan* [Materials on Pollution Problems Collected by Ui Jun, 1, Reprint: 'Independent Lectures', Third Distribution, Vol. 2] (Tokyo: Suirensha, 2006), 70.

42   Aoyama, 'Nikkan jōyaku', 68.

43   ibid.

Aoyama observed how remarkably different the new mobilisations were from the earlier domestic anti-pollution movements. Whereas these earlier movements were begun by victims who gathered supporters and through joint struggle achieved legal, political and social recognition, the new movements were initiated and spearheaded by a cadre of anti-pollution export advocates who were not themselves direct victims. This was an entirely new phenomenon in postwar Japanese environmental activism because the initial motivation for action stemmed not from a desire for individual or communal retribution and compensation but out of concern for others.[44] Ui Jun's ILP movement was a pioneer in this respect, opening the way for later transnational movements involving Japanese, Thais, South Koreans, Filipinos and others from East Asia. For Aoyama, the rise of such advocacy for fellow East Asians promised to be a truly revolutionary force in Japanese environmental activism because it overlaid a victim-focused agenda with an outward-looking, other-focused rubric (i.e. a reflexive outlook). The result, concluded Aoyama, could be a movement 'beyond our wildest dreams'.[45]

Aoyama's exuberance is admirable if not a little overstated, but he was on target with respect to the powerfully transformative impact of the new transnational movements on Japanese environmental activism and the consciousness of activists. Pollution export demanded that Japanese activists deal with the aggressor within as a necessary element of any new transnational alliance. Indeed, this was the very crux of the matter, and its urgency pushed Japanese environmental thought beyond the somewhat insular earlier focus on Japanese victims. Only when Japanese activists exposed the aggressor within and, from this position of vulnerability, attempted to fashion ties of equality with their East Asian counterparts, did genuine border-crossing sentiment begin to take root. To be sure, this process unfolded at first only in a handful of Japanese environmental movements. But I believe its effects on activist identity and civic activism in Japanese were more widespread. After these movements it was no longer possible to consider Japanese environmental problems or activist identity within the narrow framework of the national state, national citizenship or national victimisation. The problems and the responses now transcended borders and, hence, demanded a new mentality that in a similar way transcended the confines of the nation alone.

---

44   ibid., 67–8.
45   ibid., 68.

# Conclusion: Transnational Activism and Japan's Reflexive Modernity?

For around two decades now, Ulrich Beck and his colleagues have been pointing to the global-historical significance of an emergent reflexive modernity worldwide. They argue that 'when modernisation reaches a certain stage it radicalises itself' and 'begins to transform, for a second time, not only the key institutions but also the very principles of society'.[46] First modernity (or simply, modernity) Beck and his colleagues describe as a 'container' form of industrial society that was based upon the 'territorial framework' of the national state, consisting of many 'interlocking social institutions' such as 'a reliable welfare state, mass parties anchored in class culture, and a stable nuclear family' all supportive of and supported by 'a web of economic security woven out of industrial regulation, full employment and life-long careers'.[47] This was an order based on distinctions and boundaries: 'between society and nature, between established knowledge and mere belief, and between the members of society and the outsiders'.[48] Modernity, they explain, was constructed around a number of core (yet ultimately fragile) assumptions about the individual and the physical world. Subjectivity was assumed to be 'calculable' because of a 'fundamental assumption' that 'subject boundaries' were independently assigned and indisputable—a 'breadwinner' was a breadwinner, a housewife was a housewife, and a citizen was a national-state citizen.[49]

But, according to Beck and colleagues, it is precisely at this zenith that the radicalisation of modernity begins due to a 'critical mass of unintended side effects', which bring into question its 'touchstone ideas'.[50] The 'global victory of the principles of modernity (such as the market economy)' has resulted in global environmental degradation, financial crises, and a whole range of new uncertainties that, quite ironically, are rendering the institutions of modernity 'ineffective or dysfunctional for both society and

---

46   Ulrich Beck, Wolfgang Bonss, and Christoph Lau, 'The Theory of Reflexive Modernization: Problematic, Hypotheses and Research Programme', *Theory, Culture, and Society* 20, no. 1 (2003): 1.
47   Beck et al., 'The Theory of Reflexive Modernization', 2, 5.
48   ibid., 2.
49   ibid., 23–4, 27.
50   ibid., 8.

individuals'.[51] It is at this historical juncture, argues Beck, that a critical reflexivity begins to germinate in which society 'becomes a theme and a problem for itself'.[52] The moment is marked by the rise of a 'self-conscious politics that is self-critical and has its own reshaping perpetually in mind'.[53] Under these conditions of second or reflexive modernity, individuals and societies increasingly 'reflect upon and chart their own course into the future rather than adapt to the fate or the flow of events'.[54] Needless to say, contemporary environmentalism from its very origins worldwide in the 1960s was very much a reflexive modern phenomenon because, unlike earlier nature conservation movements in which society ('here') was seen to be destroying nature ('over there'), environmentalism was primarily a movement addressing self-destruction: society was mutilating itself.

So how then does the development of Japanese activists' involvement in East Asian environmental issues substantiate or otherwise resonate with these ideas about the onset of reflexive modernity worldwide? On this question I tend to agree with the political theorist and environmental thinker John Dryzek, who acknowledges that while 'reflexive political action is on the rise, the degree to which this heralds the arrival of a reflexive modernity is more contestable'.[55] The case of Japanese environmental engagement in Asia seems to suggest that, although we by no means have the complete transformation to reflexive modernity, we undoubtedly see the emergence of reflexive modern identities, especially in activist communities. Beck's theory of reflexive modernity was conceptualised in the framework of Western history where modernisation was, relatively speaking, 'stretched' out compared to other regions such as Northeast Asia.[56] As Han and Shim point out, countries such as South Korea and China have experienced a kind of 'compressed modernisation' in which 'the development of first modernity and the transition to second modernity happen[ed] almost at once'.[57] Japanese modernisation falls

51    Ulrich Beck and Edgar Grande, 'Varieties of Second Modernity: The Cosmopolitan Turn in Social and Political Theory and Research', *The British Journal of Sociology* 61, no. 3 (2010): 415.

52    Beck, 'The Reinvention of Politics', 8.

53    Jeffrey Berejikian and John S. Dryzek, 'Reflexive Action in International Politics', *British Journal of Political Science* 30 (2000): 212–13.

54    John S. Dryzek, 'Transnational Democracy', *The Journal of Political Philosophy* 7, no. 1 (1999): 37.

55    Dryzek, 'Transnational Democracy', 38.

56    Munenori Suzuki, Midori Ito, Mitsunori Ishida, Norihiro Nihei, and Masao Maruyama, 'Individualizing Japan: Searching for its Origin in First Modernity', *The British Journal of Sociology* 61, no. 3 (2010): 517.

57    Sang-Jin Han and Young-Hee Shim, 'Redefining Second Modernity for East Asia: A Critical Assessment', *The British Journal of Sociology* 61, no. 3 (2010): 467–8.

somewhere between the Western and South Korean/Chinese versions, being both less 'stretched' and less 'compressed'.[58] But Japan's First Modernity has arguably had more in common with its Northeast Asian neighbours because of the prominence of the national state in directing and managing growth—the so-called 'developmental state'. Because of the predominance of what they call the 'bureaucratic-authoritarian state', reflexive modernity in East Asian states according to Han and Shim has its own unique dynamics. First, it has been about recognising the 'deficiencies' and 'pathological consequences' for humans and for the society–nature nexus caused by state-led development and, second, it has been about engaging in a 'critical project' involving 'conscious efforts to go beyond the highly bureaucratic, state-centred authoritarian pattern of development'.[59]

The development of transnational environmental activism in Japan indicates the emergence of critical mentalities associated with reflexive modernity from around the mid-1960s to the early 1970s. Most indicative is the way activists involved in transnational initiatives began to reconceptualise (i.e. reposition) both environmental problems and their individual and movement identities beyond the boundaries of the nation, national-state citizenship, and victimhood. Japanese activists and their allies abroad were clearly struggling against the environmental and human side-effects of a modernity shaped by Japan's global economic ascent. To be sure, Japanese intellectuals and radicals had problematised 'modernity' some years earlier, but this was a modernity equated with the 'West' and, hence, understood—or, at least, portrayed—as something inherently foreign. But the modernity Japanese environmental activists addressed from the 1960s was absolutely internalised and universally shared (although not in the same formation everywhere). The activists involved in transnational environmental initiatives challenged this modernity in terms of their subjectivity and identity. They recognised the ethically problematic limitations of victim consciousness and, in turn, aspired to post-national, cosmopolitan ideals that coupled notions of entitlement with ideas of self-responsibility. They began to display the kind of 'bricolage biographies' and 'nonlinear individualism' characteristic of reflexive modernity in which the sources of subject formation have greatly multiplied and subjects are not only *produced by* but also become

---

58    Suzuki et al., 'Individualizing Japan', 517.
59    Han and Shim, 'Redefining Second Modernity for East Asia', 481.

*producers of* their boundaries—they may simultaneously be 'victims', 'perpetrators', 'Japanese citizens', 'Asians', 'Pacific inhabitants' and 'global citizens'.[60] In this sense, Japanese transnational involvements in East Asia of the 1970s and beyond mark an important geographical and intellectual transition in the postwar struggle against the dual pillars of modernity in the country—namely, state-supported developmentalism, on the one hand, and national-state citizenship on the other.

---

60    Beck et al., 'The Theory of Reflexive Modernization', 27.

5

# Animism: A Grassroots Response to Socioenvironmental Crisis in Japan

Shoko Yoneyama

## Introduction

Socioenvironmental crises, such as global warming and nuclear disaster, indicate that modern industrial civilisation contains in itself a seed of self-destruction. While awareness of these problems is widespread, the problems themselves are so deeply imbedded in our civilisation that trying to find solutions within existing paradigms is almost a contradiction in terms. The knowledge base of the social scientific community, too, is formed around paradigms that seem incapable of addressing the fundamental crisis faced by contemporary civilisation. In this context, the discussion that follows examines two socioenvironmental catastrophes in contemporary Japan—Minamata disease and the triple disaster of 11 March 2011 (or 3.11)—from the perspectives of the local residents. I argue that animism has (re)emerged as a grassroots response to the two historical disasters in postmodernising Japan.[1]

---

1   This chapter, by permission, draws on and develops my article that appeared in 'Life-world: Beyond Fukushima and Minamata', in *The Asia-Pacific Journal: Japan Focus* 10, issue 42, no. 2 (2012) apjjf.org/2012/10/42/Shoko-YONEYAMA/3845/article.html and in *Asian Perspective* 37, no. 4 (2013). The inspiration to connect modernity, animism and Minamata came from the work of sociologist Tsurumi Kazuko (1918–2006). In particular, *Tsurumi Kazuko Mandara VI: Tamashii no maki – Minamata, animizumu, ekorojii* [Tsurumi Kazuko Mandala Volume VI: About the Soul – Minamata, Animism and Ecology] (Tokyo: Fujiwara Shoten, 1998).

Animism is defined here as an approach to life that presupposes the presence of a soul or spirit in animate and inanimate things in nature, covering all life (living, dead and yet to emerge), as well as other things such as water, air, soil, rocks, rivers and mountains. It is defined as a *philosophy* that allows the *possibility* of the presence of such things as soul or spirit, regardless of one's belief as to whether such an unseen world exists or not. My main concern here is to explore the relationship between modernity and the epistemology of animism, and its implications in considering the relationship between humans and nature in the world risk society—a world where life has become organised around risk, and where risk itself is generated for political gain.

The chapter consists of four parts. First, Minamata and Fukushima (as the 'epicentre' of the triple disaster of 2011) are positioned in the historical context of postwar Japan. I argue that both disasters represent cases where the 'connectedness that supports life' was severed not only in the biological sphere, but also in the social sphere and that, as a corollary, the pursuit of 'connectedness' emerged as the legacy of both disasters. Second, I present a discussion of the philosophy of 'life-world' (*inochi no sekai* いのちの世界) developed by Minamata fisherman Ogata Masato, whose critique of modernity is that its epistemology fails to address the question of the soul (*tamashii* 魂).

The third section covers what I refer to as 'the Ishimure Michiko phenomenon': a dramatic increase in recognition of and interest in the work of Minamata writer Ishimure Michiko since the mid-1990s. Positioning Ogata and Ishimure as 'twin advocates' from Minamata, I argue that the phenomenon reflects a significant social change in Japanese society, i.e. the steady rise in post-materialistic values and increasing reflection on the limits of modernity. I argue that the Minamata discourse of animism, presented by Ishimure, addresses the needs of Japanese society as it matures into a postmodern society, especially after 3.11 when people became particularly interested in the relationship between humans and nature, or more precisely, in the question of life, nature and soul.

After exploring the animistic discourse from Minamata and the increased interest that it evokes, I introduce three examples where animistic tradition became a powerful resource for reconstructing communities in the disaster-stricken areas of Japan after the 3.11 triple disaster. They are: the case of folk festivals, the meaning of shrines as tsunami marker, and the significance of sacred forests (*chinju-no-mori* 鎮守の森). I argue that animistic epistemology, an intangible cultural heritage of Japan, was a common thread in grassroots responses to the triple disaster.

The conclusion of the chapter is this: in order to face the self-destructive tendencies of modernity, the philosophy of animism, reframed as an *informal, grassroots life philosophy* in post-industrial and post-3.11 Japan, opens up a new theoretical space to discuss relationships between humans, nature, and the unseen world. The grassroots responses to world risk society in Japan illuminate a lacuna in current Western-made social science: its inadequacy in fully addressing the questions of nature, spirituality, and life.

## Minamata, Fukushima and Connectedness: A Lacuna in Modernity

German sociologist Ulrich Beck stated that Japan plunged into the 'world risk society' as a result of the nuclear accident in Fukushima.[2] Beck's phrase 'world risk society' refers particularly to things such as nuclear accidents and global warming, unfortunate and unwanted byproducts of modernity, which threaten the very existence of our civilisation. In order to minimise the risk, Beck postulates that it is essential to transform the system itself—but the question is what to change and how to change it.

World risk society occurs in what sociologists call late,[3] second,[4] or liquid[5] modernity, the main characteristic of which is individualisation, where the connection between the individual and social institutions weakens. The moral and ethical foundations of society are also eroded. This raises the question of what moral and ethical foundation could be used to protect modern societies from the self-destructive tendencies of modernity. One reference we can draw on for considering this question is a report produced by the Ethics Committee for a Safe Energy Supply

---

2   Ulrich Beck, 'Kono kikai ni—Fukushima aruiwa sekai risuku ni okeru Nihon no mirai' [On This Occasion—Fukushima or the Future of Japan in World Risk Society], in Ulrich Beck, Suzuki Munenori, and Ito Midori eds, *Risuku ka suru Nihon shakai* [Japanese Society That Becomes a Risk] (Tokyo: Iwanami, 2011).

3   Anthony Giddens, *Modernity and Self-Identity: Self and Society in the Late Modern Age* (Stanford: Stanford University Press, 1991).

4   Ulrich Beck, *World Risk Society* (Cambridge: Polity, 1999).

5   Zygmunt Bauman, *Liquid Modernity* (Cambridge and Malden: Polity Press, 2000).

in Germany, of which Beck was a member, in response to the Fukushima nuclear accident. Based on the report, Germany decided to decommission all its nuclear plants within 10 years. The report reads: 'A special human duty towards nature has resulted from Christian tradition and European culture'.[6] This begs an immediate question of what might be an Asian principle of environmental ethics.

When I think about the nuclear disaster in Fukushima from this perspective what puzzles me most is this: the 'Minamata problem' was studied by some of the best and the most critical social scientists in Japan, to the extent that they established what is now called 'Minamata Studies' (*Minamata-gaku* 水俣学). My question is why, then, after all this study, were we unable to prevent Fukushima? The question is not just about power and political economy, but also about epistemology. Have we not missed something important that is the key to understanding Minamata and Fukushima?

Minamata disease, one of the worst cases of industrial pollution in human history, was caused by organic mercury contained in effluent from the Chisso chemical factory in Minamata. It was officially recognised in 1956, which also marked the beginning of Japan's high economic growth period. After the official recognition, however, neither Chisso nor local or national governments took adequate measures to reduce the discharge for 12 years. In those 12 years, the production of acetaldehyde, for which organic mercury was used as a catalyst, increased threefold, exacerbating the poisoning.[7] The Japanese Government finally recognised organic mercury as the cause of the problem in 1968, the year when Japan became the second-largest economy in the world. Subsequently, the organic chemical industry lost its edge, superseded by the petrochemical industry.[8]

The human cost of the Minamata problem is immeasurable. While the extremely stringent criteria required for government recognition as a Minamata disease patient has limited official numbers to about 3,000 (mostly deceased), an additional 11,000 sufferers received a payout in 1995, and another 65,000 or more people applied for 'relief measures'

6    Ethics Commission for a Safe Energy Supply, *Germany's Energy Transition – a Collective Project for the Future* (Berlin: Offices of the Ethics Commission on a Safe Energy Supply in the Federal Chancellery, Germany, 2011).

7    Harada Masazumi, 'Minamata Disease as a Social and Medical Problem', *Japan Quarterly* 25, no. 1 (1978).

8    Ui Jun, 'Minamata Disease', in Ui Jun ed., *Industrial Pollution in Japan* (Tokyo: United Nations University, 1992).

in 2012 when the Japanese Government launched what they called the 'final' compensation scheme.[9] Epidemiological studies by independent medical researchers conducted in the 2000s estimated that some two million people in the Minamata region are still affected by low-level methyl mercury exposure.[10] In addition to the human cost, the devastating impact upon other lives, such as fish, cats, pigs, birds, and the ecosystem has been immeasurable.[11]

The nuclear accident in Fukushima, on the other hand, occurred only days after China officially displaced Japan as the world's second-largest economy.[12] The human cost of the nuclear disaster in Fukushima is also immeasurable. As of 2015, four years after the accident, there are almost 120,000 'nuclear refugees',[13] who are at high risk of 'nuclear-accident-related death' (*genpatsu jiko kanrenshi* 原発事故関連死). Within three years of the disaster, over 1,700 (mostly elderly) deaths were related to the accident. Seven hundred of these deaths occurred more than a year after the accident while in the same time period, in the two other prefectures devastated by the tsunami, the number of disaster-related deaths was less than 20.[14] In addition, by February 2016, 116 cases of thyroid cancer among youth had been confirmed.[15] Using the incidence rate of thyroid cancer in the general population, around four cases would have been expected.[16] The cost to other life forms was also immeasurable. Almost 3,000 cows, 30,000 pigs and 600,000 chickens and unaccounted numbers of pets were left behind to starve to death in the nuclear exclusion zone.[17] Within five months of the accident, over 3,400 farm animals were

---

9    'More Than 65,000 Apply for Relief for Minamata Disease', *Asahi Shimbun* (English Digital), 1 September 2012.

10    Shigeru Takaoka, 'Minamata kara Fukushima e no kyōkun' [Lessons from Minamata to Fukushima], *Shinryō Kenkyū* [Clinical Research] 470 (August 2011).

11    Ogata Masato, *Chisso wa watashi de atta* [Chisso Was I] (Fukuoka: Ashi Shobō, 2001).

12    Robert Guy, 'It's Official, China Is No.2', *The Australian Financial Review*, 15 February 2011.

13    Ganjoho [Cancer Information Service Japan], *Fukushima kara kengai e no hinan jōkyō* [The Current State of Evacuation from Fukushima to Other Prefectures] (2015), www.pref.fukushima. lg.jp/uploaded/attachment/117392.pdf. Accessed 1 June 2016.

14    'Shimbun Kyōkai Shō honshi "Genpatsujiko kanrenshi' kyanpēn"' [Newspaper Association Award to Fukushima Minpō for 'Nuclear Accident-related Death' Campaign], *Fukushima Minpō*, 14 September 2014.

15    'Gan kakutei hitori mashi 16-nin, 2-junme kodomo kōjōsengan chōsa' [Confirmed Cases of Cancer Increased by One to be 16 in the Second Survey of Thyroid among Youth], *Fukushima Minpō*, 16 February 2016.

16    Ganjoho [Cancer Information Service Japan], 'Graph Database Tyroid Incidence Age-Specific Rate for 2010', ganjoho.jp. Accessed 14 June 2015.

17    'Ushi 3-zen to, buta 3-man biki, genpatsu 20-kiro ken ni – gashi ka' [3,000 Cows and 30,000 Pigs in the 20 Kilometre Zone – Death by Starvation Suspected], Yomiuri Online, 19 April 2011.

'euthanised'.[18] Genetic and ecological impacts on other species, such as birds, butterflies, cicadas have also been reported.[19] Although the nuclear disaster was triggered by the earthquake and tsunami, the official report of the National Diet of Japan judged that the accident at Tokyo Electric Company (TEPCO) Fukushima Daiichi Nuclear Plant was 'manmade' in that it resulted from 'the collusion between the government, the regulators and TEPCO, and the lack of governance by said parties. They effectively betrayed the nation's right to be safe from nuclear accidents'.[20] (See also Chapter Six.)

Minamata and Fukushima thus symbolise the beginning and the end of the period of Japan's economic development and its trajectory of modernisation. Both signify catastrophic environmental and social disasters, the impact of which is still current. Between 1956 and 2011, social science research in Japan has contributed enormously to understanding the structural problems associated with modernity as symbolised by Minamata. As a result, even though they are 55 years apart, we can see that there are fundamental commonalities between Minamata and Fukushima. From the perspective of political economy, the commonalities include the fact that both problems were based on relentless pursuit of profit; collusive relationships between industry, governments, bureaucracy, and the media; marginalisation of critical scientists; manipulation of scientific data; discrimination against rural people; and destruction of the food production base. In other words, Fukushima confronted us with the reality that the structures that caused and exacerbated the Minamata problem have continued almost intact, despite the knowledge gained in social sciences, allowing more 'manmade' devastation to happen, this time making Japan a world risk society. Here we come back to the question again: have we not missed something important, the key to understanding Minamata and Fukushima? What kind of knowledge can contribute to bringing about a fundamental change in society to prevent similar disasters from happening again?

---

18    'Anrakushi shobun no kachiku 3,422' [3,422 Farm Animals Euthanised], *Fukushima Minpō*, 31 August, 2011.

19    Atsuki Hiyama, Chiyo Nohara, Seira Kinjo, Wataru Taira, Shinichi Gima, Akira Tanahara and Joji M. Otaki, 'The Biological Impacts of the Fukushima Nuclear Accident on the Pale Grass Blue Butterfly', *Scientific Reports* 2 (2012). Timothy A. Mousseau and Anders P. Møller, 'Genetic and Ecological Studies of Animals in Chernobyl and Fukushima', *Journal of Heredity* 105, no. 5 (2014).

20    The National Diet of Japan, The Official Report of the Fukushima Nuclear Accident Independent Investigation Commission: Executive Summary (2012), 16.

# Breakdown of Connectedness

Seen from a different angle, the commonalities between Minamata and Fukushima can be summarised as a breakdown of connectedness at a multitude of levels: family (e.g. the impact of death or health impairment of a family member, loss of housing, land, and other possessions); work (e.g. loss of a job and livelihood); food production (farming and fishing); traditional and local ways of life; and the sense of connectedness with nature, past and future, ancestors and descendants. Both disasters caused deep schisms and paralysis in the affected communities depending on the residents' position vis-à-vis the company responsible for the disaster and how each person wanted to respond to the crisis—in the case of Fukushima, typically a mother wanting to move to a safer place with the children while her husband and in-laws stayed put, leading to 'nuclear divorce' (*genpatsu rikon*).

The breakdown of connectedness occurred not only in sociological spheres, but also in biological dimensions. In the case of Minamata disease, connectedness in the nervous system of the brain was severed. Mercury disrupts the growth of neurons in the brain, and this severing of connectedness of the nervous system was visually captured in a video by researchers from the University of Calgary.[21] The effect is the same for *organic* mercury that causes Minamata disease.[22] Radiation, on the other hand, destroys DNA and severs connectedness among cells. A photo of DNA taken from Ōuchi Hisashi, who died after being exposed to an excessive amount of radiation in a localised nuclear accident in Tokaimura in 1999, shows that his DNA was completely torn into pieces by radiation. As a result, his body lost the connectedness that is necessary to maintain life, i.e. lost the memory required to regenerate cells, eventually turning his body cells into a pulp.[23] If one of the characteristics of modernity is the weakening of connectedness, Minamata and Fukushima epitomise it to its extreme. They show how industrial nationalism, the most efficient capitalist system in modernity, ended up destroying the very core of life itself.

---

21    F. L. Lorscheider et al., 'How Mercury Causes Brain Neuron Degeneration', 2013, www. youtube.com/watch?v=Z1RHWfJSo6w. Accessed 16 June 2015.

22    M. Aschner et al., 'Metallothionein Induction in Fetal Rat Brain and Neonatal Primary Astrocyte Cultures by in Utero Exposure to Elemental Mercury Vapor (Hg0)1', *Brain Research* 778, no. 1 (1997).

23    NHK TV Crew, *A Slow Death: 83 Days of Radation Sickness* (New York: Vertical, 2008).

Is it any wonder then that words that mean connectedness emerged as a legacy of both Minamata and Fukushima? In the case of Minamata, the key word is *moyai* 舫い, which means tying boats together. For the Fukushima/triple disaster it is *kizuna* 絆, meaning bonds. It is clear that people in Japan felt the need for more connectedness with society after Fukushima. This has been captured by official statistics as well. A public opinion survey conducted in 2012 by the Cabinet Office shows that 80 per cent of over 6,000 respondents indicated that, after the 2011 disaster, they came to realise the importance of connectedness with society to a greater extent than they did earlier.[24]

Feeling a sense of connectedness with everything around us, that is spirituality in the broadest sense.[25] In this sense, the legacy of Minamata and Fukushima, namely *moyai* (tying ships together) and *kizuna* (bonds), can be considered as a discourse of spirituality. In other words, the civil discourse of Minamata and Fukushima can be considered to be a discourse of spirituality.

## 'Life-world': A Critique of Modernity from Minamata

Minamata fisherman Ogata Masato (緒方正人) is the person who coined the term *moyai* (tying ships together) as the legacy of Minamata.[26] His critique of modernity is extensive,[27] but his most profound insight is that:

> The Minamata disease incident has left a question that cannot be dealt with as a political issue. It is the biggest and most fundamental question, a question that cannot be transformed into a question of politics or institutions. That is the question of the soul (*tamashii* 魂).[28]

---

24   Cabinet Office of Japan, *Shakai ishiki ni kansuru yoron chōsa* [Survey on the Perceptions of Society] (Tokyo: Naifukaku, 2012).
25   Marian De Souza et al., 'General Introduction', in M. de Souza et al. eds, *International Handbook of Education for Spirituality, Care and Wellbeing* (Dordrecht: Springer, 2009).
26   Ogata Masato, interview by author, digital recording, Minamata, 16 January 2012.
27   For details see Shoko Yoneyama, 'Life-World: Beyond Fukushima and Minamata', *The Asia-Pacific Journal: Japan Focus* 10, issue 42, no. 2 (2012).
28   Ogata, *Chisso*, 67.

Ogata says that we need a more substantive expression of what soul is. He writes:

> I have been thinking lately how we can convey what soul is, and what we can say about the soul … Previously I stated that it is *another name for life*, but in a way, I think it can also be called 'the stamp of humanity' (*ningen no akashi* 人間の証). Especially after the war, various things have been modernised and mechanised so they can be integrated into the system-society. *This has devoured the soul, which is the basis for the connectedness among people, between humans and other living things, and between humans and the sea, rivers and mountains …* I think that the promise of being human is to sense life (*inochi o kankaku suru* 命を感覚する) and to manage life (*inochi o tsukasadoru* 命を司る). Human beings are that sort of life-existence (*seimei sonzai* 生命存在) and, essentially, we are never a mechanical or institutional existence (emphasis added).[29]

How can soul be 'another name for life' and at the same time 'the stamp of humanity'? Underlying this is Ogata's notion of 'system-society' (*sisutemu shakai* システム社会) and 'the life-world' (*inochi no sekai* いのちの世界 or *seimei sekai* 生命世界), the two sides of our modern living. By 'system-society' Ogata means a composite of institutional (legal, economic, political and to some extent social) aspects of modern society,[30] which have a tendency to mechanise and institutionalise humans. 'The life-world' on the other hand represents the world from which we as human beings have emerged as 'life-existence', the world to which we return after death, the world that enables us to connect to other people, other forms of life and inanimate things in nature in a non-institutional way (i.e. simply as life) and the world that enables us to see the problems of system-society.[31] By saying that soul is another name for life, Ogata poses soul as the essence of life, the essence of our existence, or the stamp of humanity that enables us to feel and manage life in such a way as to prevent us from being completely mechanised and institutionalised in the system-society, and perhaps, if we use the terminology of Beck, prevent us from being destroyed in the world risk society. Ogata's notion of the life-world thus refers to the *entirety of life–soul–nature nexus* that defies modernity.

---

29   ibid., 192–3.
30   ibid.
31   Yoneyama, 'Life-World'.

What connects us to the life-world, in Ogata's philosophy, is the 'memory of life' (*inochi no kioku* 命の記憶). He writes:

> In the age of 'modernity', we have standardised, institutionalised and mechanised many things in the name of modernisation. In the process, we reclaimed the sea of Minamata that was full of life saying that it was polluted by mercury. But perhaps it was not just the sea we buried. We have created a system of concealment to continue institutional and mechanical burying. That can be summarised as the creation of a 'false memory system' (偽りの記憶装置). By doing so, we have perhaps moved away from the essence of life, and the memory of the essence of life. I cannot help but feel that various social problems we face today happened because we have lost the 'memory of life' (命の記憶).[32]

For Ogata, 'memory of life' first means his own memory of the life he had as a child in a Minamata unpolluted by organic mercury, a memory also shared by other locals:

> Once Minamata Bay was the treasure chest of our sea. Here schools of fish came to spawn. The young fry matured here and then returned to repeat the cycle. The bay was like a womb. In what is now landfill between Hyakken Port and Myojin Point, the silver scales of sardine and gizzard shad shimmered in the sunlight. Mullet leapt. Shrimp and crab frolicked in the shallow. At low tide we collected shellfish. At the edge of the waves we gathered seaweed – *wakame* and *hijiki*. These were the things that nourished us.[33]

This memory of life, where everyday living was almost entirely supported by the blessings of nature, was at one with the notion of *gotagai,* a word from the local Minamata dialect that means 'we're all in this together'. It is a name given to the sense of connectedness of all life within nature. Ogata writes:

> [*Gotagai*] doesn't mean simply that we humans rely upon each other for our existence but that plants and animals are also partners in this life. *Gotagai* includes the sea, the mountains, everything. Human beings are part of the circle of *gotagai*; we owe our existence to the vast web of interrelationships that constitute life.[34]

---

32   Ogata, *Chisso*, 63.
33   Oiwa Keibo and Ogata Masato, *Rowing the Eternal Sea: The Story of a Minamata Fisherman,* trans. Karen Colligan-Taylor (New York: Rowman & Littlefield, 2001), 122.
34   ibid., 164.

This 'web of interrelationships that constitute life' goes beyond his personal life. It also refers to the vast continuum of life, millions of years in the past as well as in the future. It is best portrayed by 'The Image of Biohistory', an artwork developed by the Osaka-based Biohistory Research Hall, which illustrates the history and diversity of life that came into being from a common genome over the course of 3.8 billion years.[35] Biologist Nakamura Keiko, who was invited to the 50th Anniversary of the Official Recognition of Minamata Disease, stated that all living things share the same origin (genome); that human beings are only one of the diverse species that share the same history of development; and that human beings are *in nature* (i.e. not outside it). In her speech she stressed the importance of regaining our sense of being as living things (*ikimono to shite no kankaku o torimodosu* 生き物としての感覚をとりもどす).[36]

'Regaining our sense of being as living things' was also the main point of Ogata's keynote speech at the conference. The aim of the conference was to present recommendations from Minamata to the world about how to achieve a sustainable future, transcending victimhood. The conference proceedings are titled 'Minamata for New Genesis: Recommendations for the Future' (*Sōseiki o Mukaeta Minamata: Mirai e no Teigen* 創世記を迎えた水俣: 未来への提言).[37] Ogata concluded his keynote speech by saying that:

> Although we live in the system-society where economy is based on insatiable wants and desires (*yokubō keizai* 欲望経済), I think that there will be a way to transcend it with a new meaning. A hint can be found in our sense of life as a living being (*ikimono to shiteno inochi no kankaku* 生き物としての命の感覚). For that, I think it is time for each of us to return to the starting point as one life-existence (*seimei sonzai* 生命存在), from where we re-live a life … The new 'genesis' (*sōseiki* 創世紀) included in the title of this conference, *Minamata for New Genesis*, is also *sōseiki* 創生紀, an era to create life.[38]

---

35   Nakamura Keiko, Dan Marina, and Hashimoto Ritsuko, 'The Image of Biohistory', JT Biohistory Research Hall, www.brh.co.jp/imgs/about/emaki/emaki.jpg. Accessed 20 June 2015.

36   Nakamura Keiko, 'Seimei kagaku: Ikimono kankaku de kangaeru' [Bioscience: To Think about it with Senses of a Living Creature], in Saitō Yasuhiro et al. eds, *Sōseiki o mukaeta Minamata: Mirai e no teigen* [Minamata for New Genesis: Recommendations for the Future] (Minamata: Minamatabyō Kōshiki Kakunin 50-nen Jigyō Iinkai, 2007).

37   Ogata Masato, 'Keynote Speech: Sōseiki o mukaeta Minamata: Mirai e no teigen' [Minamata for New Genesis: Recommendations for the Future], in Minamatabyō Kōshiki Kakunin 50-nen Jigyō Jikkō Iinkai ed., *Sōseiki o mukaeta Minamata*.

38   ibid., 31.

More practically, though, Ogata asks 'how [can we] break ourselves from our own spell and liberate ourselves'[39] from the spell of 'system-society' driven by the pursuit of affluence? He does not suggest that we should give up living in system-society in order to pursue living in the life-world. Rather, he sees the relationship between the two as 'right foot and left foot': both indispensable for walking. The question is how to live within this potentially contradictory dual structure.

> We need to think how to live with the dual structure. In the global-capitalist-market economy, we are controlled by a view of the world dominated by the economy and we cannot escape from it. It is a world regulated by clock-time, and we feel as if everything is controlled by the overwhelming power of the economy and politics. But precisely because of this, I think it is necessary to have our own time in 'cosmic-time', in order to relax and refresh, and find and regain a sense of our true selves. I think that each person is like a small universe and that it is possible for each of us to find our own way, existentially, to connect to the cosmic-time where life is eternal. It seems to me that living this duality provides a very important hint for us to remain and regulate ourselves as humans. To put it differently, we work in the system-society to earn our living, and we live in the life-world to live our life. It's like doing two-sword fencing, or having two different, top and bottom, streams of wind, or a double helix structure in one's life.[40]

For Ogata, to recognise this duality means understanding that he himself was part of the 'Chisso-ish' society and to recognise that he was 'another Chisso' in a sense that he is part of history where it is not possible to live without relying on materials and systems supported by companies like Chisso. Ogata emphasises, however, the importance of knowing where each of us 'stands', i.e. 'where you put your centre of gravity' (*jūshin* 重心) and 'where you point your soul'.[41]

> Sadly, I myself cannot escape from the money economy or the economic system. I use my mobile phone, and my boat is equipped with GPS, for instance. Although I cannot escape from the system, I am still resisting stubbornly. What is it that I am defying? *There is only one point ultimately. It is where you put your 'trust'* (*shin o doko ni oku ka* 信をどこに置くか, with *shin* as in *shinrai* 信頼). *In the end, it is the question of where you place your trust, the system-society or the life-world.*[42]

---

39    Ogata Masato, telephone interview by author, digital recording, Sydney to Minamata, 25 August 2012.
40    ibid.
41    ibid.
42    ibid.

For Ogata, the life-world presents an *absolute, ethical frame of reference* in which he, as human being, has a responsibility to nature even though he is living in the system-society. What empowers humans to do this task, according to Ogata, is our soul, our memory of life, the life that makes us human, the stamp of humanity, i.e. the life-world as the *life–soul–nature nexus* that defies modernity. Ogata presents a philosophy, a foundation for environmental ethics that addresses human responsibility vis-à-vis nature/life at this historical crossroad when the globalising world faces the life-threatening reality of 'self-reflexive' modernity.

In the terminology of Morris-Suzuki, Ogata's philosophy of life-world is a voice of 'informal life politics' or 'survival politics' that arises from grassroots Japan. In the terminology of Lyotard, it is a little narrative that can produce a new kind of knowledge that opens up our imagination to the unknown, something that has been outside the epistemological boundaries of existing knowledge.[43]

The new space Ogata opens up is the space to address life (*inochi* 命), soul (*tamashii* 魂) and nature as a single mutually entwined relational entity. The concept of *moyai* (tying ships together), a legacy of Minamata, is part of this philosophy. His notion of the life-world is a strong critique of modernity in that it questions a key empirical reality of modernity. He argues that modernity 'devours the soul' from everyday life and 'de-spiritualises' cultures.[44] He also challenges modernist epistemology: the secularist premise of social science that puts matters related to spirituality (or the unseen world) outside its boundary. Although Ogata himself does not use the word animism, his philosophy of life-world is a contemporary version of animism 'armed' with deep insights into modernity. And it is precisely the issues of animism that have been treated in sociology 'with the utmost reserve, if not disdain',[45] as if it was 'magic'. The elimination of 'magic', according to Max Weber, is 'one of the most important aspects of the broader process of rationalisation',[46] that is to say, it is the key to modernity.

---

43   J. F. Lyotard, *The Postmodern Condition* (Minneapolis: University of Minnesota Press, 1979), 60–7.
44   Kieran Flanagan, 'Introduction', in K. Flanagan and P. Jupp eds, *A Sociology of Spirituality* (Farnham: Ashgate, 2007), 1.
45   ibid.
46   Talcott Parsons, 'Translator's Note (Chapter IV, Endnote 19)', in *The Protestant Ethic and the Spirit of Capitalism by Max Weber* (London: Unwin University Books, 1930–1974), 222.

Lyotard defines postmodern as 'incredulity towards the metanarrative'[47] of modernity, and the principle of postmodern knowledge to be 'not the expert's homology, but the inventor's paralogy'.[48] In that sense, the life-world is postmodern knowledge or, more precisely, a postmodern version of animism that emerged as a grassroots response to the socioenvironmental disaster that hit a periphery of Japan at the height of its industrialisation. While Ogata illuminates and articulates the relationship between the system-society and the life-world in lucid and powerful language, the sociological significance of his work is better understood in conjunction with the works of the writer Ishimure Michiko, in the context of what I call the 'Ishimure Michiko phenomenon'.

## The Ishimure Michiko Phenomenon: An Animistic World to Pine for

Ishimure Michiko (石牟礼道子) is a Minamata writer, often referred to as an environmental novelist, or the Rachel Carson of Japan, and is one of the key members of the Minamata movement. Her signature piece, *Kugai Jōdo: Waga Minamata Byō* [Paradise in the Sea of Sorrow: My Minamata Disease 苦海浄土 わが水俣病] illustrates the plight as well as the beauty of life of those affected by the disease/poisoning, in a novel that is based on factual information about Minamata. Like Ogata, Ishimure's work is fundamentally a critique of modernity, and like him, life, soul and nature are at the core of her work.[49] Unlike Ogata, however, Ishimure uses the term 'animism' whereas Ogata, as mentioned earlier, uses the phrase life-world. Ishimure writes:

> With what sort of human character should we describe the immoral behaviour of the modern industry that exacted and continues to exact harm to nature and to the very basis of life therein, in the remote villages of Minamata? It surely was another form of the ruthless exploitation of people and nature by monopolistic capitalism. Yet, simply to point that out will not be sufficient. Living spirits and dead spirits hover over my hometown without being able to attain Buddhahood. I consider

---

47   Lyotard, *Postmodern*, xxiv.
48   ibid., xxv.
49   Ishimure Michiko, *Ishimure Michiko zenshū* [Complete Works of Ishimure Michiko] (Tokyo: Fujiwara Shoten, 2004–2014).

the words of these spirits as the pristine language of their social class. I therefore must become a shaman for modernity by fusing my notion of animism and pre-animism.[50]

Although Ishimure does not use the word animism often in her literary work, an animistic ambiance runs through her work, in her descriptions of nature and people. The one closest to the definition of animism is the following passage from *Kamigami no Mura* [Villages of the Gods 神々の村].

> A communal village well almost always was located in a place where camellias and other evergreens grew thick. Trees would collect water for the spring and the spring in turn would nourish the trees. Time immemorial dwelled in the spring and in the trees.
>
> Each well had its own *kami* (deity/god/spirit カミ); mountains had a *kami*; ships had a *kami*; rocks had a *kami*; rice paddies had a *kami*; sea had a *kami*; rivers had a *kami*; each *kami* dwelled in its own place and had a unique and lovable character.
>
> The cheeky careless *kami* of the river, who had a plate attached to the top of its head, would go up the river, deep into the mountains, and sneak into, in the depth of the night, into a miner's hut at the Fuke Gold Mine in Satsuma …
>
> When people wanted to have a *kami* for their rice field, they would find a suitable stone, pour lots of *shōchū* (potato wine) onto it, and thus imbue a soul into the stone. The villages were protected by impromptu *kami* such as these. The little *kami* in fact were also the people themselves.[51] (Author's translation)

Although *Paradise in the Sea of Sorrow* was published in 1969, Ishimure was marginalised for a long time as a literary figure, until the 1990s.[52] Since then, there has been a substantial increase of recognition and interest in her work in Japan, which then created a snowball effect and what might be called the 'Ishimure Michiko phenomenon' occurred. The change is

---

50   Ishimure Michiko, *Kukai jōdo sekai bungaku zenshū III-04* [Paradise in the Sea of Sorrow, World Literature Series III-04] (Tokyo: Kawade Shobō, 2011–2012), 44.

51   ibid., 236.

52   Watanabe Kyōji, 'Ishimure Michiko no jiko keisei' [The Establishment of Self of Ishimure Michiko], in Iwaoka Nakamasa ed., *Ishimure Michiko no sekai* [The World of Ishimure Michiko] (Fukuoka: Gen Shobō, 2006).

indicated clearly by the number of times her name appeared in the *Asahi* newspaper as shown in Figure 4. (This data was collected using the Kikuzo II database of both eastern and western Japan versions of the *Asahi*).

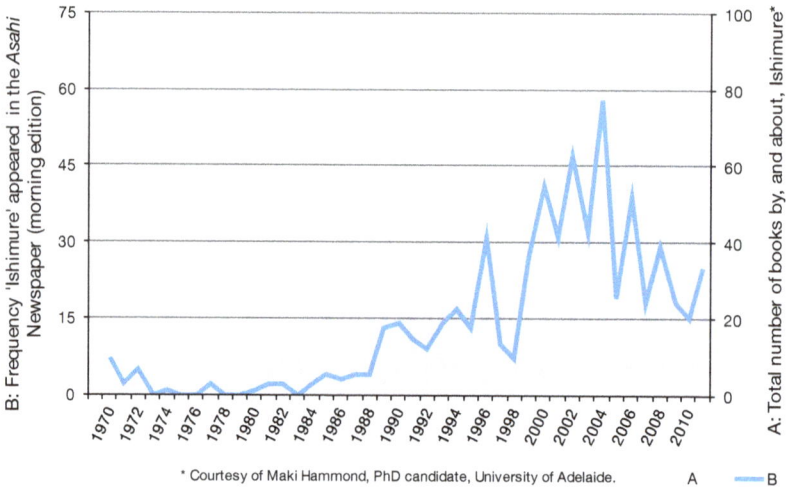

* Courtesy of Maki Hammond, PhD candidate, University of Adelaide.    A    ▬▬ B

**Figure 4: The 'Ishimure Michiko Phenomenon': Ishimure Michiko in the mainstream media (1970–2014).**
Source: Author's work.

Another strong indicator of the Ishimure phenomenon is the succession of awards she has received since the 1990s. In 1993, she received the Murasaki Shikibu Literary Award, with commendations by Umehara Takeshi, the then Director of the International Research Center for Japanese Studies, and Setouchi Jakushō, a renowned writer. This award connected Ishimure for the first time officially with the mainstream literary world of Japan. She then received a 2001 Asahi Award, together with Miyazaki Hayao and others; followed by a 2002 Minister of Education and Science Award for the Promotion of Art; 2013 Avon Award for Women; and, in 2014, the 32rd Hanatsubaki Award for Contemporary Poetry by Shiseido and the prestigious 8th Gotō Shinpei Award.

The recognition of Ishimure's work took different forms as well. Her long-term friendship with sociologist Tsurumi Kazuko, a grandchild of Meiji statesman Gotō Shinpei, led to a chance to talk in length with Empress Michiko at Tsurumi's memorial service, which subsequently led to a visit by the Heisei Emperor and Empress to Minamata in 2013. For the first time in history after the outbreak of Minamata disease in the 1950s, a Japanese emperor visited Minamata, and following Ishimure's request, the royal couple met congenital Minamata disease sufferers who were in their 50s.[53] The *Asahi* newspaper twice reported the role Ishimure played in the royal visit, in such a way that generated a sense of reconciliation and healing between Minamata sufferers and the imperial family.[54]

There seem to be three intertwined factors behind the Ishimure Michiko phenomenon. First is the steady publication of her highly original work.[55] In addition to literary works, Ishimure produced numerous collections of poems, picture books and essays, including a column in the *Asahi* newspaper, *Chotto Shinkokyū* [Taking a Big Breath] that lasted from 1999 to 2005.

The second factor explaining the Ishimure Michiko phenomenon is the development of the Minamata movement itself, in which Ogata and Ishimure have been key players. The first big spike in Figure 4 coincides with the 1996 Minamata Tokyo Exhibition that was held to mark the 40th anniversary of the official recognition of Minamata disease. One of the key features of the exhibition was an old, barely seaworthy fishing sailboat, the *Nichigetsu maru* [Sun Moon Boat 日月丸], which Ogata sailed from Minamata to Tokyo 'in order to push the poison back to the capital'.[56] This exhibition heralded a new era whereby Minamata became connected at a new level to the civil society of Japan. For instance, Minamata Forum, a Tokyo-based non-profit organisation that organised the Tokyo Exhibition, has continued to show the exhibition at 23 other venues since the original event in 1993, attracting over 130,000 visitors

---

53    Kitano Ryūichi, '"Ima mo kurushimu Minamata no kanja ni atte" – Ishimure-san kōgō-sama ni tegami' [Please Meet Still Suffering Minamata Patients – Ishimure Wrote a Letter to the Empress], *Asahi Shimbun*, 25 October 2013, Tokyo.

54    Kitano Ryūichi, 'Ishimure-san ga miokuri – Kōgō-sama kara dengon "Okarada taisetsu ni"'[Ishimure Saw Them Off – a Message from the Empress – Please Take Care], *Asahi Shimbun (Seibu)*, 29 October 2013.

55    This includes compilations of her work: an 18-volume *Ishimure Michiko zenshū* [Complete Works of Ishimure Michiko] published by Fujiwara Shoten between 2004 to 2014; and another series, a seven-volume *Ishimure Michiko shibun korekushon* [Ishimure Michiko Literary Works] published also by Fujiwara in 2009 and 2010. In 2011, just before the triple disaster, Ishimure's flagship work, *Kukai jōdo (Trilogy)*, was published as part of *Sekai bungaku zenshū* [World Literature Series], as the only Japanese entry in the series. The trilogy included 1969 *Kugai jōdo* [Paradise in the Sea of Sorrow], 1997 *Tenko* [Lake of Heaven] and 2006 *Kamigami no mura* [Villages of the Gods], which altogether took 40 years to complete.

56    Ogata, *Chisso*, 122.

by 2015.[57] In May 2016, a special memorial lecture series to mark the 60th anniversary of the official recognition of Minamata disease, held by the Minamata Forum at the University of Tokyo, was attended by nearly 2,400 people including some 90 volunteers.[58]

At the same time, key players of the Minamata movement began to express themselves in different ways. Ogata's two books were published in 1996 and 2001, the latter being *Chisso was I*.[59] Ishimure's Noh play was performed in Tokyo, Kumamoto and Minamata in the early 2000s. The 50th anniversary of the official recognition of Minamata disease was titled 'Minamata for New Genesis', reframing the Minamata incident as a historical experience with a significant message for the future. A field of study, Minamata Studies, was established in the 2000s by Harada Masazumi, a doctor who had devoted his entire working life to the care of Minamata disease patients. Kumamoto Gakuen University where Harada taught became the mecca of Minamata Studies and the five-volume *Minamata Gaku Kōgi* [The Minamata Studies Lectures 水俣学講義] was published between 2004 and 2012. The Minamata incident has thus entered a new phase since the mid-1990s and has flourished. In Ogata's words, Minamata is no longer a 'movement' but an 'expression'.[60] Through these developments since the mid-1990s, Minamata disease has become established as a robust reference point of civil society Japan. The work of Ishimure Michiko has been the key medium to connect Minamata and civil society, and the Ishimure Michiko phenomenon is an indication of the strength of that connectedness.

The third factor behind the Ishimure Michiko phenomenon is a broader social change in Japanese society.[61] World Values Surveys show that 'postmaterialist values' are one of the strongest indicators of the cultural

---

57    Minamata Forum, 'Minamata Forum katsudō naiyō' [Minamata Forum Activities], www.minamata-f.com/activity.html. Accessed 29 June 2013.

58    Minamata Forum, Minamata-byō kōshiki kakunin 60nen kinen tokubetsu kōenkai [Special Memorial Lecture Series to Mark the 60th Anniversary of the Official Recognition of Minamata Disease], www.minamata-f.com/evt_201605.html. Accessed 2 July 2016.

59    Ogata Masato and Tsuji Shinichi, *Tokoyo no fune o kogite* [Rowing the Eternal Sea] (Tokyo: Seori Shobō, 1996); Ogata, *Chisso*.

60    Ogata Masato, interview by author, digital recording, Minamata, 25 January 2013.

61    This paragraph first appeared in Shoko Yoneyama, 'Spirituality in Life Stories in Postmodernising Japan', Elizabeth Morrell and Michael Barr eds, *Referred Conference Proceedings, the 18th Biennial Conference of the Asian Studies Association of Australia*, ASAA (Adelaide: Asian Studies Association of Australia, 2010).

transformation from modern to postmodern[62] and that Japan was part of this major shift in the highly industrialised world.[63] This value change has been captured in public opinion polls that are conducted annually by the Cabinet Office. In the early 1980s, the proportion of those who considered the 'richness of heart/mind' (*kokoro no yotakasa* 心の豊かさ) to be more important than 'material affluence' (*mono no yutakasa* 物の豊かさ) exceeded those who valued the 'material' over the 'mind/heart', and the gap became wider, reaching 64 per cent for 'mind/heart' and 30.1 per cent for 'material' in 2012.[64] For many people, the meaning of existence has become more important than what they possess. Japan has been very much part of the rise of a 'new spiritual culture' in industrialised societies, which surfaced in Japan as the rise of interest in 'mind/heart world'.[65] The word *supirichuaru* (spiritual) became a buzzword in the 2000s, and played a pivotal role in the discourse of the new spirituality culture. A linguistic study of *supirichuaritii* (spirituality) as a loan word found that the word 'spirit' has been translated as *tamashii* (soul 魂), *kokoro* (heart こころ or 心), or *inochi* (life いのち or 命), suggesting the close relationship between the notions of 'soul' and 'life' in Japan.[66]

This broad value change that began in the 1980s has been amplified by a major shift in Japanese society since around 1990, which pushed people to reflect on the meaning of prosperity in a society that had reached its growth plateau. It started with the 1989 death of the Shōwa Emperor, Hirohito, who symbolically represented the 'postwar' development. This was followed by the 1990 bubble burst, the collapse of an excessively speculative money economy based on the construction industry that was the mainstay of Japan's economy in the 1980s. At the time when Japan became a post-industrial society in 1995 and the labour force in the service industry exceeded that of manufacturing, Japanese society was awash with incidents that pushed its citizens to ask existential questions. These incidents included the Hanshin-Awaji Earthquake in Kobe, the

---

62  Ronald Inglehart, *Modernization and Postmodernization* (Princeton: Princeton University Press, 1997), 86.

63  ibid., 333.

64  Ministry of the Environment (Japan), *Kankyō hakusho, junkangata shakai hakusho, seibutsu tayōsei hakusho* [White Paper on the Environment, Recycling Society and Bio-Diversity] (Tokyo: Ministry of the Environment, 2013), chapter 2, section 1, www.env.go.jp/policy/hakusyo/h25/html/hj13010201.html. Accessed 2 July 2016.

65  Shimazono Susumu, *Spirichuaritii no kōryū* [The Rise of Spirituality] (Tokyo: Iwanami Shoten, 2007).

66  Harumi Minagawa, '"Spiritual" Interpreted: A Case of Complex Lexical Borrowing in Japanese', *Japanese Studies* 32, no. 3 (2012).

terrorist sarin-gas attack by the Aum Supreme Sect in the subway near the government district of Tokyo, and a series of horrendous crimes committed by youth, starting with the decapitation of a boy by a 14-year-old 'school killer' in Kobe.[67] The level of anxiety in society was amplified by economic stagnation since the early 1990s, a major policy shift for casualisation of the workforce in 1995, and the spread of neoliberalism, which had broad implications (e.g. the prevalence of the culture of bullying in Japanese society in general).[68]

The Ishimure Michiko phenomenon occurred against this backdrop of growing scepticism about economic development, broader value changes in postindustrial and postmodern Japan, and increasing need to respond to existential questions. It was also in this context that people in Japan were confronted with the 3.11 triple disaster, and Ishimure was no exception. The nuclear accident in Fukushima in particular provoked her sense of mission, and raised the significance of her work to a new height. A documentary film on Ishimure Michiko, released in 2013, 'Hana no okudo e': Ishimure Michiko rasuto messēji [Towards the Paradise of Flowers: Ishimure Michiko's Last Message 花の憶土へ], opens with an introductory statement:

> Ishimure Michiko has kept questioning the 'poison of modern civilisation'. In post-3.11 Japan, she extends her questions to the destiny of the Earth.[69]

Sociologist Mita Munesuke, Emeritus Professor of Tokyo University, captured the relevance of Ishimure's work as follows:

> 'Minamata Disease' represents nothing but the malady of Japan's capitalism as a whole. And if the collapse of the 'life-world' constitutes the malady of the modern world as a whole, the essence of Ishimure Michiko's work is that it provides *spiritual medicine that heals the body and the soul of the modern world* (My translation. Emphasis added.)[70]

---

67    Shoko Yoneyama, *The Japanese High School: Silence and Resistance* (London and New York: Routledge, 1999).

68    Shoko Yoneyama, 'The Era of Bullying: Japan under Neoliberalism', *The Asia-Pacific Journal: Japan Focus* 6, issue 2, 1 December (2008).

69    Kin Taii, *Hana no okudo e* [Towards the Paradise of Flowers] (documentary film), 2013.

70    Mita Munesuke, 'Ijutsu toshite no sakuhin: "Ten no Io" o yomu' [Literary Work as a Medical Art: Reading the Fish of Heaven], in *Shiranui: Ishimure Michiko no kosumolojii* [Shiranui: The Cosmology of Ishimure Michiko] (Tokyo: Fujiwara Shoten, 2004).

The Ishimure Michiko phenomenon can be considered as an indication that Japanese society has been in need of 'spiritual medicine' as an antidote to modernity. She made this evident through her illustrations of the world where humans live as part of nature, as part of the continuum of life, or the life-world where life and 'soul' (*tamashii*) are connected. And this is the world that was destroyed by Chisso, a company that represented modernity and the domination of money and materials over life, soul and nature. In the context of Japan, the cultural reference that addresses the life–soul–nature nexus is animism. The Ishimure Michiko phenomenon suggests that even before the triple disaster, there was an increasing interest in the life–soul–nature nexus vis-à-vis modernity. As in the case of Ogata, Ishimure's work has provided a robust discourse on life–soul–nature, or discourse on animism as a grassroots response to the first socioenvironmental crisis in post-war Japan.

It is on the basis of this idea that I now turn to the final section of the chapter, which introduces three developments that suggest animistic tradition has regained relevance in post-3.11 Japan. The developments are renewed appreciation of folk festivals, local shrines, and sacred forests (*chinju-no-mori*) in the disaster-stricken areas.

## Reconnecting with the Cultural Heritage of Animism in Post-3.11 Japan

**Folk Festivals**: Folklorist Akasaka Norio (赤坂憲雄), who specialises in Northeast Japan, points out that folk festivals/arts (*minzoku geinō* 民俗芸能), though they had been in decline before the triple disaster, were the very first thing to be revived in many tsunami-struck communities.[71] Akasaka introduces the case of the Deer Dance in Minamisanriku, which is particularly relevant here. Minamisanriku is in the area where the tsunami was most ferocious, and in this town alone more than 800 people, or one in 20 of the population, lost their lives. The whole town was reduced to rubble, and the community was decimated. How was it possible to reconstruct a local festival in such a situation? Akasaka writes about a local fisherman, Muraoka Kenichi, who lost everything and wandered through the rubble for months, searching for anything related to his life. He found only two things. One was a shell ring he had made for his wife, and

---

71  Akasaka Norio, *3.11 kara kangaeru 'kono kuni no katachi'* [Post 3.11 Reflections on the Way We Are in This Country] (Tokyo: Shinchō Sensho, 2012), 85.

the other was a *taiko* drum used in the traditional Deer Dance.[72] Before the tsunami, Muraoka had played a key role in preserving the dance. He thought that the *taiko* would have been washed away, together with everything else, because of its light weight. When he found the drum in the mud, he thought: 'Okay, I might be able to start again'.[73] Eventually, locals managed to find all but one of the drums along with costumes and outfits for the dance, all buried in the mud. The first person keen to do the Deer Dance was a 12-year-old boy, Onodera Shō, who persuaded his friends, who were scattered among various shelters, to learn the dance together.[74] When the revived Deer Dance was finally performed, local people watched it with tears in their eyes.[75]

Akasaka remarks that folk festivals/arts played a significant role in uniting people in the disaster-stricken communities that were divided by numerous private differences: were there deaths in the family, were the bodies found or not, and was the family house lost, etc. Festivals were particularly effective in uniting people because acts of sacrament for the dead as well as repose for dead souls are strong themes of local festivals in Northeast Japan. Also, the festivals are open to everyone, unlike Buddhist funerals, which are strictly a family matter. [76]

Significantly, the dead souls in this context include those of animals. Concerning the Deer Dance, for instance, a memorial stone erected approximately 300 years ago reads: 'This dance is dedicated to the repose of the souls of all creatures living or dead'.[77] In addition to the Deer Dance in Minamisanriku, there are various other versions of the dance as well as other animal-related festivals/arts in the region. Akasaka holds that animism is an intrinsic part of the festivals and is also associated with the Buddhist notion of *shikkai jōbutsu* (悉皆成仏).[78] In Japanese Buddhism, *shikkai jōbutsu*, the long version of which is *sansen sōmoku shikkai jōbutsu* (山川草木悉皆成仏), means universal enlightenment not only for humans but for all entities, living and dead (i.e. humans, animals, birds, insects, etc.), including grass and trees, as well as other

---

72 ibid., 84–5 and 154–5.
73 Ishino Nahoka, 'Furusato ni hibike, bokura no kodō to yakudō' [May Our Heart Beat and Our Energy Reverberate in Our Hometown], *Kokoro Puresu* [The Heart Press], 2014, kokoropress. blogspot.com.au/2014/01/blog-post_24.html. Accessed 2 July 2016.
74 ibid.
75 Akasaka, *3.11 kara*, 155.
76 ibid.
77 ibid., 158.
78 ibid., 159.

inanimate things such as mountains and rivers. To what extent people engaging in the recovery of folk festivals/arts were conscious of such cultural traditions is unknown. As pointed out by Akasaka, however, folk festivals/arts functioned as a latent cultural mechanism connecting people divided by the disaster.[79]

**Shrines as Tsunami Markers:** Imamura Fumihiko (今村文彦), a specialist in tsunami engineering and disaster archives, presents a picture of a tiny wooden shrine surrounded by several trees, standing miraculously undamaged in the middle of a vast sea of mud left by the tsunami.[80] He points out the significance of local shrines acting as ancient landmarks of safe haven during tsunami and stresses the importance of transmitting the memory of disasters to descendants as part of disaster prevention measures.[81] The example Imamura draws on is Namiwake shrine (浪分神社), the name of which suggests a place where 'waves are divided (i.e. stopped)'. Local legend is that the god of the sea appeared on a white horse at the time of the Jōgan tsunami (860 AD) and controlled the surging wave by dividing it to the north and the south. Imamura's research team's analysis of alluvial deposits found data consistent with the legend. The Jōgan tsunami stopped just a few hundred meters from the shrine.[82]

A striking illustration showing the significance of shrines as landmarks of the 'tsunami line' was broadcasted by TBS TV soon after the triple disaster (*Hōdō Tokushū*, 21 August 2011). The report was based on the investigation by a local environmental surveyor Kumagai Wataru who became curious about the fact that many shrines withstood the tsunami. Further investigation of an area stretching 30 kilometres to the north from Minamisōma, the area most affected by tsunami, revealed that out of 84 shrines in the area, 67 stood undamaged. These undamaged shrines were almost exactly on the line that showed how far inland the tsunami came.[83]

---

79  ibid., 161.

80  Imamura Fumihiko, 'Miyagiken Sendaishi Wakabayashiku engan shūhen' [The Coastal Area of Wakabayashi Ward in Sendai City, Miyagi Prefecture: Photo Image], *Gakujutsu no dōkō* [Academic Trends] July 2012 (2012).

81  Imamura Fumihiko, 'Daishinsai no jittai to kyōkun no seiri ni mukete' [Facts About the Great Earthquake and Lessons to Be Learned], Presentation at Higashinihon Daishinsai Shakai Shihon Saisei Fukkō Shinpojium [Northeast Japan Disaster Symposium for Social Capital Reconstruction and Recovery] (Miyagi Prefectural Office, 2012).

82  Takase Hiroshi, Yoshida Kazushi, and Kumagai Wataru, *Jinja wa keikoku suru* [The Warning from Shrines] (Tokyo: Kōdansha, 2012), 76.

83  ibid., 38.

They were all small 'village shrines' (*sonsha* 村社), many nameless and no more than tiny wooden structures, that had been cherished and cared for by local people for hundreds of years. Data available from the Association of Shinto Shrines (*Jinja Honchō* 神社本庁) further indicated that it was the old shrines that tended to survive the 2011 tsunami. Of 100 shrines in the disaster region that were listed in the imperial survey of Shinto shrines compiled in 927 AD (meaning they are more than 1,000 years old), only three were damaged by the 2011 tsunami. A public relations officer of the association hypothesises that the Jōgan tsunami of 860 AD influenced the location of these ancient shrines.[84] Research on the Jōgan tsunami deposit has revealed that the frontline of the area inundated by the tsunami more than 1,000 years ago is almost exactly the same as that in 2011.[85]

Figure 5: A small village shrine stands intact in the area completely devastated by the tsunami including the tide-water control forest. The coastal area of Wakabayashi Ward in Sendai City, Miyagi Prefecture.

Source: Courtesy of Professor Imamura Fumihiko, Director, International Research Institute of Disaster Science (IRIDeS), Tohoku University.

84   ibid.
85   ibid., 93.

It is not yet clear whether the small shrines located on the tsunami line were built to mark the safe haven, or if they are there because they survived the devastation of the tsunami over 1,000 years ago. Either way, what is significant here is the meaning people find in this line of surviving shrines. This is clearly expressed in the words of the mayor of Sōma, a city also devastated by the tsunami. In his own neighbourhood many people survived by escaping to a local shrine that was believed by the locals to enshrine 'the god of tsunami'. Many ran to the shrine following the teaching of their ancestors: 'tsunamis come up to the shrine, and if you reach the shrine you are saved'. The mayor describes the shrine as a monument of past tsunami experience and says it is there to transmit knowledge to descendants: 'I felt most grateful to the ancestors'.[86]

As with the case of the local folk festival, the significance of this post-3.11 experience lies in the sense of being connected with the past, by realising anew the significance of the old, often small and nameless shrines, while at the same time feeling the sense of care of ancestors. It is possible that in the disaster-stricken areas where much was lost, quite paradoxically, people found a deeper sense of connectedness with the past. Shrines can at times be associated with state Shintoism, but in this context, the political dimension is hardly relevant. Rather, the meaning of shrines as a symbol of folk religion and local community comes across strongly. And as was the case with the tradition reflected in the notion of 'sansen sōmoku shikkai jōbutsu' in Buddhism, Shinto as the most ancient spiritual heritage of Japan is also deeply animistic. The (re)discovery of the significance of shrines in the aftermath of the 3.11 disaster is all about the nexus between nature (tsunami), life (of the living) and souls of the dead (people and all other forms of life that once existed), and in that sense it strongly represents the animistic essence of Shinto as folk religion.

In the recovery effort after the triple disaster, another significance of shrines was reappreciated, and provided theory and practice for a project that aims to protect future generations. Shrines have provided a foundation for the project, which now constitutes a new trend of civil society Japan. It is the appreciation of the trees surrounding shrines, the sacred forests, or *chinju-no-mori*.

---

86   ibid., 54–5.

**Chinju-no-mori Project:** A project to create a green seawall along the coast of the tsunami-affected region began soon after the disaster. It is called the Chinju-no-mori (Sacred Forest 鎮守の森) Project.[87] It is a grand-scale project that aims to create a 20 to 25-metre-high, and 300-km-long seawall, which is likened to the Great Wall in China. It is a combination of public works, to create the 5-metre-high mound using a gigantic amount of tsunami debris that is otherwise hard to dispose of, and volunteer work, to plant local trees on top of the mound. This organic seawall is expected to grow up to 20 metres high to provide a flexible, robust and beautiful, low-maintenance and sustainable buffer to mitigate tsunami impact and to prevent people and objects from being washed away into the sea.

The project consists of independent subprojects led by different administrations, such as prefectural governments, the Forestry Agency, and the Ministry of Land, Infrastructure, Transport and Tourism, all of which are in charge of the public works to prepare the mound. The volunteer work on the other hand includes gathering local seeds and nuts, preparing seedlings, planting them, and removing weeds. Between 2012 and 2016, a total of 38,451 people participated in the project as volunteers, collecting local seeds and nuts, and nurturing and planting 336,200 trees.[88]

The impetus for the project comes from ecologist Miyawaki Akira (宮脇昭), Emeritus Professor at Yokohama National University, who has devoted his life to the tree-planting movements around the world. He is the vice-president of the Chinju-no-mori Project, a public interest incorporated foundation (公益財団法人), presided over by former prime minister Hosokawa Morihiro. It is an umbrella organisation that arranges tree planting, after receiving requests from governments, corporations and citizens' groups. Miyawaki received the 2015 Gotō Shinpei Award, following Ishimure Michiko's award in 2014.

Miyawaki had always stressed the importance of a forest having a mixture of native trees indigenous to the area, especially evergreen broadleaf trees such as castanopsis, machilus and oak. The impact of the tsunami confirmed his theory to a much greater extent than he originally

---

87　The name of the project was changed from 'Great Forest Wall Project' to 'Chinju-no-mori Project' in June 2016.

88　'Chinju-no-mori Project', morinoproject.com. Accessed 19 June 2016.

anticipated. He witnessed that the native machilus (Japanese bay trees) not only survived the tsunami but were able to regenerate and regrow. In clear contrast, mono-culture forests of non-indigenous trees such as the pine forest along the coast of Minamisanriku were not only destroyed completely by the tsunami, but the severed trunks became projectiles that harmed people and damaged buildings. The non-indigenous forests failed to stop people being washed away into the sea, and were also unable to regenerate.[89]

Miyawaki calls forests that consist of a mixture of indigenous evergreen broadleaf trees *inochi no mori* (forests of life 命の森). He argues that these forests preserve DNA specific to the local area, cultivate the sensitivity, creativeness and intelligence of local people, help to stimulate the local economy, and collectively contribute to a sustainable global ecology. He also argues that these forests tend to survive natural disasters (such as earthquake, typhoon, fire, tsunami) and live for thousands of years because they are anchored around a group of tall trees whose roots go deep into the ground. These anchor trees are surrounded by multiple layers of trees of varying heights, which in turn are surrounded by shrubs and grasses.[90] Miyawaki emphasises that the prototype of the 'forest of life' is the *chinju-no-mori*, the sacred grove that surrounds shrines, consisting of a mixture of broadleaf evergreen trees and shrubs indigenous to the local area. As he remarks, the sense of sacredness is also significant as it prevents trees from being cut down.[91]

Just as shrines were built to protect their ancestors from tsunamis, people are building forest seawalls, using the knowledge gained from the sacred groves surrounding a shrine. This movement is the complete opposite of the national government's project to build a gigantic concrete seawall along the coast of the Tohoku region. Many people feel that a concrete seawall is an imposition of a huge, costly construction project that cuts the connectedness between people and nature (especially those who work at sea). Concrete seawalls become old and weak with time whereas forest seawalls grow bigger and stronger. Forest seawalls reconnect people with nature and protect them for generations to come. It is possible

89    Miyawaki Akira, *Gareki o ikasu 'mori no bōhatei' ga inochi o mamoru* [Forest Seawall Built on Debris Protects Life] (Tokyo: Gakken Shinsho, 2011); Miyawaki, Akira, 'The Japanese and Chinju-no-mori: Tsunami-Protecting Forest after the Great East Japan Earthquake 2011', *Phytocoenologia*, 44, issue 3–4 (2014): 235–44.
90    Miyawaki, *Gareki*, 33–4.
91    ibid.

that the project represents a new phase of civil society Japan where administration, citizens and cultural heritage are all connected to the theme of protecting life.

Anthropologist John Clammer points out that the celebration of local festivals distinguishes folk Shinto from the more institutionalised state and sect Shinto.[92] This is a significant remark as 'shrine' or localised folk Shinto played a pivotal role in all the previously discussed post-3.11 recovery efforts: local folk festivals belong to folk Shinto; most of the shrines on the tsunami frontline were small ancient shrines; and sacred groves represent the ecology of folk Shinto as indicated by the anti-shrine-consolidation protests by Japan's first ecologist, Minakata Kumagusu, at the end of Meiji period. Clammer holds that before the late 19th century when a more institutionalised form of Shinto was introduced with the aim of promoting nationalism, Shinto was better understood as 'an ecology'. Folk Shinto provided a way, after 3.11, for people to reconnect with each other (through the folk festivals), to connect with ancestors (by becoming aware of the significance of ancient shrines as tsunami markers) and to form a connection with their descendants (by constructing the great forest seawall using the seeds from, and knowledge of, the sacred forests surrounding folk shrines). The key words used here are exactly the same as the descriptors of the ecology of folk shrines: 'local', 'small', 'diverse' and 'grassroots'. Clammer claims that folk Shinto is nothing but a sophisticated example of animism.[93]

According to Clammer, animism in shrine Shinto comes with radical epistemological implications arising from a permeable sense of human–nature boundaries, which allows 'the positive forces that exist on the other side of the boundary … [to] pass through into the human realm'.[94] The sense of wonder encapsulated in all three examples seems to suggest, in Clammer's words, the 'permeable sense of human-nature boundaries': the Deer Dance costume being found in the tsunami mud and debris, the string of 67 small ancient shrines on the tsunami line, and the miraculous survival of local machilus trees, species that constitute sacred groves. This sense of wonder was felt not only by locals but also by visiting specialists: the folklorist Akasaka, the tsunami engineer Imamura, and the ecologist

---

92   John Clammer, 'The Politics of Animism', in John Clammer, Sylvie Poirier, and Eric Schwimmer eds, *Figured World: Ontological Obstacles in Intercultural Relations* (Toronto: University of Toronto Press, 2004), 90.
93   ibid., 102.
94   ibid., 93.

Miyawaki. So, do these examples suggest the presence of helpful forces that can pass through into the human realm as explained by Clammer? We do not have the answer to this question, but these episodes are strong examples of radical epistemology that animism can bring about to empower people confronted with socioenvironmental disaster.

## Animism as Grassroots Response for a New Modernity

Clammer points out that animism is 'still widely used [in Japan] as a way of explaining the distinctiveness of the national culture and as a vehicle for constructing a model of Japanese society'.[95] Indeed, the polytheistic/pantheistic world of Shinto that accommodates an infinite number of *kami* (deity/god/spirit) as natural life-forces within objects or places can be understood as classical animism. The Buddhist notion of '*sansen sōmoku shikkai jōbutsu*', which preaches that the Buddha resides not only in humans but in all things, living and dead, animate and inanimate, can also be regarded as classical animism. The availability of this cultural heritage was a precondition of Ogata's philosophy of the life-world, Ishimure's literature, and the Ishimure Michiko phenomenon, as well as the grassroots responses to the triple disaster as discussed above.

The contention of this chapter, however, is that the significance of animism has actually gone beyond that of cultural heritage. I argue that animism (re)emerged as a grassroots response to socioenvironmental crises in increasingly 'postmodern' (i.e. post-materialist) Japanese society, and that this has two significant political and epistemological implications.

Firstly, in political terms, one undeniable characteristic of the discourse on animism in Japan is that it has been part of what Morris-Suzuki calls 'eco-nationalism', a strong intellectual current that locates nature at the core of Japan's national identity.[96] Recently, animism has been used to criticise monotheist cultures, saying that Japan's tradition can fix environmental problems and bring about a sustainable future,[97] i.e. a new version of eco-nationalist inspired *Nihonjinron* (theories about the Japanese). In this

95   ibid.
96   Tessa Morris-Suzuki, *Re-Inventing Japan: Time, Space, Nation* (New York: M.E. Sharpe, 1998).
97   Yasuda Yoshinori, *Isshinkyō no yami: Animizumu no fukken* [The Darkness of Monotheism: Revival of Animism] (Tokyo: Chikuma Shobō, 2006).

chapter, animism has been located clearly at the other side of the political spectrum: a 'worm's-eye level' rather than a 'bird's-eye level'. This has enabled us to discuss animism sociologically, as a grassroots response to the political economy of Japan and, more broadly, to modernity itself. Animism has been presented not as a question of ontology in an ethnographic context, but as grassroots discourse of survival. As pointed out earlier, Ogata's philosophy of life-world is nothing but a postmodern version of animism, and so is Ishimure's literature, which has catered for the emotional and spiritual needs of Japanese society today.

In an article titled 'The Politics of Animism', Clammer goes one step further and argues:

> animism has profound political implications [since] it contains a model of human–nature relationships beyond the sociological categories of the state; it is extremely difficult to codify or to convert into any easily administrable theological system; and when it is linked with expressions such as shamanism it can become subversive, a form of power residing in implicit knowledge, a counter-discourse … and indeed a way of undermining the categories of conventional science.[98]

As Clammer asserts, the 'increasing significance of ecological, feminist, and New Age thinking in effecting intellectual currents suggests that such ideas, long current in Japan, are, despite their no doubt very different sources, becoming more and more widely diffused'.[99] The rise of the field of study called post-humanism is an indication of the perceived need to completely reconsider the human–nature relationship. Clammer's insight suggests that animism that (re)emerged in Japan as a citizens' discourse of survival has the political power to appropriate 'cultural heritage' to present a view of 'the new world from below', and that this has even broader potential to accommodate the needs of a world that is painfully aware of the contradictions and limitations of modernity.

This leads us to the second significance of animism that emerged from the grassroots quest for survival in Japan. That is, it can help us address the question of soul in social science and beyond. In the field of social science, the question of the soul constitutes a big lacuna. This is because social science itself is the product of modernity, and secularism has been its most fundamental premise. Matters regarding the soul therefore have

---

98   Clammer, 'Politics', 84.
99   ibid.

been epistemologically strange in the social sciences. As a consequence, animism was treated for a long time as if it were magic, and its elimination was considered key to modernity. At the same time, notions of nature and life have been quite limited in the social sciences. Is it possible for the discourse on animism that emerged from Minamata and Fukushima (or post-3.11 Japan) to fill this lacuna and provide a new/old kind of principle of environmental ethics?

Animism is not unique to Japan. Its primordial-indigenous tradition merged with Daoism from China and is now the basis of the strong cultural heritage of East Asia and beyond. Ogata's philosophy can be considered as a late modern and grassroots version of this cultural heritage and thus has the potential to provide environmental ethics that have wide relevance in Asia. If, as the German Ethics Commission for a Safe Energy Supply points out, environmental ethics should be drawn from a spiritual tradition, animistic culture might be as appropriate in the East as Christian tradition and European culture is in the West.

The World Risk Society occurs in the second/late/liquid modernity where the connection between the individual and social institutions weakens. The sociological observations presented in this chapter suggest that after the two environmental catastrophes of Minamata and Fukushima,[100] many people in Japan have come to learn to connect with each other in a new (yet, at the same time, old) way, and that a sense of animism plays an important part in this. Animism was there to make connections between different entities: the living and the dead, the past and the future, ancestors and descendants, the local area and nature, humans and animals, people, both in, and outside the community. In her 1999 seminal article titled 'Animism Revisited', Bird-David argued that animism represents relational epistemology in contrast to modernist epistemology,[101] which then stimulated a renewed interest in animism—often referred to as

---

100  To be precise, the three examples discussed as post-3.11 searches for survival have been drawn from areas, devastated by the earthquake and tsunami, which are north of Fukushima. In Fukushima where the nuclear crisis is current, it is likely to take decades, as was the case of Minamata, for any local discourse to emerge that goes beyond the present legacy of *kizuna* (bonds). However, given the very nature of the devastation—the total and direct threat to all connectedness of life, the ecosystem and community—it is likely that the vision of the life-world (or animism) will emerge from Fukushima with an even sharper focus on the themes of life, nature and the soul.

101  Nurit Bird-David, '"Animism" Revisited', *Current Anthropology* 40, no. Supplement February (1999).

New Animism.[102] This new study of animism fits very well with the understanding of animism that emerged as a grassroots response to the socioenvironmental disaster in Japan.

The search for survival in post-Minamata and post-Fukushima Japan suggests that achieving a sustainable future may demand an epistemological change in social sciences, so that we can revise concepts such as animism, as well as the concepts of soul, life and nature, in a new light. This means including the unseen in the realm of social sciences. It may sound radical, but perhaps there really is nothing new in this. After all, sociology did not exist before Durkheim established the existence of social phenomena *sui generis* that are independent of the actions and intentions of individuals. Would it be going too far to say that recognition of the existence *sui generis* of 'the life-world', the world of animism, where soul, nature and life are all connected, might be the pre-condition for a new modernity where sustainable development is possible?

---

102  See for instance, Graham Harvey, *Animism: Respecting the Living World* (London: Hurst & Co, 2005).

# 6

# Informal Labour, Local Citizens and the Tokyo Electric Fukushima Daiichi Nuclear Crisis: Responses to Neoliberal Disaster Management

Adam Broinowski

Nuclear workers are important as sentinels for a broader epidemic of radiation related diseases that may affect the general population.[1]

We live with contradictions everyday.[2]

## Introduction

The ongoing disaster at the Fukushima Daiichi nuclear power station (FDNPS), operated by Tokyo Electric Power Company (TEPCO), since 11 March 2011 can be recognised as part of a global phenomenon that has been in development over some time. This disaster occurred within a social and political shift that began in the mid-1970s and that became

---

1    Paul Jobin, 'Radiation Protection after the Fukushima Nuclear Disaster 3.11', *The Journal of Ohara Institute for Social Research*, August 658 (2013): 3 (14–30).

2    Anonymous, Association Franco-Japonaise (ASUKA), *Témoignages No.1* [Statements by *Fukushima genpatsu kokuso-dan*] (2014): 6. For a copy contact: www.asuka-association.org/contact/.

more acute in the early 1990s in Japan with the downturn of economic growth and greater deregulation and financialisation in the global economy. After 40 years of corporate fealty in return for lifetime contracts guaranteed by corporate unions, as tariff protections were lifted further and the workforce was increasingly casualised, those most acutely affected by a weakening welfare regime were irregular day labourers, or what we might call 'informal labour'.

During this period, many day labourers evacuated rented rooms (*doya* どや) and left the various *yoseba* (urban day labour market よせば, or lit. 'meeting place') to take up communal tent living in parks and on riverbanks, where they were increasingly victimised. With independent unions having long been rendered powerless, growing numbers of unemployed, unskilled and precarious youths (*freeters* フリーター) alongside older, vulnerable and homeless day labourers (these groups together comprising roughly 38 per cent of the workforce in 2015)[3] found themselves not only lacking insurance or industrial protection but also in many cases basic living needs. With increasing deindustrialisation and capital flight, regular public outbursts of frustration and anger from these groups have manifested since the Osaka riots of 1992.[4]

As Mike Davis observed, an un(der)protected informal sector in cities and industrial zones around the world occurs where there is a dilution or absence of labour rights and is characterised by 'semi-feudal kickbacks, bribes, tribal or gang loyalties and ethnic exclusion'.[5] Whether on a construction site, on the pavement, or in a domestic employment situation, informal labour comprises a surplus or reserve army of mercenary, irregular or precarious workers who pay off their debt for the opportunity to work through the availability of their cheap labour power.

---

3    Jeff Kingston, 'How to become an Activist: Start as a Japanese Part-Timer', *Bloomberg*, 29 May 2015, www.bloomberg.com/news/articles/2014-05-29/how-to-become-an-activist-start-as-a-japanese-part-timer. Accessed 16 July 2015.
4    The Osaka riots of 1992 are known as the 'anti-unemployment riots' in the Kamagasaki day labour centre in Nishinari ward. Day labourers who could no longer pay the rent demonstrated on the streets in protest. As distinct from the 1990 riots in the same location, which were specifically targeted against corrupt ties of the Nishinari police with a *yakuza* group, a large number of youths joined the day labourers in 1992 to protest against unemployment. See M. Yang, K. Haraguchi and T. Sakurada, 'The Urban Working-Class Culture of Riot in Osaka and Los Angeles: Toward a Comparative History', in B. Fraser ed., *Marxism and Urban Culture* (New York: Lexington Books, 2014), 230–31.
5    Mike Davis, *Planet of the Slums* (London and New York: Verso, 2006), 185.

In this chapter, first I outline the conditions of irregular workers at nuclear power plants and the excess burden they have borne with the rise of nuclear labour in Japan since the 1970s. I then turn to post-3.11 conditions experienced by residents in radiation-contaminated areas. Contextualising these conditions within the genealogy of radiodosimetry standards, I seek to show, through personal interviews and localised responses, how those who are regularly exposed to radiation from Fukushima Daiichi are now confronting problems similar to those faced by informal nuclear labour for decades in Japan. This analysis shows how, after 40 years or more of environmental movements as discussed in Chapter Four, the struggle continues to find viable solutions to the systemic production of the intertwined problems of environmental crises and labour exploitation, and suggests how potential alternative directions for affected populations may lie in their mutual combination.

## Conditions for Informal Labour Employed in Nuclear Power Stations

The phenomenon of assembling and recruiting a relatively unskilled labour pool at the cheapest rate possible is typical in nearly all of Japan's large-scale modern industrial projects in the 20th century. As early as the late 19th century, however, non-criminal homeless men were recruited for such projects, whether forced, coerced or voluntarily from the major day-labourer (*hiyatoi rōdōsha* 日雇い労働者) sites (*yoseba*) established in Sanya (Tokyo), Kotobuki (Yokohama), Kamagasaki (Osaka) and Sasashima (Nagoya). In pre–World War II and wartime Japan, *yakuza tehaishi* (手配師 labour recruiters) operated forced labour camps known as *takobeya* (たこ部屋 octopus rooms) for Korean and Chinese labourers who had been transported to work mainly in coal mines and on construction sites.[6]

The Dodge Line policy of 1949 stemmed rapid inflation by stabilising the yen, drastically curtailing government spending in the public sector, directly affecting education, public works and services such as the Japan National Railway (JNR), and cutting export subsidies for small businesses while expanding loans to big business.[7] Aimed at replacing the 'production

---

6    Brett Nee, 'Sanya: Japan's internal colony', *Bulletin of Concerned Asian Scholars* 6, no. 3 (1974): 14.
7    Sugita Yoneyuki, *Pitfall or Panacaea: The Irony of US Power in the Occupation of Japan 1945–1952* (New York: Routledge, 2003), 52–68.

first' with an 'export first' approach, this policy of economic liberalisation increased unemployment, lifted tariff protection and reconfigured the *zaibatsu* (財閥 industrial and financial business conglomerates during the Meiji, Taisho and Showa periods) as conglomerates without holding companies. The ranks of unemployed labour, including *zainichi* (在日 resident in Japan) Korean and Chinese, swelled in urban ghettos. During the 1950s, the new labour unions were crushed, and, with the return of the big conglomerates, agriculture increasingly faced growing competition from cheap American food imports. Urban labourers were rendered more pliable and many farmers and fisher people were forced from traditional livelihoods and communities to do seasonal work (*dekasegi* 出稼ぎ) on large-scale industrial or construction projects.[8] As the ties to their village communities and practices weakened or were lost, many became semi-nomadic, drifting from site to site and randomly collecting in *yoseba*. Like the shanty town or reservation in the colonised sectors of third world/decolonising countries as observed by Frantz Fanon, these were akin to the renewed 'disreputable places inhabited by disreputable people … [where] you die anywhere from anything … this world divided in two, is inhabited by different species'.[9]

In the 1960s and 1970s, with the closure of coal mines, as reliance on coal-fired power was replaced by petroleum, gas and nuclear-based energy generation, informal labour was in demand for the construction of tankers and ore carriers in shipyards fitted with new technologies and on projects such as the national *Shinkansen* and expressways, the 1964 Olympics and 1970 'Japan World Exposition', and nuclear power stations. Day labourers and irregular workers were vital in this period for the supply of vulnerable and flexible cheap 'unskilled' labour for menial, dirty and dangerous jobs (garbage collection, morgue work, work with animal carcasses, work involving toxic industrial materials etc.).

In the labour employment structure, the parent company (*moto-uke* 元請け) employs a subcontracting company (*shita-uke* 下請け), which employs another subcontractor (*mago-uke* 孫請け) that relies on labour brokers (*tehaishi/ninpu-dashi* 手配師／人夫出し), who are often *yakuza*-connected, to guarantee a certain number of workers per day. This nodal structure ensures the parent company penetration to the bottom social

---

8    Funamoto Shūji, *Damatte notare jinuna Funamoto Shūji ikoshū* [Don't Die Silently by the Roadside: Posthumous Writings of Funamoto Shūji] (Tokyo: Renga Shobo Shinsha, 1985), 199–200.
9    Frantz Fanon, *The Wretched of the Earth* (New York: Grove Press, 2004), 4–5.

layers while reducing their liability for the costs of labour power (accidents, health insurance, safety standards) and maintains responsiveness to the violent logic of supply and demand. Primary and secondary contractors receive money from parent companies like TEPCO to cover workers' salaries and expenses, special danger allowances and bonuses. By employing *tehaishi* who operate in a liminal zone of under-regulation, they hire cheaply, rapidly, under minimal conditions and seemingly without a direct duty of care.

The rapid build of nuclear power stations was planned in the 1960s by a consortium of major investment banks, electric utilities and construction companies and/or industry manufacturers (Mitsubishi, Tōshiba, Hitachi, Sumitomo, etc.), and was carried out in the 1970s, with increased momentum in response to the oil crisis of 1974–76. Through an intensive 'regional development' program of rural industrialisation from the early 1970s, politically disempowered communities were targeted as potential cheap labour as their environs were designated as sites for nuclear projects by investment capital. In a combination of regulatory capture and economic dependency, utilities moved in to provide employment opportunities to communities while the same communities steadily lost control over their resources and subsistence economies. In the process, they lost political agency as their political representatives often received corporate and state inducements for these projects. As TEPCO owns the electricity distribution system in Fukushima Prefecture, which includes hydroelectric and thermal power stations as well as nuclear, and is a major employer and investor in Fukushima Prefecture,[10] it has considerable sway in the political process as well as over electricity bills.

By the early 1980s, irregular workers came to comprise nearly 90 per cent of all nuclear workers.[11] As nuclear reactors grow increasingly contaminated and corroded by radiation over time, informal labour became fodder for regular maintenance, cleaning, repairing and/or venting and refuelling of these nuclear reactors to reduce exposures to permanent company employees such as scientists and engineers. As the

10    Toshihiro Okuyama, 'Radiation Doses 4 Times Larger for 'Outside Workers' at Nuclear Plants, *Asahi Shimbun*, 26 July 2012, ajw.asahi.com/article/0311disaster/fukushima/AJ201207260071 (subscription only).

11    Eighty-eight per cent of 83,000 workers in Japan's nuclear sector and 89 per cent of 10,303 workers at Fukushima Daiichi are in subcontracting service positions. See Editors, 'Radiation doses 4 times larger for "outside workers" at nuclear plants', *Asahi Shimbun*, 26 July 2012, ajw.asahi.com/ article/0311disaster/fukushima/AJ201207260071. Accessed 14 January 2015.

power station must be halted during the maintenance period, this period equates to a lack of production and profitability and is kept to a bare minimum by the operators, an approach that led to a litany of safety oversights and accidents.

Although provided less training, informal nuclear workers are paid higher over a shorter employment period than regular workers, whose insurance is taken out of their wage. Sworn to secrecy,[12] after a superficial safety education drill, they are sent into highly contaminated, hot and wet labyrinthine areas. Their work includes scrubbing contaminated areas, installing shields to reduce exposure for skilled workers, decontaminating and repairing pipes and tanks, welding, transporting contaminated materials and waste, washing contaminated uniforms and tools, removing filters and clearing garbage, inspecting gauges in high-level areas, dispersing chemicals over nuclear waste piles, pouring high-level liquid waste into drums and mopping up waste water. Although radioprotection regulations have been tightened in the last decade, working conditions for irregular workers have not necessarily improved and, without sufficient information about radiation danger, they can still be exposed to over 1 millisievert (mSv) of external radiation within minutes in high concentration areas and accumulate large amounts of internal radiation.[13]

Since 3.11, invoking the International Commission on Radiological Protection's (ICRPs) often-used ALARA (as low as reasonably allowable) principle to justify this regulatory contingency, the state also raised nuclear workers' limits from no more than 50 mSv per year (mSv/y) and 100 mSv/5 years to 250 mSv/y to deal with emergency conditions, and determined that there would be no follow-up health treatment for those exposed to doses below 50 mSv/y, while TEPCO decided to not record radiation levels below 2 mSv/y in the misplaced justification that the effects would be negligible. In December 2011, 'cold shutdown' was (erroneously) declared and the workers' limit was returned to 100 mSv/5 years. It will likely be raised again as the government expedites decommissioning to meet its estimated completion by 2030–2050.[14]

---

12   Kazumi Takaki, 'Listen to Their Silent Cry: The Devastated Lives of Japanese Nuclear Power Plant Workers Employed by Subcontractors or Labour-brokering Companies', *Bulletin of Social Medicine* 31, no. 1 (2014): 10.

13   Yuki Tanaka, 'Nuclear Power Plant Gypsies in High-tech Society', *Bulletin of Concerned Asian Scholars*, 18, no. 1 (1986): 12. See also Takaki, 'Listen to Their Silent Cry', 9.

14   For perspective, the estimated completion of decommissioning of Chernobyl is 2086.

Although very few regular workers' cumulative doses exceeded 20 mSv/y in any year prior to 3.11, by June 2015 the official number rose to 6,642[15] with doses of irregular nuclear workers often un(der)counted.

In a fast-track 40-year plan to decommission Fukushima Daiichi (i.e. removing the cores and dismantling the plant), as of August 2015 roughly 45,000 irregular workers ('front-line' workers, or 'nuclear gypsies') had been assembled at the J-Village Iwaki-Naraha soccer stadium before entering the sites. As well as jobs at the power stations, they work on decontamination and construction sites throughout the prefecture, which include those designated for the 2020 Olympics, a new school in Futaba (the town nearest to FDNPS), a large centre for radiation monitoring, a large research and training institute for reactor decommissioning, and a giant sea wall for tsunami prevention (see also Chapter Five). *Yakuza*-linked labour brokers (*tehaishi/ninpu-dashi*), eager to profit from the post-3.11 decommissioning budget (conservatively estimated at $150 billion), use social media and oral contracts to recruit these workers from the most vulnerable populations for 'clean up' work.[16] In this customary cascade of diluted responsibility, their original wage and conditions are skimmed or cut away (*pinhane sareta* ピンハネされた) by contractors (roughly 733 companies) so that some irregular workers receive as little as 6,000 yen per day and only a very small fraction of the 10,000 yen per day in danger money promised by the Ministry of the Environment (MoE) and TEPCO.[17]

Irregular workers' oral contracts with *tehaishi* are often illegal or dangerous, and are sometimes imposed on workers through threats or use of force.[18] In addition, the day labourer may become indebted to *tehaishi* for housing and/or loans for lifestyle dependencies (i.e. gambling, drugs, prostitution). As products of structural discrimination, itinerant and/or

15   Editors, 'Fukushima daiichi genshiryoku hatsudensho sagyōsha no hibaku senryōen no hibaku se ni tsuite', TEPCO, 31 July 2015, www.tepco.co.jp/cc/press/betu15_j/images/150731j0604.pdf. Accessed 1 August 2015.

16   See Hiroko Tabuchi, 'Unskilled Recruited for Fukushima Duty', *The Age*, 18 March 2014, www.theage.com.au/world/unskilled-recruited-for-fukushima-duty-20140318-hvk08.html; Saito Mari and Antoni Slodowski, 'Japan's Homeless Recruited for Murky Fukushima Clean-up', *Reuters*, www.reuters.com/article/us-fukushima-workers-idusbre9bt00520131230.

17   Michael Okwu, 'Gangsters and "Slaves": The People Cleaning Up Fukushima', *Al Jazeera America*, 8 January 2014, america.aljazeera.com/watch/shows/america-tonight/america-tonight-blog/2014/1/7/fukushima-cleanupworkerssubcontractors.html.

18   Editor, 'Yajuku rōdōsha no genpatsu hibakusha no jittai o tekisuto shite itadakimashita', Sanya Blog - Yajuku-sha shitsugyō sha undō hōkoku, 15 April 2011, san-ya.at.webry.info/201103/article_11.html. Accessed 19 January 2016.

irregular workers who are already socially isolated may find it difficult to build support networks, whether through marriage, family or solid friendships. Obligated within a semi-legal economy and stripped of rights and protections, each worker is pitted against the other, young and old, stronger and weaker, individual and family man, for basic survival.

Over the past 40 years, poor monitoring and record-keeping has meant that many former nuclear workers who develop leukaemia and other illnesses have been denied government compensation due to their lawyers' inability to prove the etiological link between their disease and employment. For example, the death of Yoshida Masao (58), the Fukushima Daiichi manager who was among the 'Fukushima 50' who remained at the plant to manage the nuclear meltdowns in their critical phase and who developed oesophagal cancer in 2013, was not recognised by TEPCO as related to radiation exposure from Fukushima Daiichi as the cancer was deemed to have developed too quickly after the initial accident.

Irregular nuclear workers have commonly relied on permanent employees to monitor, record and calibrate their doses. Denied sufficient information about radiation exposure risks, and preferring not to jeopardise their contracts and provoke physical intimidation if they complain about their conditions, many collude with company officers (who record their accumulated doses) to camouflage and underestimate their dose rates (particularly for internal doses). This allows them to extend their time and contracts at nuclear plants before they are deemed to have reached (or exceeded) the maximum annual dose limit (50 mSv/y).[19] When a nuclear worker is diagnosed with abnormalities in a routine check-up, some subcontractors may falsify nuclear workers' passbooks.[20] Despite the long lives of internalised radionuclides, it has been customary either not to measure this properly and/or to simply reset the dose record at the end of each financial year.[21] While protective clothing and procedures have grown more stringent for nuclear workers, especially after some workers died and fell ill from heat-related causes, irregular workers remain

19    On methods of dosimetry camouflage see Paul Jobin, 'Radiation Protection After the Fukushima Nuclear Disaster 3.11', *The Journal of Ohara Institute for Social Research* 658 (August 2013): 9.
20    Jobin, 'Radiation Protection', 9.
21    In the 1980s, it was standard practice at the Tsuruga plant of the Japan Atomic Power Company (JAPC) to reset accumulated doses to zero on four days of every month. See Tanaka Yuki, 'Nuclear Power Plant Gypsies', 9.

far less protected.[22] At Fukushima Daiichi, where crews are overworked and understaffed, irregular workers often commit errors leading to cases of serious injury and large leaks of radioactive materials into the environment. This is further compounded by the lack of understanding or recognition of chronic illnesses in either permanent or irregular nuclear workers. This has sometimes led to poorly explained deaths of nuclear workers.[23]

In October 2015, a welder in his late 30s and father of three from Kita-Kyushu became the first worker in four years to be awarded workers' insurance payments (medical costs and loss of income for temporary disability) while three more cases remained undecided. He was diagnosed with acute myelogenous leukaemia after having accumulated 19.8 mSv/y from exposure to a radiation leak and one year's work at Fukushima Daiichi (Reactors 3 and 4) and the Genkai nuclear plant (Kyushu) (both of which use MOX fuel).[24] While compensation was recognised under nuclear workers' compensation insurance legislation (1976), the Health Ministry maintained that a causal link between illness and employment remains to be scientifically proven. After the delayed report by TEPCO of 1,973 workers exposed to over 100 mSv/y by mid-2013, by August 2015 21,000 of the 45,000 irregular workers had been exposed to over 5 mSv/y and 9,000 workers to over 20 mSv/y.[25] TEPCO and the central government would certainly be worried about a spike in compensation claims.

Without a proper health regime, the permanent damage incurred by irregular nuclear workers far outweighs the value of their cheap labour power. With their use as filters as they move to each plant, as nuclear

---

22    Kazumi Takaki, 'Listen to their Silent Cry', 10.

23    See, for example, *Fukushima Daiichi genshiryoku hatsudensho no jōkyō ni tsuite*, 30 July 2016, TEPCO, www.tepco.co.jp/press/report/2016/1314410_8693.html.

24    Mixed-Oxide fuel (MOX) combines uranium (U238) and plutonium (Pu 239-240) in nuclear fission. The plutonium component makes the fuel even more toxic as well as producing longer-lived waste than with uranium fuel.

25    Yuri Oiwa, 'Ministry Recognizes Link between Fukushima Nuclear Worker's Leukemia and Radiation Exposure for 1st Time', *Asahi Shimbun*, 20 October 2015, ajw.asahi.com/article/0311disaster/fukushima/AJ201510200086. Since the time of writing, this article has been made unavailable online. For verification, an online mirror link can be found at: www.fukushima-is-still-news.com/2015/10/worker-cancer-case-confirmed-2.html. It is worth recalling that in 2013 TEPCO, after an earlier underestimation of 'only 178' workers, had finally admitted that 1,973 workers had been exposed to over 100 mSv/y. See 'Nearly 2000 at Fukushima No. 1 Face Higher Thyroid Cancer Risk', *Japan Times*, www.japantimes.co.jp/news/2013/07/19/national/1973-fukushima-plant-workers-show-higher-risk-for-thyroid-cancer/#.V9ff_LXgwXg.

workers grow older and sicker they become less able to commodify their labour and are unlikely to receive proper treatment and/or compensation (due to insufficient data and high radiation safety limits among other things). Although the endless production of labour willing to take on this dangerous work and the devolution of responsibility and ambiguity around radiation health effects are used to justify the continuation of these practices, if workers are knowingly placed in harmful conditions the employer is in breach of a duty of care under the Labour Standards Law. As byproducts of a discriminatory industrial labour system, these irregular nuclear workers and their families, like many elsewhere, are deprived of basic rights to health and well-being. As one labourer stated in relation to Fukushima Daiichi: 'TEPCO is God. The main contractors are kings, and we are slaves'.[26] In short, Fukushima Daiichi clearly illustrates the social reproduction, exploitation and disposability of informal labour, in the state protection of capital, corporations and their assets.

## Conditions for Residents of Post-3.11 Radiation-Affected Areas

For roughly 30 years, the exclusion zone around Chernobyl has been set at 30 kilometres. Between 1 and 5 mSv/y is the assisted evacuation level and mandatory evacuation is 5 mSv/y and above. Unlike the approach adopted for Chernobyl, which was to achieve containment (a sarcophagus was built in eight months) and permanent resettlement of 350,000 people, the government and TEPCO have adopted a 'dilution' approach— to widely disperse and redistribute ('share') radioactive materials and waste and decontaminate residential areas. To date, this has permitted the permanent release through venting, dumping and incinerating of radioactive materials into the air, land, water and sea, and circulation in the food chain and recycled materials on a daily basis since March 2011.

Over the first few days at Fukushima Daiichi nuclear power station, severity (International Nuclear Event Scale) levels were steadily raised from level 3 to level 5 to level 7, and the mandatory evacuation zone was gradually expanded from 10 to 30 kilometres. On 16 March 2011, readings in Aizu-Wakamatsu Middle School (100 kilometres from FDNPS) in Fukushima Prefecture returned 2.57 microSv/h (microsieverts

---

26   Okwu, 'Gangsters and "Slaves"'.

per hour),[27] and Kōriyama (60 kilometres) recordings returned 3.6–3.9 microSv/h. Inside people's homes in Kōriyama, levels were between 1.5 and 2.0 microSv/h and 8.2 microSv/h in the downpipes.[28] This data was made public only three months later. On 6 April, schools in Fukushima Prefecture were reopened. As the boundaries, legal limits and information were gradually altered, populations were urged to return to work. At the same time the legal safety level for mandatory evacuation for the public (radiation safety level 1972) was raised from 1 to 20 mSv/y,[29] based on a cumulative 100 mSv dose averaged over five years, suddenly shifting the parameters for 'low-level' radiation and designating the general public with the level previously designated to nuclear workers.

The US Government advised a mandatory evacuation zone of 50 miles (80 kilometres). Several nations' embassies in Tokyo evacuated their staff. Of roughly 2 million in Fukushima Prefecture, about 80,000 people from 11 municipalities were ordered to evacuate while another 80,000 evacuated voluntarily. By late 2015, about 118,862 remained evacuated.[30] Sixty thousand of these people live in temporary housing and many lacked basic needs. There were many evacuees who sought public housing

---

27    There is discrepancy on this measurement. Officially, the Japanese Government calculates 0.23 microSv/h = 1 mSv/y based on an average eight hours/day outdoors per person. The ICRP, however, calculates 0.08 microSv/h = 1 mSv/y. en.wikipedia.org/wiki/Sievert-ICRP_definition_of_the_sievert. When including normal background radiation, calculations normally vary between 0.11 and 0.18 microSv/h. This is complicated by the fact that radiation from Fukushima Daiichi has been and continues to be distributed across the entirety of Japan, so that normal background post-3.11 is in fact abnormally elevated. See See Hiroshi Ishizuka, 'Cesium from Fukushima Plant Fell all over Japan', *Asahi Shimbun*, 26 November 2011, ajw.asahi.com/article/0311disaster/fukushima/aj201111260001. Since the time of writing, this article has been made unavailable online. For verification, an online mirror link can be found at: www.infiniteunknown.net/2011/11/27/cesium-from-fukushima-plant-fell-all-over-japan-even-on-okinawa-1700-km-from-nuke-plant/.
28    Kataoka Terumi on 18 May 2012 as recorded for the *Fukushima kokusodan* (Fukushima plaintiffs) presentation to the Fukushima district attorney's office against 33 TEPCO past and present officers, government officials and medical experts made in 2013. See N. Field and M. Mizenko eds, *Fukushima Radiation: Will You Still Say No Crime Was Committed?*, Amazon Digital Services: Complainants for Criminal Prosecution of the Fukushima Nuclear Disaster, 1st edition (12 May 2015), 360.
29    The Radiation Safety Level law permits nuclear workers 100 mSv over 5 years and no more than 50 mSv in any year; female workers no more than 5 mSv in 3 months; denies citizens entry to areas of 5.2 mSv/y, women are limited to 2 mSv/y; 5 mSv is the threshold for claims of occupational disease; food in general is measured below 1 mSv/y; 5 mSv and above prohibits residence and consumption of food and water.
30    Although it was reported by the end of 2015 that this number had dropped to below 100,000, there was some discrepancy in calculation as those who had bought houses in the locations they had evacuated to were no longer included as 'evacuees'. See Editors, 'Fukushima Nuclear Evacuees Fall Below 100,000', *Japan Times*, 9 January 2016, www.japantimes.co.jp/news/2016/01/09/national/fukushima-nuclear-evacuees-fall-100000/#.VpDnE1LzN_l.

who have been turned away.[31] There are additional evacuees affected by the earthquakes and tsunami who come from other prefectures (including parts of Miyagi and Ibaraki), some of whom were also affected by radiation exposure.

The situation in many villages within contaminated areas signifies how government policies have further exposed a wide range of people—farmers, shopkeepers, taxi drivers, factory workers, mothers (as reproductive workers), school students, local public servants—to conditions informal workers have long had to endure. In several cases (i.e. Iitate, Minami Soma, Namie), the notification of residents of radiation danger was delayed and potassium iodide pills were not distributed. Similarly, data on weather patterns and distribution gathered by the SPEEDI monitoring system[32] was suppressed. These populations were not adequately informed of what the dose readings meant in terms of health risk. When people did seek measurement and treatment for their likely exposures, hospitals and other institutions with the requisite measuring technologies refused to measure them, as it was deemed 'there was no reason for internal contamination and so there was no reason to measure'.[33] These people unwittingly became *hibakusha* (被曝者), broadly defined as victims of radiation exposure.

Even though the Fukushima Daiichi nuclear disaster has caused near-permanent pollution, the conflation of the radiation problem with tsunami and earthquake destruction to be managed as a single large-scale 'clean-up', reconstruction and revitalisation operation as instituted by the National Resilience Council 2013 has occluded the materiality of radiation. Informal workers on 'decontamination projects' washed down public buildings and homes and scraped up and replaced soil and sludge contaminated at levels found for example at between 84,000–446,000

---

31    By the end of 2015, Fukushima Prefecture had built housing for around 17 per cent of the 43,700 Fukushima households that remained without a permanent home. This was based on the categorisation of 'long-term evacuee' as only pertaining to those who only wanted to remain evacuated until evacuation orders had been lifted. Those who wanted to remain evacuated permanently or until safety had been proven were not considered 'long-term evacuees'. Editors, 'Nuclear evacuees surveyed about living in public housing later became non-eligible', *The Mainichi*, 5 December 2015, mainichi.jp/english/articles/20151205/p2a/00m/0na/013000c. Since the time of writing, this article has been made unavailable online. For verification, an online mirror link can be found at: dunrenard. wordpress.com/2016/page/153/.

32    SPEEDI monitoring system is the computer-based emergency response system linked to the Japan Weather Association and Science and Technology Agency of Japan to predict radiological impacts in local and workplace areas due to nuclear accident.

33    Takahashi Kei in Allain de Halleux, *Fukushima e yōkosō*, vol. 1 (at 4 min 40 sec), 14 June 2013, www.youtube.com/watch?v=bjv1b6Zn9DY. Accessed 15 May 2015.

Becquerels per kilogram (Bq/kg) in Kōriyama (60 km from Fukushima Daiichi).[34] They also collected waste that included radioactive debris, uniforms and tools. The organic waste is stored on government-purchased land in black industrial bags piled in large walls and mounds to create a sort of buffer zone on town margins and in areas determined as long-term irradiated zones.[35] Other contaminated waste is burned in newly constructed incinerators in towns nearest the plant (such as Futaba, Okuma, Naraha, Tamura, Tomioka, with more planned) in addition to the incineration already underway in major cities since 3.11, even while evacuees are being compelled to return to some of them (Tamura, Kawauchi, Naraha) where evacuation orders have been lifted. In addition, in June 2016 the Ministry of the Environment approved radioactive soil of up to 8,000 Bq/kg to be reused in national public works. Although stipulated to be used for roads and barriers (such as sea walls) under a layer of non-contaminated materials, there is concern that these will corrode over time leading to recirculation in the environment.

As compensation schemes are contingent upon where evacuees come from (whether these are areas where there are plans to lift evacuation orders, areas pending decontamination in the shorter term, or those deemed difficult to return to), those mandatory evacuees without property have received on average 100,000 yen per month while voluntary evacuees have received 60,000 yen per month, even if radiation levels in their residential areas were high. The return to towns that received over 50 mSv/y (Futaba, Namie, Okuma) remains unlikely for decades, but if evacuees do return to other villages, they risk lifetime re-exposures of up to 20 mSv/y. In late 2015, Iitate village, for example, was divided into Areas 1 and 2, which

---

34 Wada Nanako (Hanawa-machi liaison for the incineration of radioactive debris and member of Fukushima kokuso-dan) in Anonymous, *Témoignages No.1*, Association Franco-Japonaise ASUKA 2014: 13 (1–18). For a copy, contact www.asuka-association.org/contact/. The calculation of radiation distributed in soil as it translates to potential damage to the human body has significant variables and is contested. The provisional safety limit was 500 Bq/kg, which was lowered to 100 Bq/kg in Japan after Fukushima. The ICRP calculated that a total body activity of 1,400 Becquerels would correspond to 20 Bq/kg of body weight in a 70 kg adult and is equivalent to 0.1 mSv/y exposure. That would make the internationally accepted limit of 1 mSv/y equate to 200 Bq/kg in a 70 kg adult or 14,000 Bq in soil. See Stephen Starr, 'Implications of the Massive Contamination of Japan with Radioactive Cesium', 11 March 2013, *Helen Caldicott Foundation Symposium*, New York Academy of Medicine. For an alternative calculation see fn 61.

35 Watanabe Miyoko (Tamura) observed that in spite of their protests, '400 tons per day of irradiated waste is burned everywhere. [This is planned] in our village factory'. 'Témoignages No.1', 2014. Further, Wada Nanako testified that 'Incinerators have been built, sometimes secretly, in Samegawa, Sōma, Fukushima, Kōriyama [and Miyakoji in Tamura]. There will be 20 built in total'. 'Témoignages No. 1', 2014: 13.

are being prepared for repopulation (54,000 people), and Area 3, which so far remains out of bounds. Although the topsoil contaminated with Caesium was stripped and replaced (i.e. returning 0.6 microSv/h) and its houses and roads were washed down, 96 per cent of Iitate remained at 1 microSv/h. As Iitate is 75 per cent forest, which trapped a large stock of contamination, the land re-concentrates through radiation circulation (hence, quickly returned to 2.6 microSv/h).[36] If the majority in Iitate, who are primarily agricultural workers, can no longer harvest vegetables, rice, wild mushrooms and vegetables (*sansai* 山菜) or burn wood for heat, and their houses are re-irradiated, then only the semi-autonomous elderly are likely to return. By August 2015, less than 10 per cent of roughly 14,000 eligible had applied for temporary return.[37]

So-called 'decontamination' and 'remediation' has been deployed to justify redefining evacuation boundaries and lifting evacuation orders so as to cut compensation payments. Following the 37th National Emergency Response Headquarters meeting held at the Prime Minister's Office in June 2015 in which the Prime Minister decreed that 'evacuees must return to their hometowns as quickly as possible and start new lives',[38] in late August 2015 evacuees were told if they chose to return home they would receive a one-off payment of 100,000 yen per household. If they did not, once evacuation orders had been lifted, 'free rent' (*yachin hojo* 家賃補助) for voluntary evacuees would be cut by March 2017 at the very latest.[39] Further, the government announced its intention to partially lift the restriction on the 'difficult-to-return zone' by 2022 so as to counteract the negative image of the area and its produce.[40] Without alternative income, and with a significant housing shortage due to the restriction

---

36  Greenpeace, 'Investigation Exposes Failure of Fukushima Decontamination Program', 21 July 2015, www.greenpeace.org/japan/ja/news/press/2015/pr20150721/20150721-Press-Release-Greenpeace-investigation-exposes-failure-of-Fukushima-decontamination-program-/. Accessed 22 July 2015.

37  In other towns such as Naraha, where an estimated 46 per cent of 7,368 registered evacuees hope to return while only 780 are willing to return immediately, personal radiation monitors were distributed and radiation monitoring of tap water and water filtration systems implemented to reassure them that it was safe. See 'Evacuation Order Lifted Completely in Naraha near Wrecked Fukushima Plant', *Japan Times*, 5 September 2015, www.japantimes.co.jp/news/2015/09/05/national/japan-to-lift-evacuation-order-for-fukushima-town-of-naraha/.

38  Government of Japan (GoJ), The Prime Minister of Japan and his Cabinet, June 2015, japan. kantei.go.jp/97_abe/actions/201506/12article1.html.

39  Editors, 'Fukushima Prefecture Looking to End Free Rent for Voluntary Disaster Evacuees in 2017', *The Mainichi*, 16 June 2015, mainichi.jp/english/articles/20150616/p2a/00m/0na/015000c. Accessed August 2015.

40  Otsuki Noriyoshi, 'Ban to be Lifted on Fukushima's Worst Affected Zone by 2022', *Asahi Shimbun*, 1 September 2016, www.asahi.com/ajw/articles/AJ201609010066.html.

of new public housing, many have been and will be forced to return to contaminated areas, to endure radiation exposure without compensation. If only the elderly return, there will be few prospects for young families in such towns where there is little local business and infrastructure, and public facilities and housing are in disrepair.

In Naraha, between May and August 2015, ambient readings in populated areas officially determined as 'low or moderate' returned 0.3–0.7 microSv/h and soil samples returned 26,480–52,500 Bq/kg of Caesium 137 and 134 combined (and 18,700 Bq/kg in the town's water reservoir).[41] While the majority of former residents are more likely to either pull down their houses and sell the land or maintain their homes as vacationers, there is additional private and state pressure to industrialise these former idylls as 'reconstruction hubs'. As part of the 'Innovation Coast' plan, for example, 1,000 irregular workers have resided on the town's outskirts as they built a giant research facility (estimated cost: 85 billion yen) to train hundreds of workers in reactor simulations and use of specialised robots. As industry colonises and transforms such towns, the pressing concern of unmitigated radiation levels in soil, forests and water, whether from distribution or recirculation, remains due to the long-lived decay and harmful effects of these radionuclides.

Similarly, in the effort to stimulate business, highways (Route 6) and train lines (Jōban line) passing directly through the (former) evacuation zone were reopened in 2015, although traffic must still travel with closed windows at the time of writing. Regular users of these corridors such as railway and transport workers and irregular nuclear workers accumulate higher doses from regular exposure while radioactive particles attached to vehicles are dispersed beyond contaminated areas. Clearly, a containment and permanent resettlement approach has been deemed untenable in the belief it would disrupt economic productivity levels. As one high school student insightfully observed, 'Sensei … If they [really wanted to turn] Fukushima into an evacuation zone they'd have to block the Route 4 highway, Tōhoku expressway and *Shinkansen*'.[42] Nevertheless, in lieu of overall reconstruction costs less conservatively estimated at half a trillion dollars, it may have been cheaper in the longer term to adopt permanent resettlement, education, health treatment and work creation strategies.

---

41   Iwaki Monitoring Centre, www.iwakisokuteishitu.com/pdf/weekly_data.pdf.
42   Kazuki Jinno (35 years old) in *Fukushima Radiation*, 2015: 537.

# Official Medicine: The (Il)logic of Radiation Dosimetry

On what basis have these policies on radiation from Fukushima Daiichi been made? Instead of containing contamination, the authorities have mounted a concerted campaign to convince the public that it is safe to live with radiation in areas that should be considered uninhabitable and unusable according to internationally accepted standards. To do so, they have concealed from public knowledge the material conditions of radiation contamination so as to facilitate the return of the evacuee population to 'normalcy', or life as it was before 3.11. This position has been further supported by the International Atomic Energy Agency (IAEA), which stated annual doses of up to 20 mSv/y are safe for the total population including women and children.[43] The World Health Organisation (WHO) and United Nations Scientific Commission on the Effects of Atomic Radiation (UNSCEAR) also asserted that there were no 'immediate' radiation related illnesses or deaths (*genpatsu kanren shi* 原発関連死) and declared the major health impact to be psychological.

While the central and prefectural governments have repeatedly reassured the public since the beginning of the disaster that there is no immediate health risk, in May 2011 access to official statistics for cancer-related illnesses (including leukaemia) in Fukushima and southern Miyagi prefectures was shut down. On 6 December 2013, the Special Secrets Protection Law (*Tokutei Himitsu Hogo Hō* 特定秘密保護法) aimed at restricting government employees and experts from giving journalists access to information deemed sensitive to national security was passed (effective December 2014). Passed at the same time was the Cancer Registration Law (*Gan Tōroku Hō* 癌登録法), which made it illegal to share medical data or information on radiation-related issues including evaluation of medical data obtained through screenings, and denied public access to certain medical records, with violations punishable with a 2 million yen fine or 5–10 years' imprisonment. In January 2014, the IAEA, UNSCEAR and Fukushima Prefecture and Fukushima Medical University (FMU) signed a confidentiality agreement to control medical data on radiation. All medical personnel (hospitals) must submit data

---

43 IAEA, 'Actions to protect the public in an emergency due to severe conditions at Light Water Reactor', May (2013): 97, accessed August 2015, www-pub.iaea.org/MTCD/publications/PDF/EPR-NPP_PPA_web.pdf.

(mortality, morbidity, general illnesses from radiation exposures) to a central repository run by the FMU and IAEA.[44] It is likely this data has been collected in the large Fukushima Centre for Environmental Creation, which opened in Minami-Sōma in late 2015 to communicate 'accurate information on radiation to the public and dispel anxiety'.

This official position contrasts with the results of the first round of the Fukushima Health Management Survey (October 2011 – April 2015) of 370,000 young people (under 18 at the time of the disaster) in Fukushima prefecture since 3.11, as mandated in the Children and Disaster Victims Support Act (June 2012).[45] The survey report admitted that paediatric thyroid cancers were 'several tens of times larger' (*suitei sareru yūbyōsū ni kurabete sūjūbai no ōdā de ōi* 推定される有病数に比べて数十倍のオーダーで多い) than the amount estimated.[46] By 30 September 2015, as part of the second-round screening (April 2014–March 2016) to be conducted once every two years until the age of 20 and once every five years after 20, there were 15 additional confirmed thyroid cancers coming to a total of 152 malignant or suspected paediatric thyroid cancer cases with 115 surgically confirmed and 37 awaiting surgical confirmation. Almost all have been papillary thyroid cancer with only three as poorly differentiated thyroid cancer (these are no less dangerous). By June 2016, this had increased to 173 confirmed (131) or suspected (42) paediatric thyroid cancer cases.[47]

The National Cancer Research Center also estimated an increase of childhood thyroid cancer by 61 times, from the 2010 national average of 1–3 per million to 1 in 3,000 children. Other estimates of exposure to radiation, obtained from direct thyroid measurements in Namie town in April 2011, although discontinued under government pressure, also returned much higher results than official estimates (i.e. 80 per cent

---

44 Editors, 'Gan tōroku hō no seiritsu, kuni ga zenkoku no kanja jōhōhan wo database ni', *Huffington Post*, 6 December 2013, www.huffingtonpost.jp/2013/12/06/cancer-datebace-japan_n_4396656.html. Accessed 15 July 2015.

45 The Act stipulates expanded health checkups; assessment of doses and their health effects; alleviation of health concerns; long-term support for radiation effects; support for choice of residence and settlement; provision of regular medical care; reduction of medical expenses for children (unborn included) and pregnant women; lifelong medical checkups for those from contaminated areas.

46 Fukushima Prefectural Government, 19th Prefectural Oversight Committee Meeting for the Fukushima Health Management Survey, Fukushima Prefecture, 18 May (2015): 1, www.pref.fukushima.lg.jp/uploaded/attachment/115335.pdf.

47 Yuri Oiwa, '15 More Child Thyroid Cancer Cases Found in Fukushima', *Asahi Shimbun*, 7 June 2016, www.asahi.com/ajw/articles/AJ201606070042.html.

positive, 1 at 89 mSv, 5 over 50 mSv, 10 at 10mSv or under).[48] In April 2014, Dr Tsuda Toshihide, an epidemiologist at Okayama University, declared this a 'thyroid cancer epidemic' (*kōjōsen densenbyō* 甲状腺伝染病), and predicted multiple illnesses from long-term internal radiation below 100 mSv/y and advocated for a program of outbreak (emergency or rapid) epidemiology in and outside Fukushima.[49] Similarly, a Tokyo-based physician, Dr Mita Shigeru, circulated a public statement notifying his colleagues of his intention to relocate his practice to Okayama due to overwhelming evidence of unusual symptoms in his patients (roughly 2,000). Given that soil in Tokyo post-Fukushima returned between 1,000 and 4,000 Bq/kg, as compared to an average of 500 Bq/kg (Cs 137 only) in Kiev soil, Mita pointed to a correlation between these symptoms and the significant radiation contamination in Tōhoku and metropolitan Tokyo.[50]

While results from the Fukushima Health Survey demonstrate flaws in the official dosimetry model and public safety campaign, the survey itself also has clear limitations. It is limited to subjects in a specific age bracket in one prefecture and one non-fatal illness (thyroid cancer, which can be treated with surgery but has lifelong side effects) from the ingestion of one radionuclide (Iodine 131) with a relatively short half-life (eight days) that comprised only 9.1 per cent of the total releases. Its dosimetry is based on the National Institute of Radiological Sciences (NIRS) model,[51] which is for external exposure only, does not account for exposures in the initial days of the disaster and uses Japanese Government data that has been criticised for underestimating releases and exposures.[52] Further, the survey ignores the damage from the bulk of the total inventory including longer-

48    The most contaminated area is Nakadōri (605 per million, 50 times higher than total) while other parts are 12 times the total. Editors, 'Fukushima Government Terminated Iodine 131 Exposure Study, Citing it Might Concern Residents', *Simply Info*, 14 June 2013, www.fukuleaks.org/web/?p=6243. Accessed January 2015.

49    Ministry of the Environment (MoE), 8th Expert Meeting, Status of Disaster Victims' Health Management, 16 July 2014, in Editors, 'Running Backwards on Health Support after the Nuclear Accident: Ministry of Environment Expert Meeting', *Tokyo Shimbun*, 22 July 2014.

50    Mita Shigeru, 'Why did I Leave Tokyo' [letter to Association of Doctors in Kodaira, *WNCR*, 16 July 2014, www.save-children-from-radiation.org/2014/07/16/a-tokyo-doctor-who-has-moved-to-western-japan-urges-fellow-doctors-to-promote-radiation-protection-a-message-from-dr-mita-to-his-colleagues-in-kodaira-city-t/. Accessed 17 July 2014.

51    Keiichi Akahane et al., 'NIRS External Dose Estimation System for Fukushima Residents after the Fukushima Dai-ichi NPP Accident', *Nature Scientific Reports* 2013 (3): 1670, www.ncbi.nlm.nih.gov/pmc/articles/PMC3628369/.

52    See 'New Radiation Release Estimates Compiled', *Simply Info*, 4 November 2013, accessed January 2015, www.fukuleaks.org/web/?p=11668.

lived radionuclides (such as Plutonium 239, Caesium 137, Strontium 90, Americium 241, among others), some of which are more difficult to measure on ordinary and less sensitive Geiger counters and which have been distributed and continue to circulate across a wide area. It also ignores other organ diseases, unusual chronic illnesses and premature births and stillbirths, voluntary terminations and birth deformities occurring in and beyond Fukushima prefecture.

In addition to the control of relevant data, the government has used other methods to encourage residents to stay in radiation-contaminated areas. In May 2011, Dr Yamashita Shunichi, then co-director of Fukushima Medical University and the Fukushima Health Management Survey and a specialist from Nagasaki on radiation illness in Chernobyl, declared there was a 1 in 1 million chance of children getting any kind of cancer from radiation and there would be negligible health damage from radiation below 100 microSv/h, and prescribed smiling as an aid to living with radiation to a public audience in Fukushima.[53]

Dr Yamashita is only one among a host of politicians, bureaucrats, experts and advertising and media consultants who support the post-3.11 safety mantra of *anshin* (secure 安心), *anzen* (safe 安全), *fukkō* (recovery 復興). Through public meetings, media channels, education manuals and workshops,[54] local citizens in Fukushima Prefecture were inundated with optimistic and reassuring messages, also known as 'risk communication discourse', and central and prefectural government-sponsored 'health seminars' encouraging a 'practical radiation protection culture' in which they have been urged to take responsibility (*jiko sekinin* 自己責任) for their own health (e.g. wearing glass badges, self-monitoring, avoiding hotspots), form bonds of solidarity (*kizuna* 絆) with their community and participate in the great reconstruction (*fukkatsu* 復活) for the revitalisation of a resilient nation (*kyōjinka kokka* 強靱化国家) as a whole. To counteract baseless rumours (*ryūgen higo* 流言蜚語) and the negative impact of gossip (*fūhyō higai* 風評被害) of radiation in contaminated

---

53 See 'Unbelievable Comment by Mr. Yamashita', 8 May 2011, accessed 15 August 2015, www.youtube.com/watch?v=UOgaBUDFeb4&feature=related. Another physician, Dr Arai from Asahi Nairyō Clinic, Kōriyama, who subscribes to the hormesis theory, augmented the description of 'low level radiation' (up to 50 mSv/y) as 'an angel's smile', while claiming that food with small amounts of radiation would attract a premium, and that Fukushima would become the number one health land in the country. See Asahi Nairyō Clinic, December 2012, e.oisyasan.ne.jp/asahi-cl/topics/radi.html.

54 Such as 'Public Opinion Policy Related to Nuclear Power' by JAERO (Japan Atomic Energy Research Organisation/Nihon Genshiryoku Bunka Zaidan); 'The Nuclear Power Story' by the Ministry of Education (MEXT); 'Nuclear Fuel Cycle lectures' by the Ministry of Finance (MoF).

Fukushima produce, citizens in and beyond Fukushima Prefecture, and even non-citizens, have been encouraged to buy and consume Fukushima produce as an expression of moral and economic support (through slogans such as '*Ganbare Fukushima!*' がんばれ福島!). At the same time, to reduce 'radiophobia' and anxiety, while focusing on the psychological impact from stress, health risks from radiation exposures have been trivialised and/or normalised for the general public.[55]

This approach is backed up by international nuclear-related agencies. As stipulated on 28 May 1959 in the 'WHA12-40' agreement, the WHO is mandated to report all data on health effects from radiation exposures to the IAEA, which controls publication. On no other medical health issue is the WHO required to defer publication responsibilities to another institution. Scientific expertise at the IAEA primarily lies in nuclear physics (radiology and dosimetry) as opposed to epidemiology and medical expertise on radiation effects to living tissue. The IAEA and its related UN bodies are informed by the International Commission of Radiation Protection (ICRP) recommendations on radiation dose assessments derived from the Atomic Bomb Casualty Commission/Radiation Exposure Research Foundation (ABCC/RERF) lifetime studies of *hibakusha* (被爆者) in Hiroshima and Nagasaki. This dosimetry is primarily based on an average exposure of a 20–30-year-old 'reference man' (originally modelled on a US Army soldier) mainly to short-term one-off acute gamma radiation exposure. While it recommends caution, the ICRP continues to maintain that anything below 100 mSv/y is a 'low dose' and that the risk of 'stochastic effects' are yet to be scientifically proven beyond doubt. Within this framework, it would seem reasonable to raise the level from 1 to 20 mSv/y.

The ABCC/RERF studies ignored, however, biological contingencies of sex, age, constitution, other health conditions and the variegated effects (including complicating chemical and metabolic dynamics)

---

55   MEXT booklets designed for students at all levels assert that (a one-time external exposure dose) below 100 mSv/y is negligible; natural and man-made radiation have the same effect; cancer has multiple causes and is difficult to trace; and that radioactive materials are no longer harmful after they bond with soil. See www.mext.go.jp/b_menu/shuppan/sonota/attach/1313004.htm. Further, Kataoka Terumi testified that public health leaflets in Kōriyama were distributed stating, 'In the future, one in two children in your class will have a cancer, and ten of them will die', as part of a program to familiarise children to the realities of cancer. Kataoka reports that the leaflets were subsequently withdrawn from circulation due to a negative public response.' Association Franco-Japonaise (ASUKA), *Témoignages No.1* [Statements by *Fukushima genpatsu kokuso-dan*] (2014): 7. For a copy contact: www.asuka-association.org/contact/.

from both internal and external exposures to different radionuclides of all types ('low level' internal radiation is at least 20 times greater). After Chernobyl, the WHO and IAEA used the ICRP dose model to conclude that there were up to 56 deaths of 'liquidators' (clean-up workers) from acute radiation sickness and 4,000 additional cancers;[56] and that environmental effects such as lifestyle (i.e. parental alcoholism, smoking) and 'radiophobia' (stress and depression) contributed to excess illnesses in 80 per cent of adult cases. It also concluded that no harm would be received by the 2 million farmers and more than 500,000 children who continued living in radioactive areas in Belarus.

Nevertheless, it is no longer possible to ignore a significant body of research, including 20 years of scientific studies compiled in Belarus and Ukraine that show serious depopulation, ongoing illnesses and state decline.[57] These studies have found genetic effects within a radius of 250–300 km from Chernobyl, while children's health in Belarus has declined from a situation where 80 per cent of the child population was healthy prior to the Chernobyl disaster to a situation post-Chernobyl where only 20 per cent are healthy.[58] In 1995, Professor Nechaev from the Ministry of Health and Medical Industry (Moscow) stated that 2.5 million people were irradiated from Chernobyl in the Russian Federation, the Ukrainian Prime Minister Marchuk stated that 3.1 million had been exposed to Chernobyl radiation and Professor Okeanov from Belarus observed a spike in leukaemia and cancers among liquidators in Gomel relative to duration of exposure.[59] By 2001, of 800,000 healthy Russian and Ukrainian liquidators (with an average age of 33 years) sent to decontaminate, isolate and stabilise the

---

56    The Chernobyl Forum, 'Health effects of the Chernobyl accident and special health care programmes', Vienna, April (2006): 113, accessed July 2015, www.who.int/ionizing_radiation/chernobyl/WHO%20Report%20on%20Chernobyl%20Health%20Effects%20July%2006.pdf.

57    See Alexey Yablokov, Vassili Nesterenko, Alexey Nesterenko, *Chernobyl: Consequences of the Catastrophe for People and the Environment* (New York: Annals of the New York Academy of Sciences, 2009). This was recognised by President of the Academy of Sciences in Belarus in December 1999, and confirmed in April 2000 by Vice–Minister of Health of Belarus at a parliamentary hearing about the Chernobyl disaster. See also Wladimir Tchertkoff, 'The Crime of Chernobyl – a Model for Fukushima', *IndependentWHO* [April 2013], 5 February 2014, independentwho.org/en/2014/02/05/chernobyl-model-fukushima/. Accessed 10 July 2015.

58    Statement from the President of the Academy of Sciences in Belarus, in December 1999, confirmed by the Vice-Minister of Health of Belarus at a parliamentary hearing about the consequences of the Chernobyl disaster, in April 2000. See Tchertkoff, 'The Crime of Chernobyl', 2014.

59    Nechaev and Okeanov presented at the 1995 WHO-Geneva Conference, the Proceedings of which have remained inaccessible to the public. See Michel Fernex, 'The Chernobyl Catastrophe and Health', 3 May (2000): 5, accessed 1 July 2015, independentwho.org/media/documents_autres/michel_fernex_the_chernobyl_catastrophe_and_health_03may2000_en.pdf.

reactor, 10 per cent had died and 30 per cent were disabled. By 2009, 120,000 liquidators had died, and an epidemic of chronic illness and genetic and perigenetic damage in nuclear workers' descendants appeared (this is predicted to increase over subsequent generations).[60] The full extent of the damage will not be understood until the fifth generation of descendants. By the mid-2000s, 985,000 additional deaths between 1986 and 2004 across Europe were estimated as a direct result from radiation exposure from Chernobyl.[61]

Given this background of regulatory capture and radical discrepancies in methods and estimates prior to the Fukushima disaster, it is less surprising that there may be a process of regulatory capture and cover up underway in response to Fukushima Daiichi. In December 2011, a Cabinet Office Working Group chaired by RERF chairman Nagataki Shigenobu consisted of 18 Japanese ICRP members (including Niwa Otsura and Yamashita Shunichi). The experts invited Mr Jacques Lochard to provide external expertise. Lochard is an economist, ICRP member, Director of the Center of Studies on the Evaluation of Protection in the Nuclear Field (CEPN) (funded by Electricité de France EDF), and co-director of the CORE-ETHOS Programme in Chernobyl (1996–1998).

The CORE (Cooperation and Rehabilitation in the Belarusian territories contaminated by Chernobyl) Programme organised a takeover of radioprotection health centres in Ukraine and Belarus, and delayed a health audit beyond five years while it produced the ETHOS report outlining a 'sustainable system of post-radiological accident management for France and the European Union'.[62] While local scientists (led by Yuri Bandazhevsky and Vassili Nesterenko) recommended whole body counts (WBC) for each child (in which 50,000 children would be tested with

60    R. I. Goncharova and N. I. Ryabokon, 'Dynamics of Gamma-emitter Content Level in Many Generations of Wild Rodents in Contaminated Areas of Belarus', Radiobiological Consequences of Nuclear Accidents 2nd International Conference, 25–26 October 1994.

61    Yablokov et al., *Chernobyl*, 210.

62    ETHOS and CORE are products of the French nuclear industry, financed through Centre d'étude sur l'Evaluation de la Protection dans le domaine Nucléaire (CEPN), formed in 1976 by EDF, the Autorité de Sureté Nucléaire (ASN) and/or the Commissariat à l'Énergie Atomique et aux Énergies Alternatives (CEA). The ETHOS co-directors (M. Henry Ollagnon, l'Institut National d'Agronomie Paris-Grignon; Gilles Hériard-Dubreuil, Mutadis Consultants; Jacques Lochard, CEPN) initiated the European CORE program, with the support of the Chernobyl Committee of the Government of Belarus, the United Nations Development Programme, French and German embassies, the European Commission, the Swiss Agency for Development and Cooperation of Switzerland, United Nations Educational, Scientific and Cultural Organization (UNESCO), the World Bank and four districts of Belarus.

spectrometers), food measurement, dietary radioprotection (prophylaxis through adsorbents) and resettlement of those exposed to radiation over 1 mSv/y,[63] the ETHOS manual concluded that in a similar radiological event in western Europe, resettlement would be restricted to those exposed to more than 100 mSv/y. By factoring in 'social, economic and political' costs, ETHOS proposed ways for populations to live with radiation, and identified psychosomatic illnesses derived from 'stress' based on unfounded fears (i.e. 'radiophobia') of radiation as the greatest health risk. After a prolonged delay, in 1996 the IAEA and WHO finally settled on 5 mSv/y as the mandatory evacuation limit in a compromise between the Soviet (1 mSv/y) and western European (100 mSv/y) recommendations after Chernobyl.[64] These agencies targeted 'alarmist' reports (including social protests) as encouraging 'radiophobia', stressing the psychological impacts of radiological events.

In post-3.11 Japan, the Japanese Cabinet Office Working Group[65] reinforced the IAEA dosimetry regime by reiterating that cancers only emerge four to five years after exposure, that increases in cancers within

63   Professor Vassili Nesterenko (Institute of Nuclear Energy of the Academy of Sciences of Belarus) was removed from his post after demanding a 100 km mandatory evacuation zone in July 1987. He formed the Institute of Radiation Safety (Belrad) and organised 370 radiological monitoring centres in contaminated villages in Belarus to train doctors, teachers, nurses, parents and children in radioprotection ecanthropogammetric measures, pectin diets and information. Dr Yuri Bandazhevsky (Gomel Medical Institute) identified the etiology of low-level radiation impacts on organs and tissues. In 1994, Nesterenko and Bandazhevsky worked in the contaminated territories. Bandazhevsky found above 50 Bq/kg would lead to irreversible lesions to vital organs. From 1996, Belrad Institute measured internal contamination with spectrometers in the villages and Nesterenko used apple pectin as an absorbent of Cs137. This reduced Cs137 in the child's body by 60–70 per cent. See Tchertkoff, 'The Crime of Chernobyl', 2014.
64   IAEA Conference, 'One Decade after Chernobyl: Summing up the Consequences of the Accident', 8–13 April 1996, www-pub.iaea.org/mtcd/publications/pdf/te_964v1_prn.pdf.
65   Nagataki stated that 99.8 per cent of 1,080 children measured in March 2011 were under 5 mSv and nobody exceeded 50 mSv. MoE Expert Group members include Nagataki Shigenobu—Emeritus Professor at Nagasaki University, former chairman of Radiation Effects Research Foundation, mentor of Yamashita Shunichi, chair of Cabinet Office Working Group; Niwa Otsura—Cabinet Office Working Group 2011, retired Kyoto University Professor (molecular biology and radiation biology), Special Professor at Fukushima Medical University, WHO Expert Group, editor *Health Risk Assessment from the Nuclear Accident after the 2011 Great East Japan Earthquake and Tsunami, Based on a Preliminary Dose Estimation* (February 2013), ICRP member, funded by Federation of Electric Power Companies of Japan (*Denjirenkai*), advocate of one-tenth of WHO estimates; Endo Keigo—Kyoto College of Medical Science president; Ban Nobuhiko and Honma Toshimitsu—2013 UNSCEAR Fukushima report authors; Sasaki Yasuhito—former Expert Group chairman.

this period could not be attributable to the accident,[66] and that illnesses in people exposed to radiation below 100 mSv/y could be concealed by other carcinogenic effects and other factors (rendering them statistically negligible), and thus could not be proven to be radiation related. In fact, in July 2014, Nagataki Shigenobu declared that it would be 'disastrous to conclude [from the survey findings] an increase in thyroid cancer' was due to radiation exposure.[67] Consequently, privileging a government study of the thyroid glands of 1,080 children in late March 2011 (a very small sample), Nagataki claimed that almost none had exceeded 50 mSv for internal exposure and that 99.8 per cent of the population in Fukushima Prefecture could be estimated to have received an external dose below 5 mSv. Nagataki dismissed the need for further medical screenings, regular check-ups or internal radiation tests (whole body counter, urine and blood tests) at hospitals and clinics in Fukushima Prefecture or elsewhere.

Instead, the government appears to have adopted the ETHOS model: 'improving' community life in radiation-contaminated areas through local education and support groups; encouraging proactive self-responsibility (i.e. self-monitoring with government monitors) for children and parents (including pregnant women); stamping out 'stigma' attached to 'Fukushima' residents, the area and its produce while stigmatising 'radiophobia'; and encouraging evacuees' return after and even prior to 'decontamination'.[68]

---

66   This contradicts Ban Nobuhiko's finding on leukaemia one to two years after irradiation of lab mice, www.oita-nhs.ac.jp/member/cat5_top/cat193/cat351/post_20.html; www.labome.org/expert/japan/oita/ban/nobuhiko-ban-572788.html. Leukaemia and thyroid tumours within one or two years was found in Belarus. See International Physicians for the Prevention of Nuclear War (IPPNW), *Health Effects of Chernobyl: 25 years after the Reactor Disaster*, April 2011, www.chernobylcongress.org/fileadmin/user_upload/pdfs/chernob_report_2011_en_web.pdf. Accessed March 2015.
67   Hiranuma Yuri, 'Questioning the Very Status of the Ministry of the Environment Expert Meeting Regarding the Status of Disaster Victims' Health Management', *Fukushima Voice* version 2e, 3 August 2014, fukushimavoice-eng2.blogspot.com.au/2014/08/questioning-very-status-of-ministry-of.html; 'Genpatsu jiko go no kenkō shiji de gyakusō: Kankyō shō' no Senmonka kaigi', *Tokyo Shimbun*, 22 July 2014, www.tokyo-np.co.jp/article/tokuho/list/CK2014072202000168.html.
68   See, Yuri Oiwa, 'NRA Plan to Implement Use of Personal Dosimeters No Easy Task', *Asahi Shimbun*, 21 November 2013, ajw.asahi.com/article/0311disaster/fukushima/AJ201311210067. Since the time of writing, this link is no longer available. For verification, an online mirror link can be found at: www.fukushima-is-still-news.com/article-personal-dosimeters-easier-said-than-done-121232568.html.

By September 2015, an officially estimated 3,407 people (up from 3,194 the previous year) had died from 'effects related to the great east Japan earthquake' (*Daishinsai kanren shi* 大震災関連死).[69] In March 2015, about 1,870 deaths of those who had evacuated due to the overall disaster were deemed to have been from ill-health and suicide. By March 2016, this had increased to 2,208 deaths, while 1,386 deaths were estimated to have been caused by effects related specifically to the nuclear disaster (*genpatsu kanren shi*).[70] Further, a statistically significant 15 per cent drop in live births in Fukushima Prefecture in December 2011, and a 20 per cent spike in infant mortality were found to have been caused mainly by internal radiation from the consumption of contaminated food.[71] Nor do statistics on abortions seem to have been factored into official accounts. As the statistics are so temporally specific, anxiety (disruption, evacuation) is unlikely to have been the major factor as the spikes would be more prolonged. It has also been extrapolated from the conservative UNSCEAR 2013 estimate of a 48,000 person Sv collective dose, that another 5,000 are expected to die from future cancers in Japan (and larger numbers to become ill).[72] Using the Tondel model, however, the European Commission on Radiation Risk (ECRR), in contrast to the ICRP dose model, which estimates 2,838 excess cancers within 100 km radius over 50 years excluding internal radiation, estimated that 103,000 excess cancers within 100 km would be diagnosed within 10 years and 200,000 in the next 50 years.[73]

69    See GoJ, Reconstruction Agency, 25 December 2015, www.reconstruction.go.jp/topics/main-cat2/sub-cat2-6/20151225_kanrenshi.pdf. See also, www.reconstruction.go.jp/topics/main-cat2/sub-cat2-1/20141226_kanrenshi.pdf; Editors, 'Death toll grows in 3/11 aftermath', *Japan Times*, 5 March 2015, www.japantimes.co.jp/news/2015/03/15/national/death-toll-grows-in-311-aftermath/.
70    'Genpatsu kanren shi 1368 nin ni honshi shūkei 1 nen de 136 ninzō', *Tokyo Shimbun*, 6 March 2016, www.tokyo-np.co.jp/article/national/list/201603/CK2016030602000127.html.
71    Alfred Körblein, 'Increased Infant Mortality and Decline in Birth Rate after Fukushima', 6 February 2014, accessed 15 June 2015, www.strahlentelex.de/Koerblein_infant%20mortality%20after%20Fukushima.pdf; Alfred Körblein, 'Decline of Live Births Nine Months after Fukushima', February (2016), www.researchgate.net/publication/292540026_Decline_of_live_births_in_Japan_nine_months_after_Fukushima; Alfred Köblein, 'Perinatal mortality after the Fukushima accident', February 2016, www.researchgate.net/publication/291818329_Perinatal_mortality_after_the_Fukushima_accident.
72    Ian Fairlie, 'Summing up the Effects of the Fukushima Nuclear Disaster', August 2015, www.ianfairlie.org/wp-content/uploads/2015/08/Summing-up-the-Effects-of-the-Fukushima-Nuclear-Disaster-10.pdf. Accessed August 2015.
73    Chris Busby, 'The Health Outcome of the Fukushima Catastrophe: Initial Analysis from Risk Model of the European Committee on Radiation Risk (ECRR)', 30 March 2011, *Green Audit*, Occasional Paper, presented at ECRR/ GSRP conference, Charite Hospital Berlin, July 2011.

As with informal and formal nuclear workers, if these deaths were officially recognised as being tied to radiation from Fukushima Daiichi, then the family of the deceased as main income earner would be eligible for a 5 million yen 'consolation' payment (half for others). Further, it would also imply the need for stricter radiological protection standards and a greater number of permanent evacuations and official health treatment program that would effectively limit the so-called 'benefits' associated with nuclear power generation.[74] In short, it is not surprising that the overwhelming emphasis in scientific studies and public reports has been placed on psychological impacts rather than disease and deaths (particularly but not limited to nuclear workers and children) and the argumentation over the significance of thyroid cancers. The same pattern occurred after Chernobyl and Three Mile Island.

## Local Responses to State–Corporate Suppression and Lack of Public Health Protection

Faced with the post-3.11 reality of government (and corporate) policy that protects economic and security interests over public health and well-being, the majority of the 2 million inhabitants of Fukushima Prefecture are either unconscious of or have been encouraged to accept living with radioactive contamination. People dry their clothes outside, drink local tap water and consume local food, swim in outdoor pools and the ocean, consume and sell their own produce or catches. Financial pressure after 3.11 as well as the persistent danger of social marginalisation has made it more difficult to take precautionary measures (i.e. permanent relocation, dual accommodation, importing food and water) and develop and share counter-narratives to the official message. Nevertheless, some continue to conceal their anxiety beneath a mask of superficial calm.

As Fukushima city resident Shiina Chieko observed, the majority of people seem to have adopted denial as a way to excise the present danger from their consciousness. Her sister-in-law, for example, ignored her son's 'continuous nosebleeds', while her mother had decided that the community must endure by pretending that things were no different from

---

74  See for example, the ICRP 2005 draft recommendations, www.icrp.org/docs/2005_recs_ CONSULTATION_Draft1a.pdf.

pre-3.11 conditions.[75] Unlike the claim that risk is evenly distributed, it is likely that greater risk is borne by those who eat processed foods from family restaurants and convenience stores, as well as infants, children and young women who are disproportionately vulnerable to internal radiation exposures. Most mothers, then, have an added burden to shield their children while maintaining a positive front in their family and community.

Some, such as Yokota Asami (40 years old), a small business owner and mother from Kōriyama (60 km from FDNPS), demonstrated initiative in voluntarily evacuating her family. She decided to return (wearing goggles and a mask, she joked) in September 2011 when her son's regular and continuous nosebleeds (in 30-minute spells) subsided. The Yokotas found themselves the victims of bullying when they called attention to radiation dangers, and were labelled non-nationals (*hikokumin* 非国民) who had betrayed reconstruction efforts. Her son was the only one to put up his hand when he was asked along with 300 fellow junior high school students if he objected to eating locally produced school lunches. He also chose not to participate in outdoor exercise classes and to go on respite trips instead. When it came time to take the high school entrance exam, he was told by the school principal that those who took breaks could not pass. He took the exam and failed. When he asked to see his results he found that he had, in fact, enough points to pass (the cut-off was 156 while he received 198 out of 250 points). The Yokotas decided that it was better to be a 'non-national' and protect one's health. Their son moved to live in Sapporo.[76]

In March 2015, Asami reported that doctors undertook paediatric thyroid operations while denying any correlation (*inga kankei* 因果 関係) with radiation exposures. They also urged their patients to keep their thyroid cancer a secret to enhance their employment or marriage prospects, although it would be difficult to conceal the post-operation scar.[77] Yokota also indicated she knew of students having sudden heart attacks and developing leukaemia and other illnesses.[78]

---

75    Shiina Chieko, interview with the author, digital audio recording, 23 March 2015.
76    Yokota Asami, interview with the author, digital audio recording, 6 February 2015.
77    See Editor, 'Fukushima Children's Thyroid Examination: How Shunichi Yamashita Would like Doctors to Deal with the Results', *Fukushima Voice*, 4 May 2012, fukushimavoice-eng.blogspot.com. au/2012/05/fukushima-childrens-thyroid-examination.html. Accessed 12 June 2015.
78    Yokota Asami, interview with the author, digital audio recording, 6 February 2015.

This seems to be supported by Mr Ōkoshi, a Fukushima city resident, whose two daughters experienced stillbirths after 3.11. While Ōkoshi found that doctors have regularly advised women in the area to abort after 3.11, presumably to avoid miscarriages and defects, they do not discuss direct causes. He also observed regular illnesses experienced by many of his friends, and some sudden deaths. After a friend (62 years old) started saying strange things, he was diagnosed with brain dysfunction. He died quickly. Another friend (53 years old) was advised by a doctor to monitor a polyp in her breast. When she sought second opinions, she discovered she had accumulated an internal dose of 22 mSv and had a rapidly developing liver cancer. She also died quickly.[79] There are many more such stories that are being actively ignored by the authorities. As Shiina put it, 'we're getting leukaemia and cataracts and we die suddenly. The TEPCO registrar has been inundated with complaints'.[80]

While radiation contamination is clearly a health and environmental issue, state-corporate methods deployed by executives to protect (transnational) financial, industry and security interests and assets also make it a political issue.[81] As things do not change by themselves, rather than turning one's frustration inward in self-blame, turning to prayer or deceiving oneself into returning to pre-3.11 lifeways in contaminated areas, Shiina states that people, particularly those most affected, must develop political consciousness.

To achieve this ambitious objective is not as complicated as it might sound. Nishiyama Chikako (60 years old), for example, returned to Kawauchi village to run for the local assembly after the mandatory order was lifted in December 2011. She found, as she commented in her blog, a link between TEPCO and the tripling of the Kawauchi budget post-3.11. Subsequently, she reported that her blog was shut down by unknown hackers on several occasions.[82]

This sort of information and communication control appears to be widespread. After 3.11, the central government hired advertising companies Dentsū and Hakuhōdō (formerly McCann Ericson Hakuhodo) to run a 'public acceptance' campaign. Young teams were dispatched nationwide to conduct 'public opinion guidance' (*yoron yūdō* 世論誘導).

---

79    Mr Ōkoshi, interview with the author, digital audio recording, 24 March 2015.
80    Shiina Chieko, interview with the author, digital audio recording, 23 March 2015.
81    Shiina Chieko, interview with the author, 23 March 2015.
82    Nishiyama Chikako, interview with the author, digital audio recording, 24 March 2015.

The teams consisted of casual labour (earning 2,000–4,000 yen per hour) hired under a confidentiality clause (*shuhi gimu* 守秘義務) to manipulate information (*jōhō kōsaku* 情報工作) and harass internet users.[83]

Media professionals have been subjected to similar tactics. The Asahi TV journalist Iwaji Masaki (Hōdō Station), one of the few mainstream journalists covering the Fukushima Daiichi nuclear accident in depth, for example, was intimidated by police for interviewing (December 2012) informal nuclear workers who showed shoddy decontamination practices that entailed contaminated waste disposal rather than removal and the mother of a child with thyroid cancer. Airing the program was delayed until August 2013. Before he could complete his planned segments on the US$1 billion class action for compensation for unusual and serious illnesses filed against TEPCO, General Electric, Hitachi and Tōshiba in 2015 by sailors from the USS *Ronald Reagan* (which provided assistance quickly after the disaster, and among whose crew 250 were ill and three had died),[84] on 29 September 2013, Iwaji was reportedly found dead in his apartment (having suffered carbon monoxide poisoning in a sealed room as he slept). Much speculation followed on social media, including both plausible reasons for suicide and testimonies from friends that knew him well that Iwaji himself stated he would never commit suicide, but the story was conspicuously ignored by major news channels.[85]

The former mayor of Futaba village Idogawa Katsuichi was harassed on social media for calling attention to illnesses and for the resettlement of pregnant women and children. When Kariya Tetsu characterised Idogawa in his popular manga series (*Oishinbo* 美味しんぼ), and depicted the manga's main character as suffering from nosebleeds after visiting Fukushima, Kariya's editors shut the series down following accusations of 'spreading rumours' from some readers, media commentators and high-

---

83  'Netto kōsaku-in no seitai (Truth About Net Managers)', 16 September 2014, ameblo. jp/64152966/entry-11925550749.html. Accessed 1 August 2015.

84  The class action also intends to prove that up to 70,000 American citizens were exposed to radiation from Fukushima Daiichi. See Charles Bonner, lawyer for the USS Ronald Reagan class action plaintiffs, www.youtube.com/watch?v=V0zGbG2dTvo.

85  See non-government organisation founder of Social Uplift and journalist, and personal friend of Iwaji, Beverly Findlay-Kaneko at 12–17.45 mins. on *Nuclear Hotseat*, 16 September 2014, nuclearhotseat.com/2014/09/13/nuclear-hotseat-169-beverly-findlay-kaneko-on-journalist-iwajis-death-karl-grossman-on-nukes-in-space/. See also Beverly Kaneko-Findlay, 'Update on Fukushima', 14 September 2014, www.youtube.com/watch?v=xm2oibl00ie. See also Imanishi Noriyuki, 'Asahi TV Rage: Big Battle with Police at the Shoddy Decontamination Interview Site', 21 December 2013, www.imanishinoriyuki.jp/archives/35811450.html.

level politicians. Similarly, Takenouchi Mari, a freelance journalist and mother who evacuated from Fukushima in 2011, received thousands of slanderous messages and threats to her two-year-old son and her property after criticising the co-founder of Fukushima ETHOS on her blog in mid-2012. She too reported that her internet account was suspended and her request for a police investigation ignored. She was counter-sued for harassment and subjected to a criminal investigation and civil law suit.[86]

Among the activists who have been arrested for anti-nuclear protests, the academic Shimoji Masaki of Hannan University (9 December 2012) was arrested by Osaka Prefectural Police and charged with 'violating the Railway Operation Act' for walking through an Osaka station concourse while participating in a demonstration against radioactive waste incineration (17 October 2012). Shimoji had reiterated that residents, due to radioactive incineration (which was due to commence in Osaka in February 2013), would be forced to bear the burden of air, food and water contamination.[87]

Despite such obstacles to developing a political consciousness as well as the obvious difficulties in permanently resetting large populations, it has been not only evacuees who have had to think about their fundamental life priorities after the Fukushima Daiichi nuclear distaster. Some have adopted real (not only psychological) self-protection mechanisms. The voluntary Fukushima Collective Health Clinic (*Fukushima Kyōdō Shinryōjo* 福島共同診療所), for example, is founded on three principles: respite (*hoyō* 保養), treatment (*shinryō* 診療) and healing (*iryō* 医療). Co-founder Dr Sugii, advocates a return to the 1 mSv/y limit, and seeks to inform those who for whatever reason cannot move from contaminated areas in Fukushima Prefecture.[88] This is modelled on Belrad, the independent health clinic in Belarus run by Alexey Nesterenko, which prioritises knowledge, safety and open information on radiation and its health impacts.

86    Takenouchi Mari, '2nd Consultation to Kyoto Bar', April 2014, accessed 1 July 2015, savekidsjapan.blogspot.jp/2014/04/2nd-consulation-to-kyoto-bar.html.

87    Shimoji Masaki, 'Demand for the immediate and unconditional release of Associate Prof. Masaki Shimoji', Civic Activity – an Organization Supporting Citizens Opposing Spread of Radiation, 15 December 2012, keepcivicactivity.jimdo.com/english/. See also, 'Press Conference for the Apology and Immediate Release of Professor Masaki Shimoji and other People Unjustly Arrested for Opposing Debris Incineration in Osaka', 15 December 2012, iwj.co.jp/wj/open/archives/46334; 'Statement from Mr. Shimoji during unjust detention', 13 December 2012, goo.ne.jp/garekitaiho1113/e/79c68fd4e86da4ec02b2e01a5188052b.

88    Dr Sugii, interview with the author, digital audio recording, 24 March 2015.

To counteract the misinformation residents were exposed to post-Chernobyl, over time and with limited resources, Belrad and other organisations have disseminated information and organised respite trips for children in affected areas. In 2015, for example, subsidised respite trips were organised for 50,000 children, and results have shown that over two continuous years of respite those who accumulated 25–35 Bq/kg had reduced the amount to 0 Bq/kg. Unlike the flat limit of 100 Bq/kg of Caesium in food in Japan (50 Bq/kg for milk and infant foods, 10 Bq/kg for drinking water), Belrad recommends an internal radiation limit of 10–30 Bq/kg in the body (although it advises below 10 Bq for infants to avoid lesions and heart irregularities).[89] It should be noted that these limits do not guarantee safety against the effects of repeating internal radiation exposure from consuming contaminated foods, which is relative to the length of time the radiation remains and its location in the body.

While some communities, such as the town of Aketo in Tanohama, Iwate Prefecture, have struggled to block the siting of nuclear waste storage facilities,[90] others are also organising to reduce radio-accumulation in their children through respite trips,[91] as well as concentrating on indoor activities, measuring hotspots and decontaminating public areas and pathways, pooling funds for expensive spectrometers to monitor internal exposure and food and water, incorporating dietary radioprotection, as well as finding ways to reduce anxiety.

Many local farmers cannot admit the already near-permanent damage to their land (which may continue for hundreds of years) because it would imply the devaluation of their property and produce as well as threatening their ancestral ties to the land, commitments and future plans. While many are keenly aware of their responsibilities, the push by the Fukushima and central governments to identify and gain access to markets for produce from irradiated areas would make it easier to overlook uncomfortable factors. Some have argued that given the reassurances of safety from the highest authorities, these offical figures should therefore relocate to

---

89    See Kamanaka Hitomi, *Canon Dayori*, vol. 4 (2015) (Independent DVD documentary, dir. Kamanaka Hitomi).

90    Toshihide Ueda, 'Women in Tohoku Village Refused to Play Host to Nuclear Plant', *Asahi Shimbun*, 2 September 2015, ajw.asahi.com/article/views/column/aj201509020011. Since the time of writing, this link is no longer available. For verification, an online mirror link can be found at: www.fukushima-is-still-news.com/2015/09/tanohata-women-against-nukes.html.

91    Sasaki Michinori (38 years old) in *Fukushima Radiation*, 848.

contaminated areas and consume these products regularly. Despite the fairness of this statement, a more utilitarian logic has prevailed. In the name of reconstruction and revitalisation of Fukushima and the nation, the dilution of Fukushima produce with unirradiated produce to return measurements just under the required limits, radiation spikes in soil and food or the mutation of plants as Caesium replaces potassium (K40), for example, tend to be minimised. In this climate, the distribution and relabelling of Fukushima produce for urban and international markets (i.e. in a black market of cut-price bulk produce picked up by *yakuza* and other brokers) is likely to continue.

To date, the majority of evacuees have refused to return to (de)contaminated areas. Some claim they are yet to receive accurate information to justify it. Independent specialists such as Hosokawa Kōmei (Citizens' Commission on Nuclear Energy), who develops models for transition to renewable alternatives, anticipate an increase in evacuee populations as they predict increased resettlement of Fukushima residents over 20–30 years.[92] As some evacuees recognise the potential for second or third Fukushimas, they have sought to strengthen their collective identities and rights. Through local organisation and alternative life practices, whether in micro-scale ecovillages and transition towns[93] with communal occupancies and squats, parallel currencies and local exchange systems (roughly 70 substantive projects), organic food co-ops, self-sufficient energy systems, local production and recycling, carpools and free kindergartens, such groups are seeking to reconstruct and model core social priorities, focusing on clean food, health and community cooperation rather than the internalised and dreary competition for material accumulation.

Although the accountability of authorities with prior knowledge has yet to be properly investigated, one of the largest groups of collective legal actions to be mounted in Japanese history includes some 20 lawsuits by 10,000 plaintiffs. The *Fukushima genpatsu kokuso-dan* (Group of Plaintiffs for Criminal Prosecution 福島原発告訴団), formed on 20 April 2012, filed a criminal case (lodged 3 September 2013, Fukushima District Court) against 33 previous and present officers of TEPCO, government officials and medical experts for 'group irresponsibility' and the neglect of duty of care, environmental damage and harm to human health. Mutō Ruiko, one of the key plaintiffs, declared the main aim to be

---

92     Hosokawa Kōmei, interview with the author, digital audio recording, 30 March 2015.
93     Uno Saeko in Kamanaka, *Canon Dayori*.

symbolic: to publicly record injury, reclaim the victims' sense of agency and protect the next generation. In short, they were seeking recognition of wrong and harm done rather than primarily financial redress. This moderate aim was undoubtedly tempered by recognition of regulatory capture: those who were cavalier with safety procedures 'were now in charge of restarts; those responsible for the "safety" campaign were now in charge of the Health Survey; [there has been] no responsibility for the SPEEDI cover-up; and TEPCO is not being held responsible for [faulty] decontamination'.[94]

The judgement of this case was handed down at the Tokyo District Court on the same day as the announcement of Tokyo's successful Olympics bid (9 September 2013). The case was dismissed on the grounds that the disaster was beyond predictability (*sōteigai* 想定外), which made negligence hypothetical.[95] A citizens' panel (Committee for inquest of Prosecution) overturned the dismissal and renewed the claim against three TEPCO executives on 18 December 2013. They demanded, alongside a ruling of negligence against three former TEPCO executives, the inclusion of physical, economic, social and psychological harms: illness, paediatric underdevelopment (radiation exposures, excessive isolation indoors), financial losses (unemployment, loss in property value, rental costs of two homes, relocation, travel, etc.), family and community division, *ijime* (bullying いじめ) and stress. Many plaintiffs also claimed that their disrupted reliance upon nature,[96] as inviolable and precious,[97] should be recognised as harm. This too was dismissed and again a citizen's panel found against the three TEPCO executives.[98] In May 2015, 10 groups of plaintiffs formed a network named Hidanren (被弾連, Genpatsu Jiko Higaisha Dantai Renrakukai) comprising 20,000 people. The *Fukushima kokuso-dan* again made a claim to another citizens' panel, which found in

94    Mutō Ruiko, *Fukushima Radiation*, 268.

95    Hamada Kentaro, 'Fukushima Operator's Mounting Legal Woes to Fuel Nuclear Opposition', *Reuters*, 17 August 2015, uk.reuters.com/article/japan-nuclear-tepco-legal-idUKL3N10E2G820150817. Accessed 17 August 2015.

96    Asada Mariko (63 years old), 27 April 2012, *Fukushima Radiation*, 303.

97    Furukawa Machiko (64 years old), 1 June 2012, *Fukushima Radiation*, 400.

98    Editors, 'Indictment of TEPCO trio encourages Fukushima nuclear accident victims', *Asahi Shimbun*, 1 August 2015, ajw.asahi.com/article/0311disaster/fukushima/aj201508010032. Since the time of writing, this link is no longer available. For verification, an online mirror link can be found at: www.fukushima-is-still-news.com/2015/08/teoco-s-indictment-a-sense-of-justice.html. Yayoi Hitomi (54 years old), 11 May 2012, *Fukushima Radiation*, 343; Matsutaka Chiwaki (41 years old), 8 June 2014, *Fukushima Radiation*, 343.

July 2015 in favour of indicting the three TEPCO executives for trial.[99] In addition, a civil case filed in June 2015 by 4,000 plaintiffs from Iwaki seeking to prove negligence and not just harm sought to use previously withheld evidence to show fair warning of a 3.11-type scenario was given. This case focused the court on the operator's calculation of risk probability of a tsunami of that size and, rather than aiming at financial compensation, it sought to deter nuclear operators from future negligent practices if ruled in favour. In anticipation of out-of-court settlements, the Japanese Government increased the budget for compensation payments to 7 trillion yen (US$56 billion).

## Conclusions

From this discussion, it is evident how an advanced capitalist nation-state deploys a disposable population of informal labour to absorb the dangers inherent to the use of large-scale nuclear technologies and its private extractive and accumulation practices. Since its inception, nuclear power has been regarded by some as a symbol of Japan's postwar civilisational progress.[100] At the same time, the health of many thousands of people has been endangered in exposures to radiation while harms have been perpetrated upon local communities and nuclear workers and the environment more broadly as millions of people have been integrated within the centralising and concentrating dynamic of the transnational nuclear power industry.

On the mediated surface, Fukushima Daiichi has been used to prove to the world that a nuclear disaster of significant scale can be overcome and that people can survive and return to their normal lives. The government has concentrated on proving that it is safe for the Olympics, safe for tourism, safe to consume local produce, and safe to restart nuclear reactors (with 25 reactors expected to be supplying 20 per cent total energy by 2030). The neoliberal disaster model adopted, in which the state prioritises the profit of private corporations and their wealth-creating strategies while

---

99    For more on this see Norma Field, 'From Fukushima: To Despair Properly, to Find the Next Step', *The Asia-Pacific Journal: Japan Focus* 14, issue 11, no. 3, September 2016.

100   Kasai Yoshiyuki, Chairman of Central Japan Railways, described nuclear power as the nation's 'bloodstream of economic activity' and the only way to obtain sustainable baseload electric power. Kasai Yoshiyuki, 'Nuclear Energy is Indispensable for Japan's Future', November, Association of Japanese Institutes of Strategic Studies, Commentary No. 165, 2012, www.jiia.or.jp/en/commentary/201211/13-1.html. Accessed March 2014.

minimising public services and pursuing deregulation (e.g. of labour conditions), is indicated not only in the official intention to rebuild the local economy of Fukushima Prefecture, but also to expand, including through its transnational nuclear industry, Japan's financial, military and industrial sector after Fukushima. This reflects the priority given to both the interests of the utilities, banks and construction companies involved in the reconstruction program, and those of multinational corporations, foreign governments and international regulatory and financial institutions involved in this sector.

At the same time, the sovereign duty to protect the fundamental needs of the population and reflect majority will is secondary to these priorities. Unlike a natural disaster, owing to the materiality of radiation that continues to be dumped and vented into the environment, facilitating the return to pre-disaster conditions by forgetting and rebuilding communities in contaminated areas is a practice of illusion. Despite the claims of the Abe administration and other nuclear promoters, Japan's safety standards cannot adequately insure against the seismic activities or extreme weather events and their impacts on that archipelago. The authorities have furnished people with the means by which to normalise sickness and pathologise anxiety to justify the return to nuclear power reliance, while suppressing those who seek to resist it. The wealth of a healthy society and environment cannot be traded for the putative convenience and economic benefits of nuclear power generation as they are not comparable values. Official denial of the steady accumulation and exposure to 'low-level' internal radiation in a growing segment of the population only aggravates rather than protects the affected communities from the stresses related to Fukushima Daiichi. This inescapably leads to the need to address greater systemic problems that underlie such disasters.

As the previous organic life of village communities in contaminated zones is transformed into retirement villages and ad-hoc industrial hubs for temporary workers, this alienation from food, land, community, history, the human body and nature itself is a warning of the growing negative costs of the rapid expropriation and consumption of the planetary commons under a globalised system. Just as nuclear energy is not the solution to climate disruption caused by reliance on fossil fuels in a global capitalist economy, nor are radiation exposures comparable to everyday risks in modern society (i.e. transport accidents). If introducing 'mistakes' into the human genome is to be wagered against the daily conveniences of 'modern' life then this aspect of modernity is unsustainable. Although somewhat anthropocentric, it is a timely reminder that the Nobel Prize laureate (1946) Herman Müller stated in 1956, 'the genome is the most valuable treasure of humankind. It determines the life of our descendants and the harmonious development of the future generations'.[101]

And so we return to the basic problem that no nuclear reactor can operate without radiation-exposed labour, particularly of informal or irregular workers. If these populations refused to work and joined in support with a network of translocal groups on informal and alternative life projects for greater self-sufficiency such as micro-financing, small-scale and permaculture farming on non-contaminated land, renewable and decentralised energy production and distribution, or campaigns for greater distribution of wealth, better public education and health improvement, these communities and workers could be active agents in devising models that could eventually become viable for adaptation to larger human populations. This application at scale cannot come too soon in the present context of imminent exhaustion of the planetary commons from the systemic demands for relentless economic growth and accumulation of wealth and power for the few.

## Acknowledgement

Research for this chapter was made possible by the author's ARC DECRA project, 'Contaminated Life: 'Hibakusha' in Japan in the Nuclear Age' (DE130101746).

---

101  Herman Müller, 'Radiation and Heredity', *American Journal of Public Health* 54, no. 1 (1964): 42–50.

# 7

# National Subjects, Citizens and Refugees: Thoughts on the Politics of Survival, Violence and Mourning following the Sewol Ferry Disaster in South Korea

Cho (Han) Haejoang

## Introduction: One Incident That Made People Ask 'What is a State?'

Don't politics exist so that the people and the state do not engage in a naked clash for power? Don't politics lead two opposing parties, who would otherwise have no place to meet, to a common ground? Those currently in power, however, seem to have risen to their positions because of their lack of empathy and compassion. To avoid responsibility and climb even higher upon the rungs of power, they appear ready to step on more bodies… The most important thing, therefore, is the recovery of the political. However, this notion of political does not involve begging the state for power but making a public for ourselves. (Lee Gye-sam, social activist)[1]

---

1    Lee Gye-sam, 'Chamsi mŏmch'wŏsŏja' [Let's Stop for a Moment and Stand Up], *Hankyoreh Newspaper*, 8 May 2014.

Though I am not a particularly accomplished storyteller, I wish to share with you a story about a particular incident 事件, not accident 事故, that of the *Sewol* ferry in South Korea.[2] Since South Korea's founding as a nation in 1948, many incidents—both large and small—have occurred on the Korean peninsula. However, this incident, which took place in 2014, was special in prompting many of its citizens to ask, 'What is a state?' This incident has forced many intellectuals and grassroots activists to contemplate more deeply about society, nation and the future of humankind. Furthermore, it has compelled many 'ordinary' citizens to seriously address the issue of 'survival politics'. It also compelled many young people to ponder whether they should continue supporting this state or shift their allegiance to another one, by emigration for instance. This incident has not ended but is still unfolding.

After the devastating civil war of 1950–53, South Korea transformed itself into the world's 13th-largest economic power in the short period of 60 years. Though Koreans often pride themselves on this fact, with the Sewol Ferry Disaster they seem to realise that there is something they could have done better. They have come to realise not only that South Korea is a highly risky society, but also that their 'loving nation state' has been feeding the avaricious market, while caring little about its people. Observing the collapse of Korean society after the Asian financial crisis in 1997, I wrote an essay arguing that there are 'no citizens but only a national subjects' and 'no individuals but only families'.[3] The subjects that I found during the financial crisis and the ensuing recovery process were not the 'individual citizens (*simin* 市民)' but the 'national subjects (*kukmin* 國民)'. Rather than opening up a public/civilian space to discuss, reflect upon and resolve the crisis, the national subjects were desperately trying to overcome the crisis within the paradigm of the developmental authoritarian state. Moreover, they were doing so only as members of a family, not as individual citizens. There were few debates about the

---

2    There is an ongoing struggle between those who wish to view the *Sewol* tragedy as an unfortunate 'accident 事故' and those who wish to view it as a socially noteworthy historical 'incident 事件'. In a segment of the online forum of 'Slow News', started by some youth on 28 April 2014, they ask, 'Was Sewol tragedy an accident? Or an incident?' Warning against the irresponsible behaviour of the existing media outlets that have forsaken their duty of delivering accurate information, they declare that the *Sewol* tragedy was an 'incident' that has resulted from the 'overall failure of the system' within South Korea created by gross negligence. At the same time, they warn against the totalising perspectives implied by the term 'overall failure of the system', and, instead, emphasise the particular perspectives on this incident. plus.google.com/101120182737860073943/posts/c1QwKkc9riN.

3    Haejoang Cho, 'You are Entrapped in an Imaginary Well: The Formation of Subjectivity Within Compressed Development – a Feminist Critique of Modernity and Korean Culture', *Inter-Asia Cultural Studies* 1 (2000): 49–69.

widening social divisions within society or about changing the direction of modernisation. Around 1997, however, there was still a certain amount of trust and loyalty in the state and family. Now, it seems difficult to find these. In an Organisation for Economic Co-operation and Development (OECD) survey, only 24.8 per cent of Koreans stated that they trusted the government. The average for OECD countries was 42.8 per cent, while 82.2 per cent of the Swiss said they trusted the government. Moreover, with the rapid disintegration of families, growing class polarisation, rising youth unemployment, and skyrocketing elderly poverty and suicide, South Korea seems one of the most wretched among the OECD states. If anything, the Sewol Ferry Disaster seems to have crushed any remaining faith in the state. As articulated by activist Lee Gye-Sam above, it has resulted in a standoff between the state and the people. How can people recover trust in their nation when all sense of public sentiment and politics seems irretrievably lost, or replaced by acrimonious cynicism? Dwelling on this question, South Korean people/citizens have been undergoing a profound experience of learning through the agony and anxiety produced by the Sewol Ferry Disaster. Rather than lamenting this seemingly hopeless situation, I view it as a time and space for self-reflection where people can fundamentally retool their consciousness. That is, I believe that catastrophic events, in providing a profound sense of 'social catharsis', can transform into 'emancipatory catastrophism'.[4] As a Korean citizen and resident, who has, for the past two years, experienced the grief and depression of emancipatory catastrophism, I want to share some thoughts on modernity, violence and survival politics, and introduce terms such as 'citizens of compassion' and 'cosmopolitan refugees'.

# The Events Near Jindo Island, 16 April 2014

After crossing the line of unimaginable pain, P'aengmok Harbor has become a mortuary of corpses. When the bodies arrive from the shipwreck, an hour and ten minutes away, the medical examiners call them out one by one using not names but rather only numbers and other details – 'Female # 75, 168 centimeters, white short-sleeve shirt, black Adidas track pants, thin build, long hair, braces, birthmark on the right

---

4    Ulrich Beck, 'Haebangjŏk p'akuk: kŭgŏsŭn kihubyŏnhwa mit wihŏmsahoee ŏttŏhan ŭimiga itnŭnka?' [Emancipatory Catastrophism: What Does it Mean to Climate Change and Risk Society?], paper presented at The Seoul Conference 2014 with Professor Ulrich Beck Public Lecture. Organised by Joongmin Foundation for Social Theory, Center for Social Sciences of Seoul National University, 8 July 2014.

side of face.' When some parents, who, upon hearing these words, cry out, 'Oh, that's my child!' and run off to identify the child, everybody cries. Parents who are waiting for the corpse of their child, congratulate those who have recovered theirs. Parents, who have recovered their child's body, feel sorry because other parents are still waiting to recover their own. As you can see, it's an unimaginable scene of pain and suffering with parents who have recovered their dead child, parents who are still waiting for their missing children, and volunteers who are helping both groups of parents. (Ju Jin-u, from Green Review)[5]

The 'Sewol Ferry Accident' or 'Disaster' occurred at 8:48 am on 16 April 2014 when the *Sewol*, a passenger ferry carrying 476 passengers and cargo, capsized off South Korea's southern coast near Jindo County. Initially, in the breaking news of the accident, all passengers were reported to be alive and to have been rescued. After these initial reports were quickly discounted, the country sat down to seemingly endless hours of live coverage of the ferry slowly sinking to the bottom of the cold spring ocean. Passengers on this ferry were mostly students from Danwon High School in Ansan, Kyung-gi Province, on a long-awaited field trip. Of the 325 students in total, only 75 of them survived the accident.[6] Among the 15 teachers in charge, three survived. Two days later, one of the three surviving teachers, the head teacher—overcome with grief and guilt—hanged himself from a pine tree. As for the surviving families, they forged strong bonds of sorrow and grief as they shared scenes like the one described above at P'aengmok Harbor.

Amidst the sorrow and grief, there was hot, molten anger—anger on the part of surviving families who heard that the passengers on the ill-fated ferry were told, in an onboard announcement, to put on their life jackets and sit tight in their cabins until further notice. While the children who disobeyed the crew's instructions and came immediately onto the deck after the accident survived, those who obediently followed the announcement perished. Also enraging the surviving families and the public was the fact that the captain and ferry crew abandoned their youthful passengers and were the first to board the rescue boats. Finally, there was the irresponsible attitude of the president and her high-

5    Kim Jong-chul, Kim Young-ok, Ju Jin-woo, and Ha Seung-woo, 'Roundtable Discussion: Hangukiranŭn nara, hŭimang ŭn itnŭnga?' [Is There Hope Within a Country like South Korea?], *Noksaek Pyungrone* [Green Review] 137 (2014): 41–2.
6    Lee Young-ji, '"Sewŏlho ap'ŭm" tanwŏn'go chorŏbsik… saengjonhaksaeng do chorŏpsaeng do urŏtta' ['The Pain of Sewol' and the Graduation Ceremony at Danwon High School: Even the Surviving Students Cried], *Yonhap News*, 9 January 2015.

ranking officials when they visited the accident site. Rather than lamenting the untimely deaths and worrying about the state of grief of other people in the country, they appeared to be more concerned about avoiding public blame. According to reporter Ju Jin-u, with the government doing little to defuse public anger and alleviate suffering, it was mostly bystanders and volunteers who carried the torch of hope for the grieving families.[7]

At the same time, mysteries involving mind-boggling acts of ineptitude remain unresolved. On that morning, when the youthful passengers were texting their families for help or to say goodbye, the Korean Coast Guard sent out no rescue boats. Soon after the accident, the public also learned that *Sewol* had been a decrepit ferry with an extended lifespan. The ferry *Sewol* (meaning to 'transcend the world' in Korean) had been owned by a 73-year-old CEO named Yoo Byung-un, who was later discovered to be the leader of *Kuwon-p'a*, a religious sect awaiting the millennium. Like many successful business leaders, he had built his company through corrupt relations with politicians. For instance, due to the deregulation of the shipping industry by the previous Lee Myung Bak administration, Mr Yoo was able to import an 18-year-old ship from Japan in 2012 and modify it in order to add more room for passengers and cargo. He managed to carry out these modifications despite their violation of various safety regulations. The public also became incensed when they learned about the short-term contract for the captain, indicative perhaps of his level of experience or reliability, and lack of safety training for the crew. Still, it was not until they learned about the missing CCTV tapes and internal communication records that they began to ask a more fundamental question: 'Where was the state, responsible for the safety of its people, during all this?' Prior to the accident, many had prided themselves on being members of an advanced nation. Adding to their frustration was the lack of information, which gave rise to wild rumours and deepened the public's sense of misgiving and distrust of the government. While the government remained tight-lipped about the accident, the mainstream media focused its attention on an extensive manhunt for Mr Yoo, who had gone into hiding. The country's mood became further agitated when a body was discovered in a village garlic field on 12 July, giving rise to wild rumours on the internet that it was Mr Yoo's.

---

7    Kim Jong-chul et al., 'Roundtable Discussion', 8–9.

Earlier, on 19 May—several weeks after the prime minister took the blame for the accident and resigned—President Park Geun-hye took to the podium to address the nation. As she wiped away tears and called out the names of the adult passengers who had died on the ferry while trying to rescue other passengers, she said she took full responsibility. Then, addressing the widespread rumours of collusion between the government and private sector, she announced the dismantling of the Korean Coast Guard and the establishment of the Ministry of National Safety in its place. Through such reforms, she vowed to dig out the poisonous roots of *Kwan-p'ia* (Bureaucratic Mafia) that had 'held the lives of the nation for ransom'.[8] Finally, she proposed setting up a Truth Commission to investigate the causes of the accident and the failure of the rescue effort. Rather than reassuring the surviving families and public, however, the president's address further aggravated them. Many wondered whether the dismantling of the Korean Coast Guard would bring those responsible for the botched rescue effort to justice or let them off scot-free. Instead of investigating the many questions that the public had about the accident, the prosecutors also focused their energy on guaranteeing the death penalty for the ferry captain, as if that would solve all the mysteries surrounding this accident. Finally, in order to demand a thorough investigation of the accident—i.e. what had happened, how it happened, and how tragedies like this could be prevented in the future—the surviving families began a vigil in Seoul's downtown plaza.

In the aftermath of the accident, the surviving families lived like refugees, sleeping on the floors of makeshift accommodations within gyms, tents, and funeral homes near the site where the ferry sank. As they shared grievances and tried to make sense of this senseless tragedy, the parents of the students at Danwon High School bonded like no other victims of any tragedies before.[9] Together, they engaged in various protests and marches to make sure that a similar accident would not reoccur within Korean society. In one protest, they marched to the headquarters of the Korean Broadcasting System (KBS), a public corporation that had been heavily criticised for its highly distorted accounts of the disaster. After that, they marched to the Blue House, home of the Korean president, to demand the passage of a special law to guarantee the political neutrality of the Truth Commission proposed by President Park. However, not only

8    article.joins.com/news/blognews/article.asp?listid=13414472.
9    Refer to the early CNN news coverage. www.youtube.com/watch?v=4i_qKM7SMn8
24 April 2014.

did the president refuse to meet the families, KBS's biased coverage of the disaster continued, prompting the families to carry out another protest on 14 May calling for the resignation of its CEO Gil Hwan-young. While KBS reporters at the site of their protest shed tears of sorrow, the KBS editorial office refused to allow coverage of the demonstration.[10] Moreover, while KBS's CEO did eventually resign, he was quickly replaced by another CEO who shared a similar background and views.

After camping for 76 days outside the Blue House, the families moved their protest to Kwanghwamun Square—a large open area that sits amidst tall government buildings in the administrative core of Seoul. Overnight, these families, who had been living ordinary lives as middle-class people waiting for their children to grow up, attend college, and pursue their dreams, became activists as they began to lose their previously held trust in the government. Vowing to avenge their children's deaths and prevent a similar accident in the future, they approached *Min-pyŏn* (Lawyers for a Democratic Society) to ask for their help in launching a Special Investigation Committee. The aim of this committee was to pressure the government to set up a Truth Commission as soon as possible and pass a special law to grant it strong investigatory and prosecutorial powers. In order to ensure the political neutrality of this commission, they also proposed that half of its members be composed of individuals nominated by the government and the other half of individuals nominated by the committee. Throughout the entire process, the surviving families and the Special Investigation Committee tried to maintain a neutral position vis-à-vis the government and utilise official channels. Neither proved to be an easy task as society was already too polarised and corrupt.

Along with an ultra-right wing group of conservative nationalist Christian organisations, some radical right-wing young people soon emerged to express their open hostility towards the surviving families and their street protests. These conservative groups began to put forth a counter-discourse, accusing the families of making 'unreasonable' and 'excessive' demands on the government that sowed social disorder and contributed to economic stagnation. After exhaustively covering their

---

10    "'Chega kachog iŏdo…" KBS kicha ŭi nunmul' [Even if I'm a Family Member, the Tears of a KBS Reporter], YouTube video, 0:22, posted by 'Newstapa', 5 May 2014. www.youtube.com/watch?v=iFzK2hjpbms.

activities, the mainstream media began to pressure the families to just 'let things be'. Deploying the expression 'public fatigue', it began to assert that people were tired of hearing about the families' protests.

According to Han Wan-sang, a respected academic and intellectual, this type of discourse that employs expressions referring to 'public fatigue' can be considered a form of linguistic censorship, comparable to Nazi propaganda employed during the totalitarian period.[11] Indeed, quotations from master Nazi propagandist Joseph Goebbels, such as the following, could be easily found circulating on the internet:

> It would not be impossible to make people believe that a square is in fact a circle with sufficient repetition and a psychological appeal. They are mere words, and words can be molded until they clothe ideas and disguise … One cannot determine theoretically whether one propaganda is better than another. Rather, good propaganda has the desired results and bad propaganda does not lead to the desired results. It does not matter how clever it is, for the task of propaganda is not to be clever, its task is to lead to success.[12]

While grieving continues to occur in Ansan, where the students had gone to school, similar protests and vigils have spread among diasporic Koreans, especially mothers, in cities around the world.[13] This essay, however, will focus less on these social activities of grieving and healing than on the discourses that have emerged and surround this disaster. In prompting many people to question the state's ability to safeguard the safety of its people, the Sewol Ferry Disaster has become a key political issue that has rent the nation in two. While one group claims that the country can only move on from this disaster after properly mourning the deaths of these children, the other claims that it was a simple 'accident'. They condemn the surviving families and their supporters for 'pestering' the government. In the next section, let us examine the positions of these polarised groups more carefully.

---

11    Han Wan-sang, 'P'iro tamron' p'ŏttŭrinŭn i ttang ŭi 'sŏnjangdŭl' [The 'Captains' of this Land who are Propagating the 'Fatigue Thesis], *Hankyoreh Newspaper*, 11 September 2014.

12    Kim Jae-han, 'Sŏndong en chŭngo ŭi taesang p'ilsu … koepelsŭ, chŏnsŏn nŏmu hwagdaehae chamyŏl' [Instigation Necessitates the Target of Hatred … Goebbels's Aggrandising of the Enemy Line led to Self-Destruction], *Joong-ang Daily*, 25 April 2014.

13    For example, there is a Sewol Ferry Disaster protest as part of a peace rally held every Wednesday in Minneapolis, US, and there is a Remembering Sewol UK team (rememberingsewoluk.wordpress.com) that holds candlelight rallies, makes social media postings, organises study groups, etc.

# Grieving Citizens and the Politics of Compassion

It's not as if we heard about the Sewol Ferry Disaster afterwards. Rather, it was like we were there with the students on the ferry as it slowly sank into the sea. With images of the ferry accident transmitted to us in real time through the media, the whole country saw its sinking last April. So it wasn't something that we 'heard' or 'read about' afterwards but something that we 'saw' directly with our eyes as we sat or stood where we were in our everyday lives. Day-by-day, achingly slowly, we saw it unfold on the morning news, the evening news, and on the Internet. While people responsible for the disaster were busy calculating their losses and avoiding blame, we saw the ferry sink further into the sea. Eating, sleeping, working, walking, we saw it. And even now we continue seeing it and it is likely we will be made to continue to see it whether the ferry breaks up, rusts away, or becomes metal in a scrap yard. (Kim Ae-ran, excerpt from 'Slanted Spring, What We Have Seen')[14]

Observing the unfolding Sewol Ferry Disaster and its grief-stricken families, the entire nation was given an important opportunity to reflect on their lives. Viewing this disaster as an important window into Korean society, Jeon Gyu-chan, a media scholar, called it a 'remote visual event'—an event that unfolded before the eyes of the nation like 'a horrible nightmare with nothing to veil it'.[15] During its unfolding, the mainstream media—operating under strict government censorship—earned the title of *ki-re-ki* (journalist garbage) for its highly distorted coverage. Even so, through its 'outstanding affective and intellectual perception', the viewing public, Jeon Gyu-chan argues, was able to grasp the essence of the situation with just a passing glance. Perhaps realising that they too live in an era overshadowed by death, the viewers formed a 'grieving community' in front of their television screens. Psychotherapist Carl Jung argued that when a community experiences a tragedy, it becomes afflicted by a 'big dream' that serves as a collective warning. Certainly, the Sewol Ferry Disaster was one such event in South Korea, making everyone aware of the fragility of their everyday lives within which a tragedy like this could befall anyone at any time.

---

14   Kim Ae-ran, 'Kiunŭn pom, uriga pon kŏt' [Slanted Spring, What We Have Seen], in Kim Ae-ran et al., *Nunmŏn chadŭl ŭi kukka sewŏlhorŭl paraponŭn chakkaŭi nun* [A Country Gone Blind: Writers' Perspectives on the Sewol Ferry Accident] (Paju: Munhak Dong-nae, 2014), 12.

15   Jeon Gyu-chan, 'Yŏngwŏnhan chaenansangt'ae: Sewŏlbo ihuŭi sikanŭn ŏpta' [Perpetual Calamity: There is No Time After Sewol], Kim Ae-ran et al., *Nunmŏn chadŭl ŭi kukka*, 154–5.

As people converged around the surviving families' protests, many others around the country refrained from drinking, singing and dancing, and set up similar altars for grieving. Every night, groups of citizens—mothers of young children, in particular—held candlelight vigils in their respective neighbourhoods with banners that read 'We Will Never Forget', 'Let Us Fly to Where There is No More Corruption, Calculation and Conspiracy!' and 'Once a Happy Family, We Have Lost Everything'. During this national grieving, Lee Chul-soo, a print artist and a highly respected public intellectual, engaged in an artistic performance of sending online postcards to his fans, mourning the children's deaths. Here is his first postcard, postmarked 16 April:

> There were too many—too many and too young. Some agonies, growing pains, and many dreams. Some just starting their first love, some trying to make their dreams come true. Meeting only death in that southern sea, you are now lost. What was that moment like when you were drawn to your death? So many people wailing in despair for you. If your death weighs so heavily upon our hearts, how unbearable it must be for your families. The possibility of a miracle to save you hanging by a single thread as the dark night descends. We can't even find words to offer our condolences.

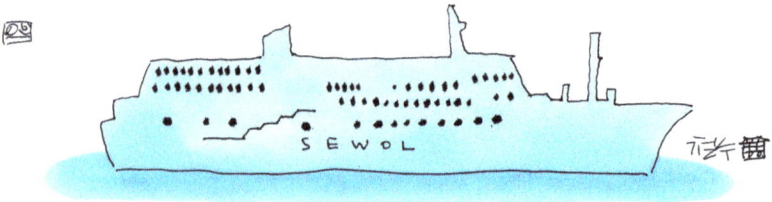

너무 많았습니다. 너무 많고 너무 어렸습니다.
어쩌느라 갈등도 고민도 많고, 꿈도 많았을 나이.
이제 막 사랑도 생각하고, 어른이 되어 살 미래를
서툴게 연습하던 아이들이 저 남쪽 바다에서 이미
죽음에 이르렀거나 실종되었습니다.
아이들 앞에 닥쳤을 절망의 순간이 어땠을까
생각하고 통곡한 사람들 많았을 겁니다.
너무 잔인하고 너무 무서운 일입니다. 그 어린
아이들에게는 있어서 안 될 일이었습니다. 우리가
무거워진 마음을 감당하기 이렇게 어려운데, 가족들
오죽하실까요. 실낱같은 기적의 가능성을 지우는듯
밤이 깊어갑니다. 차마 조의를 말하지 못하겠습니다.

Figure 6: 'Too Many. Too Many and Too Young.'
Source: Courtesy of Lee Chul-soo.

On 25 April, he sent another postcard with the following inscription, 'Fly from the Depths of the Sea to the Heavens!'

> The world is weeping. Farewell. Farewell. To a land without collusion, without endless calculations of profit, without bribery. To such a place, go, you beautiful souls. There is no such place here. There is no such place here.

Figure 7: 'Farewell. Farewell.'
Source: Courtesy of Lee Chul-soo.

On 5 May, he wrote still another postcard with the following quote from one of the surviving families:

> We were poor but happy. But, now that you have gone, we are completely destitute.

With the establishment of the Task Force for the Families of Victims/Missing/Survivors and the Citizens Task Force for Sewol Ferry Disaster, the 10-million signature petition for the passage of Sewol Special Law began. By 7 June 2014, the petition had collected one million signatures. By the first-year anniversary of the disaster, that number had ballooned to six million.[16] On 8 July, two bereaved fathers also began a 750-kilometre

---

16 Jang Sul-gi, '"600-man sŏmyŏng muryŏkhwahanŭn sihaengryŏng", kilkŏri nongsŏng sichak' ['The Ordinance Neutralising the Power of 6-Million People Petition', The Start of the Sit-Down Protest], *Media Today*, 30 March 2015.

trek across the country from Danwon High School to Paeng-mok Harbor carrying a cross. During this long trek of mourning, tens and hundreds of citizens, who wished to share their grief and consolation, greeted them. On 14 July, urging the adoption of a proper Sewol Special Law, the Sewol Ferry Disaster families began fasting. This drew people who wanted to show their solidarity not only to Kwanghwamun Plaza, but also onto online spaces, where individuals posted pictures and shared stories of their own fasting. On YouTube, people began to upload videos of *Sewol* commemorations, such as fields of yellow ribbons to express people's grief. Nationwide, citizens held protests with banners that read 'Life before profit!' and 'People before money!', as well as open forum discussions, which prompted many to reflect on their fast-paced lifestyles and question the cherished concepts of 'nation', 'compressed modernity', and 'unbridled neoliberalism'. Soon, these acts of grieving took on more artistic and cultural forms. While the *Hankyoreh Newspaper* printed stories and sketches of children who had passed away by cartoonist Bak Jae-dong, an art gallery exhibited the keepsakes of a girl who had dreamt of becoming a fashion designer before dying in such an untimely manner.

On the 100th day after the sinking, various commemorations took place nationwide, including a concert by the Paris-based and world famous pianist Paik Kunwoo. After cancelling a world tour, he held a concert on Jeju Island (the destination of the ill-fated ferry) instead, to mourn the children's deaths. In front of Seoul Plaza at City Hall, over 50,000 grieving citizens gathered under the slogan 'A Day of Promise to Never Forget'. On the stage, Kim Jang-hoon, a popular activist singer, sang a duet with the recorded voice of a girl who had died on the ferry but left behind an audition tape, bringing the audience to tears. At the end of the concert and memorial service, everyone applauded when popular singer, Lee Seung-hwan said, 'I suddenly realize that we are such pitiful people with a state that is either unable or unwilling to protect its people. Instead of avoiding this ugly truth, however, let us eat well and stay strong so that we may never forget what we have seen and learnt from this tragedy'.[17]

---

17    '[NocutView] 'Kimchanghun- Yisŭnghwan, nunmul ŭi k'onsŏt'ŭ "4.16 chŏltae itchi ankesssŭmnida"' [Kim Jang-hoon & Lee Seung-hwan, the Concert of Tears, 'We Will Never Forget 04/16], YouTube video, 3:03, posted by 'NocutV', 25 July 2014. www.youtube.com/watch?v=1HER muciE0s&feature=youtu.be.

Overseeing this act of mourning were over 10,000 police and military troops as part of 130 squadrons that were deployed to control the grieving public.[18]

In addition to these spontaneous acts of civic gathering, a flood of writings began to appear on the disaster. Declaring that the Sewol Ferry Disaster was 'not an omen but the result of accumulated events', novelist Bae Myung-hoon writes: 'Though there have been many warnings, the strange and unsavory ways in which the nation state has been operating have been made crystal clear by this accident'.[19] Viewing the Sewol Ferry Disaster as more than an 'accident', rather a momentous 'event' that has unveiled the state's corrupt inability to protect its own citizens, novelist Pak Min-gyu wrote a highly metaphorical account of 'The Sinking Ferry of South Korea', likening the nation to the doomed *Sewol*, a vessel that was built and originally operated in Japan, and then ineptly refitted to enable it to carry a dangerously large load. Analogously, Pak depicts Korea's system as being shaped by Japanese colonialism, dangerously 'retrofitted' under postwar US auspices, and then operated by a crew of politicians and citizens who failed to acknowledge that their ship was sinking.

Looking back, 10 years was too short a time to build a democratic nation, which had a distorted concept of 'public interest' from the beginning. Since the colonial period, the most ardent desire of Korean people has been to become the confident and dignified members of an independent nation. Unlike citizens in the West, who had built their cities and publics since the 12th century, Koreans became 'colonial' citizens of a modern nation only in the 19th century. Identifying the public with the state, they became readily mobilised by the state during its modernisation process. During this process, they continued to view the public as a state-dominated community rather than a voluntary community of communicative citizens. This perception of the public also appears within the language. The terms, 'people' and 'citizen', have very different connotations. To be more precise, 'people' referred to 'national subjects', a collective body of mobilised people rather than 'citizens', who can make and change the nation from below. Through the Sewol Ferry Disaster, Korean public intellectuals have realised the folly of identifying the public

---

18  Im Jong-myung and Kim Yae-jee, 'Sewŏlho 1chugi sŏulkwangchang 5manyŏ unchip… ch'umoche mach'igo haengchin' [50,000 Citizens Who Have Gathered for the 1st Anniversary of Sewol Diaster in Seoul Plaza Commemorating That Day], *NEWSIS*, 16 April 2015.

19  Bae Myung-hoon, 'Nuka tapeya halkka?' [Who Should Answer?], Kim Ae-ran et al., *Nunmŏn chadŭl ŭi kukka*, 105–6.

with the state. For instance, some people have responded to the demand of the surviving families 'to investigate and prosecute those responsible for the accident' with the statement that it is like 'handing a knife to the victim of a crime'. In reply, Pak Min-gyu retorted, 'Does that mean that we should give the knife back to the killer instead?' In a nation dominated by the state, he asks, 'Who should stand as the judge of the public when the state is a criminal suspect and the public enemy is the public itself?'[20] Following the accident, protestors have cited Article 1, Clause 2 of the Constitution most frequently within their protests: 'the sovereignty of the Republic of Korea shall reside in the people, and all state authority shall emanate from the people'. This chapter, once again, expresses the strong will of protestors to recover the 'state for the people'.

The Sewol Ferry Disaster has dredged up acute feelings of sadness and anger within the Korean people.[21] If, as cultural critic Kim Young-ok argues, politics is the transformation of everyday feelings, emotions and consciousness into public speech, then this disaster has done exactly that. It has forced people to take the small moments of self-awareness that have formed from gazing into the black hole of despair and transform them into public speech. Shuttling back and forth between the public and private spheres, the surviving families and mourning citizens are recovering the practices of empathy and mourning that were either suppressed or excluded from the phallocentric political sphere. One such ritual drew upon shamanistic and Catholic practices. Upon hearing that the parents' hearts were heaviest when they were sorting through the box of possessions of their deceased child recovered from the accident, a group of nuns set out to alleviate the sorrow of one mother who had lost her son in the Sewol Ferry Disaster. As the mother took her son's clothes out of the box and into the bathroom to wash them one by one, the nuns sat on the floor lit with a candle and sang hymns. As the mother dried, ironed, and folded the clothes, other mourners recited poet Chun Sang-byung's *Kui-ch'un* ('Returning to Heaven') and wailed in grief. The mother thus bid farewell to her child with utmost love and devotion. Although few parents could partake in this kind of mourning ritual attended to by the nuns, various other forms of mourning and healing have taken place in Ansan. Though I do not cover these rituals of mourning extensively within this essay, I wish to emphasise the ways in which the Sewol Ferry Disaster

---

20   See Kim et al., *Nunmŏn chadŭl ŭi kukka*, 53.
21   Kim Jong-chul et al., 'Roundtable Discussion', 6.

has given rise to these collective practices of grieving that allow people to recover their sense of mutual dependency and ethical responsibility.[22] Also providing great condolence was Pope Francis's visit to South Korea from 13–18 August,[23] which prompted many people to begin asking how they could share another's pain.

Following the public outpouring of grief and protests, intellectuals and social scientists went on to develop further discourses about the relationship between the Korean state and neoliberalism, arguing that this disaster represented not a glitch but a basic flaw within the entire system. Scholars ranging from economist Woo Sun-wook[24] to sociologist Han Byung-chul claimed that the real culprit behind the children's murder was not the ferry captain or its owner but neoliberalism. They claimed that the Sewol Ferry Disaster was the natural culmination of 50 years of compressed modernisation during which the pursuit of economic growth became privileged above everything else. Scholarly publications, including those by Jin Jang-duk, argued that this tragedy disclosed the 'dual nature' of South Korea's risk society: its structural deficiency in terms of the shipping industry and the broader problems of Korean society caught in the tidal wave of privatisation.[25] Historian Park Myung-rim has brought up the issue of modernisation without social welfare by pointing out how Western countries became neoliberalised only after having enjoyed a social welfare state for many decades. In contrast, South Korea, in adopting neoliberal ideals almost immediately after the overthrow of military dictatorships, continues to have weak social welfare programs and is experiencing what he terms 'malicious neoliberalism'.[26]

---

22    'Many people think that grief is privatizing, that it returns us to a solitary situation and is in that sense, depoliticizing. But I think it furnishes a sense of political community of a complex order, and it does this first of all by bringing to the fore the relational ties that have implications for theorizing fundamental dependency and ethical responsibility.' Judith Butler, *Precarious Life: The Powers of Mourning and Violence* (Verso, 2004), 22.

23    'P'ŭranch'isŭk'o kyohwang, sewŏlho danshik 34-il Gim yŏng o-ssi wiro' [Pope Francis Comforting Kim Young-oh's 34-day Sewol Disaster Fasting] YouTube video, 1:21, posted by 'MediaVOP', 15 August 2014. www.youtube.com/watch?v=A-81bkiuQYk.

24    Woo Suk-hoon, *Naeril su ŏmnŭn pae* [A Boat That One Cannot Get Off] (Paju: Oong-jin Jishik House, 2014).

25    Chang Duk-jin et al., *Sewŏlhoga urieke mutta chaenangwa konggongsŏng ŭi sahoehak* [Sewol Disaster Asks Us: Sociology of Disasters and Publicness] (Paju: Han-ool, 2015).

26    Lee Sae-young, 'Saramŭi kach'irŭl chik'iryŏ…tasi konggongsŏngida' [People are the Centre. A Country with a Collapsing Public: What Caused the Sewol Ferry Accident?], *Hankyoreh Newspaper*, 14 May 2014.

These academic discourses, however, fail to sway ordinary citizens who grieve. Part of the reason for this gap between academic discourses and popular sentiment is the control of media and information by the state power. Another reason is the highly judgemental language used by intellectuals as well as ordinary citizens. The intellectuals, as members of the post-Enlightenment generation, pretend that they know the truth. The tone of their discourse closes down—rather than opening up—a dialogue. As discussions of the Sewol Ferry Disaster continued to be framed through the discourses of nationalism and familism, the majority of citizens, who initially felt the 'heart of heaven' descend upon them, find themselves increasingly estranged from the protests. I consider this unfortunate trend to be the result of South Korea's modernisation process, which has paid little attention to the formation of a public sphere where citizens could voluntarily meet and solve their collective problems. Now there are people with hatred in their hearts who protest against the opening of the public sphere of grieving. In the next section, let us examine these growing voices of opposition.

## National Subjects of Animosity and the Politics of Fear

The political climate after the Sewol Ferry Disaster has become infinitely more complicated. Observing the unfolding events of the Sewol Ferry Disaster, social critic Gang June-man, from the perspective of a progressive and concerned citizen, has identified five stages of despair.[27] The first was realising that none of the involved parties—the ferry owner, captain, or crew—considered life more important than money. The second was witnessing the disappointing attitudes and responses of public authorities, including the maritime police. The third was seeing the president and politicians reflect similarly irresponsible attitudes. The fourth was noting that not all shared the indignation of the grieving families and citizens. The fifth was tallying the results of the regional elections, which took place 49 days after the accident. Intellectuals had expected people to turn their backs on the conservative politicians, not one of whom had a sensible plan to ease the nation's sense of loss and hopelessness. Instead, the re-election of these same politicians shattered the intellectuals' own naive belief in the people. After this series of disappointments, the Sewol Ferry

---

27    Gang June-man, *Ssakachi ŏmnŭn chinbo* [The Worthless Progressives] (Inmulgwa Sasang, 2014), 129–31.

Disaster became stuck in the opposing logics of the two political parties. While the left-wing opposition party tried to use the issue to expand its own power, the right-wing government, tense at the possibility of being blamed for the disaster, tried to bury it altogether. When a certain segment of civil society joined the opposition party's call for the resignation of the president, the Sewol Ferry Disaster simply spawned more controversies.

Adding fuel to the fire have been the controversies around the Sewol Special Law. When the surviving families demanded a closer examination of this law, some netizens began to make sensationalist claims in order to oppose them. Among them were: 'The surviving families are demanding the designation of all victims as national martyrs'; 'Are Sewol families some kind of government?'; 'The efforts of the surviving families to extract one more cent from the government are now exposed'. Through this smear campaign, they tried to portray the families as selfish individuals out for personal gain.[28] Even though these claims are groundless, they have become the primary way to understand the Sewol Ferry Disaster.

In fact, one of the growing problems within Korean society is the inability to distinguish fact from fiction, with struggles for truth giving rise to further falsehoods. These falsehoods are then further manipulated to exacerbate an already tense political situation. For instance, when one man, identifying himself as the descendant of a Korean War veteran, proposed the formation of a group to oppose the passage of the Sewol Special Law, he was soon joined by the ultra-right Fathers' Coalition. Not only did they make ridiculous claims about these surviving families demanding special privileges for their deceased children, they also compared the Sewol Ferry Disaster to an ordinary traffic accident that neither the state nor the nation was responsible for. In their words, the children had simply died on a school trip, which they undertook out of their own volition and for their own pleasure. When the parents of the *Sewol* victims began a hunger strike on 17 July to demand a fair and speedy investigation of the accident, anti-Communist and ultra-right wing groups, including the Fathers' Coalition and fundamentalist Christians, gathered to denounce them as bad parents. They also claimed that giving the surviving families the power to hold an independent and impartial investigation would shake the legal foundation of the country. Portraying the fasting parents

---

28    Lee Ju-young, 'Sewŏlho yugachok tulrŏssan ŭihok 3kachi, chinsil ŭn?' [Three Doubts Surrounding Sewol Disaster's Surviving Families: The Truth?], *Ohmynews*, 16 July 2014.

as a pro-Communist and pro-North Korean force bent on toppling the government, some even warned the president of a second Kwangju Uprising.[29]

At the hunger strike, joining the Fathers' Coalition were the 'Volunteer Battalion of Mothers'—a team of middle-aged women in vests who carried picket signs with incendiary messages on them, such as 'How much financial compensation do you want, that you are out here fasting and protesting instead of quietly crying at home?' or 'How well do you want to live that you're willing to sell [the bodies of] your children?' As groups like these waved these signs in front of the fasting parents,[30] wild rumours began to spread widely, especially among senior citizens. Among them were accusations that the surviving families were putting forth political demands only to wrestle more compensation from the government. Taxi drivers and shopkeepers often asked me whether the protests of the families were not prolonging the economic recession. Others stated that the state should not compensate these families since their children had died in a 'boating accident' and taxpayers had not agreed to use their taxes to compensate them. In 2015, when the amount of the families' compensation was finally determined, an old lady in my neighbourhood asked me, 'I heard that if a person gets hit by a car, he receives US$200,000 (200 million won) in compensation. Why is it then that the surviving families are getting US$800,000 (800 million won)?' She then added, 'I heard that the costs of recovering the sunken ferry are astronomical. So why bother trying to recover it at all?' When I asked her about the source of this information, she answered, 'Kakao Talk', which is a phone and messaging service similar to WhatsApp or Skype. In a mediascape of smart phones and internet shared by all generations, these distorted rumours spread quickly even among the older generation of grandparents in their 60s and 70s.

The group that concerns me most is that of young people who show strong animosity toward the surviving families. As one example of their obnoxious behaviour, on 6 September, in a so-called '100 Pizza Party' sponsored by a businessman, they sang, danced and gorged on food in

29   *Yonhap News*, 23 April 2014; The Kwangju Uprising, also known as Kwangju Democratisation Movement, was a popular movement crushed by government troops under Chun Doo-hwan in May 1980 in the city of Kwangju, South Cholla Province, killing more than 600 civilians.
30   Bak Bo-na, 'Anchŏnsahoenŭn ŏttŏhke kanŭnghanka? "Chasik p'ara hogangharyŏ hanya" nŭn pibang e tapanda' [How is a Safe Society Possible? Responding to Slanderous Accusations of 'Selling One's Children to Live Well'], *Ohmynews*, 29 July 2014.

front of the fasting families outside their Kwanghwamun shelter. Further fomenting hatred have been the actions of 'Ilgan Best' (Ilbae), an online community originally known for their political satire, which is now promoting hatred against social minorities including women, people from Cholla Province (the home region of president Kim Dae Jung who fought against president Park Jung Hee's military regime, often a target of discrimination by people from other regions) and foreign migrant workers.[31] Ilbae members, who consider social minorities to be free riders, say that they are fed up with helping them. They make spurious claims that '[i]f the Sewol Special Law gets passed, the surviving families will get too many benefits' and '[i]mpure forces are using the unfortunate deaths on Sewol ferry to siphon off national resources'. In such a manner, they express their concern for the country.[32] Even a few years ago, this kind of behaviour was socially unacceptable.[33] However, by widely reporting on these hateful protests, conservative news outlets not only condone them but also exploit them to try to turn public opinion against the surviving families' struggle for justice.

Another target of public attacks was a father, who, after losing his daughter, began a month-long fast to demand the passage of the Sewol Special Law. When the fact of his previous divorce became public knowledge, all types of smear campaigns began to surface. While some claimed that the father, Kim Young-oh, 'had not once changed a diaper in his life', others accused him of 'enjoying the high-class sport of archery even though he had never paid one cent in alimony'. In the face of media attacks that portrayed him as an unfit father because he was divorced, Kim Young-oh was forced to reveal a copy of his empty bank account. Within it were figures for the money that he had wired to his ex-wife for their daughter's living expenses, including health insurance and cell phone bills.[34] According to sociologist

31   For Ilbae, refer to Kim Hak-june, The Emotional Fellowship of Hatred and Wildness in Internet Community's 'Ilbae Storage Site'. Master's thesis, Seoul National University, Sociology (2014); Yoon Bo-ra, 'Ilbae and Hatred Against Women', *Jinbo Pyungrone*, Issue 57 (2013): 33–56. Bak Seun-young, 'Wigi ŭi namsŏngdŭl "yŏsŏng ŭn paeryŏ anin ch'ŏkkyŏl taesang" twit'ŭllin chŏkkaesim' [Men in Crisis: Women as Objects not of Consideration but of Eradication: A Misdirected Hostility], *Hankook Ilbo*, 30 May 2015.
32   'Wigi ŭi namsŏngdŭl "yŏsŏng ŭn paeryŏ anin ch'ŏkkyŏl taesang" twit'ŭllin chŏkkaesim' [Men in Crisis: Women are not Subjects of Care but Elimination], *Hankook Ilbo*, 26 May 2015.
33   Chae Gyung-june, Kim Si-yuen and Lee Hee-hoon, 'Ilbae, Sewolho tansiknongsŏngjang chupyŏnseo" "pizapati' kkaji"' [Ilbe: Even a 'Pizza Party' Near Sewol Disaster's Fasting Family Members], *Ohmynews*, 6 September 2014.
34   Lee Hyun-jeong, 'Ingansŏng, kachok, kŭriko kiŏkhanŭn haengwi e kwanhayŏ' [Humanity, Family, and the Practice of Remembering], in No Myung-woo et al. eds, *P'aengmokhangesŏ pulŏonŭn parlam* [The Wind Blowing from P'aengmok Harbor] (Hyunshil Munhwa, 2015), 113.

Kim Dong-choon, President Park Geun-hye and her administration have used various tactics, including employing the Korean state intelligence agency, to spread vicious rumours and pit the surviving families against each other. These tactics, he argues, constitute a form of informational warfare aimed at protecting their power and authority.[35]

Like others, I remain highly critical of efforts by the Park Geun-Hye administration and mainstream media to discredit the surviving families and bury the truth of what had happened on the *Sewol*. I also consider it necessary to better understand those citizens who so readily believe their lies. Dwelling on a similar issue, Kim Dong-choon attributes the animosity of the older generation to their wretched lives. According to him, people in their 60s and above have a tremendous amount of anger and resentment that they are unable to express as legitimate grievances. Even though they consider themselves the main agents behind the country's rapid economic ascent under the military government, many continue to live impoverished lives. Therefore, having never asked for nor received any compensation from the state, they feel a severe sense of relative deprivation when they hear the surviving families demanding reparations.[36] Moreover, to the 'Cold War' generation, the term 'redistribution' automatically evokes feelings of repulsion. They consider it selfish and corrupt to talk about compensation when reviving the stagnant economy remains such an urgent task. Therefore, they repeatedly assert that the Sewol Ferry Disaster was simply an accident that neither the state nor government is responsible for. They also declare that the bereaved should not do anything to promote social disorder and deepen the economic recession. Still, despite the animosity that these far right–leaning seniors share with their younger counterparts, their root of discontent does not lie in unbridled neoliberalism but the Cold War system.

Contrary to many people's perception of Ilbae as young fanatics, many are, in fact—according to sociologist Kim Hak-june, who has done extensive field research within this community—kind and polite young men with

---

35 Kim Dong-choon, 'Kukka puchaewa kamchŏngchŏngch'i: sewŏlho ch'amsa ihuŭi hankuksahoe' [The Absence of the State and Politics of Emotion: Korean Society after the Sewol Ferry Disaster], No et al., *P'aengmokhangesŏ pulŏonŭn parlam*, 188.

36 ibid., 186.

great respect for their self-made fathers.[37] What most distinguishes Ilbae is their sense of righteousness. Many say they prefer the corruption of the conservative government to the incompetence and hypocrisy of the leftist government. They also harbour resentment against women who demand equal treatment despite not having served in the military. These women include their girlfriends who make them pay for going on dates but offer little 'service' in return. To them, people with disabilities, foreign workers and mothers who get child support from the state are all parasites who feed off hard-working and tax-paying citizens. As such, these young people ignore structural inequalities and emphasise the values of self-reliance and individual responsibility. Within this framework, they view the birth of children into well-to-do families, for instance, as part of their personal 'ability'.

By virtue of some 20,000 people, who gather on its website every hour to curse, act in a rowdy manner, and vent their anger by calling each other losers, Ilbae has become South Korea's most powerful online community. Growing up in the aftershock of the IMF crisis, most Ilbae members have experienced cutthroat competition to get into college. As consumers of private after-school education since youth, many have internalised the 'winner-take-all' mentality of neoliberalism. Without any alternative role models, few have had a chance to cultivate a sense of belonging. To them, everything is 'private' and a 'matter of fact'. Despising anyone who talks about 'truth' without supporting 'facts', they dismiss *kkon-dae* (derogatory term for older people who always try to teach) who, in their minds, merely preach without providing any evidence. 'What is your real motive in bringing up the issue of compensation?' they ask the sympathetic and warm-hearted citizens who support the grieving families. Is it any surprise that people should be unable to care for others who are suffering when they have not received such care themselves? From a student, I heard of one 30-year-old woman, who, passing by the protest site of the surviving families, started screaming at them to stop 'nagging' the government. Having not received love and support themselves during their youth, they are unable to understand the suffering of others.

---

37   Kim Hak-june, 'Int'ŏnet kŏmyunit'i 'ilbejŏjangso-esŏ nat'ananŭn hyŏmo wa yŏlkwang ŭi kamchŏngtonghak' [The Emotional Dynamics of Hatred and Wildness in Internet Community's 'Ilbae Storage Site'], Master's thesis, Seoul National University, Sociology, 2014. Chun Gwan-yool, 'Iche kukka ap'e tangdanghi sŏn "ilpe ŭi ch'ŏngnyŏndŭl"' ['Ilbae Youth' Who Stand Proudly Before the Nation], *Sisa-in*, Issue 367 (29 September 2014).

Considering themselves to be smarter and more sophisticated than gullible citizens who support the grieving families, these radicalised youths spend their days engaging in satirical discourse. Claiming 'You are an idiot, I'm an idiot', they refuse to take anything seriously. How are we to understand these radicalised youths who, after 30 bloody years of democracy protests, have emerged as cynical narcissists and conservative egoists, who dismiss the past decade of democratic politics as 'the lost decade'? According to sociologist Kim Hong-jung, the reason that these youths have emerged as cynical narcissists is because they have internalised the imperative to survive at all costs.[38] Having adopted survivalism as their modus operandi, many youths not only fail to empathise with the pain of society's losers but also heap scorn and hatred upon them. In a slightly different context, philosopher Renata Saleci argues that when life becomes a brutal war for survival, the young generation, in particular, experiences a form of 'neurotic anxiety'.[39] Just like post-traumatic stress disorder experienced by soldiers returning from battle, this neurotic anxiety can be seen as the result of a combination of factors. In evaluating the relationship between survivalism and conservatism, we may view it as the result of youth adapting themselves to a reality in which they feel social change is impossible.

Also undeniable is how effectively the conservative government has managed to manipulate both law and media within this gloomy environment to further their agenda. In aligning itself more strongly with the market, the Korean state seems to believe that it no longer needs to pay any attention to its more enlightened citizens. Instead, it can rely on money and power to pursue its political agenda. State manipulation of the media has become more sophisticated under the conservative regime of President Lee Myung-bak (known as the 'Economy President' because of his background as the former CEO of Hyundai Construction) and President Park Geun-hye, the daughter of Park Chung-hee, the military dictator responsible for the nation's economic development in the 1960s and 1970s. Under these two administrations, government control of political demonstrations has strengthened to the point that it is becoming

---

38 According to Kim, 'survivalism' is a collective psychology formed by people to respond effectively to the various problems created by the conditions of late modernity. Kim Hong-jung, 'Survival, Survival Ethics, and the Youth Generation', *Hangook Sahoe-hak* 49, Issue 1 (2015), 179–81.

39 Here, 'realistic anxiety' refers to a known danger while 'neurotic anxiety' refers to an unknown one. Renata Seleci, *Puran* [On Anxiety], trans. Bak Gwang-ho (Paju: Humanitas, 2015), 48–9.

impossible to participate in them.[40] With political parties needing only 30 per cent of the popular vote to win an election (because of low voter turnout), the right-wing party has focused on 'economic recovery' and 'threat of North Korean invasion' while the left-wing party has focused on the corruption and immorality of the right. Together, these two political stances mean that real issues affecting the country remain unaddressed. Within a political environment in which many citizens are becoming increasingly cynical, I fear the growth of a movement similar to Nazism in Germany during the early part of the 20th century. The likelihood of such movement emerging is very high when the 'industrial generation'— who did not have the time or the leisure to cultivate a humanitarian consciousness—meets the 'neoliberal generation'—who are struggling to survive within the cruel and competitive society—under the umbrella of state power. As for the Sewol Ferry Disaster, after the government's successful recruitment of young foot-soldiers from the ranks of the calculating consumer generation, there appears to be no solution in sight. It is precisely because of this mounting sense of crisis that I highlight the issues of a 'weak state' and 'capitalism that has run out of steam', as well as of the politics of survival that must cultivate global citizens.

## People, Citizen, Refugee and the Politics of Survival

On 16 April 2014, many citizens of South Korea became mesmerised by the scenes of a ferry sinking. Images of text messages and video footage—sent by the students to their parents and friends hours and even minutes before their death—kept the country glued to television sets and smartphones. What made this disaster particularly notable was the participation of the whole nation during its unfolding. Via its mediated representations, people participated in 'real' time, both in the unfolding events on the ferry and the ensuing rescue efforts. In the process, they became simultaneous 'witnesses' and 'survivors' of this disaster. With the sinking of the *Sewol* ferry, people have witnessed a chain reaction of crises in South Korean society.

---

40   On 29 September, the National Police Agency declared that a person would be arrested right away should they cross the police line. They also stated that they were pursuing legal amendments to double the penalty to a 'minimum of 6 months of imprisonment and a fine of $500 (500,000 won) and below'. Kim Seung-hwan, 'P'olrisŭ lainman nŏmŏdo kŏmgŏ… kyŏngch'al, chiphoe siwimunhwa okchoena' [Arrest for Even Crossing the Police Line … Police Stranglehold of Rally and Protest Culture], *Hankook Ilbo*, 30 September 2015.

It was during this period of growing intolerance that I became aware of the Syrian refugee crisis. On 2 September 2015, the world was gripped by the photo of a three-year-old child whose drowned body had washed up on the shores of the Mediterranean Sea in a resort town. Wearing a red T-shirt and navy blue shorts, face down in the sand, he was later identified as Aylan Kurdi, a child of a Syrian family who had been fleeing the country's five-year civil war for Europe.[41] In the past five years, the Syrian refugee crisis has resulted in over 240,000 deaths, 4,013,000 refugees, and 7,600,000 displaced persons within its borders—representing the biggest displacement of people since the two world wars.[42] Following the drowning of more than 2,000 boat people in the Mediterranean Sea in 2014, another 800 people drowned in April 2015 in the Libyan Sea. More than all these deaths, however, this one photo of a drowned child, which circulated widely over the internet with the hashtag 'Flotsam of humanity', struck at the hearts of people around the world.

When 20,000 Syrian refugees arrived in northern European cities such as Vienna and Munich, residents greeted them with hugs, gifts and welcoming applause. In Iceland, in an online discussion started by a group critical of the government's policy to accept only 50 refugees, 10,000 people volunteered to find housing for the refugees.[43] A photo of a Syrian father selling ballpoint pens on the street while he cradled his sleeping daughter in his arms circulated on social media networks, and raised $140,000 to help him. Liberalisation of refugee policies followed within some European nations. Buoyed by the outpouring of humanitarianism among her people, Germany's Prime Minister Angela Merkel, who had been so firm and tough about the recent Greek financial crisis, announced the country's acceptance of all Syrian refugee applicants. Relenting on his earlier anti-immigration stance, Denmark's Prime Minister Lars Lokke Rasmussen also announced the acceptance of 1,000 refugees. Watching

41    Cho Il-joon, 'P'atae Milryŏon 3sal Siria nanmin aiŭi chukŏm … Chŏnsekye "Kongpun"' [The Corpse of a 3-year-old Syrian Refugee Child Swept up to the Beach by Waves … world 'outrage'], *Hankyoreh Newspaper*, 3 September 2015.
42    Yul Lee, 'Five Years of Syria's Civil War … 240,000 Deaths and 4 Million Refugees', *Yonhap News*, 7 August 2015.
43    Seo-young Ha, 'Refugee-Refusing European Governments, Citizens who Invite Refugees to Their Home', *Joongang Daily*, 3 September 2015.

the European Commission's move 'to avoid a humanitarian tragedy'[44] amid an outpouring of compassion, Korean media pundits exclaimed, 'This is the miracle that Aylan has bestowed upon humanity'.[45]

In collectively experiencing this tragic moment between life and death, human beings feel a sense of compassion that, previously deeply buried within their hearts, springs forth. While Korean Buddhist monk Tobŏp, during the Sewol Ferry Disaster, called this sense of spiritual awakening the 'heart of heaven' or 'sacred heart (kŏrukhan maŭm)', lawyer Kim Tak-su declared it to be 'the first mind (chŏt maŭm)'. In Durkheimian terms, we might view it as the emergence of a 'collective consciousness' when grieving and fearful people gather together and transcend their individual fear and suspicion anger to a higher order—the 'sacred'. Grieving the deaths of children both during the Syrian refugee crisis and Sewol Ferry Disaster, they are engaging in efforts both large and small to make sure such tragedies do not occur again—whether that means showing up at the train station laden with flowers to welcome the Syrian refugees or signing a petition to demand the proper investigation of the Sewol Ferry Disaster. Here I am asking how long humanitarian impulses or compassion that rise out of witnessing tragedies could last. There is talk about 'compassion fatigue'; people feel fatigue because they cannot find proper 'exit' for the confrontation with the state power. Moreover, people are getting busier as disastrous incidents and crises occur more frequently.

In this essay, I tried to describe a movement of compassionate and hospitable citizens and one of fearful and hate-mongering ones. These two contrasting movements and groups of citizens coexist as if they were two nations within one nation-state. Similarly, in the case of the Syrian refugee crisis, next to the outpouring of humanitarian compassion were scenes of open hostility directed against the refugees. On 8 September 2015, people around the world were shocked by the video of a female Hungarian journalist tripping a Syrian father, who was running away from the Hungarian police with a child in his arms, and then kicking a child refugee.[46] They also became incensed when they watched a video

44    Duncan Robinson, Alex Barker, and James Politi, 'Greece Under Pressure to Set Up Facilities for 50,000 Refugees', *Financial Times*, 26 October 2015.

45    Song Young-in, 'Aillani Pakkun Sesang … Tokilsŏ Nanmin Hwanyŏngmulkyŏl' [The World that Aylan has Changed … The Wave of Welcome for Refugees in Germany], *Yonhap News*, 7 September 2015.

46    'Hungarian Camera Woman for Fascist Channel Caught on Camera Attacking Immigrants', YouTube video, 0:22, posted by 'Chewing tinfoil', 9 September 2015. www.youtube.com/watch?v=i Tasfpovhe4&feature=youtu.be.

of a young mayor in Àsotthalom, Hungary, ordering refugees to stay out of his town, while striking the pose reminiscent of a neo-Nazi thug or gun-toting cowboy.[47] Where is this open animosity coming from? And what will happen to the growing sense of antipathy brewing in northern European countries? How long can the 'heart of heaven' that sprang forth from watching the pain of others last? Can I be hopeful, believing that uncovering the miseries and disasters will open a platform of collective learning of 'social catharsis' that can open new paths of survival for humankind?

After the Sewol Ferry Disaster, many academics have called for more public-minded 'citizens'. Sociologist Song Ho-gun, for instance, argues that much of Korean society's misery can be traced to its lack of public virtue.[48] Noting that economic growth has far outpaced the development of sociopolitical virtues, he urges South Korean people to respect one another and serve the public as a community of self-governing people. I agree with his argument but feel the prescription is too simplistic. Having transformed itself from a strictly ruled colony to a leading economic power in a matter of 60 years, South Korea is pointed to as a model state for its successful 'take off'. In the maelstrom of global capitalism, however, the people caught up in this compressed rush and ruled by an unforgiving developmental state had to compromise and sacrifice many things. As novelist Park Min-gyu explains above, with the 'ferry of South Korea' having started sailing in an unbalanced state, it cannot help but grow more tilted as it continues to sail. The obsession with catching up with so-called 'advanced nations' has spawned a nationalism and statism that tries to unify the population into one powerful nation. This mass hatred appearing in later developing nations such as present-day Korea and Hungary is a product of this crippling modernisation. I have closely followed the growing phenomenon of youths in such countries, who are sympathetic to this brand of insular nationalism. Their anger and frustration has surfaced because, although they may have joined the middle class in their own countries, the dreams they had of enjoying the kind of lives of comfort enjoyed by middle-class nuclear families in earlier developed nations have been dashed. Also, in countries where you must face dying alone without anyone to help you, those demanding help from

---

47    Cho Seung-hyun, '"Nanmin hyŏppaksŏng" yŏngsang ollin hŏnggari sijang "uri tosiro omyŏn t'uok"' ['Threatening Refugees' The Video of Hungarian Mayor: Imprisonment if You Come to Our Town], *Hankyoreh Newspaper*, 19 September 2015.

48    Song Ho-gun, *Nanŭn simininga sahoehakcha Songhokŭn, simin ŭi kirŭl mutta* [Am I a citizen? Sociologist Song Ho-gun. asking about the path to citizenship] (Munhak Dong-ne, 2015).

the state or others themselves must understand the level of anger that must pervade such a society, and its blowback effects, like the woman who angrily yelled at the families of the *Sewol* victims for 'nagging' the government. Because such people, as citizens, have not had the experience of receiving 'gifts' from the state or acts of 'caring', they themselves don't know how to give of themselves or care for others. Instead, they came to think that the proper way to live one's life is to exist each for oneself, living off one's own efforts alone. For these people, the Korean phrase first popularised during the hard times of the 1960s, 'Let's all prosper [live well] together', just seems like hypocrisy.

'Creating the public' involves building trust and cooperation among individual citizens. Compared with northern Europe, when one comes face-to-face with such expressions of naked hatred as in South Korea or Hungary, it is difficult to 'create a public'. In recent years, a growing number of politicians have capitalised on people's anxiety and hostility to seize state power. Such politicians want to separate the public into opposing groups in order to produce mass anger. They pay no heed to methods for constructively gaining and holding on to state power. They tend to emphasise 'economic growth' or 'economic recovery', while spending tremendous amounts to buy new weapons. They also ignore citizens' objections to continue supporting indefensible technologies such as nuclear power plants, fracking, and long-distance oil pipelines. Even as they make international agreements to forestall climate change, they make no efforts to ensure that the measures required by those agreements are carried out.

This kind of activity is not only occurring in the later developed countries. During his 2016 election campaign, US President Donald Trump emphasised a politics that pits group against group, stirring up hatred and hostility. Employing hateful speech as his weapon, he has succeeded in generating a sensational sideshow that attracts disaffected American voters. Trump has called Mexicans 'rapists', referred to women as 'bimbos' and 'fat pigs', and promised to shut down mosques, keep a database of Muslims, and round up the children of 'illegal' immigrants. Stephen Miles of Avaaz has commented that 'Trump isn't the only politician on the global stage exploiting political alienation and fear to sow hate, but he's the only one who is doing it with $2 billion worth of media attention'. Miles said he hopes to 'use Trump's media magnetism to our advantage and trigger a massive story about the world rejecting this hate-mongering'.[49] My cousin, who sent me this anti-Trump initiative, commented that 'I thought Trump's campaign was a joke and a publicity stunt and can't believe he has gotten this far'.

What about the first 'advanced nations' in Europe? How are they faring compared to the later developed countries? With the continued stagnation of their economies, there is a growing trend towards political conservatism and radicalisation of patriotic youth in advanced nations as well. As societies become more conservative, the welcoming gestures of citizens in northern Europe towards Syrian refugees cannot but seem more precious. Their gestures of warmth and empathy are not enough to solve the situation of Syrian refugees. Are they the 'kind but incompetent' citizens that some Korean youth mock as the 'obnoxious left' or citizens who have had their consciousness 'raised'? I admire people in European social democracies in their long-term effort to overcome sheer capitalistic greed after the two world wars, but I also know that it would not be easy for them to move out of their 'comfort zone'.

Within the current world order, which is characterised by unending series of disasters, catastrophes and hostility, no place on the globe is safe. For future generations, we leave behind a devastated ecosystem, the terror of new viruses, economies on the brink of collapse, the danger of nuclear arms and weapons plants, heightened class conflicts, a widening divide between the rich and poor, high youth unemployment, low fertility, ageing societies without systems for providing adequate elder care, and the fears and anxieties that follow the collapse of national economies. Within this context, I propose that we replace the binary of '*sŏnjin-guk* vs *hujin-guk*', the 'advanced/developed nation vs undeveloped/developing nation', deeply embedded within the modern mindset, with the notion of '*sŏnmang-guk* vs *humang-guk*', the 'rapidly vs slowly collapsing/declining/burning-out nation'. This may involve replacing the indices that measure Gross National Product with indices that reflect their potential destructiveness. Such indices should take into account the number of nuclear power plants

---

49   This following letter appears on Avaaz.org: 'Dear Mr. Trump, This is not what greatness looks like. The world rejects your fear, hate-mongering, and bigotry. We reject your support for torture, your calls for murdering civilians, and your general encouragement of violence. We reject your denigration of women, Muslims, Mexicans, and millions of others who don't look like you, talk like you, or pray to the same god as you. Facing your fear we choose compassion. Hearing your despair we choose hope. Seeing your ignorance we choose understanding. As citizens of the world, we stand united against your brand of division. Sincerely.' (The petition already has approximately 5,112,000 signatures as of March 2017) avaaz.org/en/deartrump_rb_loc/?acDWXcb.

in a nation, the degree of disconnectedness and atomisation among its members, or its potential for dealing with the innumerable contingencies. In this context, the concept of 'refugee' in survival politics proves far more useful than the concepts of 'national subject' or 'citizen' in a 'politics of progress'. During the Sewol Ferry Disaster, people in South Korea who once believed in the myth of economic development begin to increasingly realise that the state is but 'a system of organised irresponsibility'.[50] After overcoming their sense of astonishment and bewilderment when gazing upon the 'unpainted face' of the nation-state, they have begun the long journey of overcoming their abject situation. Already, I have encountered many who have embarked on this journey by embracing a refugee-like existence including self-exile or psychological refuge. They ask questions such as 'Will Japan or China accept us if we also become refugees?' 'Or will we die as boat people in the East Sea/Sea of Japan?' 'Is it better to leave this country before that happens? If so, where?' In the departure of these youth for a better life elsewhere, one can find a reason for Ulrich Beck's hope in the face of countless disasters and untold miseries that characterise risk society. According to Beck, the shock administered to humanity by massive disasters will also produce the 'conditions for cosmopolitanism', resulting in countless miracle-like events, including a new social consensus on the environment. His colleague Bruno Latour has also said, 'society has never been the equivalent of a nation-state' and 'society has always meant association and has never been limited to humans'.[51] With the disappearance of one cosmos, Latour further suggests using the term cosmopolitics instead of cosmopolitan.[52] Here, I want to suggest that young people engage in survival politics by becoming 'global refugees' to transform the present catastrophe into an emancipatory one.

In October 2015, I visited International People's College in Denmark, the sister school of Haja Production School, which I founded after the Asian financial crisis in Seoul. A boarding school with approximately 100 students from over 35 countries, the International People's College is an excellent global school that aims to foster 'global citizens'. While I was there, the principal and teachers were discussing how to cultivate compassion and competence as global citizens among the students. Based on my limited observation, the problem appeared to lie in their concept

---

50 Interview with Ulrich Beck, 'System of organized irresponsibility behind the Fukushima crisis', *Asahi Shimbun*, 8 July 2011, blog.sina.com.cn/s/blog_7ab41de50100tb1n.html.

51 Bruno Latour, 'Whose cosmos, which cosmopolitics?' *Common Knowledge* 10, no. 3 (2004): 450–51.

52 ibid., 453.

of citizenship. The courses at the school covered many important topics such as the historical roots of the violence of the Australian state against its Aboriginal population and issues surrounding the multinational corporations, such as Monsanto. Still, students seemed to have a hard time personalising these issues and accepting them as their own. While students from the humang-guk—the 'slowly collapsing/declining/burn-out nations'—appeared somewhat tired of these dystopian stories, for the students from sŏnmang-guk—the 'rapidly collapsing/declining/burning-out nations'—the challenges were too real to face.

What is clear here is that these youngsters are going to have to come to terms with the fact that these local disasters and catastrophes are globally connected. From this perspective, I find the term 'global refugee' much more useful than 'global citizen'. Whether one has been physically displaced or not, the personal realisation that one is being displaced from one's country of citizenship is likely to be a good start of learning. In coming to this realisation and cultivating one's sense of being a refugee, these displaced citizens may do well to heed the words of one native woman from the Chiapas region in Mexico:

> If you have come here to help me, you are wasting your time. But if you have come because your liberation is bound up with mine, then let us work together.[53]

## Acknowledgements

I presented the draft of this essay at the symposium, 'Reflections of Humanities on April 16th Sewol Disaster and Disaster Studies', held at the Humanities Research Center at Seoul National University on 31 October 2104. I am grateful to Hirokazu Miyazaki at Cornell University, Takashi Fujitani, Jennifer Chun and Judy Han at the University of Toronto, Tessa Morris-Suzuki at The Australian National University, and Dongjun Shin at Cambridge University for providing me further opportunities to think over the Sewol Ferry Disaster. I am particularly grateful to Song-Pae Cho, Jeffrey Stark and Eun Jeong Soh for translating and making this essay filled with abrupt generalisations and emotional nuances into a readable English essay.

---

53    School for Chiapas, 'Women's Empowerment', www.schoolsforchiapas.org/advances/womens-empowerment/.

8

# Thinking of Art as Informal Life Politics in Hong Kong

Olivier Krischer

## Towards a Language of Social Action

This chapter considers artistic practices as a form of informal life politics in the context of Hong Kong, through the case of the Wooferten 活化廳 art space. Besides situating the space's emergence in the context of local cultural politics, and a 'translocal' network of regional collaborators, I also consider theoretical approaches to this form of creative action, and relate them to the often overlooked history of social movements in Hong Kong.

The challenge of thinking about collective social actions or movements in Hong Kong became clearer to me after being invited to present at a symposium organised by ZKM (Zentrum für Kunst und Medientechnologie), Germany, in January 2014, titled 'Global Activism Symposium'.[1] The roster of speakers was inspiring yet also revealing, including members of Occupy Wall Street, an activist turned politician from Iceland's Pirate Party, street artists and journalists from

---

1    'Global Activism Symposium' was held at ZKM Centre for Art and Media Karlsruhe from 24–26 January 2014, coinciding with the exhibition *Global Activism*. For details of presentations and speakers, see www.global-activism.de/global-activism-symposium.

the Egyptian and Tunisian uprisings, a South African ANC (African National Congress) veteran turned academic, American direct democracy advocates, and some artists working with 'radical' political groups.[2]

Although I had introduced a number of participants from Hong Kong when approached by the organisers, they eventually came back to ask if I would speak on their behalf. I found it awkward situating the range of actions and motivations from Hong Kong and other urban contexts in East Asia, each with their own particular history and epistemology, into a politics of 'global activism'.[3] The so-called Umbrella protests would not occur until September of that year, and I don't recall anyone at the symposium showing awareness of Hong Kong's own Occupy Central movement.[4] There was, of course, traffic in creative ideas between people facing similar pressures of the neoliberal urban economy, but the different facets of Hong Kong politics, its history and 'post-colonial but not independent' reality, seemed a world away. While I could introduce these informal sites of creative action on the other side of the world, I was afraid they would be lost in translation. Did I even know the words to make sense of them myself? Reflecting on this brings to mind the words of another border-crossing artist:

> If the language I used failed to deliver, was I to appropriate another that talked to others even though it did not talk to me? How would a universal language work when the spaces in which we dwell are not synchronised?[5]

---

2    The latter refers to the New World Summit, a project established by Dutch artist Jonas Staal, as a series of 'summits' for political organisations that have been outlawed by the governments under which they live (typically as 'terrorists'), pointing to the limits of 'democracy'. The first summit, held at the Berlin Biennale in January 2014, included representations by the Kurdish Women's Movement, the Basque Independence Movement, the National Liberation Movement of Azawad and the National Democratic Front of the Phillipines. See www.newworldsummit.eu.

3    I also found it awkward speaking on behalf of a wide group of artists whom I had discussed with organisers with the intention of their participation, rather than my own. I suspect that had the Umbrella protests of September 2014 occurred before the exhibition and symposium, participation by Hong Kong artists and activists would have been sought.

4    Part of the spread of 'Occupy' actions following Occupy Wall Street, Occupy Central was an occupation under the HSBC bank headquarters, in Central, Hong Kong, initiated 15 October 2011 and forcibly evicted on 11 September 2012.

5    Phaptawan Suwannakudt, 'Catching the Moment, One Step at a Time', in F. Nakamura, M. Perkins and O. Krischer eds, *Asia Through Art and Anthropology: Cultural Translation Across Borders* (London: Bloomsbury, 2013), 99.

Figure 8: Exhibition view from *Global Activism* at ZKM Centre for Art and Media, Germany, February 2014. Detail of an artwork by Mark Wallinger, comprising a reconstruction of a 'peace camp' in London's Parliament Square, where activist Brian Haw lived from 2001 until his eviction in 2006, in protest at the UK's participation in wars in Iraq and Afghanistan. In 2007, Wallinger's 'installation' based on Haw's encampment won the prestigious Turner Prize following its exhibition at the Tate Modern.

Source: Olivier Krischer.

How can we talk about collective actions in Hong Kong or East Asia, particularly in cases where networks of collaborators work between formally distinct political systems? Calling for less 'state-centred' understandings of politics, some recent approaches in political science recognise the integral role of 'informal politics' in various East Asian political systems. Ditttmer, Fukui and Lee's *Informal Politics in East Asia* (2000), for example, focuses on the ways informal actors, particularly kinship groups and factions, work to affect change through formal political institutions, legally or otherwise.[6] Interestingly, they note how such informal affiliations can predate the institutional systems with which they now negotiate. Examples

6    L. Dittmer, H. Fukui and P. N. S. Lee eds, *Informal Politics in East Asia* (Cambridge, UK: Cambridge University Press, 2000). This features case studies from Taiwan, China, South Korea, North Korea and Vietnam.

include the roles of former Route Army factions in China, Kuomintang (KMT) factions in Taiwan, or the oligarchic continuity bridging pre- and postwar politics in Japan. While sharing certain modes of action, such informal actors operate differently in different political systems. In China, 'submerged networks' might only become apparent during leadership changes or Party crises, whereas elsewhere they have become structural and publicly acknowledged, as in Japan.[7] While the so-called marketisation of conflicts of interest can decrease violent confrontation, it can also lead to increased corruption. Significantly, the authors point out that such informal, even 'illegal' machinations are often employed to affect legitimate change where formal channels have become difficult or unworkable.

But this analysis remains focused on formal institutions as central agents in societal change. Where Fukui recognises that an appreciation of informal politics means that 'many contemporary social issues are … neither a priori private and non-political nor a priori public and political', institutions remain the legitimate political agents.[8] For Dittmer, informal politics 'consists of the use of non-legitimate means (albeit not necessarily illegal) to pursue public ends. Thus it is conceptually sandwiched between formal politics on the one hand and "corruption" on the other'.[9] Despite expanding the notion of politics, this still seems close to the 'who gets what, when, and how' approach, in which it remains institutions that author(ise) change in 'public' life.[10] Informal politics here acts according to the limits of an existing system, even when circumventing it. Moreover, the persistence of such informal channels is attributed to the weak rule of law and weak formal institutions, while institutional democratisation is aligned with economic growth. Accordingly, for Dittmer, Fukui and Lee, the 'logical step' is to form or join institutionalised political parties, which provide more 'civil' means of settling differences.[11] But what about

---

7    Lowell Dittmer, 'Conclusion: East Asian Informal Politics in Comparative Perspective', in Dittmer, Fukui and Lee, *Informal Politics in East Asia*, 298–99.

8    Haruhiro Fukui, 'Introduction: On the Significance of Informal Politics', in Dittmer, Fukui and Lee, *Informal Politics in East Asia*, 1–20, citation from 8.

9    Dittmer, 'Conclusion: East Asian Informal Politics in Comparative Perspective', 292. Emphasis in the original.

10   See Harold D. Lasswell, *Politics: Who Gets What, When, How*, reprinted in Harold D. Lasswell, *The Political Writings of Harold D. Lasswell* (New York: The Free Press, 1951), 295–461.

11   Dittmer, 'Conclusion: East Asian Informal Politics in Comparative Perspective', 307.

attempts at redefining a formal system or of acting autonomously of formal structures, either individually or collectively, such as in the form of social movements or citizen collectives?

In the wake of the Paris student movement of May 1968, some European historians and sociologists reconsidered the role of social movements not merely as ephemeral protests but as vehicles of urban change. Building on the work of Alain Touraine, Manuel Castells in particular has theorised the relationship between cities and social change, focusing on civic movements across different times and cultures.[12] Discussing the Comunidades of Castilla (1520–22), in which citizens allied with nobles against the Spanish monarchy, Castells recognised that citizens acted collectively on the basis of common concerns rather than structural conditions such as social class. '[T]he comuneros designated their opponents in terms of their monopoly over political institutions and not on the basis of their social privileges.'[13] Castells sees this as representing the underlying structure of social movements in many times and places. This importantly casts social movements and citizen collectives as legitimate historical agents. However, it is sometimes difficult to differentiate between 'movements' and uprisings in Castells' work. In his case studies, people directly seek more equitable political representation by affecting institutional change, or through revolution, which here means the seizure of institutional power.[14] Even in his more recent work on social movements in the 'Internet age'— including civil uprisings in Iceland and North Africa, and the Occupy movement in North America—Castells remains drawn to a dualistic interaction between 'power and counterpower', an 'endless historical process of conflict and bargaining' with institutions that 'regulate peoples' lives'.[15] While he identifies a fundamental 'battle for the construction of meaning in the minds of the people', Castells seems less concerned with the ways in which people constantly renegotiate such systems

---

12    Manuel Castells, *The City and the Grassroots: A Cross-Cultural Theory of Urban Social Movements* (Berkeley: University of California Press, 1983), 291.

13    ibid., 7.

14    The other case studies are the Paris Commune (1871), the Glasgow Rent Strike (1915), the Movimiento Inquilinarios or 'Tenants Union' strike in Veracruz, Mexico (1922–27), and the 'revolt of the American cities' during the 1960s, demanding community control and racial equality in the face of a burgeoning postindustrial society. Hence, in all but the last example what Castells presents as 'movements' essentially took the form of uprisings, as direct and temporary challenges to institutional authority.

15    Manuel Castells, *Networks of Outrage and Hope: Social Movements in the Internet Age* (Cambridge, UK: Polity, 2012), 5.

at an individual level too.[16] What if actors do not form 'the majority', despite collective mobilisation? Or if collectives are tenuous, protracted or intermittent networks of loosely affiliated groups and individuals? How do we recognise collective actions that take the form of ongoing collaborations rather than rallying behind a single cause or principle?

Responding particularly to the anti-nuclear movement of the early 1980s, Alberto Melucci observed that what he called 'new social movements' had increasingly shifted 'from the "political" form, which was common to traditional opposition movements in Western societies, to cultural ground'.[17] Melucci felt the very notion of a movement is confined by the limited vocabulary of sociological discourse, which 'inherits a legacy of dualism from philosophies of history'[18] and therefore suffers from the 'epistemological challenge' of belonging to the same conceptual framework as 'progress' or 'revolution'.[19] Understood in this way, social movements are described either in terms of 'breakdown' (collective economic crisis or social disintegration), or 'solidarity' (shared interests within a common structural condition, such as class). This dualism might be expressed in terms of 'structure/motivation', where collective action derives either from the logic of the system (e.g. socioeconomic context) or from personal beliefs (e.g. ideology, values).[20]

Instead, Melucci considered movements or collective actions as social constructions, 'built by an organisational investment'.[21] By concentrating on 'systemic relationships rather than the logic of actors', he comes to describe movements as 'action systems': a structure that facilitates communication and interdependence among actors, even in apparently loose or temporary circumstances. These systems are dynamic, 'built by aims, beliefs, decisions, and exchanges operating in

---

16    ibid., 246.

17    Alberto Melucci, 'The Symbolic Challenge of Contemporary Movements', *Social Research* 52, no. 4 (Winter 1985): 789. For a comparative definition of 'old' and 'new' political paradigms as they are used here, see Claus Offe, 'New Social Movements: Challenging the Boundaries of Institutional Politics', *Social Research* 52, no. 4 (Winter 1985): 821–32. Briefly, the 'old' paradigm of the post–World War II period emphasised economic growth and security, keeping civil society at a distance from public policy participation; the 'new' paradigm, writes Offe, is action in a third space that does not conform to the binary public or private of liberal politics. The 'political' here is when both: 1. The actor claims the means of action be recognised as legitimate, and 2. The ends of action can be recognised by the wider community.

18    Melucci, 'The Symbolic Challenge of Contemporary Movements', 790.

19    ibid., 799.

20    ibid., 790.

21    ibid., 792–3.

a systemic field'. Collective identity thus becomes less a condition than 'a shared definition' of the plural opportunities and constraints offered by collective action.

> Actors in conflicts are increasingly *temporary*, and their function is to *reveal the stakes*, to announce to society that a fundamental problem exists in a given area. They have a growing symbolic function; one can probably speak of a *prophetic function*. They are a kind of *new media*. They do not fight merely for material goals or to increase their participation in the system. They fight for symbolic and cultural stakes, for a different meaning and orientation of social action. They try to change people's lives; they believe that you can change your life today while fighting for more general changes in society.[22]

Furthermore, Melucci accepted that postindustrial urban life, as it was then emerging, has not only an economic base but also a symbolic and cultural one. Collective action is not carried out simply to exchange goods or increase formal political participation, 'it challenges the logic governing production and appropriation of social resources'.[23] The organisation of such movements is more diffuse, like a network, '"informal" relationships connecting core individuals and groups to a broader area of participants and "users" of services and cultural goods produced by the movement'.[24] Increasingly autonomous, this kind of collective action is a 'point of convergence for different forms of behaviour which the system cannot integrate'—not only for conflict, but also for 'social deviance and cultural innovation'.[25] The 'movement networks' become systems of exchange, through which people and information circulate, with participation becoming a goal in itself. 'Since action is focused on cultural codes, the form of the movement is a message, a symbolic challenge to the dominant patterns.' In short, by practicing the change they are struggling for, 'they redefine the meaning of social action for the whole society'.[26]

---

22   ibid., 797. Emphasis in the original.

23   ibid., 798.

24   ibid., 798–9.

25   ibid., 799.

26   ibid., 801. Melucci developed these ideas into a general theory of collective identity and action in the late 1980s and 1990s, particularly with the increased effect of telecommunications on collective social actions. See Melucci, *Nomads of the Present: Social Movements and Individual Needs in Contemporary Society* (London: Hutchinson Radius, 1989) and *Challenging Codes: Collective Action in the Information Age* (Cambridge and New York: Cambridge University Press, 1996). For a comparative discussion of Melucci's work on theories of community as action and collective identity, see Gerard Delanty, *Community*, 2nd ed. (London; New York: Routledge, 2009), 94–9.

# The Politics of Aesthetics

How does the action of a part symbolically challenge, by its very definition, the meaning of the whole? Bearing some similarity to Melucci's reinterpretation of a movement as a dynamic 'action system', Jacques Rancière's re-reading of aesthetics has had a notable impact on current thinking in both the arts and politics. Rancière sees aesthetics not merely as 'the sensible', but rather as a certain 'modality' through which the sensible is distributed (*partagé*, literally 'shared'). This derives from Rancière's understanding of the Greek term *aesthesis* as the capacity both to perceive something and to make sense of it.[27] This situates politics as emerging from the aesthetic experience itself, because of 'the way in which aesthetic experience—as a refiguration of the forms of visibility and intelligibility of artistic practice and reception—intervenes in the distribution of the sensible'.[28]

To appreciate Rancière's notion of a politics of aesthetics, it is useful to consider his distinction between three 'regimes of identification' in art: the ethical, the poetic and the aesthetic.[29] In the ethical regime, 'art' is not valued for itself. Rather the origin and purpose of art take precedence. Judgement is based on the extent to which an image, for example, fulfils its function. The poetic regime involves representation, in that the principle of mimesis organises 'ways of doing, seeing, making, judging'. It distinguishes art as such, allowing the identification of imitations and the development of normative principles, which underpin the classical 'fine arts'. By contrast, in the aesthetic regime 'artistic phenomena are identified by their adherence to a specific regime of the sensible, which is extricated from its ordinary connections and is inhabited by a heterogeneous power, the power of a form of thought that has become foreign to itself'.[30] The aesthetic regime frees art from the rules of subject, material and genre; it removes the 'mimetic barrier' that distinguishes artistic 'ways of doing and making' from other social practices.[31]

---

27  Jacques Rancière, 'The Aesthetic Dimension: Aesthetics, Politics, Knowledge', *Critical Inquiry* 36, no. 1 (Autumn 2009): 1.
28  ibid., 5.
29  Jacques Rancière, *The Politics of Aesthetics: The Distribution of the Sensible*, trans. Gabriel Rockhill (London; New York: Continuum, 2004), 20–4.
30  Rancière, *The Politics of Aesthetics*, 22.
31  ibid.

For Rancière, the aesthetic regime is a democratic situation; it is here that politics takes place as such, because for him the *demos* is not the power of the everyone but rather of 'the whoever'. 'It is the principle of infinite substitutability or indifference to difference, of the denial of any principle of dissymmetry as the ground of the community.'[32] Dissymmetry is a structural inequality, while the democratic 'supplement' represents an inherent capacity to question the perceived or prevailing order of the system. 'This is the aesthetic dimension of politics: the staging of a dissensus—of a conflict of sensory worlds—by subjects who act as if they were the people.'[33] Rancière's concept of politics liberates democracy from the state; it also implies that politics is naturally transgressive—it points to the inherent potential of the political subject whose faculties open to them an aesthetic experience, an 'as if', in which anything is possible (or thinkable).[34] 'Politics revolves around what is seen and what can be said about it, around who has the ability to see and the talent to speak, around the properties of spaces and the possibilities of time.'[35] It is in this sense of politics as transgressive that we might discover the potential for aesthetic, creative practices to intervene in and redefine the status quo. I think it is also significant that this approach emphasises the staging of politics, the enacting of an 'as if', which (in politics) is a legitimate state of being. This function of metaphorical action is highly relevant to creative forms of activism.

## Wooferten: Community, Art and Activism

An examination of Wooferten in Hong Kong provides an opportunity to explore informal life politics from the perspective of aesthetic practice and metaphorical action. It should also be noted that it is just one example among many different initiatives that have emerged in Hong Kong during the last decade. It was by no means the first artist-run space, nor the first organisation using arts to activate or interrogate ideas of community and local heritage, but it offers a good example of the establishment, development and transformation of a fixed space for artistic and social

---

32  Rancière, 'The Aesthetic Dimension: Aesthetics, Politics, Knowledge', 10.
33  ibid., 11.
34  This has also more broadly been part of Rancière's attempts to deprivilege philosophy as the exclusive domain of sense-making. See Gabriel Rockhill, 'Translator's Introduction: Jacques Rancière's Politics of Perception', in Jacques Rancière, *The Politics of Aesthetics*, 2.
35  Rancière, *The Politics of Aesthetics*, 13.

experimentation, in years that have seen a flurry of social action. The participation of a younger generation of so-called 'Post-80s' artist-activists has also been significant in Wooferten's experience.[36]

It is difficult to succinctly describe Wooferten, as the nature of the space, its activity and 'management' has evolved in response to both the administrative system under and against which it operates, as well as to the community in and with which it acts. When I first visited, on a balmy Hong Kong night in August 2011, a Japanese activist-artist, Ichimura Misako, was about to start her presentation. Her talk was being translated from Japanese to Cantonese for a crowd of around 20 people—which at Wooferten meant the shopfront space was packed. Ichimura is a 'homeless artist' and activist who had been invited by the space to spend a couple of weeks in Hong Kong, presenting her work informally while also realising a series of actions locally. These local actions were then photographed and added to documentation she showed as an exhibition. On one wall, painted a vivid red, ran the Japanese words 'Hands off Miyashita Park!', with a megaphone positioned nearby. These seemed like a vignette, reenacted for this Hong Kong audience, from the protests in which Ichimura had been active, against plans by the Nike Corporation to 'sponsor', gentrify and commercialise a Tokyo public park used by homeless people.

Wooferten was established in September 2009 as a non-profit organisation, and successfully applied to operate the Shanghai Street Artspace, administered by the Arts Development Council (ADC).[37] This old corner shop once operated as a Chinese herbalist until the late 1990s, yet the building belongs to the Hong Kong Government. Around 2000, the government agreed to lease it to the relatively new ADC as a goodwill gesture and made it available for arts projects based on annual competitive applications. For nearly a decade it was used for a variety of

36   Lee Chun Fung 李俊峰, 'Cong bashihou de guandian kan huohuating' [Wooferten, seen from a Post-80s Perspective] 從八十後的觀點看活化廳, in Yuk Hui and DOXA Collective eds, *Creative Space: Art and Spatial Resistance in East Asia* (Hong Kong: Roundtable Synergy Books, 2014), 214–22.
37   The Hong Kong Arts Development Council is a statutory authority established in 1995 to advise the Hong Kong Government on cultural policy, distribute grants and promote various art forms in the territory.

small-scale arts programmes, ranging from art education to exhibitions, nominally inspired by the idea of 'community arts', in a renovated white-cube gallery setting.[38]

By 2009, when artist Luke Ching (b. 1972) noticed that the ADC was soliciting applications again, the local art scene, and indeed Hong Kong more generally, had significantly changed; as founding member and inaugural manager Jasper Lau put it, 'people were talking about community'.[39] Ching, whose pioneering practice actively intervenes in or 'hijacks' parts of city life,[40] saw an opportunity to focus on artistic process rather than object-making, and to interrogate the idea of community art being touted by the ADC. Ching approached artist friends whose work had engaged with political and social issues; as a result, Wooferten was established as a non-profit arts organisation, with 10 'members', nominally led by Ching and managed by critic-curator Jasper Lau.[41] The space was intended as a place in the middle of Yau Ma Tei where the community could meet art, and art could meet the local community. Yau Ma Tei is an old Kowloon neighbourhood that now finds itself at the edge of the future West Kowloon Cultural District—a massive, and controversial, HKD80 billion cultural and commercial development announced in 1996–97, designed to realise the Special Administrative Region (SAR) Government's vision of Hong Kong as a 'world city', but which has repeatedly been criticised as a typical top-down project that ignores existing communities, local needs and real cultural diversity.[42]

---

38    Unless otherwise noted, the following information is based on interviews with founding members Jasper Lau Kin-Wah and Lee Chun Fung (interviewed in Yau Ma Tei, Hong Kong, 19 January 2012) and Luke Ching Chin-Wai (interviewed at Wooferten, in Yau Ma Tei, Hong Kong, 24 October 2013), as well as articles reflecting on Wooferten. See particularly Lee Chun Fung, 'Wooferten', in Alice Ko ed., *Reverse Niche: Dialogue and Rebuilding at the City's Edge* (Taiwan, 2013), 202–11 [Chinese] and 216–24 [English]. I have generally referred to the Chinese version, as the English is an abridged translation.

39    Interview with Lau, Hong Kong, 19 January 2012.

40    Interview with Luke Ching; see also Lee Chun Fung, 'A Good Idea is Hijack', dated 2 November 2012, translated by Sumyi Li. This was apparently published for the Asia Art Award 2010 in which Ching was nominated. leechunfung.blogspot.com.au/2012/11/a-good-idea-is-to-hijack-it.html.

41    Interview with Lau, Hong Kong, 19 January 2012. The 10 founding members were Luke Ching, Jasper Lau, Kwang Sheung Chi, Doris Wong Wai-ying, Wan Yau, Clara & Gum Cheung, Cally Yu, Edwin Lai Kin Keung, Law Man Lok and Lee Chun Fung.

42    The West Kowloon Cultural District (WKCD) project is a legacy of Hong Kong's first post-handover Chief Executive, Tung Chee-hwa, and has become a much studied example of post-handover governance issues. See Agnes Shuk-mei Ku, 'Contradictions in the Development of Citizenship in Hong Kong: Governance without Democracy', *Asian Survey* 49, no. 3 (May/June 2009): 521–4; and Carolyn Cartier, 'Culture and the City: Hong Kong, 1997-2007', *The China Review* 8, no. 1 (Spring 2008): 66–9.

Ching's original idea was for Wooferten to be a short-term creative experiment, lasting only one or two years. In the first year, the group developed exhibitions and projects that actively sought to engage with and learn about the surrounding community, not only as an audience for their artwork but as participants, local experts and neighbours—or rather *kaifong* 街坊, people from the neighbourhood (a Cantonese term that repeatedly appears in Wooferten materials). The project 'Small Small Prize! Big Big Pride!' took the form of a competition where participants were asked to nominate their favourite local shops, for which DIY trophies were made by Wooferten and delivered with fanfare to the winning establishments. Another early project, 'Mastermind', connected artists with the workshops of local craftspeople and technicians, including expert activities outside the typical realm of the arts, such as electrical repairs and locksmithing. Like many of Wooferten's subsequent projects, these were bilateral: Wooferten learnt more about the area and their neighbours, while also sharing skills, resources and local history, and cultivating more trust.

The space often played with the formal concept of an institution to serve new purposes: for example, when they discovered that a flower plaque (*faapai* 花牌) maker had lost his workshop in nearby Sham Shui Po due to an urban redevelopment project, Wooferten offered him a permanent space at the back of their premises, as an 'Artist in Residence', naming him Wooferten's 'Flower Plaque Master in Residence'. Subsequently, Wong Nai-chung, the flower plaque master, adapted his commercial practice to suit his new circumstances, creating plaques with slogans of protest, as well as making public presentations and demonstrations to raise awareness of this unique local cultural practice, which has been pushed ever further from the city by rising rents and the upscaling of local businesses. Once resident at Wooferten, Wong's work became part of the space's activity; he made a large 'Wooferten' *faapai* for the shopfront, and later began contributing a regular column to Wooferten's local newsletter, becoming inextricably associated with the space.[43]

---

43    Ironically, Wong Nai-chung's work has since become better known, while the surge in projects relating to local customs and heritage has also heightened awareness of flower plaques and other local artisanal trades being pressured by urban redevelopment. Jasper Lau has published a slideshow explaining how the government repossessed Wong's shop and home, and his subsequent practice. See 'Flower Plaque (Faa Pai) Craft Master Wong Nai Chung', YouTube video, 6.30, posted by 'kin wah lau', 2013. www.youtube.com/wa tch?v=lu7JftKIHDo, accessed 18 December 2015.

Figure 9: An event at Wooferten in September 2013.
Source: Courtesy of Lee Chung Fung and Wooferten.

Wooferten's development then took a slightly different turn, with management passing to the youngest founding member, Lee Chun Fung. When the ADC seemed poised to take the space back after a year of operation, members deliberated on whether to reapply or to leave.[44] Lee and a few others chose to carry on developing the space's activities, emphasising a two-pronged approach: continuing to make experimental art projects with community relevance, while also promoting the gallery space as an informal community centre, providing amenities such as a water fountain, comfortable sofa and public computer, even posting a sign on the door that invited locals to drop by 'anytime'. Local children (including those of South Asian migrant working families in the area) stop by after school; some elderly neighbours, even volunteers from other parts of Hong Kong, started dropping in to take part in whatever was happening and to propose their own projects. This 'living room' indeed seems to be reflected in the organisation's name: 'Wooferten' is an

---

44 Jasper Lau and Lee Chung Fung, interview by author, digital recording, Hong Kong, 19 January 2012; also see Lee Chung Fung 'Wooferten', in Lee Chung Fung ed., *Wooferten's Art/Activist in Residence (AAIR) 2011-12*, (Hong Kong: Wooferten, 2014), 129.

alternative, slightly Anglophone-looking transliteration of the Cantonese words *wut faa teng*, suggesting a 'hall' or place (*teng* 廳) for 'activation or revitalisation' (*wut faa* 活化).[45]

## Lee Chun Fung and Art Activism

Born in 1984, Lee identifies as a member of Hong Kong's 'Post-80s' generation, those who came of age in the late 1990s to mid-2000s, the first decade of People's Republic of China (PRC) rule, in which issues of Hong Kong values and identity progressively came to the fore.[46] After graduating in fine arts from the Chinese University of Hong Kong, Lee worked with the Artist Commune, another community-oriented non-profit arts organisation, established in 1997 and located in the Cattle Depot Artists Village—a repurposed heritage building also administered by the ADC. Why this interest in community? One notable turning point is the year 2003, marked by the SARS outbreak, an economic downturn that dented the developmental myth of Hong Kong as a money market and, most importantly, saw massive popular protests against attempts to introduce anti-subversion laws (the notorious Article 23). For Lee, and many other 20-somethings, however, the real catalyst was the movement to preserve Central's Star Ferry Pier, in 2006.

In August 2006, Lee and a group who came to be known as 'We Are Society' began to stage weekly performances and installations at the pier, later joined by teaching artist Kith Tsang Tak-ping and his students from Polytechnic University. They hoped to raise public awareness of the government's decision to demolish the 1950s pier despite heritage reports noting its significance in public memory and the potential for an outcry.[47] While other political and conservation organisations attempted to negotiate with the government and then to apply legal pressure, as Lee has

---

45   ibid., 129.
46   Debate surrounding the definition and legacy of the Post-80s continues in Hong Kong. See Gary Wong Pui-fung and Yuk Hui eds, *Pre- & Post-80s: Beyond Social Movements—Imagining Discourse and the Generation* (Hong Kong: Roundtable Synergy Books, 2010).
47   Cartier, 'Culture and the City: Hong Kong, 1997–2007', 76.

observed, the Post-80s group deliberately chose direct action, stressing the personal concern they felt for what was at stake, and hence the need to represent themselves rather than waiting to be represented by others.[48]

In her article reflecting on cultural and urban development in the first decade since Hong Kong's handover to Chinese rule, Carolyn Cartier describes attending the protest site just prior to the final closure and demolition.

> [T]he entrance to the piers had been boarded up, and cultural activists had mounted placards, information boards and banners all around … in the middle of the roadway where taxis had queued, was a young woman sitting on top of a high ladder, dressed in taut black, looking towards the clocktower. Scissors in hand, she intermittently and methodically cut off pieces of her hair and gave them to the cold breeze. Police stood by and watched; news camera crews filmed her and bystanders with digital cameras put them on movie mode. She was having a mesmerising effect, her silent performance speaking to Hong Kong people: the loss of the Star Ferry piers is deeply personal, like losing a piece of yourself.[49]

Even as the Star Ferry pier was being finally closed and demolished in December 2006, protestors, no doubt buoyed by public support, vowed to take the fight to the nearby Queen's Ferry Pier, slated for a similar fate in April of the following year under the government's reclamation project. Attempts were made to legally challenge the government's position on demolition as the only feasible option. Yet, while the high court eventually ruled in the government's favour and police evicted the remaining protestors (some of whom had begun a hunger strike), the Post-80s had already coalesced, invigorating the pre-existing groups of social actors and inspiring new ones. By the time of the Queen's Ferry action, a certain pattern was emerging: young activists occupied the site, draping banners and tents over the building, while also hosting various creative events in situ, all well documented by the media, the participants and passersby. Meanwhile veteran activists, pan-democrat politicians and experts (e.g. conservationists and architects) pointedly questioned the government's claim of lacking viable alternatives to demolition, evidently

---

48    Transcript provided by Lee Chun Fung, from his presentation 'We Wanna Make a Change: Art and Social Actions of the Post-80s Generation', presented on 29 May 2011 in 'Backroom Conversations: Open Platform', hosted by Asia Art Archive for the 2011 Hong Kong Art Fair.
49    Cartier, 'Culture and the City: Hong Kong, 1997-2007', 77.

inspired by the Post-80s' new style of protest.[50] Eventually, some of the young protestors launched a hunger strike, but all were soon forcibly removed by police for 'illegal obstruction'.

Again in late 2009, when the government had begun to demolish parts of Choi Yuen village, in New Territories, to make way for a high-speed rail link[51]—which will terminate in the West Kowloon Cultural District development—a loose yet sizeable coalition of art workers, activists and Post-80s (many of whom had taken part in actions to preserve the Star and Queen's Ferry piers), gathered in support of the village. Some Post-80s formed the 'Post 80s Anti-High Speed Rail' group. Apparently inspired by the protests of Korean farmers against the World Trade Organization in 2005, they staged a Tibetan-style single-file walk through five districts, silently pacing, with rice in their hands, prostrating themselves in the winter wind every 26 steps, as they wove their way towards the building of the Legislative Council in the centre of downtown Hong Kong.[52] Later, back in Choi Yuen, organisers coordinated with local villagers to stage a two-day festival amid the half-demolished buildings, which became site-specific installations (including a photography show of the Post-80s walking action), ad hoc museum displays, public sculptures, as well as stages for literature readings and music concerts. Films were screened and homemade snacks were sold by volunteers, in what was dubbed 'Choi Yuen Tsuen Woodstock: An Arts Festival among the Ruins', a defiant display of grassroots cultural solidarity.[53]

One particularly important focus of Lee's artistic and curatorial work has been the history of the June Fourth protests in Beijing and subsequent crackdown, a topic that is both near and far from Hong Kong. On the

---

50    For instance, veteran 'leftist' activist Leung Foon, from the Society for Community Organisation (established in 1972), comments on this intergenerational relationship in 'West Kowloon and Star Ferry Pier', in Iman Fok ed., *Our Life in West Kowloon* (Hong Kong: Society for Community Organisation, 2007), 31–5. Also see Wong and Yuk eds, *Pre- & Post-80s: Beyond Social Movements—Imagining Discourse and the Generation*.

51    Officially known as the Guangzhou–Shenzhen–Hong Kong Express Rail Link, dubbed 'XRL', constructed by the MTR Corporation, in 2011 the project was already accused of being an unjustified public expense at HKD67 billion; whereas in 2015 this has risen to an estimated HKD85.3 billion. See www.expressraillink.hk/en/project-details/key-information.html. Accessed 18 December 2015.

52    Valerie C. Doran, 'Viewed From a Train: Glimpses of the Artist as Hong Kong Citizen', *Perspectives* (Asia Art Archive Newsletter), March 2011, www.aaa.org.hk/Diaaalogue/Details/977. Accessed 20 September 2013. The village's support group also produced a two-hour documentary film about the movement, *Raging Land: Breaking New Ground Through Thorns and Thistles* [ 鐵怒沿線－華路藍樓 *Tienu yanxian - bi lu lan lou*] (Hong Kong: V-artivist and Supporting Group of Choi Yuen Village, 2010), DVD.

53    Doran, 'Viewed From a Train'.

one hand, on 1 July every year a march is held in memory of the event, the first of which, in 1989, remains the largest collective public action in Hong Kong's history. However, Lee has been acutely aware of not having personally experienced June Fourth at the time, given his age. Unlike an older generation, which remembers the scenes on the news and took part in that first march, some Post-80s like Lee have actively sought to form their own knowledge of and relationship with this history.[54] To mark the 20th anniversary of June Fourth, in mid-2009, just prior to the establishment of Wooferten, Lee and colleagues from We Are Society organised 'P-at-riot', a project held at the Cattle Depot Artist Village, comprising exhibitions, performances and discussions to not only commemorate the anniversary of June Fourth but also to probe each participant's relationship to the event and its memory in Hong Kong. A statement from exhibition materials remains a significant reflection on the relationship of the Post-80s to such events, and their tendency to search for their own answers:

> Twenty years have passed, and we have now grown up. In our eyes, June 4th is not just a historical incident that is waiting for vindication, it is an attitude which should be passed on to the next generations. In discussing June 4th, we have decided to move from melancholy (perhaps, a melancholy which could not be totally genuine). What we should bring up again here is the attitude of rethinking about the current situation as well as the gesture of standing out for the truth.

An anecdote about the origin of the name We Are Society aptly explains this different attitude among recent social activists and artists in Hong Kong, who identify more readily as 'the people'. Jasper Lau has explained that the name derives from the 1982 film *Nomad* (directed by Patrick Tam Kar Ming). When Cecilia Yip's character asks, 'What have we ever contributed to society?', Leslie Cheung retorts, 'What do you mean, society? We *are* society'.[55]

---

54 Anecdotally, a number of Hong Kong artists I have spoken to born in the 1960s, who were in their early to late 20s at the time, recall the 1989 march as their first (and, in many cases, until recently, their only) direct involvement in public actions—despite recognising that June Fourth left them more aware of politics or current affairs. See for example Olivier Krischer, 'Wilson Shieh: Political Avatar', Wilson Shieh … Sumbody (Hong Kong: Osage Gallery, 2013), 33–48.

55 Jasper Lau Kin-wah, 'Tipping Over: Of Politics of Aesthetics as Hong Kong Demands our Art Activism', *Art Critique of Taiwan ACT* 47 (2012): 75, note 2.

In early 2011, after returning from a residency at Tokyo's 3331 Arts Chiyoda centre, Lee had the idea to launch a residency programme through which, on a shoestring budget, Wooferten would host six artists and events between 2011–12, focused on guests who used their creative work as a method of social action. From Tokyo, Lee invited Ichimura Misako 市村美佐子, who lives as a homeless person in Tokyo's Yoyogi Park. Ichimura (a graduate of Japan's prestigious Tokyo University for the Arts) had become interested in squatting after a short stay in Amsterdam in 2002, and soon decided to move onto the streets after returning to Japan. From this position she shares the experiences of fellow homeless people, particularly women. One initiative was to start a 'barter café' with fellow resident Ogawa Tetsuo in the blue-tent village where they lived, as a place where homeless and non-homeless could meet without the need for money. Ichimura has also become involved in causes related to the use of public space, such as the long protests to stop the privatisation of Miyashita Park in 2008–10, mentioned above.[56] Ichimura brought documentation from this protest to Hong Kong during her residency and organised a meal in a nearby small park, which included distributing food to anyone passing by. During her stay she tried to connect to local homeless people, to compare their situation with hers in Japan, and produced a series of photographs in which she lies down comfortably on local park benches, defying their intentionally anti-homeless designs, a common feature of gentrified urban public spaces worldwide.[57]

56   Tetsuo Ogawa 小川哲男 (trans. Chen 'Nine Zero' Jiong-lin), 'The Resistance of Miyashita Park Art Village' 宮下公園藝術村的抗爭 [gongxia gongyuan yishucun de kangzheng], in Yuk Hui and DOXA Collective eds, *Creative Space: Art and Spatial Resistance in East Asia* (Hong Kong: Roundtable Synergy Books, 2014), 164–79.
57   See Olivier Krischer, 'Lateral Thinking: Activist Networks in East Asia', *ArtAsiaPacific* 77 (2012): 99; also Misako Ichimura, 'Subversion in Parks and Streets', *Wooferten's Art/Activist in Residence (AAIR) 2011-12* (Hong Kong: Wooferten, 2014), 97–101.

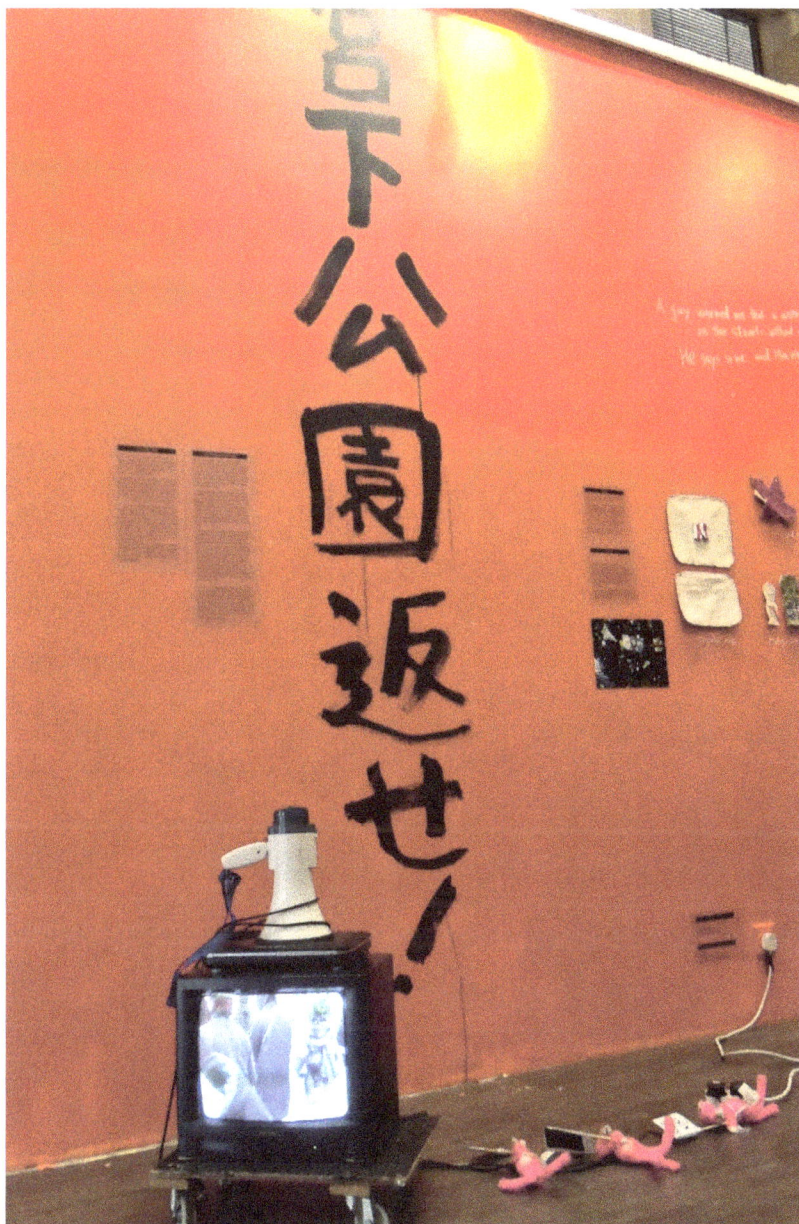

Figure 10: Installation view of Ichimura Misako's 'Homeless Artist' exhibition at Wooferten, August 2011. The slogan on the wall reads 'Hands off Miyashita Park!', referring to the ultimately unsuccessful protests by Ichimura and colleagues to save Tokyo's public Miyashita Park from private commercial development by the Nike Corporation.

Source: Courtesy Ichimura Misako and Wooferten.

The residency was also a way to build a regional network for Wooferten, connecting between locales rather than official agencies in first-tier cities, which is the typical formula for 'international' cultural projects. Lee had been introduced to Ichimura through a Korean artist-activist colleague, Kim Kang. Kang had been invited to Hong Kong in July of that year, with her collaborator and partner Kim Youn Hoan, and they led squatting workshops. Like Ichimura, Kim Kang had experienced squatting in Europe, in her case in France where she had written a postgraduate thesis on the subject. When she returned to Korea, the pair organised 'Oasis Project', targeting a building owned by Korea's largest arts association, the Federation of Artistic and Cultural Organisations of Korea, established in 1961, which has enjoyed close ties with successive conservative governments during its 50-odd year history. In 1994, the federation lobbied for funding to construct a 25-storey high-rise building in the centre of Seoul, ostensibly for artist use. By 2004, the project was still incomplete, apparently because government-allocated funds (around KRW16.5 billion, or USD14.8 million) had been redirected by the association, and also due to disputes with the contracted construction companies. The Kims argued that, as artists, this prime piece of Seoul real estate was intended for their use, so they went about organising a well-publicised squat event in which they stormed the building, with media in tow. While the federation claimed the whole project was illegal, the media attention ultimately led to an investigation and to charges relating to the federation's misuse of funds.

When Oasis Project came to an end in 2007, the Kims formed Lab39 with like-minded colleagues to investigate issues of government use of public land, producing a number of research reports. They moved into an area of Seoul known as Mullae-tong, at that time one of the few remaining light industrial areas of small-scale workshops, flanked by apartment complexes. They encouraged fellow artists and musicians to move into the area, which meant negotiating individual leases, but soon well over 100 artists had relocated. Cafes and music venues quickly popped up, even as the steel workshops continued trading. For their 2011 Hong Kong residency, the Kims adapted their project 'Squat Geography Information System (SGIS)', holding workshops to form a database of potential Hong Kong squatting sites, then undertaking an inspection of some, such as the former Oil Street Artist Village. They also documented the process of scaling the fence and symbolically 'reclaiming' this once vibrant public building.[58]

# A History for Social Movements in Hong Kong

Through the memorialisation of June Fourth as public memory, and through the development of activist residencies connecting Hong Kong urban issues to those of other metropolises in the region, Lee and Wooferten colleagues have bridged historical and national frontiers, and have reconnected with and created alternative narratives of identity and history in Hong Kong. In some cases, Lee has been surprised to discover the hidden resonance between contemporary and historical sites of social action—an example of which I will return to below. Many historians have marveled at the apparent social stability of colonial Hong Kong, described by some, for example, as an 'administrative absorption of politics'.[59] As history was often commissioned by the ruling authority or its allied elites, alternative narratives have surfaced only recently. Hong Kong's unique situation of 'decolonisation without independence' makes instances of anti-authoritarian action, even those that appear nationalistic, remain historically sensitive. Yet, even before 1997, social movements shaped politics and local identity in a variety of ways that, while distinct from the contemporary situation, nevertheless deserve to be rediscovered as parts of a longer historical arc through which to understand life politics in Hong Kong.

While the 1940s–50s saw labour strikes and reflections of the Chinese civil war, the watershed moment in postwar Hong Kong social movements was the so-called Kowloon riots of 1966–67. Most notably, the riots seem, in hindsight, to have prompted far-reaching policy shifts in the late 1960s and 1970s, through which the colonial administration invested more

---

58 Olivier Krischer, 'Lateral Thinking: Activist Networks in East Asia'; Kim Kang and Kim Youn Hoan, 'S.G.I.S. in Hong Kong', *Wooferten's Art/Activist in Residence* (AAIR) 2011–12 (Hong Kong: Wooferten, 2014), 62–67. Part of the site (No. 12 Oil Street, formerly the Royal Hong Kong Yacht Club clubhouse) was renovated and reopened as 'Oi! Oil Street Art Space' in May 2013.

59 Ambrose Y. C. King, 'Administrative absorption of politics in Hong Kong: emphasis on the grassroots level', in Ambrose Y. C. King and Rance P. L. Lee eds, *Social Life and Development in Hong Kong* (Hong Kong: Chinese University Press, 1981), 129.

earnestly in the recognition and enrichment of the local quality of life. Projects such as the highly effective Independent Commission Against Corruption (1974), the underground Mass Transit Rail system (1979),[60] even the recognition of Cantonese as an official language (1974), all date from this period and are now perceived as integral parts of local identity, generating notions such as rule of law, technology and efficiency, and Hong Kong as bastion of Cantonese heritage.

It is not my intention to claim that these riots raised the quality of Hong Kong life during the 1970s. Rather, my aim here is to deepen the context of contemporary social movements by showing the complex relationships that exist with earlier issues and sometimes even particular sites. The 1966 incident, for instance, was directly triggered by opposition to a fare increase on the Star Ferry, which escalated from general complaints and petitions when one man launched a hunger strike and openly clashed with the authorities, leading to wider protests, government repressions and then rioting.[61] Barely a year later, in May 1967, a series of labour disputes came to a head when 21 workers at a plastic flower factory in Kowloon clashed with police.[62] Within days the communist-dominated Hong Kong Federation of Trade Unions stepped in, and then on 15 May the Chinese Government made an official statement of protest to the British Embassy in Beijing. Anti-British demonstrations were staged in Beijing and Guangzhou, backed by *People's Daily* editorials, which reframed the disputes as an anti-colonial movement—echoing aspects of China's own ensuing Cultural Revolution. Seizing on this tacit endorsement, Hong Kong communists and leftist sympathisers initially launched anti-colonial demonstrations, strikes and propaganda campaigns; but when, by August,

---

60   While the first MTR line was opened in 1979, construction had begun in 1967, based on a government-commissioned study on alleviating traffic congestion.

61   Tai-lok Lui and Stephen W. K. Chiu, 'Social Movements and Public Discourse on Politics', in Tak-wing Ngo ed., *Hong Kong's History: State and Society Under Colonial Rule* (London; New York: Routledge, 1999), 104.

62   The factory was in fact owned by Li Ka-shing, then a young businessman, now one of Asia's wealthiest people, with influential stakes in all major aspects of Hong Kong life and beyond, including shipping, real estate, retail, communications and utilities. He is generally considered one of the most powerful figures in Hong Kong's capital-orientated political landscape.

the administration shut down leftist newspapers and launched raids and arrests, some leftists started a violent bombing campaign that lasted till October.[63]

Hong Kong was for many a safe haven from decades of uncertainty and conflict in China, memories easily rekindled by the Cultural Revolution. Rather than inspiring anti-colonial solidarity, such leftist violence had the opposite effect, radicalising anti-colonial politics to the point of alienating its intended constituency. The colonial administration quashed leftist agitators and quickly worked to bolster confidence in the government. The riots failed to open new channels of political participation, but they did draw attention to social issues such as labour conditions, access to housing and social services, which would inform both new government policies and grassroots pressure groups in the decade to come. In effect, 'politics had now been localised':[64] there was a shift from ideological 'Chinese politics' to more spontaneous, issue-driven actions, which— given the lack of political access inherent in the colonial 'consultative democracy' model—made protests the medium of local grievances.[65]

While Communist China may have been rejected, this did not equate to an increased identification with the colonial regime. For a younger (by then often Hong Kong-born) generation during the 1970s, the search for a new cultural identity even extended into an interest in cultural nationalism, exemplified in the 'imported' issue of the Defend Diaoyutai Movement.[66] In parallel, between 1950 and 1980, the colonial government gradually implemented stricter controls on immigration, introducing a 'Hong Kong Belonger' classification from 1971, which seemed to positively identify local identity, albeit as an offshoot of essentially exclusionary

---

63    Robert Bickers and Ray Yep eds, *May Days in Hong Kong: Riot and Emergency in 1967* (Hong Kong: Hong Kong University Press, 2009), 6–11. In preparation for *May Days in Hong Kong*, the editors organised a public forum on the riots in 2007, testimonies from which are included at the back of the book. Some who had witnessed or participated in the riots spoke of the experiences for the first time in nearly 40 years. In their study of social movements in Hong Kong, Lui and Chiu note there were no publicly available records documenting the experiences of riot participants, providing instead excerpts of a 1996 interview suggesting that non-communist students, many of them barely teenagers, had been mobilised, for example to print and distribute leftist anti-colonial materials, and were subsequently arrested by the authorities despite their young age. See Lui and Chiu, 'Social Movements and Public Discourse on Politics', 116, note 20.

64    Lui and Chiu, 'Social Movements and Public Discourse on Politics', 105.

65    Lui and Chiu, 'Social Movements and Public Discourse on Politics', 102.

66    Lui and Chiu, 'Social Movements and Public Discourse on Politics', 108. 'Defend Diaoyutai' refers to the movement to assert China's territorial right to the disputed islands known as Daioyutai in Chinese and the Senkaku Rettō in Japanese.

immigration policy shifts in the United Kingdom. This began to formalise distinctions between locals and newcomers in the face of ongoing, though more regulated, Chinese immigration. In 1980, the government assumed complete control of immigration. In her study of identity formation in relation to immigration policy, Agnes Ku has pointed out the multiple factors that contributed to identity formation in Hong Kong during this period, which include but are not limited to demographic shifts, distinction from Communist China amid the Cold War, community formation in the face of economic and social crises (such as the 1967 riots, or later the arrival of Vietnamese boat people), adherence to economic liberalism and rapid growth, or demographic shifts.[67] What is clear, however, is that the issue of Hong Kong identity was still shifting and unresolved when the colonial government formally embarked on the handover process in 1984.

In the period between the Draft Declaration of 1984 and the 1997 handover, expectations regarding political participation also significantly changed in Hong Kong. Beijing was perhaps unprepared for such a shift and largely interpreted demands for greater democratic participation as the result of British intervention in what would otherwise have been a smooth transition of sovereignty from the colonial administration to a Beijing-stamped bureaucracy of public servants with decades of local experience. Since then, at the heart of most large-scale protests have been the issues of state–capital collusion and a lack of equitable representation in the SAR's functional constituency model—most spectacularly in the recent so-called Umbrella protests, which initially rallied not for 'democracy', but the rather more concrete demand for 'real elections' (i.e. universal suffrage). Seen in this light, recent informal actions can be related to far-reaching issues of not only political representation, but more nuanced questions of local identity and values.

67    Agnes S. Ku, 'Immigration Policies, Discourses, and the Politics of Local Belonging in Hong Kong (1950–1980)', *Modern China* 30, no. 3 (July, 2004): 328.

# Post-Wooferten Postscript

From late 2013, the Arts Development Council informed Wooferten that its application for the coming year would not be approved. Lee and colleagues decided to occupy the space and they launched a media campaign to encourage debate around the closure. While the cyclical nature of ADC grants had not been surprising, they wished to draw attention to the unique position they had forged in the local community. There was a distinct irony in the way a multibillion dollar project such as the WKCD could be mired in a lack of public relevance, while a small space that worked hard to understand and be understood by its existing local community could be unceremoniously shut down. They have since formed the Wooferten Working Group to continue their activities, and through this they maintain a regular social media presence. In January 2014, with their eviction imminent, I received an upbeat email message from Lee Chun Fung, in which he noted:

> In fact, I think once we want to keep on doing something with the community we have no need to worry about not having a space to do it. And I don't need many resources either. We will do it in a more autonomous way, I'm quite confident about that. Hong Kong is an interesting place [now] because there are many artists concerned about their community. Most important is to sustain the network and keep on. That's just the very beginning.[68]

Lee's comment is reminiscent of Melucci's notion of the new social movement as an action network. Many art spaces and groups that have emerged in protests and social actions have since dispersed, but the individual artists and activists continue to share the same concerns, albeit looking for different means to articulate and act on them. Some have turned to full- or part-time farming, others to education, still others have altogether distanced themselves and their artwork from the flurry of protests. Some young artists have gone on to join longer-standing organisations engaged in urban and social research. I know one artist who has also begun intense research into religious art, setting aside his conceptual practice in the search for 'spiritual' responses to contemporary flux. In the same email conversation, Lee also wrote: 'To me, art never

---

68    Lee Chun Fung, email correspondence with author, 9 January 2014.

changes something directly. What's important is that art gives us a platform for joining together, to try to understand issues from an alternative angle, in a sustainable, intimate and subversive way.'[69]

In a more recent trip to Hong Kong, I learnt of a performance organised by Wooferten in the months after this conversation. With the space's fate apparently sealed, Lee and colleagues had nevertheless continued their work, combining their art and politics with the context of the community they had nurtured. In May and June 2014, they held two street performances near the Shanghai Street space that exemplify the complicated way in which informal life politics can affect history, identity and community. The performances were based on documentary research into a largely unknown incident forming a historical link between the Beijing protests of June 1989 and Hong Kong. Titled 'Back to 6.7.89: Pitt Street Riot—Rolling Theatre of Tiananmen Massacre', the event comprised reenactments and scripted reminiscences of 7 June 1989, just days after the news from Beijing had rocked Hong Kong. That night, on Pitt Street in Yau Ma Tei—barely 100 metres from the Wooferten space—a 'riot' had erupted; more than 7,000 people gathered, projectiles were thrown, cars were torched and looting occurred. Police bused into the scene fired 19 rounds of tear gas. One effect of this public disturbance was the cancellation of a massive rally commemorating the Beijing massacre, planned for the following day, which organisers estimated would have attracted 1.5 million people to the streets. Through this combination of street theatre and citizen history, Lee and others sought to unearth and reconnect to these missing memories and ask (as Rancière might put it), what if: What if the protest had taken place? What if we knew more about this riot, as a direct consequence of the Tiananmen protests in Hong Kong? How would the course of Hong Kong's history change? How does this change the history and possibility of protest in Hong Kong?[70]

---

69   Lee, email correspondence with author, January 2014.
70   A booklet and DVD have been produced documenting the event and this history, including short reminiscences from Yau Ma Tei locals. See *Pitt Street Riot – Rolling Theatre of Tiananmen Massacre Video & Documents* [碧街事件－六四滾動街頭劇場行動紀錄 *Bijie shijian - liusi gundong jietou juchang xingdong jilu*], edited by Lee Chun Fung (Hong Kong: Wooferten Kai Fong Wui, 2015). A selection of film clips and essays have also been collected on the project's website, to allow wider access to history of this incident: pittstreetriot.blogspot.com.au/2015_05_01_archive.html.

Figure 11: Performance still of the 'Back to 6.7.89 Pitt Street Riot – Rolling Theatre of Tiananmen Massacre', staged in Yau Ma Tei, Hong Kong, on 31 May and 7 June 2014.

Source: Image by Pak Chai; courtesy Lee Chung Fung.

In Lee's essay for the project titled 'Yesterday is Today but Also Tomorrow', he writes that the subject of this theatre was a 'missing' history, the story of this dramatic episode in Hong Kong's history of collective public action that has never been retold. Beyond immediate questions of social and economic injustice, many cases in which informal life politics take place similarly deal with missing or belated histories being sought out and retold. Given the proximity to Wooferten, and their relationships in the neighbourhood, Lee and his colleagues' 'research' consisted of interviews with neighbours, most of whom had not had the chance to discuss these events for over 20 years. Lee's own reflection on this unearthed history, then, is not only for the incident itself but rather its dormant and still potent legacy: the way it has sat silently in the hearts of a community until now.[71] Lee has actually noted how an experienced social worker friend of his once quipped that Wooferten, in its community centre approach, hadn't discovered anything, it was merely recreating the sort of community space in which their grandparents' generation would have

---

71    Lee Chun Fung, 'Yesterday is Today but also Tomorrow', in *Pitt Street Riot* (2015), 22–3.

once congregated.[72] Ideally, these were spaces in which the community was enacted, confirmed and reconstituted, acting as meeting places and forums to share concerns, histories and resources.

Wooferten's work has been an experiment in art and politics, but also many related facets of the community that the original members could not have foreseen—local history, identity, urbanisation, gentrification, labour rights, migrant workers and regional activism. In this chapter, I have situated creative social activism in Hong Kong in a broader history of social actions and cultural politics in Hong Kong. Melucci's work also alerted us to the need to recognise the limitations of existing discourse, and this remains vital if we are to recognise the kind of 'action networks' in which Wooferten work. The pressure of existing discourses always has the potential to radically redefine events. For example, just months after the Pitt Street Riot theatre piece, from late September to December 2014, the Umbrella movement occupied the streets of Hong Kong. Yet even before the last defiant occupiers had been evicted one last time from the streets, popular discussion turned immediately to the old dichotomy of success and failure. Had the movement been a success for mobilising so many diverse groups into direct, generally coordinated and incredibly sustained action? Or was it all ultimately a failure, since C. Y. Leung's government had managed to weather the storm, refusing to meet the movement's core demand of universal suffrage and, perhaps more importantly, since the movement had seemingly failed to maintain public support?

This chapter argues that the very nature of politics is to transgress such dichotomies, and this is typical of the examples of informal life politics we see practised here. Rancière's notion of creative transgressions is also useful in considering the relationship of art and politics in Wooferten. A final anecdote from Wooferten's 'Small Small Prize! Big Big Pride!' project succinctly intervenes in the question of art or politics. Lee Chun Fung recalls an episode in which one of the Yau Ma Tei locals, reflecting on the rapid changes in the community, suddenly burst into tears. Lee later observed:

---

72   Lee Chun Fung 李俊峰, 'Cong bashihou de guandian kan huohuating' [Wooferten, seen from a Post-80s Perspective], 222.

The reason she was crying was, on the one hand, the community was changing so quickly she couldn't help but forget; but on the other hand, because we were actively caring about this old district's past, it prompted her to suddenly reminisce. At that moment, it didn't really seem to matter where the 'art' was.[73]

---

73   ibid.

# 9

# Informal Life Politics of Marketisation in North Korea

Eun Jeong Soh

## Introduction

Observers of today's North Korea recognise that marketisation is a widespread phenomenon there. While the state-planned economic sector continues to persist, *changsa*[1] (a general term referring to various types of trade and business activities, on a private economic level) has become a necessity for survival. One's capacity to engage in trade activities has become a determinant of the survival and wealth of the household. Market as a mechanism of exchange is still limited to goods and services, and monetary and financial markets do not yet exist on a significant scale.[2] Nevertheless, in the everyday life of North Koreans, trade, both in marketplaces and in the underground economy, has become an absolutely crucial and fundamental means for survival and livelihood. The significance of the market not only holds for ordinary North Koreans but also for state officials at all levels, as well as for the

---

1    Lankov and Kim (2008) define *changsa* as 'dealings in the marketplace'. But in fact, *changsa* in North Korea also includes long-distance bartering and selling of goods outside of the marketplace: Andrei Lankov and Kim Seok-hyang, 'North Korean Market Vendors: The Rise of Grassroots Capitalists in a Post-Stalinist Society', *Pacific Affairs* 81–1 (2008): 53–72.
2    Lee Suk-ki, 'Change and Prospect for North Korea's Market', Unification Media Group Conference (14 September 2015), www.youtube.com/watch?v=uhVroKIUo88.

maintenance of public institutions and enterprises.[3] The market has become an essential backbone for the life of individual households as well as the entire North Korean political and economic system and thus has the potential to cause the current long-lasting regime either to fall, to muddle through, to transform, or even to thrive.

What is puzzling about the spread of *changsa* and the resultant marketisation of goods and services in North Korea is that they occurred in the absence of decisive and consistent institutional reforms necessary to facilitate marketisation. Marketisation in North Korea took place under the continued presence of state suppression of basic freedom of movement and association and the absence of property rights.[4] How have North Koreans continued to expand their private economic activities despite state authorities' persistent social controls and the selective punishments of market traders carried out in an effort to inhibit private economic activities? What social mechanisms have enabled such a formation and expansion of marketisation from below without the presence of market-inducing or market-permitting reforms?

On the phenomenon of marketisation in North Korea, Haggard and Noland most notably distinguish North Korea's form of marketisation as a 'marketisation from below'. Whereas other cases of marketisation occurred, initiated through top-down policy responses resulting from a bargaining process among elites, changes from below dominated the North Korean process and pushed the state to make incremental concessions. Marketisation in North Korea was 'a by-product of state failure', actualised by the decline of the state socialist economy in general and a more acute absence of wages and rations, which led to the full-blown famine of the 1990s.[5] Despite the central Party's efforts to crack down on market forces, state officials' corruption and exploitation of office for private gain facilitated the spiralling growth of markets.[6]

---

3    Kim Young-hwan, 'Change and Prospect for North Korea's Market', Unification Media Group Conference (14 September 2015), www.youtube.com/watch?v=Xq1SJ5nhTh0.
4    On this, see editor's remark on Andrei Lankov, 'The Limits to Marketisation: State and Private in Kimist North Korea', (14 June 2013), *Sino-NK*, sinonk.com/2013/06/14/marketization-and-its-limits-state-private-enterprises-in-north-korea/.
5    Haggard and Noland, 'Reform from Below: Behavioral and Institutional Change in North Korea', *Journal of Economic Behavior and Organization* 83 (2010): 133–4.
6    ibid., 133.

But seeing marketisation in North Korea simply as a phenomenon of state failure devalues the agency of people driven by a desire for survival. Was the private response to state failure indeed 'unintended'?[7] This conceptualisation overlooks the presence of tight state controls on freedom of movement and information and organised social life, despite which marketisation in North Korea occurred. Multiple agencies including the Public Security Bureau, the police, the Army and other ad hoc bodies created by the Centre implemented measures against anti-socialist activities including the market trade of various prohibited items. On top of these social control mechanisms, frequent ideological education and work mobilisation were supposed to divert people from fully engaging in private economic activities. In terms of policy inconsistencies, the central state swung between reluctant limited liberalisation measures in 2002 and counter-measures in 2005, followed by the disastrous currency reform in 2009. Given the state's efforts to deter and limit the growth of the market, grassroots marketisation in North Korea can more accurately be understood when the agency of individuals conducting market activities under such circumstances is taken into consideration in conjunction with the phenomenon of state failure. In fact, state failure, in the case of North Korea, did not simply occur from the top. Rather, people have helped to erode the state from below.

To highlight the dynamics of the process, this study pays attention to micro-dynamic mechanisms of the formation of collaborative relationships between law-implementing officials of the state apparatus and those who engage in trade. While distinguishing the two for analytical purposes, officials of the state apparatus, in reality, if not directly and openly, are most actively involved in trade. The relationship between the two is a dualistic one, cooperative as well as contentious. This chapter identifies practical strategies, cultural factors and normative justifications that constitute this relationship and facilitate the marketisation process under control.

Due to practical limitations on observing everyday life in North Korea, the evidence presented in this chapter comes from narratives of refugee informants in South Korea. I conducted two rounds of interviews—the first round from October to December 2013 and the second round from April to June 2015. Each round consisted of 25 interviews, in which

---

7    ibid.

interviewees spoke about their own experiences and observation of private economic activities in North Korea. The refugee informants came from a diverse range of backgrounds in terms of age, gender, hometown, occupation, and the year of defection. Inevitably, however, the pool of refugee informants who participated in this study may not be representative of the population in North Korea as a whole. The majority of informants were women and come from North Hamkyung and Ryanggang provinces, where marketisation began and spread most extensively. Therefore, allowance must be made for possible regional and gender biases in the material presented here.

Figure 12: Hyesan Market, 22 July 2015.
Source: Courtesy of Cho Chun-hyun.

## Background: Conducting Private Economic Activities under Collectivism in North Korea

The single most important feature of life in North Korea is the high degree of collectivism. North Koreanists have utilised a range of political science concepts to characterise the North Korean state. The state is often defined as being highly personalistic due to the supreme importance of the leader,[8] and totalitarian due to the extent of the state control of the society through ideology and organisation. It is also often seen, on the one hand, as a corporatist organic entity and, on the other, as neo-Confucian in its uniquely East Asian features where the family serves as a model of the state. The extent to which each of these characterisations is emphasised depends on the period of North Korea's history being examined.[9] No one model correctly represents North Korea, but rather all emphasise various features that make the North Korean society uniquely collective. The deified leader, layers of bureaucracies and social organisations, extensive surveillance, the system of social stratification, and the unifying ideology of *chuch'e* (self-reliance) all facilitate, strengthen and reinforce collective ways of life in North Korea.

Scholars describe North Korea as one of the most intensely organised societies in the world and in history.[10] This collectivism was fostered initially through its efforts to restructure society in the postcolonial period of socialist revolution from 1945, leading up to the founding of the government in 1948.[11] Suzy Kim's recent book, *Everyday life in the North Korean Revolution, 1945–1950*, describes the experience of the North Korean Revolution (1945–50) as the realisation of a socialist modernity shared with its Chinese and Soviet neighbours, but unique in its exceptionally high level of mobilisation in everyday life spaces.[12] It was understood that the well-being of the individual was achieved only through the well-being of the collective. The collectivism of North Korean society strengthened after the Korean War with Kim Il-Sung's consolidation of his unitary power by eliminating all countervailing factions. Collectivism as envisioned in North Korea was an imaginary wartime solidarity against powerful external enemies that Wada Haruki calls a guerrilla state.[13]

---

8    Linz and Stepan briefly mention North Korea as an extreme form of the patrimonialism defined by Max Weber: Juan J. Linz and Alfred Stepan, *Problems of Democratic Transition and Consolidation: Southern Europe, South America, and Post-Communist Europe* (Baltimore and London: The Johns Hopkins University Press), 51–2.

9    Charles K. Armstrong, 'The Nature, Origins, and Development of the North Korean State', in Samuel S. Kim ed., *The North Korean System in the Post-Kim Il Sung Era* (New York: Palgrave, 2001), 39–64.

10    Michael E. Robinson, *Korea's Twentieth-Century Odyssey: A Short History* (Honolulu: University of Hawai'i Press, 2007), 150.

11    ibid.

12    Suzy Kim, *Everyday Life in the North Korean Revolution, 1945–1950* (Ithaca and London: Cornell University Press, 2013), Kindle Version, 2257(7410).

13    On the use of the term 'guerrilla state', see Armstrong, 'The Nature, Origins, and Development of the North Korean State', 23–4.

Collectivism continued to be a foundation for the country's postwar recovery and socialist construction based on mass mobilisation campaigns. Most representatively, the Chollima movement initiated in 1958 resembled the Soviet Union's Stakhanovite movement and was also influenced by the Chinese Great Leap Forward. Mass mobilisation campaigns, along with aid from Chinese and Soviet allies, achieved a decade of initial success. Bruce Cumings notes Immanuel Wallerstein's regard for North Korea (the Democratic People's Republic of Korea, DPRK) as a model for the periphery: 'The DPRK shows the way in the periphery ... it never idled but always raced'.[14]

Life in the workplace, social organisations, and neighbourhood units were at the core of everyday life in North Korea. Every individual belonged to groups of youths, workers, women and peasants. The percentage of the population who are members of the state Party was higher in North Korea than in any other communist state in the 1980s.[15] Organisational life was value-ridden: recognition and advancement in the Party and related political structures was considered more precious than material gains. As one North Korean defector scholar humorously puts it, 'we were closer to our work colleagues than to our husband'.[16] In this everyday collective life, people lived simple, hardworking lives and felt generally content and secure about their livelihoods. A level of shortage existed in households under the state rations system but relative egalitarianism prevented the fear that is caused by a sense of relative deprivation. Cumings notes that the success of the leadership in cultivating communal collective life was the most striking thing about North Korea to Americans. A British diplomat described North Korea as 'one big kibbutz'.[17]

The tight culture of collectivism shaped by the North Korean state socialist revolution began to lose its almost total embrace of society with the decline of its state-planned economy. The North Korean economy was already showing signs of strain in the late 1970s. Shortage of consumer goods and deterioration in the quality and the quantity of food supplies

---

14   Wallerstein quoted in Bruce Cumings, 'Corporatism in North Korea', *Journal of Korean Studies* 4 (1983): 293.
15   Bruce Cumings, 'Corporatism in North Korea', 291–2.
16   Hyun In-ae, 'Pukhansahoe net'ŭwŏk'ŭ: sijang esŏui chuminsaenghwal' [Network in North Korean Society: Life of Residents in the Marketplace], paper presented at The 2015 Soongsil Institute for Peace and Unification Spring Seminar, Seoul, 22 May 2015, 27–46.
17   Andrew Holloway quoted in Bruce Cumings, *Everyday Life in North Korea* (New York and London: The New Press, 2004), 139–40.

were already evident from the mid-1980s.[18] Households, especially those with many growing children, supplemented food through informal coping strategies. Seven hundred grams of grain per day for office workers, 800 grams per day for manual labourers, and 300 grams for children were never adequate. Households supplemented consumption of vegetables and protein by picking and gathering greens (*namul*) in the mountains, cultivating kitchen plots, and breeding pigs and rabbits at home to sell through informal networks to gain additional income. Elderly persons in rural areas cultivated additional plots of unused land to contribute to the household food supply. Andrei Lankov notes that private space in North Korea was much smaller than that in the Soviet Union. Nevertheless, these minuscule private spaces existed and became foundational and habitual bases for coping strategies in the 1990s.[19]

As much as North Korea's collectivisation experience demonstrated totality in the unity between state authority and the people, the people's demand for private economic spaces, as it grew in scale, inflicted significant and irreversible damage on the state authority's ability to exert control over its people. The demand occurred at the margins and at the bottom of society where women and elderly and labourers and farmers, out of sheer concern for survival of their households, resorted to various private economic activities as coping strategies despite knowing that such activities were transgressive of socialist ideals. The state's easing of the spaces for private market economic activities occurred reluctantly in response to the unsettling demands for space for market trade. The following three policies demonstrate that the state yielded to the growing grassroots demands for private economic activities even prior to the full-blown crisis that began in 1995.

In the 1980s, government policies intended to co-opt informal and illegal economic activities resulted in the further opening up of spaces for private economic activities. In 1984, the state launched an 'August 3rd Movement' in an attempt to ameliorate the shortage of consumer goods that was apparent in the 1980s, by having factories and enterprises

---

18    Ch'oe Pong-dae and Ku Kap-u, 'Pukhan ŭi tosi 'changmadang' hwalsŏnghwa ŭi tonghak – 1990nyŏndae sinŭiju, ch'ŏngjin, hyesan ŭl chungsimŭro' [Changes in Vitalization of Marketplace in North Korean Cities – With a Focus on the 1990s Sinuichu, Chongchin, and Hyesan], *Hyŏntaepukhanyŏnku* 8, no. 3 (2005).

19    Andrei Lankov, *The Real North Korea: Life and Politics in the Failed Stalinist Utopia* (Oxford: Oxford University Press, 2013), 36.

source their own inputs to produce consumer goods.[20] According to Choi and Koo, this was also a policy to ameliorate growing pilfering and illegal side work by factory workers who could not feed their family and obtain household necessities by relying solely on their wages and food rations.[21] As the authorities allowed marketisation of some products to provide incentives for people to produce these goods and voluntarily supply them to the state, this resulted in the spread of markets. People demonstrated creativity.[22] Home-manufactured products flowed into farmers' markets and invigorated market trade from the mid-1980s onwards. As a result, by 1999, over 300 farmers' markets had been formed.[23]

Another policy was the resumption in 1984 of permission for ethnic Korean residents from China to visit family in the DPRK.[24] Border trade between North Korea and China had existed in the 1940s, ceased during the 1970s, and was then revived after the normalisation of DPRK–China relations in 1982. Ethnic Korean petty traders brought in food and manufactured goods to their relatives residing in the border areas of North Korea. These goods were quietly sold to neighbours and acquaintances. They became an important source of consumer goods for residents of the border area and had a major influence on the lives of these people. Those who were exposed to the border trade in the earlier period became 'early birds' in trade, and this helped them survive the famine in the 1990s by advancing in the border trade. Though legalisation of this trade was permitted only in the border areas, merchants from inner cities came to the border cities and brought China-manufactured consumer goods inland, subsequently leading to the emergence of underground trade and market networks across North Korea.

20    Ch'a Munsŏk, 'Konan ŭi haenggun gwa pukhan kyŏngje ŭi sŏnggyŏk pyŏnhwa', *Hyŏntaepukhanyŏnku* 8, no. 1 (2005): 43.

21    Ch'oe and Ku, 'Pukhan ŭi tosi 'jangmadang' hwalsŏnghwa ŭi tonghak', 166–7.

22    Yi Sŏnu, 'Sŏnkunchŏngch'iwa pukhansik kyŏngchekaehyŏk' [Military First Policy and North Korean Style Economic Reform], *Hyŏntaepukhanyŏnku* 12, no. 1 (2009): 140; Ch'oe Pong-dae and Ku Kap-u, 'Pukhan tosi nongminsichang hyŏngsŏng kwachŏngŭi ihaenglonchŏk hamŭi: 1950-1980nyŏntae sinŭichu, ch'ŏngchin, hyesanŭi sarerŭl chungsimŭro' [Formation Process of Farmers' Markets in North Korean Cities: in the Cases of Sinŭichu, Ch'ŏngchin, Hyesan, 1950–1980], *Hyŏntaepukhanyŏnku* 6, no. 2 (2003): 172.

23    Andrew Natsios, *The Great North Korean Famine* (Washington DC: Institute of Peace Press, 2001), 100.

24    Ch'oe and Ku, 'Pukhan ŭi tosi 'jangmadang' hwalsŏnghwa ŭi tonghak', 170.

As the food situation deteriorated in the early 1990s, another important institutional change facilitated the spread of private economic activities; the Central Party delegated the responsibility to manage matters of livelihood to provincial authorities. By 1957, all residents except cooperative farmers (who were instead given an annual distribution from the harvest) had become entitled to food rations.[25] Buying and selling of food was prohibited. Under this state-managed food distribution system, the moral consensus on the accessibility, availability and the price of food was essentially a relationship between the ruler (one ruler) and the rest. This consensus was withdrawn by the state in response to the food crisis. Kim Jong-il ordered city and county party and committees to resolve food matters on their own between 1992 and 1993. Between 1995 and 1996, state enterprises were also ordered to resolve their food situation on their own.[26] City and county offices then allowed their residents to engage in market and border trades and private farming as a response to the decline and the eventual disappearance of the state rations. Farming and trade became morally justified and even necessary for people as they endured the hardship of the non-ration period and struggled to survive on their own. By promoting the slogan 'the Arduous March', from the beginning of 1996, thereby recalling the country's historical memory of guerrilla fighting in Manchuria in the colonial era, the state Party demanded of the people a spirit of endurance, perseverance and revolution. The state conducted internal war mobilisation against the external enemy and, by doing so, the sense of expectation that the state ensures food security was no longer held during the height of the famine.

During the Arduous March period, the state tried to maintain its control over the people while reluctantly turning a blind eye to market and other private economic activities. During the height of the famine, propaganda vans with loudspeakers continued to make pronouncements not to engage in anti-socialist activities.[27] The heads of household, officials, health workers and teachers were obligated to remain in their workplace during the Arduous March, although all tried to negotiate with the state authorities to obtain time to devote to their families' survival by conducting difficult private economic activities in the form of

25    Kim Yang-hui, 'Ch'echeyujirŭl wihan pukhanŭi sikryangchŏngch'i' [North Korea's Food Politics for Regime Maintenance], *T'ongilmuncheyŏnku*, 16.
26    Yang Mun-su, *Pukhan ŭi kyehoekkyŏngje wa sijanghwa hyŏnsang* [North Korea's Planned Economy and Marketisation Phenomenon] (Seoul: Institute for Unification Education, 2013), 30.
27    Lee Young-ok, interview by author, Seoul, 23 October 2013.

farming and trade. By declaring the ideologically infused struggle against hardship over in 1998, the state reinvigorated its control over non-legal economic activities. In February 1999, Kim Jong-il attempted to shut all marketplaces and exhorted people to return to factories.[28] The reimposition of control occurred through the creation of special groups to inspect and enforce the eradication of anti-socialist activities and conducting anti-market campaigns. Having already seen the spread of markets and the weakening of the ideology's effectiveness as a tool of social control, Kim Jong-il tried to constrain the market through 'regulatory harassment', creating 'economic police', and increasing the role of the military in social control and surveillance.[29] Eventually, by the time of the 1 July 2002 reform, the state normalised the operations of major marketplaces and made price adjustments. This reform path was reversed from August 2005 with counter-reforms banning grain trade and some other businesses and resumption of the public distribution system. In subsequent years, the counter-reform path was reinvigorated through new restrictions on the farming of private plots, the imposition of age and item restrictions on market trades, and crackdowns on corruption.[30]

Despite the state's swing between reform and counter-reform, the marketisation process that began during the Arduous March period was never effectively reversed. Haggard and Noland's 2012 report of survey data of North Korean refugees collected in both South Korea and China demonstrates that neither reforms nor retrenchments had much impact on the significance of the market in household economy, and this reflects the state's incapacity to control the marketisation process.[31] Today, the market has become the most vital and central part of life in North Korea. It has gradually pushed the state to adopt the market as a fact of life. *The market has eroded the state.*

---

28   Ch'a, 'Konan ŭi haenggun gwa', 57.
29   Natsios, *The Great North Korean Famine*, 100; Yi, 'Sŏn'gunjŏngch'i wa pukhansik kyŏngjegyehyŏk', 145.
30   Stephan Haggard and Marcus Noland, *Witness to Transformation: Refugee Insights into North Korea*, (Washington DC: Peterson Institute for International Economics, 2011), 9.
31   ibid., 79.

## Mechanisms for the Emergence and the Spread of the Market — Cooperation and Conflict among Officials and Non-Officials

Let us look more closely at this process of erosion as it takes place in everyday life. A common pathway is to start by engaging in petty trade by selling what one can in pursuit of one's own survival. Selling off existing marketable items from home to secure seed money for petty trade or simply to buy grains or medicine for the family was a desperate strategy for survival during the period when state rations were non-existent. Among the lowest strata of market traders, people buy flour to make bread and sell it at the edge of the marketplace. Prohibited items, most commonly alcohol, are sold at home quietly to neighbours. A much more physically demanding form of trade is itinerant trading. The long-distance bartering of certain foods and manufactured goods between urban and rural areas, between coastal or inland cities and border cities, or across the North Korea–China border is an unimaginably arduous but nevertheless widespread practice. Though these petty traders do not have sophisticated management skills and structures, trading in North Korea essentially demands some level of entrepreneurial skill because of various barriers imposed on the traders. As capital accumulates, petty traders move on to more profitable items and trading that demand more sophisticated ways of managing and building relationships, acquiring modes of transportation, procuring resources, and accessing the market.

Those who started as petty traders often make enough money to obtain official connections to make their businesses more profitable and secure. Individual traders, in the course of trading, make a shift in the items and modes of exchange and in the relationships they develop to facilitate their trade activities so as to earn more profit and obtain a secure source of income. Most trade activities develop as the result of collaboration and mutual dependency between officials and marketeers. The bribery relationship develops either through the initiative of the officials who are responsible for implementing laws against market activities, or through the initiative of residents who want to embark on non-legal activities under conditions of uncertainty. Thus, the more entrepreneurial one becomes, the more risks one has to take, and the more dependent one's business becomes on individuals in the state apparatus, in the absence of market-facilitating and market-protecting institutions. The larger the scale of trade, the more essential it is to establish official connections, often with multiple law enforcement authorities. As a result, privately run businesses in North Korea almost always form state agency affiliations and the businesses make payoffs to relevant government agencies.[32] State officials often initiate the process of developing enterprises, using their status and connections to access state resources and information. In other words, one's access to material and social resources depends on access to power.

The division between officials (*kanbu*) and non-officials in North Korea was clear even before the 1990s crisis. This was because the division aligned with one's *songbun*, the social stratification category based on family background. Of the three main categories, 'core', 'wavering' and 'hostile', only those who belong to the core class could qualify to fill official positions that are considered important in the state apparatus. Wavering class members of various sorts could become *kanbu* only when the individuals faithfully proved their loyalty to the Party. The *songbun* division, which is passed on from generation to generation, clearly reinforced the division between officials and non-officials, and the discrimination and resentment were clearly recognised and internalised. Yet, because of North Korea's centrally controlled ration and wage system, as well as the egalitarianism embedded in its communist ideology, the division had never been a socioeconomic one. Only after the 1990s did the political–social cleavage became an economic and contentious one.[33]

Officials in North Korea constitute those who hold various offices in the state apparatus. Refugee informants say that in an ordinary rural city or town, around 10 per cent of the town are officials of various sorts.[34] The number of *kanbu* had expanded since the postwar period in the 1950s as the state's policy increased the number to implement its postwar reconstruction policies and consolidate the state power through entrenchment and mobilisation. With the decline of the state-planned economy and the emerging vitality of farmers' markets, corruption of the *kanbu* was already growing by the early 1990s. When the ration system

---

32    On such dynamics of state–business relations, see Andrei Lankov, 'Limits to Marketisation: State and Private in Kimist North Korea', *Sino NK*, 14 June 2013, sinonk.com/2013/06/14/marketization-and-its-limits-state-private-enterprises-in-north-korea/.

33    Adopted from Hahn Soon-young, interview by author, Suwon, 15 May 2015.

34    It is estimated that the core class constituted 28 per cent of the population in the mid-1990s and the Korean Workers' Party membership as high as 15 per cent of the population: Haggard and Noland, *Witness to Transformation*, 55.

collapsed, officials and their families, exploiting their access to state resources, diverted food, stripped enterprise assets, and conducted various forms of trade.[35] Officials who belonged to various law enforcement agencies were given incentives to remain loyal to the state through the provision of rations.[36] Regulations became beneficial to them, in the sense that they could take bribes using their authority to turn a blind eye to those who flouted the regulations.[37] Under Kim Jong-il and Kim Jong-un, law enforcement officials and the army have become the most powerful actors. Law enforcement officials are today referred to as 'those who hold the swords'.[38]

Despite the clear differentiation that developed between officials and non-officials, collaboration occurs extensively. At the local level, the majority of state officials, including those in the lower levels of the legal apparatus, are poor. One informant said, 'if the town's people are poor, so are the officials of the town'.[39] The continued existence of regulations against market activities provides the officials continued opportunities for bribery. Law enforcement officials foresee a greater long-term benefit from collaboration with those who ignore the regulations than from implementation of legal punishments against marketeers. It is also a matter of survival. Because officials are prohibited from conducting market activities, only in collusion with marketeers can they maintain their livelihoods. The collaborative relationship becomes widespread and normalised.

This collaboration in stealing state resources brought about a hollowing-out of the state-planned economy. The widespread stealing in North Korea since the 1990s is not only a result but also a constituting phenomenon of the hollowing-out of the state. Since the supply of resources and electricity virtually stopped even to top priority national enterprises at some points in the 1990s, workers and guards, out of desperation in the absence of the state rations and wages, began pilfering parts of idle factory facilities. Stealing occurred rather quietly at all levels of the society: opportunistic large-scale stealing by officials in managerial positions and small-scale

35    ibid., 52.
36    Kim Sung-Chull (1997), 'Pukhan kanbujŏngch'aek ŭi jisok kwa byŏnhwa' [Continuities and Changes in North Korea's 'Policy of Cultivating Officials'], Korea Institute for National Unification, 1–89. DBpia access.
37    Cha Kyungsook, interview by author, Seoul, 13 May 2015.
38    Choi Seungmin, interview by author, Seoul, 13 May 2015.
39    Ahn Chong-han, interview by author, Seoul, 6 June 2015.

pilfering by ordinary labourers and farmers occurring simultaneously and in collaboration. In this way, this state hollowing-out occurred quietly without the violent outbreaks of contention between the state and the people trying to survive.

What resulted from this collaboration between the officials and non-officials through bribery is the institutionalisation of illegal private economic practices. Pilfering, for example, has become so widespread that it is considered a common and morally acceptable practice despite the state's repressive control against it through the terror of imprisonment and ad hoc public execution. Refugee informants describe the act of stealing as 'deducting' or 'taking a part' of a public asset.[40] Stealing and the collusive relations through which stealing occurs are regularised and systematised. Ways of diverting state resources by selling them in a market become institutionalised. Often these informally systematised practices demonstrate similar patterns across different institutions, i.e. state enterprises, cooperative farms, schools and hospitals.

## The Role of Communal Culture

The collaboration between local officials and marketeers does not only depend on bribery and the sharing of profits. A cultural factor, traditionalism, also contributes to the formation of corrupt relationships and shaping the officials' orientation to long-term benefit. The culture of close personal relationships facilitates the formation of collaboration. The personal connections include family and acquaintances as well as new relationships formed for the sake of convenience and mutual benefit. Women who became successful marketeers 'buy' official positions in the state apparatus for their husbands by 'paying for' their higher education in order to create potential for their career advancement. Marital relationships thus become a space where a marriage between the market and the state occurs.[41] It is often the wives of officials who conduct larger-scale trade activities because they are given a greater level of protection in conducting non-legal activities. Often State Security officers are school

---

40 Kim Bun-nyu, interview by author, Seoul, 6 June 2015.
41 Park Hwa-sook, interview by author, Seoul, 20 December 2013.

friends or family members. Depending on the circumstances, personal affection and friendship overcome the official obligation to implement rules, especially when material benefits follow.[42]

The North Korean regime has fostered a culture of a family state in which constituent members of society care for one another like family members. The culture of the family state has facilitated the development and sustenance of smuggling in the border regions. Collaborative relationships formed between border control officials and female marketeers in Hyesan are facilitated by filial sentiments between son-like border control guards and motherly marketeers. Since the Arduous March period, 'mothers' have become the dominant agents of smuggling, collecting all kinds of available goods ranging from medicinal herbs to metal scraps. Border control officials are young males of their sons' age. This collaboration between the young border control officials and middle-aged women helped the border smuggling to continue in Hyesan.[43] The culture of the family state not only had the effect of strengthening the bond between the leader and the people but also of engendering filial respect and motherly care outside of the nuclear family.[44]

The culture of close communal and interpersonal relationships nullifies the highly complicated ad hoc regulations of the Centre. One effect of the existence of multiple layers of enforcement agencies is that all become complicit. For instance, a refugee informant from North Hamkyung Province recounted that she had to bribe '10 strong individuals' to safely conduct her trade business in North Hamkyung Province.[45] Individuals cannot own automobiles, thus to conduct long-distance trade using a motor vehicle, one has to borrow the vehicle from a state enterprise for a cost. But pay-offs themselves do not guarantee protection from possibly being subjected to regulations by law enforcement agencies. To protect oneself and one's business, one has to build connections with powerful individuals, including three security authorities—the Public Security, the State Security, the Army Security—as well as other authorities such as North Korean Democratic Youth League officials, the Party cell official and the prosecutor. All become complicit. For a retired army officer who

---

42 Kang Seung, interview by author, Incheon, 10 December 2013; Ahn Chong-han, interview by author, Seoul, 6 June 2015.
43 Lee Ki-wol, interview by author, Suwon, 15 May 2015.
44 On an anthropology of the family state, see Heonik Kwon and Byung-Ho Chung, *North Korea: Beyond Charismatic Politics* (Rowman and Littlefield Publishers Inc., 2012), 18–33.
45 Park Kyung-sook, interview by author, Seoul, 5 May 2015.

conducted illegal border smuggling through his connections with multiple legal authorities, his response to the news of a special inspection force coming down to his town was to defect. By disappearing, he could save all the officials who were involved.[46] Thanks to these adaptive strategies developed at the local level, the Centre's enforcement strategies have not worked effectively. There is a popular saying, 'the Centre's policy does not last more than three days'.[47]

# The Development of Contention within Hegemony

Refugee informants justify their private economic activities in terms of the hegemonic ideology of self-reliance. Under this encompassing ideology of self-reliance, North Korean people gradually negotiated their private use of time, space and labour away from extensively collective ways of life. North Korea first used the slogan of self-reliance in the early 1960s when the Sino-Soviet dispute and a resultant decline of aid from both allies jeopardised the first Five Year Economic Plan (1957–61). Self-reliance was not a motto invented by the North Korean regime. It was in fact China's guiding policy around the 1960s.[48] The slogan had a dual usage. For the nation as a whole, it delineated North Korea's basic principle of national economic reconstruction as an autonomous process with little dependence on aid from its allies. The slogan was reinforced as the economy deteriorated and when the regime took a counter-reform isolationist path since the mid-2000s.[49]

Internally, the slogan mobilised people to proactively seek ways to contribute to national economic development and socialist revolution. As observed by Suzy Kim, this theme of the individual as a proactive agent of revolution is consistent from the beginning of North Korea's socialist revolution in 1945.[50] Cheehyung Kim's work on *Chuch'e Sasang* (the ideology of self-reliance) elaborates this dynamic of the socialist economy's essential dependence on the workers' spontaneous innovations

---

46  Ahn Chong-han, interview by author, Seoul, 6 June 2015.
47  Kim Mirae, interview by author, Seoul, 15 May 2015.
48  Lankov, *The Real North Korea*, 72.
49  Cho Tongho, 'Kidae wa bigwansog ŭi charyŏkkaengsaeng chŏnryak' [Strategy of Self-Reliance in Hope and Despair], *Kukkachŏnryak* 14, no. 2 (2008): 87–114.
50  Kim, *Everyday Life in the North Korean Revolution*.

and labour heroism. Through an analysis of literary works of the 1970s, Kim concludes: 'the moments when the North Korean people are assumed to be under the greatest control may actually be the moments of agency'.[51] The flip-side of this dynamic of ownership and totality is that individual ownership of the revolution is entirely subject to the totality of the state. Individual ownership and creativity existed in essence for the cause of the nation as a whole.

The value of labour, diligence and self-reliance involve paternalistic thinking. *Changsa* (selling goods or trading) for the majority of the population had initially developed only to the extent of earning residual income through the making of bread or noodles out of flour and selling them in the marketplace. Conducting market trade, if performed to an unnoticeable and unexceptional degree, is regarded as a self-reliant effort to survive on one's own in times of hardship, and therefore does not contradict the official ideology. An informant describing everyday life in North Korea reflects in her narratives what is seemingly the state-guided discourse on the value of labour: 'the harder your physical body works, the stronger your mental facilities become. There is neither dementia nor cancer in North Korea'.[52] Private economic activities of trade and farming, in aggregate, echo the themes of collective labour, diligence and self-reliance that have long been promoted throughout the history of the country. While factories and cooperative farms are emptied out in the absence of resources, labour takes place in houses, marketplaces and in the mountains. In fact, ordinary-scale market trades and private farming are so widespread that even those who had other unconventional and non-legal sources of income conduct these activities to hide such illicit sources. One elderly refugee informant told me that while she had no need to do *changsa* nor farming because her daughter who had defected to South Korea was sending her money, she engaged in both activities on a daily basis in order to disguise her other source of income and pretend that it was her sole source of survival. *Changsa* was justified as a self-reliant coping strategy and was even promoted through peer-pressure as a form of diligence. Many informants said that those who did not engage in either

---

51  Kim Cheehyung, 'Total, Thus Broken: Chuch'e Sasang and North Korea's Terrain of Subjectivity', *Journal of Korean Studies* 17 (2012).
52  Park Hwa-sook, interview by author, Seoul, 20 December 2013.

*changsa* or farming were lazy people. Fahy observes from the narratives of defectors, 'the proper response was not depression or melancholia but action'.[53]

People strategically negotiated and acquired a greater right to conduct trade activities by distancing themselves from politics. One way to distance oneself from politics is to use one's social identity position. As we have seen, the North Korean state imposes the *songbun* system, which stratifies the entire population into categories based on family lineage background and differentiated people's access and possibilities for political careers. In return, however, officials were more restricted in conducting private economic activities than non-officials. Conversely, the more marginal one's position is in the system, the greater freedom one has. While minorities, for example, Chinese residents in North Korea and ethnic Koreans from Japan who migrated to North Korea (mostly in the 1960s) have been from time to time subject to political purges, these groups have also been selectively allowed a greater level of economic freedom, and allowed to utilise their economic resources and connections abroad to supply goods necessary, useful and desirable to officials.

For instance, returnees from Japan gained an entitlement to greater freedom in conducting market activities. Those who 'returned' from Japan faced much discrimination in the system; having come from a capitalist world, they were closely watched, often scapegoated and many perished in political prisons. While readily integrated into local communities in everyday life through work and education, they were excluded from certain duties as well as rights. Returnees or children from a returnee family in general could not expect to advance far in a political career, though exceptions existed. As a result, many pursued careers in professions such as medicine. Interestingly, they were also given a greater level of leniency in conducting non-legal activities such as trading. To borrow the words of one interviewee, 'we had more freedom in economic activities as long as we did not do anything political'. Some lived off luxury goods and money sent from their relatives, and the demand for the luxury goods came from local officials. Some returnees had household businesses, selling second-hand clothes and electronics smuggled in from Japan long before the economic crisis in the 1990s, and such businesses only increased with

---

53   Sandra Fahy, *Marching through Suffering: Loss and Survival in North Korea* (New York: Columbia University Press, 2014), 51.

the crisis.[54] When rations stopped, these groups of individuals conducted trade activities using their connections abroad, while supplying payments to law enforcement officials.

The logic of the freedom of marginalisation applies within the household too. The heads of households were obligated to remain in the workplace. Thus, it was the elderly and married women who first explored the possibilities of private economic activities, because they had a greater capacity to evade labour mobilisation by the state, and to use their time in their own way. This flexibility in carving out time and labour away from collective uses differs according to enterprise and agency units, regions and time periods.[55]

Active resistance often took place on the streets at the local level. This often involved fierce protest in the form of continuing market trade. In smaller towns, markets were kept open as a result of ongoing resistance by women. Eventually, designated market places opened. The hometown of one refugee informant had less than 1,000 households, and thus was excluded from permission to open up the marketplace. Residents protested to local officials, 'don't you have to allow us simply to live?' In May 2004 everyone went out to the streets spontaneously and formed an informal marketplace with their items on the street. It looked as though the authority would soon crush the protest, but they did not dare to do so. The county officials then ran around in efforts to persuade higher administrative levels to authorise the market. In my refugee informant's words, because the state could not provide for the people, it eventually had to permit market trade with a state-controllable boundary.[56]

There is a moral dimension to the fact that petty traders are often left to their own devices. There are implicit norms about the way the laws should be enforced. The norms depend on the scale of trade. A refugee informant said, 'there is no justification for enforcing the law upon petty traders. They are not afraid of dying'. Only when businesses become visibly significant in size do security officials appear and demand bribes. Small traders are left to grow bigger.[57] The perception that there is no justification for suppressing petty trade indicates that there is a certain

54  Kang Seung, interview by author, Incheon, 10 December 2013; Kim Taekyun, interview by author, Incheon, 10 December 2013.
55  Lee Young-ok, interview by author, Seoul, 23 October 2013.
56  Han Soon-young, interview by author, Suwon, 15 May 2015.
57  Park Kyung-sook, interview by author, Seoul, 5 May 2015.

shared moral consensus about leaving these petty trades unregulated. An informant metaphorically remarked, 'a backpack becomes a hand cart and a hand cart becomes an ox cart, and an ox cart becomes an automobile. Then the trader has to start worrying about potential risks of confiscation'.[58] Trading on a significant scale becomes a risky and nerve-racking experience. The richer one becomes, the more regulations one risks violating and the more bribes one has to pay.

## Conclusion

Marketisation in North Korea is a bottom-up phenomenon that occurred under the continued regulation of market trade activities. Market trade emerged as a survival strategy in the absence of state rations, and quietly but rapidly encroached on the state sector economy. The hollowing-out of the centralised planned economy was not only a result of the greater structural change of the end of the Cold War but also of a redistribution of social goods and attainment of autonomy achieved by people's everyday moves to conduct market trade for the simple purpose of survival.

The few attempts by the state to re-control and suppress the market force since 2005 have ended in failure. Since Kim Jong-un came to power in 2012, such efforts ceased due to the state's perceived fear of unsettling of people if market trades are restricted and oppressed. The market has become the way of life in North Korea. Demands for private economic spaces existed prior to the economic crisis. Under the guise of collectivism as the only way of life, people quietly conducted very small-scale private economic activities as a means of acquiring minimal subsistence security for their household. As the crisis deepened, the activities expanded rapidly in scale and number despite the state's continued efforts to control such bottom-up movements. This indicates that even a totalitarian state like North Korea does not have total control of the society.

Shared interests, communal culture and a collective sense of morality all become important factors contributing to the emergence of the market. Private space is demanded and is actively negotiated from continued imposition of the collective. But in the narratives of refugee informants, private economic activities are also justified as collective self-reliance actions. Continuities and changes in the North Korean state–society

---

58    Park Hwa-sook, interview by author, Seoul, 20 December 2013.

relations in everyday life spaces occur in the precarious balance between the collective management of hardship, group demands for private spaces and resources, and collaborative and contentious relations between officials and non-officials.

What is striking about the emergence and expansion of market in North Korea is the sheer scale and significance it has attained today. As much as the North Korean state building was a process of collective mass mobilisation, the people's resort to the market put an end to the revival of the state-planned economic system. This demonstrates that the totalitarian state depends on the compliance of people. The North Korean people have turned the totalitarian system upside-down. Marketisation in North Korea demonstrates the agency of ordinary people even in the total absence of institutionally guaranteed economic freedom and even under the presence of control by fear and terror implemented through selective punishment. To this extent, the authorities indeed are 'the prisoners of people'.[59]

## Acknowledgements

I would like to thank Tessa Morris-Suzuki and Jong-Sung You for their valuable comments.

---

59   E. P. Thompson, 'The Moral Economy of the English Crowd in the Eighteenth Century', *Past and Present* 50 (1971): 79.

# 10

# Social Innovation in Asia: Trends and Characteristics in China, Korea, India, Japan and Thailand

The Hope Institute[1]

## Introduction

Social innovation is often defined as 'the process of inventing, securing support for, and implementing novel solutions to social needs and problems'.[2] Since the practice of social innovation usually tackles unmet social needs that cannot be solved solely by the government or certain stakeholders in a given society, the concept implies a unique approach to solve the social problem. As an activity or a specific case, social innovation often takes the form of collaboration across public, private and citizen

---

1    This chapter is based on *The Social Innovation Landscape in Asia,* the final report of the research that was conducted by the research team of The Hope Institute, based in Seoul, in 2013–14. The research was funded by the Rockefeller Foundation for a better and systematic understanding of social innovation practices in Asia. This chapter was presented at the conference 'Grassroots Regionalisation and the Frontiers of the Humanities in East Asia: Korea as a Hub', held by The Australian National University and was revised by one of the principal investigators, Dr EunKyung Lee, a research fellow in The Hope Institute.
2    James A. Phills Jr, Kriss Deiglmeier, and Dale T. Miller, 'Rediscovering Social Innovation', *Stanford Social Innovation Review* Fall (2008), ssir.org/articles/entry/rediscovering_social_innovation#sthash. LuXlirzX.fjh2JKLM.dpuf. Accessed 20 March 2016.

sectors, dissolving traditional boundaries.[3] Implicit in the concept is the notion that its impact should be good for society and enhance society's capacity to act.[4]

In various parts of Asia, there has been growing interest in the processes of European and North American social innovation. Many successful social innovation cases and practices in those areas are well known. Such cases have been shared in our region—for instance, Charter Schools as an alternative educational avenue, the fair-trade movement to address indigenous farmers' labour conditions and create a sustainable environment, microfinance to include those who are unable to gain access to major financial services, and so on. However, few studies have explored the ways in which the transcultural adaptation of social innovation practices has taken place. The Hope Institute research team, with the support of Rockefeller Foundation, has investigated how social innovation practices have been put into effect in Asian countries and how they have influenced Asian societies.

In the process of compressed industrialisation after World War II, many Asian societies adopted Western-style capitalism, usually in a top-down way. Many industrialised Western social and economic practices were imposed on Asian countries. Transplanted democratic systems and unsettled civil societies characterise many Asian countries. This has led to socioeconomic malfunctioning, the underdevelopment of civil sectors, a lack of government legitimacy, and unequal access to information and technology. Given these distinct underlying conditions, it is necessary to redefine social innovation from an Asian perspective. Our task has been to collect significant cases from the Asian experience, and to analyse the characteristics of social innovation practices in Asia. In this sense, this research strongly supports the core principle that social innovation is neither context-free nor value-neutral.[5]

3    Geoff Mulgan, Tucker, S., Ali, R., and Sanders, B., *Social Innovation: What it is, why it matters and how it can be accelerated*, working paper of the Skoll Centre for Social Entrepreneurship (Oxford Said Business School, 2007) eureka.bodleian.ox.ac.uk/761/1/Social_Innovation.pdf. Accessed 30 March 2015.
4    The Young Foundation, *Social Innovation Overview: A Deliverable of the Project. The Theoretical, Empirical and Policy Foundations for Building Social Innovation in Europe* (TEPSIE), European Commission – 7th Framework Programme (Brussels: European Commission, DG Research, 2012), www.tepsie.eu/images/documents/TEPSIE.D1.1.Report.DefiningSocialInnovation.Part%201%20-%20defining%20social%20innovation.pdf. Accessed 30 March 2015.
5    The Young Foundation, *Social Innovation Overview*, 2012.

This chapter presents some of the results of our research, which began with the question: Social innovation practices have had considerable success in the West. What about Asia? This seemingly simple question actually requires the demanding work of establishing a context for Asia as a region where social innovative practices are performed, as well as redefining social innovation in developing or less-developed countries. The complexity is two-fold: social innovation is a multilayered, practice-led field; and, more importantly, Asia is not a homogeneous region. Asia's diverse paths to democratisation and industrialisation add to the complexity.

Considering the context-specificity of social innovation, the research had three aims: (1) to conduct country background surveys on political, economic and social dimensions; (2) to identify social needs for such innovations, examine social innovation cases and identify their innovative features; and (3) to define common characteristics of the selected cases and identify features distinctive to Asia. This chapter focuses particularly on the third task, and so considers the following question: What are the common characteristics found in the social innovation cases in Asia?

Given the variety of social innovation ecosystems in Asia, this chapter examines whether common characteristics exist across Asian countries and how they are distinct from the Western models, which have been the main focus of international research to date. Answering this question will contribute to understanding the big picture of Asian countries' social innovation ecosystems and to examining the applicability of pre-existing projects, which mainly originated from the West, in an Asian context.

## Understanding Social Innovation in Asia

This chapter begins with a review of existing definitions of social innovation. It delineates core elements and features of social innovation for research purposes. We then go on to explore how the core elements and features are adopted in Asian social innovation cases. Social innovation discussed in the Asia NGO Innovation Summit (ANIS)[6] is particularly emphasised, because it has a foundational impact on the diffusion of social innovation across Asia.

---

6    Asia NGO Innovation Summit (ANIS) is a platform for sharing and exchanging the social innovation practices and accomplishments among social innovators in Asia. It has held annual conferences since launched in 2010 by The Hope Institute with the partnership of Intel Asia-Pacific.

Various definitions of social innovation have been suggested and discussed by researchers, activists, policy makers and academic institutions. No commonly shared definition exists, and any search for a clear-cut, specific definition of social innovation is quickly overwhelmed by a multiplicity of contending interpretations. The diversity among social innovation definitions shows that social innovation is a practice-led, field-specific phenomenon. In addition, social innovation is multidimensional from the outset and covers many sectors and fields.[7] The richness and openness of definitions of social innovation, however, make the debate about it hard to regulate, and it tends to fall into circular discussions. Thus, instead of attempting to pinpoint a singular definition of social innovation, for the purpose of the research, it is more appropriate to draw upon existing definitions and then to use core elements of our working definition for our selection of Asian social innovation cases presented in later sections.

Among the many definitions of social innovation, our research team particularly focused on the one used by TEPSIE[8] for this study. That definition is:

> Social innovations are new solutions (products, services, models, markets, processes etc.) that simultaneously meet a social need (more effectively than existing solutions) and lead to new or improved capabilities and relationships and better use of assets and resources. In other words, social innovations are both good for society and enhance society's capacity to act.[9]

We chose this definition for three reasons. First, while definitions used in most social innovation research are primarily drawn from academic perspectives, TEPSIE's definition embraces many aspects of experiences and decisions of social innovators and their practices. Second, it takes into consideration multiple dimensions of social innovation: the core elements, the common features, the sectors and the processes.[10] Third, the TEPSIE definition has been adopted by leading social innovation researchers in the most recent studies, and thus reflects current social innovation trends.

---

7    The Young Foundation, *Social Innovation Overview*, 2012.
8    TEPSIE is a project exploring the Theoretical, Empirical and Policy foundation for Social Innovation in Europe, and it is being carried by a consortium of six partners.
9    The Young Foundation, *Social Innovation Overview*, 2012.
10   ibid.

# Social Innovation: The Core Elements and Common Features

The core elements listed in TEPSIE's social innovation definition are: (1) meeting a social need, (2) effectiveness, (3) novelty, (4) moving from ideas to implementation, and (5) enhancing society's capacity to act.[11] In other words, social innovations are something new to the field, sector, region, market or user, and are to be applied in a new way. There should be an implementation or application of the new ideas. Such processes are explicitly designed to meet social needs in a more effective way than existing solutions for a measurable improved outcome.[12] As a result, the innovation enhances society's capacity to act by developing assets and capabilities.

According to TEPSIE's study, social innovations defined by such core elements usually present the following common features. They tend to be cross-sectoral; they build new social relationships and capabilities; they are open, collaborative and experimental; they are grassroots and mutual in character; they make better use of resources; and they develop capabilities and assets.[13]

The core elements are defining factors of all social innovations, whereas common features of social innovations are the features found in most social innovation cases. Thus, common features are not the prerequisite elements of social innovations, but they represent the summation of various trends and approaches in social innovations practised. Distinguishing the core elements from the often-found common features of social innovations gave the research team a useful perspective. It allowed us to focus on what makes the social innovation, rather than how to implement it. In the following paragraphs, TEPSIE's five elements are presented in an Asian context, recontextualised according to the Asian social innovation environment. We applied these elements as our criteria for the selection of our Asian social innovation cases, which will be presented in a later section.

---

11 ibid., 18–21.
12 Jürgen Howaldt and Michael Schwarz, *Social Innovation: Concepts, Research Fields and International Trends* (Universitat de Barcelona, 2012), www.ub.edu/emprenedoriasocial/ca/social-innovation-concepts-research-fields-and-international-trends. Accessed 30 June 2016.
13 The Young Foundation, *Social Innovation Overview*, 2012, 24.

## Meeting a Social Need

This element clarifies the goal of social innovation in any given case. We prioritised how well the social innovation case met a social need. In order to do so, we also examined each society in Asia to identify what kinds of social needs exist and which ones are urgent unmet needs. We then selected cases of social innovation that address such needs.

## Effectiveness

This element focuses on the idea that social innovation should be more effective in terms of outcomes (such as quality, satisfaction, costs or impact) than existing solutions. We examined various outcomes of the selected cases in the given society or region. If the case met a social need and was an effective outcome, then the case was marked as an initial candidate in the group of Asian social innovations. As part of this process, we conducted a basic literature review, on-site and online interviews, and field visits.

## Novelty

The element of novelty does not mean universal or absolute newness. It is rather the 'perceived novelty to the unit of adoption'.[14] We thus tried to decide if an innovation is new in the political, social or cultural context in which the social innovation cases arise. For instance, some Asian countries in our research project are not full-fledged democratic societies, so traditional or old-fashioned Western democratic methods can be perceived as innovative or new to the people there. Thus, even if some methods are already diffused or fully adopted outside the nation or region concerned, these methods can be regarded as new or reimagined on a local level.

## Moving from Ideas to Implementation

This element entails practical implementation of the idea of social innovation. Hence, even though an idea is created and experimented with, it should be applied to the field to qualify as a social innovation. This also implies that such application has to be sustainable. Adopting this

---

14   The Young Foundation, *Social Innovation Overview*, 2012.

element, we distinguished the sustained implementation cases from one-time or temporary events or experimental cases when selecting Asian social innovation cases.

## Enhancing Society's Capacity to Act

Social innovation is accomplished not only by fulfilling unmet social needs in an effective way, but also by applying the innovative process throughout society. Indeed, social innovation concerns inclusive processes involving users, beneficiaries, minorities and marginalised people in order to improve the society's capacity as a whole. Because it ultimately relates to the empowerment dimension of social innovation and societal resilience,[15] this element becomes an important point, especially in the Asian context.

# Understanding Asia

Asia is not a homogenous region; it includes many countries, cultures, religions and sociopolitical systems. Around 50 countries are located in Asia, and its diversity of social environment spans a greater range than any other continent in the world. While Asian nations share some common history, the level of economic and democratic advancement in the region varies dramatically, as is particularly clear when we examine Asia by subregion. There are economically advanced countries (e.g. Japan, Taiwan, Singapore, Hong Kong and South Korea), but at the same time many other countries are still suffering from severe poverty and an underdeveloped political or social system, such as dictatorship or hereditary classes.[16] The diversity of the region is also reflected in both the social problems and their possible solutions.

Despite the variety of social landscapes throughout the Asian continent, some similarities emerge in the region in terms of social development and its side effects. For instance, rapid economic growth strategies, based on imported capitalism and led by a central government, are commonly found in many nations of the Asian region. This typical Asian strategy

---

15    Frances Westley, *The Social Innovation Dynamic* (University of Waterloo, 2008), sig.uwaterloo. ca/sites/default/files/documents/TheSocialInnovationDynamic_001.pdf. Accessed 14 May 2012.

16    IMF, International Monetary Fund. *World Economic Outlook: Transitions and Tensions* (IMF, 2013), www.imf.org/external/pubs/ft/weo/2013/02/pdf/text.pdf. Accessed 5 December 2014.

causes a number of social problems in the region, such as a wide economic gap between the rich and the poor, oppressed civic freedom, dependency on foreign capital and political instability, etc. These problems are often addressed in Asian social innovation programs, in ways that would be less likely to be found in regions where the transitions of societal modes were relatively steady and smooth.

Some problems can be solved by applying the existing programs or models that have been successful in other regions, such as Europe or other Western countries. However, social problems that appear to be similar in nature could have very different cultural, political and social backgrounds depending on the country where the problem occurs. As a result, the replication of social innovation models that have worked successfully in other nations may be ineffective in handling social problems in an Asian country. For instance, many social innovation programs of developed countries in Europe or North America have flourished based on collaboration between the public sector and civil sector. Many nations in Asia, however, are experiencing political turmoil in the transition period, and it is not uncommon to see that Asian governments become major barriers to adopting innovative models. It is not always expected that the simple replication of successful social innovation models from Western societies would efficiently and effectively work in solving social problems in Asian countries.

Social innovation in Asia has emerged as a response to growing challenges often resulting from the 'failure' of modern welfare states and free market capitalism, and to numerous other problems beyond the current problem-solving capacity of existing institutions.[17] These challenges exceed existing problem-solving capacity because they are complex, multifaceted and appear to be impossible to solve by conventional means.[18] Such problems typically involve a range of stakeholders, so they must be addressed collaboratively amongst previously independent sectors such as government, civil society or private enterprises. Thus, the notion of 'social innovation' was introduced as a new way to address the challenges facing contemporary capitalist economies.

---

17  Example of such problems can be resource scarcity, climate change, an ageing population, impact of globalisation, impact of mass urbanisation, and so on.
18  A. Nicholls and A. Murdock eds, *Social Innovation: Blurring Boundaries to Reconfigure Markets* (Palgrave Macmillan, 2012).

# Social Innovation Initiatives in Asia

Social innovation is still an unfamiliar concept in Asia. Until a few years ago, there had been neither a leading government nor a civil organisation that had a social innovation vision or sought to diffuse the social innovation movement in Asia. Serious interest in Asian social entrepreneurs' activities arose partly due to the success of Grameen Bank. In addition, countless social entrepreneurs throughout the world have been learning lessons from such Asian innovators.[19] But apart from these few conspicuous social enterprise models, other types of social innovation programs in Asia have not been sufficiently promoted, and little effort has been made to comprehend the landscape of Asian social innovation and its distinctive features.

It is well known that social innovation flourishes best when there is effective partnership among grassroots organisations, social innovators (who are fast, mobile, creative and practical) and sponsoring organisations (which can strategically and financially support innovative models to scale up).[20] It is obvious that new initiatives are needed to foster social innovation in Asia, but it is not clear what strategy would be appropriate to achieve this. In order to define pragmatic visions and strategies in such a challenging environment, there is a need to understand similarities and differences among the diverse nations in Asia in terms of cultural, political and social background and the overall landscape of social innovation. Our study aims to address this gap in knowledge and expertise, and build a base to understand the social innovation ecosystem in Asia. To this end, The Hope Institute in South Korea actively sought social innovation networks in Asia, by founding ANIS in 2010.

ANIS was organised to share examples and experiences among Asian social innovators. It aims to solve the social issues and problems of each nation in the region through solidarity and cooperation. In practical terms, the innovative and creative projects in the region are showcased, and the ideas and feedback from Asian social innovators are actively exchanged, while new trends in Asian social innovation are presented, discussed and forecasted through ANIS. Throughout the four years of its existence

---

19    The Young Foundation, *Social Innovation Overview*, 2012.
20    Mulgan et al., *Social Innovation*, 2007.

(see Table 1), the work of ANIS has demonstrated that social innovators in Asia are groundbreakers, creating new solutions in spite of a lack of serious support from public and private sectors in a very weak civil society.

Table 1: ANIS Annual Meetings from 2009 to 2013.

| Stage | Annual Meeting | Theme | Participation |
|---|---|---|---|
| Beginning | Nov. 2009 (Hope Inst. & Intel Asia Agreement) | Series of initial discussion aiming at capacity-building opportunity for Asia NGOs | The Hope Institute, Intel Asia |
| Launching | Sept. 2010 (1st, Seoul, South Korea) | Innovate, Connect & Build Asia: Building Capacity for Changing Asia | 65 participants, 47 organisations from 14 countries |
| Promotion | Oct. 2011 (2nd, Jeju Island, South Korea) | Promoting Social Innovation in Asia: Strategies and Methods | 85 participants, 41 organisations from 14 countries |
| Collaboration | June, 2012 (3rd, Seoul, South Korea) | Connect, Collaborate & Co-create Asia: Collaboration across Sectors for Social Innovation | 195 participants, 54 organisations from 16 countries |
| Practical Solution | Oct. 2013 (4th, Bangkok, Thailand) | Social Innovation Meets Technology: Scaling Social Impact and Enriching People's Lives | 146 participants, 72 organisations from 16 countries |
| Shift for Future | Nov. 2014 (5th, Seoul, South Korea) | Strategic Plan for Future Direction | 13 participants 9 organisations from 7 countries |

Source: The Hope Institute research team.

The Hope Institute research team conducted a series of literature searches to gather information for country overviews and about numerous potential social innovation cases in selected Asian countries (China, India, Japan, South Korea and Thailand). Based on this, the research team drew up an overview of the five countries. These five countries—China, India, Thailand, South Korea and Japan—were selected based on in-depth analysis of the conditions and potential of their social innovation environments. The main criteria for this selection were regional representativeness, potential for social innovation and the existence of visible social innovation cases. The team's in-depth literature searches were used to assess the preconditions for and potential of social innovation in each country, and to identify potential social innovation cases from those countries. More specific reasons for selecting each country include richness of cases found in a country, importance of the social innovation in a given society, and convenience to access the information and the actual fields. For instance, India was selected for having relatively rich examples of and studies on its social innovation in addition to its leading role in the region in terms of social innovation. China demonstrates high potential for social innovation but also increasing need for the role of civil society. Thailand has various social innovation projects and movements, information about which came to light at the ANIS conferences. South Korea and Japan were selected since the research team had considerable understanding of the cases of both countries, and also because a variety of cases were visible in both countries, but had so far received little attention from researchers.

For a more extensive and systematic case selection, The Hope Institute research team created the Asian social innovation case bank and clustered social innovation programs in Asia according to nations or subregions and the social issues addressed. The ANIS network was used for the case bank collection as well. The research team collected the social innovation cases through the ANIS 2012 conference meeting and conducted case surveys among the attending members. Additional Asian social innovation cases were also collected through the surveys conducted during the conference.

The research team then defined the key features and the core elements of social innovation in Asia. Using them as criteria, this study selected a total of 46 cases (China 15, India 10, Japan 6, South Korea 6, and Thailand 9) of social innovation from the five countries.

Key aspects that this research focuses on when selecting cases from each country are: 1) the case should focus less on ideological and/or theoretical issues than on practical ways of satisfying the unmet social needs in citizens' daily life; 2) the innovation should be led by citizens (in other words, by the local people who live in the region), not by social activists or politicians; and 3) cases should actually be implemented and have yielded substantial result. Key examples of social innovation in Asia include new approaches of civic participation to achieve democracy in countries with a low level of democracy and cases driven by internal forces without much external support (e.g. without the help of or direction from global non-profit organisations or outside experts). In the case of social enterprise and government–business collaborative projects, the benefits should go to local residents and citizens at large. Other important examples are innovative projects using new technology to secure people's participation, which has been difficult to encourage otherwise.

Data analysis was conducted through comparison, grouping and thematic categorisation, which are based on the grounded theory technique. Drawing on this analysis, we identified key elements and factors for understanding social innovation in Asia, and then identified the shared characteristics in Asian social innovations. Acknowledging that the driving force behind meaningful social change and sustainable innovation is voluntary citizen participation that bridges different sectors, the analysis focused on how different groups of people participate in the efforts to create new models for addressing social issues.

The research team conducted a series of interviews with primary players in the identified cases. A total of 45 interviews were carried out, most of them face-to-face interviews through field visits and ANIS meetings, in addition to some phone and email interviews. Interview participants were mostly social innovators, academics, organisation-based researchers (e.g. the branch offices of Ashoka Foundation, Intel China, etc.) or civic activists. The participants were recruited through the ANIS network, and additional interviews for the cases of China and India were held at the International Conference on Creativity and Innovation at Grassroots (ICCIG).

The Hope Institute research team conducted field visits to the selected countries. The field visit was one of the most important methods in this study. The main purpose was to visit the relevant organisations and collect the field information and experiences of the cases and the countries as well. During the field visits, interviews were also conducted with experts who have insights on the various countries' social issues, sectoral relations (government, business and civil society) and the role of civil society in social innovation. The networks of ANIS and Rockefeller Foundation as well as SIX (Social Innovation Exchange) served as useful initial contact points to prepare the field visits and conduct follow-up. Expert advisory conferences aimed at assessment of the social, political and economic environments of each country and the suitability of the selected cases. Advisory meetings were held either through conferencing or interview visits. The specific information on the field visits are shown in Table 2.

Many interesting innovation cases were explored in this research. Relatively successful and characteristic cases were included such as Honey Bee Network of India, focusing on small-scale technology and knowledge sharing solutions for ordinary people; Carepro, which offers an innovative approach to health services for poor and marginalised citizens in Japan;

Hongsung Pulmu cooperative movement and the Wonju community for sustainable village development in South Korea. An interesting online '1kg More' campaign, which carries stationery to school children in remote villages in China, was found and many active implementations of innovative social ideas by Seoul City in South Korea were included as well. Some cases are distinguished by their cross-sectoral and local government leaders' initiatives for social innovation. Information and communication technology have also become particularly important elements in social innovation, as shown in the cases of alternative political podcasts in South Korea and an online candidacy movement in China, which we studied.

Table 2: Field visits by The Hope Institute research team.

| Country | Field visits | Dates |
| --- | --- | --- |
| China | 7 | 26 November–5 December 2012 |
| Hong Kong | 8 | 1–7 November 2012 |
| India | 11 | 6–12 December 2012 |
| Thailand | 13 | 13–24 May 2013 |
| South Korea | 6 | 1–30 August 2013 |

Source: Compiled by The Hope Institute research team.

# Seven Characteristics of Social Innovation in Asia

The social innovation cases from the five selected countries were categorised according to trends that reflect the overall landscape and ecosystems of social innovations of the nations in Asia. The research team identified keywords from each country's social innovation trends and listed those key words based on how frequently they appeared. A word cloud tool showed 'development', 'community', 'engagement' and 'cross-sector collaboration' as the most frequent keywords (see Figure 13). This shows that social innovations in Asia revolve around the development of urban and local areas, and sustainable development in those areas, community building and citizen engagement and cross-sector collaboration to enact effective innovative approaches.

Figure 13: Keyword cloud of social innovation.

Source: The Hope Institute research team.

As another way of characterising social innovations in Asia, this study listed all the key themes and key words drawn from the country analyses, and then categorised them, using two steps. In the first step, the themes and key words were sorted according to their relevancy, and then the resulting themes were categorised into three groups—Goals, Agents and Strategies—as shown in Figure 14.

Figure 14: Two-step categorisation of keywords and themes of social innovation in Asia.

Source: The Hope Institute research team.

This figure shows that social innovation in Asia is carried out by the people directly encountering the social problems, and by governments, intermediary organisations and funders. The goals of the social innovations in Asia have in general targeted the tasks of increasing earnings, solving local issues, expanding social welfare services and reforming undemocratic social systems. The parties to the social innovation projects often try to achieve these goals by directly tackling such social problems and adopting technologies in an innovative way. They use cross-sectoral collaboration as a working method and apply social economy models so that the problem-solving processes can gain sustainability.

Finally, this study goes on to present seven characteristics of social innovation in Asia, as follows.

## People-centred Development

One of the major characteristics of social innovation in Asia is that Asian societies face problems resulting from rapid and compressed sociopolitical development, and there is growing awareness that these problems need to be solved by the citizens by themselves. Most Asian countries have achieved some degree of economic development and democratisation. Capitalist development models and the rules of procedural democracy have been implemented. But the autonomous formation of nation-states, independent capital accumulation, the historical appearance of bourgeois and citizenry and people's awareness of citizenship have often been delayed or distorted. Though there has been considerable development through industrialisation and modernisation, the benefits have not been socially shared for sustainable development, and thus the gap between the rich and poor has deepened. According to the Asian Development Bank, the Asia and the Pacific regions remain home to the largest number of the world's poor.[21] In 2008, around 63 per cent of the poor worldwide lived in the region. The number of poor people in developing member countries of Asia is 658.07 million.[22] Most of them are engaged in low-waged manual labouring and lacking access to education. In particular, rural areas experience low productivity and slow technological advancement. These people also lack social welfare services, and especially suffer from poor health care.

---

21 Asian Development Bank (ADB), *Overview of Civil Society Organisations: India* (Manila: Asian Development Bank, 2009).
22 Guanghua Wan and Iva Sebastian, *Poverty in Asia and the Pacific: An Update,* Asian Development Bank Economics Working Paper (Manila: Asian Development Bank, 2011), 22–5.

Such unbalanced economic and social development produces marginalised people who are excluded from the mainstream. This becomes the starting point for Asian innovators to share knowledge, information, financial resources and technology, and so to create a self-reliant economic ecosystem, which enables people to improve their social conditions for themselves. People-centred development expresses the ways in which socially aware citizens identify their own social issues and create their own solutions by actively participating in social planning and decision-making processes. Innovative strategies for alternative development 'of the people, by the people, and for the people' further have an impact on local and central policies. In identifying the significance of people-centred development in Asia we found two key points.

First, marginalised people themselves help to achieve their own empowerment. This is done by redefining their knowledge, creativity and the value of their experience. Networking plays a crucial role here. Through redefinition, recognition and sharing, people invent occupational or survival solutions with little reliance on official or professional expert systems. Under these circumstances, marginalised people build up an informal knowledge network connecting like-minded individuals, innovators, farmers, scholars, policy makers, entrepreneurs and NGOs to nurture creativity. For instance, India's Honey Bee Network has emphasised people-to-people learning, the 'small technology' solutions of ordinary people, and new collaborative ways to solve problems. The activities of the Honey Bee Network are connected to other organisations such as the Society for Research and Initiatives for Sustainable Technologies and Institutions (SRISTI). SRISTI is a registered charitable organisation in India, founded in 1993 in response to the need to provide systematic support to knowledge-rich but economically poor people by adding value to their creative activities. One of the interesting activities carried out by SRISTI is *Shodh Yatras*, which is a traditional method of learning by walking together. The practice aims to seek knowledge, creativity and innovations at grassroots through seven to 10 days of journey on foot to reach remote areas of the country. It is a journey of mutual exchange and sharing of knowledge.

Second, people-centred development focuses on the building of self-reliant alternative economic communities. While pre-existing Asian development strategies have heavily concentrated on industrialisation and urbanisation, rural areas have been degraded to become a mere source of supply of low-waged labourers and basic food. The population and incomes of rural areas have rapidly shrunk. Some areas have been left devastated. In order to address such issues, farmers and local residents have created farmers' cooperatives. The cooperatives make efforts to increase members' income by setting up direct trading, adding values to products. They also make sure that part of the profits are reinvested in local improvement.[23] This approach is well demonstrated in the cases of Wonju Social Economy Network and Hongsung Pulmu Village in South Korea.[24]

## Community Empowerment

Community empowerment refers to the process of enabling communities to increase control over their lives. Community empowerment, therefore, is more than the involvement, participation or engagement of communities in developing social programs. It implies community ownership and action that explicitly aims at social and political changes.[25] Community empowerment is the process of building a stronger community through skills training, capital and logistics availability and capability. In this way, the community is able to sustain livelihood or similar projects that tend to benefit the community and its constituent members. As a social innovation trend in Asia, community empowerment comes in two forms.

First, community empowerment has been carried out mainly through urban projects for slum upgrading and community rebuilding activities. Rapid industrialisation and urbanisation have resulted in the collapse of traditional communities in many places. Many Southeast Asian countries are in the course of a development process led by mega-capital investment and industrialisation. Agricultural workers are forced to become low-waged workers in cities, and they often end up amongst the urban poor in slum areas. They frequently suffer from problems of insecure residential status. When government plans for these people proved ineffective, groups of people took the issue as their own task and came up with innovative solutions. The Bann Mankong Community Upgrade Program in Thailand

23  Kwon Seong-moon, 'A Study on Development Case in Rural Area: Focusing on Hongdong village, Hongsung County, Chungcheongnam-do'[Nongch'onjiyŏk ŭi paljŏn *sarye e kwanhan yŏn'gu: Ch'ungnam Hongsŏnggun Hongdongmyŏn ŭl chungsim ŭro* 농촌지역의 발전 사례에 관한 연구 : 충남 홍성군 홍동면을 중심으로] (Master's diss., Sungkonghoe University, 2011), 5–7.

24  Kim Heung-ju, 'A Study on Socio-economic Characteristic of Pulmu Co-op Farmers' [P'ulmusaenghyŏp saengsanja ŭi sahoegyŏngjejŏk sŏnggyŏk e kwanhan yŏn'gu 풀무생협 생산자의 사회경제적 성격에 관한 연구], *Korean Agricultural Society* 18 (2008): 45.

25  Fran Baum, 'Foreword', in Ronald Labonte and Glenn Laverack, *Health Promotion in Action: From Local to Global Empowerment* (London: Palgrave Macmillan, 2008), xiii–xv.

is a good example. In this project, slum dwellers called for a forum among themselves, community groups, civil activists, community networks, civic group entrepreneurs and government officials to discuss their residential issues and potential solutions. This project was not only focused on upgrading their living conditions, but also on engaging the slum dwellers and other residents in the process. They became aware of their role and power as members of a community. In that way, this project exemplifies people-driven community development and community empowerment projects.

Second, community empowerment has been achieved by implementing self-reliant local economic ecosystems. As mentioned in the previous section, farmers' cooperatives have been promoted to create earning routes and constant reinvestment, and this has contributed to enhancing sustainability for local economies. Such autonomous systems have helped local people to raise their voices on other issues so that they can actively pursue innovative solutions. Their innovative programs for community empowerment often encounter the challenges of dominant capital. For instance, local farmers' cooperatives in South Korea often challenge the big corporations' unfair trading or interference practices. The case of consumer cooperatives in Japan, which we also examined, is somewhat different from the case of South Korea's cooperatives in that the goal of the Japanese co-ops focuses on securing everyday foodstuffs for consumers, and so does not directly target the task of raising members' income, but it does also entail activities that empower the local community. The work of these Japanese cooperatives has been centrally concerned with problems of consumers' loss of control over their own well-being, including the safety of foodstuffs. The cooperatives especially challenge big conglomerates' monopoly over the market for food and other essentials.

Most of all, community empowerment is closely connected to community rebuilding, because 'community' does not just mean the group of residents living in a region. Rebuilding community ultimately relates to building up social capital such as trust, solidarity and cooperation among members. By doing this, residents and neighbours create their own community, where their everyday concerns and economic life are shared, supported and developed. This transformation cannot be taken for granted: the residents of urban areas, members of cooperatives, local small merchants, and others people in the community are required to identify the issues and find out the best way to solve them. Only by such participation and struggle can the transformation of dwelling place to community be achieved.

## ICT-based Civic Engagement

Information and communications technology (ICT) provides useful tools for efficient public participation in the democratic process and the dissemination of opinions and ideas. It is also frequently utilised for rallying social action about issues of concern to citizens. The technological advantages can easily be shared in societies where technological infrastructure is well established.[26] In Asia, many countries are on the path to democratic transition, which has been delayed at the expense of economic development. Thus, many Asian activists adopt ICT as a strategic tool for social innovation in an environment where civil rights and civic services are severely suppressed.

ICT-based civic engagement has been made easier by advances in the ICT industry in Asian countries such as China, Hong Kong, India, Japan, South Korea and Thailand. In Asia, the internet user growth rate was 841.9 per cent for the period from 2000 to 2012. This is much faster than Europe's 393.4 per cent or North America's 153.3 per cent growth rate.[27] Mobile technology has also been also rapidly popularised in Asia: the number of mobile phones per 100 citizens is 89.2 in China, 70.96 in India, 108.1 in South Korea, 95.1 in Japan and 105 in Thailand, as compared to the world average of 87.[28] ICT-based civic engagement appears in two ways in Asian social innovation cases.

First, many ICT-based social innovations in Asia are related to citizens' political participation, which often encounters an authoritarian regime and/or undemocratic government policies. Some countries in this study are considered as low-ranked countries in terms of level of democracy realisation (e.g. China as an authoritarian regime; India and Thailand

---

26   Hong Hyojin, *IT rŭl t'onghan sahoe hyŏksin sarye: Pin'gon, hwan'gyŏng, chaenan, pup'ae, chŏgaebal kukka chiwŏn, illyu ŭi nanche haegyŏl* [IT를 통한 사회혁신 사례 - 빈곤 · 환경 · 재난 · 부패 · 저개발 국가 지원 · 인류의 난제 해결 Social Innovation Cases through IT: Approach for Poverty, Environment, Disaster, Corruption, International Support, Global Issues] (Seoul: National Information Society Agency, 2012).

27   www.internetworldstats.com/stats.htm. Accessed 5 December 2014.

28   en.wikipedia.org/wiki/list_of_countries_by_number_of_mobile_phones_in_use. Accessed 5 December 2014.

as flawed democracies). These nations are still suffering from political oppression, strict censorship and other limitations of civil rights. Countries such as Japan and South Korea are regarded as relatively highly democratised; however, there are still some oppressive political practices and limitations to civic freedom. In this social environment, ICT was actively adopted by citizen groups in order to challenge the dominant communication systems and to disseminate counter arguments and alternatives.

For example, the online candidacy movement for local elections in China from 2011 onwards was mainly carried out via SNS. The movement was initiated online to break the government's suppression of the non-communist party members' candidacy. This case demonstrates that ICT can enable citizens to develop potential ways to promote democratic elections. Another case in South Korea, the alternative podcast broadcaster Nakomsu exemplifies the successful use of ICT for social innovation. Nakomsu effectively utilised podcast technology in order to tackle mainstream media power. It successfully played the role of a political critic of the existing regime's unethical and unjust conduct. Such cases imply that democratic improvement and enhancement of civic society are still pressing needs for many Asian societies, and that ICT can become a useful strategic tool for social innovators to address these issues.

Second, the handy and accessible features of ICT facilitate people's participation and civic awareness. The fast speed of internet and/or mobile communications prompts the dissemination of civic discourse, argument and discussion. It helps to lead less-informed people, or those who are reluctant to express their opinions in public, into more active civic engagement. Cases like '1kg More' in China are well promoted by the ICT-based strategies, which disseminate information about their practices nationwide.

## Public Sector Leadership and Local Governance

A major economic crisis beset Asia in the late 1990s. Beginning in Thailand with the collapse of the Thai baht, the financial contagion critically affected Indonesia, South Korea, Hong Kong, Malaysia, Laos and the Philippines. Though China, Taiwan, Singapore, Brunei and Vietnam were less affected, most countries experienced recession and government financial deficits. On the other hand, citizen awareness in those countries kept growing, while the governments faced various civic challenges including questioning of the legitimacy of regimes and of inequality, and demands for democracy and the expansion of social welfare.

Under these circumstances, Asian countries have made efforts to improve governance and to bring efficiency to governmental activities. These efforts are linked to social innovation, which is becoming a kind of global trend, as was shown by the Obama administration's establishment of an Office of Social Innovation and Civic Participation in 2009. However, few Asian countries have made such full-scale moves. Instead, the idea of 'innovation' in Asia has been approached mainly in the context of economic restructuring or goal setting. Thus 'social innovation' has not been energetically pursued as a governmental policy. However, it is acknowledged by many Asian governments as a meaningful practice that requires cross-sectoral collaboration embracing industry, civil society, and government.

Thus, many Asian governments recognise the necessity of collaboration with the civic sector. They have gradually expanded support for civil society organisations (CSOs) and developed policies and other institutional support for these organisations. For instance, the Japanese Government enacted a Non-Profit Organisation (NPO) Law in 1998, which promotes NPOs' activities and programs. Since then, more grassroots groups have been able to establish their legal status, and many local administrations have set up NPO support centres and/or various intermediaries to facilitate the provision of staff, funds and information for social innovation. China, where many civic organisations were controlled and censored, also reformed social welfare service systems so that local governments took on a greater role relative to the central government. As a result, CSOs' participation in the social welfare sector is increasing. Thailand's government set up a National Social Enterprise Committee (NSEC) under the Prime Minister's Office. The NSEC created a Social Enterprise Master Plan to support social enterprise and facilitate the incubation of various social enterprise ideas. India also established National Innovation Council and set up a National Innovation Fund in order to promote grassroots level innovations.

In addition to these supportive policy initiatives and efforts by central governments to create a favourable environment, local administrations have taken more specific actions to adopt practical social innovation policies. This reflects the fact that many Asian countries are in the course of decentralisation. So local governments welcome social enterprise and related innovation activities because these eventually contribute to strengthening local financial independence and effective policies, as well as promoting citizens' participation at the local level. Therefore, local governments in Asia try to seize opportunities to collaborate with civic sectors by establishing various supportive measures for community business. They also become more active in adopting participatory decision-making processes. The City of Seoul, South Korea, provides a good example of such engagement. In Japan, some local governments have also implemented municipal ordinances for community making to encourage local citizens' participation. Chinese governments too are putting forward social innovative programs under the banner of 'Social Management Innovation', to reinforce transparency and citizen participation.

## Social Entrepreneurship

Most Asian countries have experienced rapid industrialisation and other social transformations in the short period of less than a century, or in some cases even in a few decades. This rapid industrialisation has caused many sociopolitical problems. Social innovation in Asia necessarily confronts such problems and seeks to address them through innovative programs. One salient approach to this is social entrepreneurship. The emergence of social entrepreneurs is, in general, seen as a consequence of the failure of the modern welfare state and/or of flaws in conventional market capitalism. In other words, social entrepreneurs have emerged to provide solutions to the issues that lie beyond the capacity of the government or market alone. However, in Asia, space for the birth of social entrepreneurs has yet to emerge. Japan and South Korea have to some extent experienced economic development followed by the introduction of social welfare measures, but there still exist unaddressed basic needs such poverty, malnutrition, disease and lack of educational opportunities in many Asian nations. In such circumstances, the emergence of social entrepreneurs in Asia tends to fill gaps in the state social welfare system itself. Social entrepreneurs often take on the tasks that have been performed by the government in traditional welfare states.

Another characteristic of Asian social innovation in relation to social entrepreneurs is that a business model is actively adopted as a means for NGOs' profit-making, or for profit-driven enterprises to promote public values. An example for this appears in the case of social enterprise in India, where almost 40 per cent of the population live below the national poverty line.[29] In fact, approximately three-quarters of Indian social enterprises target the base of the pyramid (BOP) as consumers of critical goods and services. Those new business models rely on multitiered pricing or cross-subsidisation, which means (for example) that paying patients subsidise those who cannot afford the cost. Another example of this trend can be found in the Japanese health initiative Carepro, which provides self check-up services at low cost—about $5. This shows how a social welfare service (health care) was taken over by a combination of the market approach and a 'public good' business model. In Japan it was possible for such a business model to appear in social services mainly as a result of social welfare system reform: a long-term care insurance scheme was created, and this allowed NPOs and other cooperatives to enter service areas such as human care and long-term care service for the elderly people.

The proliferation of social enterprise in Asia is also related to the ups and downs of CSOs. Gradual democratisation and the growth of the middle class contributed to an increase of CSOs as well. However, those civic organisations soon faced hard times in terms of financial sustainability when economic recession arrived. Many non-profit organisations changed into social enterprises to find better opportunities for self-financing, and this change was also encouraged by government policies to support social enterprise. In China, almost 20 per cent of social enterprises are actually registered as CSOs and thus there is no clear distinguishing line between the two forms of program. It should also be noted that the global rise of social enterprise, particularly successful examples such as Grameen Bank, influenced many young entrepreneurs to move in this direction. Young professionals who have experience of working in industries also often move into social venture and related areas (e.g. social impact investment).

---

29   Melissa Ip, 'Exploring India's Social Enterprise Landscape', Social Enterprise Buzz, 19 April 2012, www.socialenterprisebuzz.com/2012/04/19/exploring-indias-social-enterprise-landscape/. Accessed 1 December 2014.

## Intermediary Organisations

Intermediary organisations[30] provide support financially and policy-wise. Thus, they help to create the environment for social innovation. In fact, many cases selected for this study displayed the importance of the intermediaries. The Honey Bee Network in India is a good example in that the network has led many grassroots innovations. It successfully created various projects to facilitate indigenous knowledge, experience and creativity.

In the cases of China and Thailand, intermediaries played a crucial role in the development of social enterprise. In particular, intermediaries such as the British Council and the Ashoka Foundation introduced the concept of social enterprise and actively spread its outcome by holding competitions and forums.[31] They also connected social enterprises to funding bodies and expanded opportunities for various social enterprises to implement their ideas. Moreover, intermediaries have played an important role when Asian governments embarked on supporting social innovations. The case of City of Seoul in South Korea illustrates this: the city promoted social innovation more effectively by utilising various intermediary organisations (e.g. a hub for young job-seekers, a creativity lab, a centre for local community support, centres for youth like the innovative Haja Center, also mentioned in Chapter Seven, which provides education for young people seeking an alternative from the standard school system, and so on).

When civil society is sufficiently developed to stand alone as a partner in collaboration with government in Asia, intermediaries play an important role to connect the two sectors. This has been done by way of education, enhancement programs, grassroots empowerment, etc.

---

30   Intermediary organisations play a fundamental role in encouraging, promoting and facilitating linkage between state/local governments and non-governmental organisations (NGOs, NOPs, community groups, civic groups, academic institutions and private corporations). Infrastructure organisation, umbrella organisation, local development agency, intermediary support organisation are the terms to identify such role and actitivity in the countries like the US, UK and Japan.
31   Ashoka Foundation. Ashoka innovators for the public: Prayong Doklamyai, 2012, www.ashoka.org/fellow/prayong-doklamyai. Accessed 30 October 2012.

## Cross-sectoral Partnership

Social innovation is cross-sectoral by nature; it is often achieved through partnerships and collaborations among four sectors: the non-profit, public, private and informal sectors. Asian social innovations too display 'more than one sector' collaboration, though there are variations in the role of the various sectors. However, as pointed out in the previous section, the civic or non-profit sector in Asia has not been strong enough to lead the partnership. In addition, some governments too lack strong governance. Under these circumstances, Asian social innovation is characterised by the active role of informal participants and their leading contribution to cross-sectoral collaboration. Notably, professional experts (professors, scientists, engineers, architects, medical doctor, etc.) made up much of this informal sector, and their participation has contributed to the success of many social innovation cases. For instance, architects played an important role in the Residential Innovation Project in Thailand. These architects were closely connected to the project and held housing design workshops in addition to their consulting tasks. Most of the grassroots innovations in India have been based on the participation of scientists, engineers and IT professionals, who provide practical support such as the enhancement of farm equipment and agricultural production processes. Their contributions are not limited to simple volunteering; they become a kind of pro bono work, in that their professional abilities serve social goals and contribute to public services. This kind of informal sector plays a crucial role in enabling social innovation to come up with practical solutions and to sustain social innovation practices in Asian context where the number of social innovators is still small.

# Conclusion

Social innovation is defined as a process whereby all sectors in a society, namely, the government, business and citizen, join in collaborative efforts to address issues facing the society. The mainstream discourse of social innovation that emerged from Western society stresses the importance of innovative ways of cooperation among different social sectors to meet social needs. In addition, it emphasises the sustainability of society and voluntary citizen participation. However, the contexts of Asia are quite different. Many countries in Asia demonstrate 'weak governance' with a low level of government transparency and accountability, which means that the government has a lack of capacity to deal with social problems in trusted and transparent ways. This is often coupled with a shortage of available finance. The majority of Asian countries suffer from a democracy deficit, which is clearly one of the key barriers to citizen participation in addressing pressing social challenges. Asian citizens are still struggling with poverty, public health, problems of a wide gap between rich and poor, restricted civil rights and dictatorship. Compressed development and top-down industrialisation through government-driven strategies have caused many of the existing problems. Asian countries have to cope in their own way with crucial social needs in order to improve daily lives and promote democratisation and civil liberty.

However, this does not mean that Asian societies are not ready for social innovation. Rather, because of these multilayered problems, social innovation projects are crucial in Asian societies. Many cases from the five countries we studied demonstrate how effectively social innovation projects contribute to citizen awareness, bottom-up action, self-reliant business, the pursuit of civil liberty and community rebuilding. Asian social innovation often overlaps with social movements and/or democratic reform. Social innovation in Asia on the one hand presents 'continuity' from sociopolitical democratisation movements, which are based on grassroots, bottom-up civic action. On the other hand, the innovation movement implies 'discontinuity' from the conventional movements, such as class-based political struggles, hierarchical forms of resource mobilisation or ideology-centred activism. It is problematic to identify the social innovation movement of Asia simply in terms either of continuity or of discontinuity from earlier social movements. There is much scope here for further discussion and follow-up research on this burgeoning area of social action.

# Epilogue

## Tessa Morris-Suzuki

We are mad, of course. From the point of view of those who defend their armchairs and discuss the arrangement of the furniture in the run-up to the next election, we are undoubtedly mad, we who run about seeing cracks that are invisible to the eyes of those who sit in armchairs (or which appear to them, if at all, as changes in the wallpaper, to which they give the name of 'new social movements'). The worst of it is that they may be right: perhaps we are mad, perhaps there is no way out, perhaps the cracks we see exist only in our fantasy. The old revolutionary certainty can no longer stand. There is absolutely no guarantee of a happy ending.[1]

The small and diverse experiments in informal life politics that we have explored in this volume might seem, from a more conventional political perspective, to be mad, or at least marginal, irrelevant and doomed to failure. They are idealistic efforts to change very small corners of the world, driven often by sheer pressures of circumstance, but also sometimes by a belief that minor autonomous actions can ultimately flow into wider processes of social and political change.

The stories we have encountered here are very varied, but placing them side-by-side has also helped to make certain common threads more visible. In all of these stories, it proves remarkably difficult to define the participants in terms of conventional identity categories: class, status, gender or even ideology. Though the groups are small and often community based, they almost invariably consist of networks bringing together both 'locals' and 'outsiders', as well as people with differing social backgrounds and life experiences. It might be tempting to see these groups as practising middle-class 'lifestyle politics', and certainly some participants might be called 'middle class', and some might be labelled

---

1    John Holloway, *Crack Capitalism* (London: Pluto Press, 2010), 8–9.

'intellectuals'. But the clearest motif is diversity. Farmers and fishers were active protagonists in the informal life politics described by Sho Konishi's account of early 20th-century Japan (Chapter One), in the life of the Bishan commune (Chapter Two), the Nagano Prefecture endogenous development projects (Chapter Three) and grassroots responses to the disasters of Minamata and Fukushima (Chapters Five and Six). Factory workers engaged in the cooperatives of 1920s Japan and in the reactions to the 2011 nuclear disaster (Chapters One and Six). Shopkeepers and traditional craftsmen cooperated with professional artists and others in the Hong Kong art activism described by Olivier Krischer (Chapter Eight). People from all walks of life shared in the search for a response to the *Sewol* disaster (Chapter Seven), and have taken part in groups like India's Honey Bee Network and Thailand's Bann Mankong Program (Chapter Ten).

The potential to bring together the talents and experience of diverse people is clearly important to the practices of informal life politics. At the same time, though, this diversity suggests a need to explore new ways to observe and understand these actions. Like the forms of politics discussed by John Holloway, these are ways of 'doing' rather than ways of 'being'. People engaged in informal life politics develop their sense of self in the process of 'doing', rather than being impelled to take political action by a pre-existing sense of identity. The creation of skills for observing and understanding improvisatory 'doing' remains an important frontier for future research.

A further common thread that emerges from the chapters in this book is a desire to 'push back' against the seemingly endless expansion of a commercial system that reduces all life to a matter of economic value and profit. These forms of informal life politics can be seen as one side of the 'double movement' described by Karl Polanyi in his classic *The Great Transformation*. According to Polanyi the apparently relentless expansion of the market provokes a countermovement to protect parts of human life from the invasive forces of commercialisation and commodification: 'the market expanded continuously, but this movement was met by a countermovement checking the expansion in definite directions'. This countermovement is not just 'the usual defensive behaviour of a society faced with change', but is rather 'a reaction against a dislocation which attacked the fabric of society, and which would have destroyed the very organisation of production that the market had called into being'.[2]

As early as the 1920s, as we have seen, the Japanese villagers of Arishima Farm and of the New Village Movement were experimenting with practices of shared ownership and communal living, and Chinese rural reformers were rediscovering the agrarianist visions of their forebears as a response to the inroads of commercial modernity into rural life. This push back continues in responses to disasters generated by unbridled commercialism, examined in Chapters Four to Seven, and in the search for autonomous forms of community building explored in Chapters Eight and Ten. For, as Polanyi also observed, the expansion of the market is always underpinned and made possible by the action of the state: 'the road to the free market was opened and kept open by an enormous increase in continuous, centrally organised and controlled interventionism'.[3] So too today, those who confront the damage to daily life done by corporate development schemes, industrial pollution, nuclear radiation and human-generated 'accidents' confront the power of the state as well as the power of the market.

The case of North Korea, discussed in Chapter Nine, seems to be an intriguing counter-example. Here, instead of people pushing back against the intrusive power of the market economy in their lives, ordinary people use the power of the market to push back against the intrusions of a repressive state. But this counter-example helps to highlight an important point. The central issue is not the practice of market exchange itself. Markets can take many forms and serve many purposes. Rather, as this case reminds us, we need to re-politicise our understanding of the market, and to re-examine its diversity of forms. The expansionary and invasive nature of an ever-expanding system of commodification, intertwined as it always is with the 'continuous, centrally organised' workings of state power may threaten the foundations of life. Yet small-scale exchange systems controlled by groups of local traders may be socially empowering for participants while also contributing to longer-term processes of nationwide change.

---

2    Karl Polanyi, *The Great Transformation: The Political and Economic Origins of our Time* (Boston: Beacon Press, 2001) (original published in 1944).
3    ibid., 145–6.

How can we judge the success or failure of the stories we have encountered here. None, of course, has transformed national or international society. Some (like the Bishan commune) have faced state repression. Others (like the actions of the *Sewol* families) have faced fierce counterattacks from ideologically opposed sections of society. In an age of the emptying of democracy, the forces stacked against small actions to restore human autonomy and agency seem almost insurmountable. Yet, as we saw in Chapter Three, even groups that seem to wither in the face of repression may prove to have sowed the seeds for future informal political action. By placing these stories together, we hope that we have been able to bring them into dialogue with one another, and with some of the many other minor actions of people around the world who seek to shape their lives according to their own hopes and visions. Informal life politics, as we have seen, has a long history. In a world without promises of happy endings, its future is also uncertain. The only certainty is that this future lies in the hands and actions of the people who enact—who live—this quiet and often invisible form of politics: and those people include ourselves.

# Author Information

**Simon Avenell** is Associate Professor in History and Associate Dean (HDR) in the College of Asia and the Pacific, The Australian National University. He is the author of *Making Japanese Citizens: Civil Society and the Mythology of the Shimin in Postwar Japan* (University of California Press, 2010) and *Transnational Japan in the Global Environmental Movement* (University of Hawai'i Press, 2017).

**Adam Broinowski** is a visiting research fellow at the School of Culture, History and Language at the College of Asia and the Pacific, The Australian National University. His monograph *Cultural Responses to Occupation in Japan: The Performing Body During and After the Cold War* was published with Bloomsbury Academic in 2016.

**Cho (Han) Haejoang** is Emeritus Professor of Cultural Anthropology, Yonsei University and Director of the Haja Center (Seoul Youth Factory for Alternative Culture). Her works in Korean include *Men and Women in South Korea* (1988), *Reflexive Modernity and Feminism* (1998) and *Back to the Classroom: Reading Text and Reading Everyday Lives in the Neoliberal Era* (2009).

**The Hope Institute** is a Seoul-based 'Think & Do' tank that focuses on alternative policy research on various agendas in South Korea, and puts ideas into action. Established in 2006 without any funding from the government or the corporate sector, The Hope Institute is devoted to the development of policy research and educational programs to encourage social innovation.

**Sho Konishi** is Associate Professor in Modern Japanese History at the University of Oxford, and author of *Anarchist Modernity: Cooperatism and Japanese-Russian Intellectual Relations in Modern Japan* (Harvard University Press, 2013).

**Olivier Krischer** is a postdoctoral fellow at the Australian Centre on China in the World (CIW), The Australian National University, and currently Visiting Fellow at Academia Sinica, Taiwan. He researches the role of art in modern and contemporary China–Japan relations, and networks of artistic activism across East Asia. He is co-editor of *Asia through Art and Anthropology: Cultural Translation Across Borders* (Bloomsbury, 2013). His recent curatorial projects include 'Zhang Peili: from Painting to Video' (2016) and 'Between: Picturing 1950–60s Taiwan' (2015), both held in the CIW Gallery.

**Ou Ning** is a multidisciplinary practitioner from China who now teaches at the Columbia University Graduate School of Architecture, Planning and Preservation in New York. He lived in a small village in Anhui Province and founded the Bishan Commune (2011–2016) and School of Tillers (2015–2016), to join the new rural reconstruction movement in China, and is known for urban research and documentary projects such as *San Yuan Li* (2003) and *Meishi Street* (2006).

**Tessa Morris-Suzuki** is Distinguished Professor of Japanese History and Australian Research Council Laureate Fellow in the College of Asia and the Pacific, The Australian National University.

**Eun Jeong Soh** researches health and marketplace economy in North Korea, and was a Postdoctoral Research Fellow in the College of Asia and Pacific, The Australian National University, from 2014 to 2016.

**Shoko Yoneyama** is Senior Lecturer in the Department of Asian Studies, University of Adelaide. Her research interests include the politics and philosophy of education, alternative education, organic farming, food and environment, and alternative social movements, and her publications include *The Japanese High School: Silence and Resistance* (Routledge, 1999).

www.ingramcontent.com/pod-product-compliance
Lightning Source LLC
Chambersburg PA
CBHW050807270326
41926CB00026B/4610